MERTON & SUFISM

OF RELATED INTEREST
FROM FONS VITAE

Letters of a Sufi Master by Shaykh al-'Arabî ad-Darqâwî
translated by Titus Burckhardt

The Sacred Origin and Nature of Sports and Culture
by Ghazi bin Muhammad

Islam in Tibet, featuring the illustrated narrative
Tibetan Caravans by Abdul Wahid Radhu

Alchemy: Science of the Cosmos, Science of the Soul
by Titus Burckhardt

Mary the Blessed Virgin of Islam by Aliah Schleifer

Ibn 'Arabi's *Divine Governance of the Human Kingdom*
interpreted by Shaykh Tosun Bayrak

Suhrawardi's *Hayakal al-Nur (The Shape of Light)*
interpreted by Shaykh Tosun Bayrak

Motherhood in Islam by Aliah Schleifer

The Ornaments of Lhasa: Islam in Tibet, video
produced by Gray Henry

FORTHCOMING

*On the Invocation of the Name: The Jesus Prayer as Practiced in the
Western Church* by Rama Coomaraswamy

Autobiography of a Moroccan Sufi Saint: Ahmad Ibn 'Ajiba
translated from the Arabic by J. L. Michon, and
from the French by David Streight

Moorish Culture in Spain by Titus Burckhardt

Early Sufi Women of as-Sulami translated by Rkia Cornell

The Stations of the Wayfarer: Manazil as'Sa'irin, al Harawi,
translated by Maryam al-Khalifa Sharief

Siena: City of the Virgin by Titus Burckhardt

A. K. Coomaraswamy's *The Traditional Doctrine of Art*

Al-Ghazali's Deliverance from Error and Other Works
[formerly *Freedom and Fulfillment*] by R. J. McCarthy

The Seen and the Unseen Worlds: Jinn Among Mankind
by Amira El Zein

The Architectural Glory of Cairo, Caroline Williams (video series)

MERTON & SUFISM

The Untold Story

A COMPLETE COMPENDIUM

*Edited by Rob Baker
and Gray Henry*

FONS VITAE

Printed in the United States of America

ISBN-1-887752-07-2

This edition published by
Fons Vitae
49 Mockingbird Valley Drive
Louisville, KY 40207-1366
email: grayh101@aol.com
website: www.fonsvitae.com

Library of Congress Catalog Card Number: 99-62299

Permissions for published and unpublished material for this volume
can be found starting on page 339.

THE COVER

"Yesterday afternoon I finished a remarkable book—the biogra-phy of the Shaikh Ahmad al-'Alawi, who died in Algeria in 1934. One of the greatest religious figures of this century, a per-fect example of the Sufi tradition in all its fullness and energy. This is one book that I want to read again. The excerpts from his writings are most impressive and I know I have not begun to appreciate their content."

—THOMAS MERTON, JOURNALS, VOL. V

"The book was an inspiration to me and I often think of this man with great veneration. He was so perfectly right in his spirituali-ty. Certainly a great saint and a man full of the Holy Spirit. May God be praised for having given us one such, in a time when we need many saints."

—THOMAS MERTON LETTER TO MARTIN LINGS

"With Shaikh Ahmad, I speak the same language and indeed have a great deal more in common than I do with the majority of my contemporaries in this country. In listening to him I seem to be hearing a familiar voice from my "own country" so to speak. I regret that the Muslim world is so distant from where I am, and wish I had more contact with people who think along these lines."

—THOMAS MERTON, THE HIDDEN GROUND OF LOVE

*Dedicated to
furthering
mutual respect
among the world's
sacred traditions
by sharing matters of
spiritual sustenance.*

Personally, in matters where dogmatic beliefs differ, I think that controversy is of little value because it takes us away from the spiritual realities into the realm of words and ideas. In the realm of realities we may have a great deal in common, whereas in words there are apt to be infinite complexities and subtleties which are beyond resolution. It is, however, important, I think, to try to understand the beliefs of other religions. But much more important is the sharing of the experience of divine light, and first of all of the light that God gives us even as the Creator and Ruler of the Universe. It is here that the area of fruitful dialogue exists between Christianity and Islam. I love the passages of the Quran which speak of the manifestations of the Creator in His Creation.

—THOMAS MERTON
IN A LETTER TO
THE PAKISTANI SUFI, ABDUL AZIZ

Sufism looks at man as a heart and a spirit and a secret, and the secret is the deepest part. The secret of man is God's secret; therefore, it is in God. My secret is God's innermost knowledge of me, which He alone possesses. It is God's secret knowledge of myself in Him, which is a beautiful concept. The heart is the faculty by which man knows God and there Sufism develops the heart.

This is a very important concept in the contemplative life, both in Sufism and in the Christian tradition: To develop a heart that knows God, not just a heart that loves God, but a heart that knows God. How does one know God in the heart? By praying in the heart. The Sufis have ways of learning to pray so that you are really praying in the heart, from the heart, not just saying words, not just thinking good thoughts or making intentions or acts of the will, but from the heart. This is a very ancient Biblical concept that is carried over from Jewish thought into monasticism. It is the spirit which loves God, in Sufism. The spirit is almost the same word as the Biblical word "spirit"—the breath of life. So man knows God with his heart, but loves God with his life. It is your living self that is an act of constant love for God and this inmost secret of man is that by which he contemplates God, it is the secret of man in God himself.

—THOMAS MERTON SPEAKING TO A GROUP
OF CATHOLIC SISTERS IN ALASKA
TWO-AND-A-HALF MONTHS BEFORE HIS DEATH

EDITORS' NOTE

The editors wish to especially thank the following persons and institutions for their assistance in the preparation of this volume:

- Jonathan Montaldo, Director of the Thomas Merton Center, for advice and assistance at all stages of our research, as well as his careful reading of a number of the original chapters. His knowledge of the location of archival material and his grasp of Merton's handwriting proved absolutely essential to the preparation of this volume, as did the assistance of Theresa Sandok, Jennifer Mick, and William Armstrong at the Center;

- Erlinda Paguio, for assistance in planning the volume from its inception;

- Anne McCormick, Mrs. Frank O'Callaghan III, and Robert Giroux of the Merton Legacy Trust for their encouragement of this project and their permission to quote from unpublished material from the Merton archives at Bellarmine College;

- Brother Patrick Hart and Father William H. Shannon for their advice and their help in clarifying certain mysteries along the way;

- Bernadette Dieker for handling endless details, including typing and helping edit and proofread the volume;

- Catherine (Mrs. Frithjof) Schuon for clarifying certain details of contact between her husband and Merton through Marco Pallis, as well as for the photo of Shaikh al-'Alawî on the cover of this book;

- Brother Paul Quenon of Gethsemani for photographing the ikon from Marco Pallis that was in Thomas Merton's hermitage and other photography, as well as assisting us (along with Brother Joshua Brands) in selecting photos from the Gethsemani archives for this volume;

- The photographer Darryl Jones for assistance in the photo section, and to Brynn Bruijn of *Aramco World* and Glen

Markoe of the Cincinnati Museum of Art for other photos used in the book;

- Scott L. Kelien, of Plaschke Design Group, for his creative participation - particularly the cover and photo essay design.

- Michael Drury, Christopher Bandy, and Molly Rannells for their help typesetting, designing, and proofreading this volume.

- Anthony Zarowski of Farrar, Straus & Giroux; Daniel Allman of New Directions; and Judy Durham of HarperSanFrancisco; Deborah Casey of World Wisdom Books; Father Terrence Kardong, O.S.B., of *The American Benedictine Review*; and again Jonathan Montaldo of *The Merton Seasonal* and *The Merton Annual* for their assistance in securing permissions for this volume.

Regarding the transcription into English of Arabic names and terms, we have taken the middle course (following in most cases the style used by the journal *Sophia*) halfway between academic literalism (the system of dots and lines under and over letters so confusing to general readers) and no accents at all, retaining only the long marks over letters (here rendered as circumflexes) and the Arabic *ayn* and *hamsa* (here rendered as open and closed single quotes). We have tried to standardize spellings in an area where no standard exists, for such words as "Qur'an" (but "Quranic"), "*tarîqah*," "*zâwiyah*," and hadith.

ROB BAKER AND GRAY HENRY

CONTENTS

MERTON & SUFISM

WHAT ATTRACTED MERTON TO SUFISM

Seyyed Hossein Nasr

Every authentic spirituality has its distinct perfume which is an extension of the perfume of paradise and reflects the celestial archetype that is the primal reality of the spirituality in question. Such is also certainly the case of Sufism, to which Thomas Merton was attracted deeply during the last part of his life. If we were to ask what attracted Merton to Sufism, the first answer would be that he was attracted to its spiritual perfume much like a person who, entering a garden, might be especially attracted to a particular species of flower found in that garden. This question, however, also can be answered on a more detailed and analytical level that entails examining the whole issue of the relationship between Merton and Sufism; many of those aspects are examined in the essays and selected texts that comprise this book.

In this brief preface I shall begin with an autobiographic note which involves Merton. For several years Marco Pallis, mutual friend of both Merton and myself, was the link between us and conveyed to me the ever greater interest of Merton in Sufism and my own exposition of it after he had read my *Three Muslim Sages* and *Ideals and Realities of Islam*. Arrangements were in fact made to have Merton spend a month in Persia, where I then lived, to be with me and to observe the various manifestations of Sufism from nearby. I made all the necessary preparations and it was only a few weeks before his planned entry to Tehran that he died in Southeast Asia. The opportunity never therefore arose for us to discuss Sufism together in person, but through many indirect discussions in London and an exchange of letters with Pallis as well as my own reading of Merton's books, I gained some ideas as to what within the

Sufi tradition, with its multifarious manifestations containing nearly all spiritual possibilities, attracted this Catholic contemplative to
the extent that he had said that he wanted to devote much of his
time to the study of Sufism and to write extensively about it.

Let it be said first of all that Merton's knowledge of Sufism was
authentic and genuine and not derived from either sentimental
pseudo-Sufi writings nor from dry scholarly analyses of Sufism by a
certain class of scholars who are interested in Sufism only if the spirit of Sufism is taken out of it, scholars who are much more at home
dissecting cadavers than studying living beings. Merton had read
many of the traditional books dealing with Islam and Sufism,
including those of Frithjof Schuon, Titus Burckhardt, and Martin
Lings, and thanks to his own perspicacity was able to discover their
authentic character. He had also read some of the best of Sufi poetry that was available to him in English translation and moreover
had personal contacts with certain representatives of that tradition.
Altogether, he was fairly well acquainted with Sufi doctrine, practice, and art, all of which attracted him greatly.

It is not possible to enumerate all the characteristics of Sufism
which caused Merton to be attracted to it, but at least some of the
main ones can be cited. As Merton deepened his studies of the contemplative life and his own practice of that life, he became ever
more aware of the fact that in Christian mysticism, as it had been
practiced in Western Christianity during the past few centuries,
most of the spiritual techniques that still survive in Yoga, Zen, and
Sufism had been lost. He saw in Sufism a living tradition, belonging
to the climate of Abrahamic monotheism rather than to the more
alien world of Indian religions, in which techniques of meditation,
concentration, contemplation, and invocation had been well preserved leading ultimately to principial and unitive knowledge (al-
ma'rifah) which ultimately transcends the realm of multiplicity.
Reading about these methods combined with detailed analyses of
the landscape of the inner world—a journey made possible by
means of initiation and initiatic guidance by a spiritual master—was
deeply meaningful to him. He saw in the climate of Islamic esoterism the continuation of contemplative orders which had preserved
their spiritual method and the presence of spiritual masters which
made the practice of such methods possible. This reality was highly

attractive to him as he tried to go beyond the realm of passive and individualistic mysticism.

Since the Renaissance, much of what survived of Christian mysticism became in fact mostly individualistic, sentimental, and passive. While Merton understood the value of this type of mysticism on its own level, his gaze was set upon the great medieval Christian contemplatives whose vision was not limited in any way by the individualism that was one of the characteristics of the Renaissance. The Sufi path, in which the adept plays the active role as wayfarer upon the way that finally leads to the Beloved, like the hero in quest of the Holy Grail, while remaining passive before the grace of Heaven, was certainly attractive to Merton who was himself moving in this direction. He also thirsted for the kind of structured mystical life which the Sufi path offered in which the active and passive modes of the mystical life could be balanced on the basis of a reality that transcended the accidentality of individual existence.

Sufi literature is replete with symbols on whose wings the soul is able to journey from this lowly realm to the celestial abode. Merton had become ever more interested in mystical symbols and this aspect of Sufism was therefore of great appeal to him. Furthermore, being a fine writer with great literary gifts, he was dazzled by the literary beauty of much of Sufi literature and the richness of Sufi poetry, not to mention other arts such as music associated with Sufism. There is perhaps no other mystical tradition that has produced so much first-rate poetry as Sufism. The greatest poets of Persian, Turkish, and most other Islamic languages were Sufis. As for Arabic, which possessed a powerful poetic tradition before the rise of Islam, the most universal poetry is that written by Sufis. Merton felt perfectly at home in the world of Rûmî and Hâfiz, Ibn 'Arabî and Ibn al-Fârid, or for that matter Yûnus Emre or Shah 'Abd al-Latîf of Sindh.

Also Merton turned more and more to an appreciation of the spiritual significance of nature of which Taoism, Zen, and Sufism speak so often. The Sufi perspective which views nature as the self-revelation, unveiling, and theophany of God and which sees all phenomena as Divine Signs (*vestigia Dei*), as a number of earlier Christian mystics had also asserted, was deeply attractive to Merton who found in this view of Sufism—which saw the supernaturally natural *barakah* (grace) flowing through the arteries of the cosmos and refused to separate nature completely from the grace of the supernatural—a profound confirmation of his own most intimate vision of creation as God's handiwork and the theater for the manifestation of His qualities.

Sufism combines the paths of action, love, and knowledge while providing a diversity of paths for the realization of the One in order to be able to cater to the needs of the differences in nature and temperament of those who wish to undertake the spiritual journey. As the esoteric dimension of the last major religion of the history of present humanity, Sufism contains within itself all the different possibilities of esoterism, resulting in the incredibly rich and diverse aspects of the Sufi tradition. This trait was not at all lost on Merton who had also studied Buddhist and Hindu contemplative disciplines in addition to Christianity before turning to Sufism. Merton felt deeply enriched in the profuse garden of Sufism, where he could find something of great beauty in whatever direction he cast his vision.

Finally, it must be remembered that by turning seriously to the study of the spirituality of other religions, including Buddhism which is non-theistic, Merton was acknowledging the truth of the "transcendent unity of religions" to use the term made famous by Frithjof Schuon. Merton saw in the classical Sufi tradition in the writings of such figures as Ibn 'Arabî and Rûmî a clear assertion of this truth, which goes back to the explicit teachings of the Qur'an itself. He was also aware that its contemporary formulation and exposition especially in the hands of René Guénon and Schuon also issued from the background of Sufism. This universalism of Sufism, reflected in so much Sufi poetry, was of deep interest to Merton who saw in it the confirmation of a truth that he had come to discover after a long period of study and contemplation.

What would have happened if Merton had been able to come to Persia and to continue his study of Sufism, only Heaven knows. In any case that was not to be. Perhaps he would have written major works of Sufism in its relation to Christian spirituality. But even what he did write and the thoughts that he did express to friends reveal the inner *sympatheia* he had towards the Islamic spiritual universe. Any study of the relation between Merton and Sufism is therefore of much value not only for a better understanding of

Merton himself but also for the creation of deeper modes of comprehension between the inward and contemplative dimensions of Islam and Christianity. Merton, like a number of Catholic contemplatives and mystics before him, such as Père Charles de Foucault and Louis Massignon, took important steps in laying the foundation upon which an authentic understanding can be achieved between the followers of Christ and followers of the Prophet and the Quranic revelation, which created a world in whose Islamic firmament the light of Christ as Sayyidnâ 'Îsâ (Jesus)—upon whom be peace—continues nevertheless to shine.

Bethesda, Maryland
January 1999
Shawwal 1419 (A.H.)

DRAMATIS PERSONAE

Thomas Merton (1915–1968): Cistercian monk (at the Abbey of Gethsemani in Kentucky) and writer greatly interested in non-Western religious traditions. Author of *The Seven Storey Mountain* and many other books read by religious scholars and laymen alike. He died at a religious conference in Bangkok, Thailand, on December 10, 1968.

Abdeslam (c. 1900–1980): Sufi teacher from Tetuan, Morocco, who visited Merton at Gethsemani in the fall of 1966. He was a disciple of Hadj Adda Bentounes, the North African successor of Ahmad al-'Alawî.

Ahmad al-'Alawî (1869–1934): Algerian Sufi master who was the subject of Martin Lings' *A Moslem Saint of the Twentieth Century*, a book which made a tremendous impression on Merton. Al-'Alawî founded a *tarîqah* that is a branch of the Darqawî–Shâdiliyya Order; Merton came into contact with representatives of two different branches of this *tarîqah*.

Abdul Aziz (1914–): Pakistani scholar of Sufism who corresponded with Merton from 1960–68; he sent Merton many books on Sufism from his own library.

Louis Massignon (1883–1962): French Islamicist and devout Catholic with whom Merton corresponded from 1960–62.

Marco Pallis (1895–1989): Author, mountain climber, scholar of Tibetan Buddhism and Sufism, and a leading member of the traditionalist school of thought associated with Frithjof Schuon. He corresponded with Merton frequently starting in early 1963.

Frithjof Schuon (1907–1998): Preeminent traditionalist thinker, scholar of world religions, and leader of a branch of the 'Alawiyyah *tarîqah*. Author of such works as *Understanding Islam* and *The Transcendent Unity of Religions*. Merton never met him, but they were in contact through several mutual friends, especially Marco Pallis.

SUFISM:
NAME AND REALITY

William C. Chittick

A great deal has changed since Thomas Merton discovered Sufism. At that time, only someone pursuing academic studies would have been likely to run across a name like Rûmî, whereas today any bookstore carries a few collections of his poetry. The "whirling dervishes" were known only as one of the bizarre manifestations of the Orient, but today people take courses on Sufi dancing at the local health club. "Sufism" was a piece of exotica, but today it is mentioned in daily newspapers and best-selling novels. Thirty years ago, someone not writing for a specialist audience would have had to assume that his readers had never even heard the name *Sufism*, but today one has to assume that everyone has some idea of what the word means.

What Thomas Merton discovered was an opening into a spiritual universe parallel to his own, but most people today think that Sufism is one of the New Age fads. So, despite the fact that the word is much more familiar, one still has to assume that most people know nothing about it, and one also has to free the word from all the detritus.

Already a thousand years ago, a Sufi teacher called Bûshanjî (d. 959) complained about the misunderstandings of his times. "Today," he said, "Sufism is a name without a reality, but it used to be a reality without a name." Nowadays, in North America, the name has become relatively well known, but the reality has become far more obscure than it ever was in the past. The divide between our own times and the times of Bûshanjî—when the various phenomena that came to be named "Sufism" were just beginning to have a shaping effect on Islamic society—is so deep and stark that I doubt that it is possible to recover anything more than a dim trace of the "reality" about which Bûshanjî was speaking. Nonetheless, even the trace of such a reality—in an age that knows little of "reality" in this sense—is certainly worth pursuing.

First, however, I need to say something about the name. Anyone who has looked at the various teachers and groups that go by this name in present-day America will have been left with the impression of a great heterogeneity of beliefs and practices. In fact, it is difficult to suggest what exactly it is that ties them all together, other than a connection—sometimes quite tenuous—to the religion of Islam and a tendency toward what might be called "mysticism" or "esoterism" or "spirituality."

It probably does not help us much, however, to employ these terms, because they are almost as elusive and difficult to pin down as the name *Sufism* itself. Suggesting, as is often done, that Sufism is "Islamic mysticism" or "Islamic esoterism" simply puts one unknown in place of another. People do not agree, after all, on what the words *mysticism* and *esoterism* mean, but everyone has a good sense of their connotations and is likely to have a positive or negative reaction to them. The term *spirituality* may be a bit better, but it also is notoriously vague, and in fact it is simply a contemporary way of saying "religion," a term that is less than fully respectable in polite society. In order to make sense of naming Sufism with our home-grown labels, we would first need to provide a detailed and careful definition and analysis of the meaning of these labels, and then we would find that the labels are still far too vague and far too specific to explain the reality of Sufism. I think that we are better off stating from the outset that, although indeed there may be family resemblances among Sufism, esoterism, mysticism, Yoga, Zen, and many other such phenomena, each of these terms needs independent examination, and none of them per se will help us get closer to Sufism's "reality."

The use of the name *Sufism* itself already presents us with several difficulties, and we do not need the added complication of explaining how a Western-language term does or does not coincide with what is designated by this name derived from Arabic. Although the Arabic term is widely used in the classical texts of Islamic civilization in several different languages, before the present century it always had a rather limited definition and was rarely used in the broad sense that it has now acquired. Nor is there any agreement in the texts as to what exactly the word means, and it is common for authors to argue both about its meaning and its legitimacy.

For those authors who use the term *Sufism* in a positive sense, it is associated with a broad range of ideas and concepts all having to do with achieving human perfection through following a path that leads to God. Moreover, it is usually employed to point to a certain moral and spiritual transformation that the travelers on this path should be striving to achieve. But, as Carl Ernst has pointed out in his important recent book, *The Shambhala Guide to Sufism*, the actual term *Sufism* was given prominence not by the classical Islamic texts, but rather by British Orientalists, who wanted a word that would refer to the various dimensions of Islamic teachings that they found attractive and congenial and that would avoid the negative stereotypes associated with Islam itself—stereotypes that were often propagated by the same Orientalists.

In short, scholars in the field of Islamic Studies do not agree about what exactly the term *Sufism* means or should mean, and their disagreement is a fair reflection of the use of the term over Islamic history. Personally, I use this rather obscure term because we need a name to refer to a certain something that surfaces throughout Islamic history, and the alternatives that have been offered to designate it are more problematic than *Sufism* itself.

Having said all this, I am, of course, not about to provide a nice, succinct definition of Sufism. As I understand the issues, the reality of Sufism is far too subtle and elusive to lend itself to neat delineation and classification. Nonetheless, we do need the word in order to differentiate a certain more inward approach to Islamic teachings and practices from other approaches, all of which have their own designations.

In searching for Sufism's reality, we first have to bring out what the name represents in relation to the names of other phenomena that have appeared in Islamic history. As should be obvious to everyone—though it is often forgotten in the rush to pin labels on things we don't know much about—the religion of Islam, numbering today over a billion followers, has been and remains a vastly diverse and complex tradition, whether historically, geographically, culturally, linguistically, politically, or whatever. Nonetheless, it is not difficult to argue that the name *Islam* points more or less adequately to a core or an essence that is shared by diverse manifestations over history. To begin with, what properly deserves this name must be rooted in the Qur'an, the revealed book that lies at the foundation of the tradition, and the Hadith, which are the teachings given by the recipient of the Qur'an, the Prophet Muhammad.

The Qur'an and Hadith cover a vast range of topics, ranging from God, angels, and prophets to toothbrushes and toilet training. The "religion of Islam" represents the attempts of Muslims over history to understand the wisdom offered in the Qur'an and to put it into practice on the basis of the model—called the "Sunnah"—provided by the Prophet. It was the natural calling of those who took their religion seriously to attempt to embrace all the knowledge and right conduct handed down from the Qur'an and the Prophet. But it was also natural that people were attracted to what corresponded to their own talents and aptitudes, which is to say that some Muslims focused more on practical teachings, some focused more on intellectual teachings, and some focused more on spiritual teachings. It was a rare individual who was able to focus on all three levels and bring them into the harmonious balance that was achieved by the Prophet himself.

In terms of the literary sources of Islam, the process of understanding and assimilating the teachings of the Qur'an and the Prophet came to be reflected in the gradual development of several different intellectual disciplines, each supported by many scholars who investigated and clarified the nature of the sources and the manner of putting them into practice. Already in the earliest sources, in fact, there are clear precursors for the work of giving order to the diversity of Islamic learning and to classifying the various elements in terms of their order of importance. This process of investigation, classification, and clarification, and the resulting specialization to which it naturally gave rise, can be observed among learned Muslims throughout Islamic history. By Islam's third century (that is, the ninth Christian century), one can find a great variety of approaches to Islamic learning, each of which was considered by its proponents to be focused on the most important elements of the Qur'an and the Hadith. It is around this time that certain people were calling themselves "Sufis" for the first time, although the same people were also calling themselves by other names, such as "knowers" and "ascetics" and "renouncers." What is peculiar about the term *Sufi* is that its derivation is not completely clear, so it took on the aura of a proper name. But, if the name was new, the focus and interests of the Sufis were not by any means new. The "reality," as Bûshanjî pointed out, was there from the beginning of Islam. Only when this name appeared and began to be discussed—even by those who were in no way qualified or prepared to understand what the reality was—did the reality become elusive, if not lost.

Sufism, then, is one of the terms that was applied to a certain interpretative approach to the teachings of the Qur'an and the Hadith, an approach that had specific, concrete applications in the daily practice of the religion. To clarify what sort of teachings these were, it is necessary to clarify the basic components of Islamic teachings. In doing so, I will use one of the oldest and most traditional of methods, one that goes to the Prophet himself. This is the division of the whole religious enterprise called "Islam" into three basic dimensions, corresponding to practice, knowledge, and interiority; or body, mind, and heart.

On the most external level, Islam is a religion that teaches people what to do and what not to do. Right and wrong practices are clearly delineated and codified in a system of law that gradually came to be known as "Shariah," a word that originally designated a road that leads down to water. The Shariah is a great compendium of systematic law, based squarely on Quranic teachings and Prophetic practice, but adjusted and codified by generations of scholars. The Shariah is like the body of Islam in that it designates proper activities, all of which are performed by the body, and in that it is utterly essentially for the existence of the mind and heart. The most important of the activities and practices that it delineates must be observed by all Muslims, and for this reason they are called the "Five Pillars" of the religion.

On a deeper level, Islam is a religion that teaches people how to understand the nature of things. This second dimension, which corresponds to the mind, has traditionally been called "faith," because its fundamental focus is to grasp and understand the objects to which faith attaches. These objects are God, the angels, the scriptures, the prophets, the Last Day, and the "measuring out" of good and evil. These are mentioned several times in the Qur'an and the Hadith, and investigation of their nature and reality became the domain of various disciplines, such as theology, philosophy, and theoretical Sufism. Any serious attempt to investigate these objects globally cannot fail to enter into an investigation of every human concern, whether in this world or the next. The great scientists of Islam who have been studied and admired by Western historians were invariably trained in this dimension of the religion. So also, the most famous of the Sufis were thoroughly grounded in the theoretical knowledge of the objects of faith.

On the deepest level, Islam is a religion that teaches people how to transform themselves so that they may come into harmony with the ground of all being. Neither activity nor understanding is humanly sufficient, nor are both together. Activity and understanding must both be focused in such a way that they bring about human goodness. This goodness is inherent and intrinsic to the original human nature, made in God's image, and it does not depend on outward activity for its presence. If the first dimension of Islam has in view the activities that must be performed because of our relational situation with others and with God, and the second dimension has in view right understanding of the nature of things, the third has in view seeking out constant presence with God. For those with any sensitivity to the interior life, the various terms that are employed in discussing the focus of this third dimension are immediately recognizable as the *raison d'être* of religion itself. These include sincerity, love, virtue, and perfection.

All three dimensions of Islam have been present wherever there have been Muslims, because Muslims cannot take their religion seriously without putting it into effect in their bodies, their minds, and their hearts; or in their activity, their thinking, and their being. But these dimensions became historically embodied and institutionalized in a large number of forms, the diversity of which has all sorts of causes, about which historians have written no end of books. After all, we are talking about how Muslims practice their religion, how they conceptualize their faith and their understanding of the nature of things, and how they express their quest to be present with God. We are talking about various schools of Islamic law and institutions of government, diverse schools of thought investigating the nature of God and the human soul, and multifarious institutions that guide people on the path of spiritual aspiration and crystallize their vastly different experiences of God's presence in their lives.

These diverse expressions of Islam, which have undergone tremendous historical and regional variation, have been given many names over Islamic history, and the whole situation has become much more complex because of the investigations of modern scholars, who have had their own programs, agendas, and goals. More often than not, the scholarly community has had little sympathy for the object of its study and for the way in which Muslims have understood themselves. One of the most obvious and striking characteristics of Thomas Merton's mentions and discussions of Islam is precisely his ability to see through the obfuscations of the scholars and his recognition that Islam represents an enterprise of the human spirit as complex and deep as Christianity. It is somewhat less remarkable today to hear a non-Muslim take this position than it was a few years ago, but it is still the position of only a minority of the supposedly qualified observers.

It should be clear from what I have said that Islam, like any religion, embraces the whole range of human activities and concerns, and the Islamic approach to these has become manifest in a great variety of forms and institutions over history. In contrast to the stereotypes, Islam has a special affinity for diversity of expression. Part of this has to do with the fact that it has nothing to compare to the centralized authority of the Christian church. Instead, it has produced a great variety of institutional forms that come and go, all with the function to transmit and inculcate the necessities of practice, understanding, and the interior life.

There has always been a good deal of diversity among the schools of Islamic law, of which there are five that still play major roles today. And there has been no end to disagreement and debate among the three major intellectual perspectives—theology, philosophy, and theoretical Sufism—each of which has several schools. But perhaps the greatest diversity of Islamic expression has been found on the third level, that of the heart, or the domain that can be called "Sufism" in the most general sense of term. In this broad sense, "Sufism" can be understood to refer to the inner life of practicing Muslims. It is an essential part of the religious experience of most serious Muslims in one way or another. It is also the most personal and private dimension of the religion and by nature the least given to explication and exact expression. It refers, in short, to the secret quest for God in the inner castle, and any attempt to explain precisely what this is or should be can only be the proverbial finger pointing at the moon. Of course, I do not mean to imply that all devout Muslims consider themselves "Sufis" of some sort or another. Quite the contrary, for a wide variety of reasons, the name itself — which has always had its critics and detractors—has become especially suspect among modern-day Muslims. Nonetheless, it would be rare indeed to find any Muslim who denies the value of sincerity in observing the divine commandments, love for God, and virtue, and these are precisely the focus of Sufi learning and practice throughout Islamic history.

One of the most common terms that is used to designate what I have just named "Sufism" in Islamic texts is *ma'rifah* (or *'irfân*), a term which means simply "knowledge" or "recognition." However, the term connotes a special, deeper knowledge of things that can only be achieved by personal transformation. Often the goal and fruit of this type of knowledge is explained by citing the Prophet's saying, "He who knows [*'ârafa*] himself knows his Lord."

In short, *ma'rifah* demands knowing one's own innermost self, and this self-knowledge is the prerequisite for knowing God. The texts tell us repeatedly that *ma'rifah* cannot be found in books. In fact, it is already present in the heart, but it is hidden deeply beneath the dross of forgetfulness and ignorance. Recovering this knowledge from the heart is the most difficult of tasks. The famous theologian, philosopher, and Sufi al-Ghazâlî (d. 1111) compares the heart to a pond, fed by a hidden spring that has been clogged by mud and debris, so that the pond receives water only from rain. Through practice of the pillars of Islam, purification of self, and remembrance of God, one gradually removes the debris and mud from the bottom of the pool. Eventually, the hidden spring opens up and finishes the task of purifying the water. Then one has no need to go outside of self in search of God, for the water of the divine life and knowledge flows freely in the heart.

Generally speaking, those who have become famous in the West as "Sufis"—such as al-Hallâj, Rûmî, and Ibn al-'Arabî—represent a few of the more outstanding Muslims who have spoken for the innermost dimension of the religion. But it should be kept in mind that despite the constant publication of Sufi texts throughout the Islamic world ever since the introduction of printing, the vast majority of Sufi authors have never been published, and even those who have been published remain largely unstudied and unread. The literature is vast, and the modern interest is scant, especially among contemporary Muslims. For every Hallâj who has been studied in modern times there are dozens of other major figures waiting to be investigated.

Moreover, it is important to remember that what has been written down by the Sufis, or about the Sufis, represents only a tiny fraction of the phenomenon of Sufism, since the vast majority of Muslims devoted to God—including most of those who were known in their own time or by later generations as great Sufis and knowers—did not have the vocation of writing. The literary output represents only the "name" of a much deeper and broader reality that by nature cannot be known from the outside.

*

* *

I spoke earlier of "theoretical Sufism" without any explanation other than to say that it represents one of the three main approaches to the objects of faith, or to Islamic understanding. What differentiates the Sufi approach from that of philosophy and dogmatic theology is mainly that the Sufi authors rely on ma'rifah—the direct knowledge of self and God that flows freely in the purified heart. In contrast, both the theologians and philosophers affirm the necessity of 'ilm, which one can translate as knowledge, science, or learning. They insisted that the primary means of gaining knowledge was reason, and the theologians added that reason had to submit to the givens of revelation. Like the theologians and unlike the philosophers, the Sufis gave pride of place to the Qur'an and the Hadith, but they also held that the only way truly to understand the revelatory message was the inner purification that made a person worthy to be taught directly by God Himself. They like to quote the Quranic verse, "Be wary of God, and God will teach you" (2:282). Since "being wary of God" (taqwâ) is designated by the Qur'an itself (49:13) as the highest human attribute in God's eyes, this verse was a powerful scriptural support for the Sufi position. Abû Yazîd al-Bastâmî, a ninth-century figure looked back upon as the "sultan" or chief authority of those who receive their knowledge directly from God (sultân al-'ârifîn), is reported to have said to certain scholars who were objecting to his formulations of Islamic teachings, "You take your knowledge dead from the dead, but I take my knowledge from the Living who does not die."

The Sufis sometimes called direct knowledge of God "unveiling" (*kashf*). Partly because unveiling usually takes the form of a vision-ary, imagistic knowledge, they made frequent use of poetry to express their teachings about God, the world, and the human soul. Many of them felt that poetry was the ideal medium for expressing the truths of the most intimate and mysterious relationship that human beings can achieve with God, that is, loving Him and being loved by Him. In Islamic civilization in general, poetry is the most important literary form, and it has always been widely popular among the both the literate and illiterate classes. I would argue that in the vast majority of the Islamic world—that is, wherever Arabic was not the mother tongue—the various poetical traditions of the Islamic languages were far more important for propagating the teachings of the Qur'an than the Qur'an itself. And most of the really great and popular poets were either Sufi masters or spokesmen for the teachings of this innermost dimension of Islam.

If we look at the content of Sufi teachings rather than at the pecu-liarities of Sufi methodology, we can see that the key element that differentiates their approach to explaining the Qur'an's message is to stress the nearness, presence, and immanence of God rather than his distance and transcendence. There are many Quranic verses that speaks of God's nearness, such as, "And We are nearer to him than the jugular vein" (50:16) or "And He is with you wherever you are" (57:4). The general approach of the theologians was to interpret these verses as metaphors so as to emphasize God's transcendence and to remove any suggestion of a personal nearness. In contrast, the general Sufi approach was to stress the importance of a more literal understanding of these verses in order to grasp God's concern for human welfare and the ultimate destiny of the human soul. They held that such "anthropomorphic" verses should not be taken as mere metaphors, but rather as statements of the actual situation—though the Sufis never fell into the trap of ignoring the comple-mentary teaching, that is, that God is also distant and transcendent.

The Sufi attempt to balance the demands of transcendence and immanence helps explain why they are especially fond of paradox-es—statements that ignore the law of non-contradiction—which they tend to express as aphorisms and employ frequently in their poetry. One of the functions of these paradoxical explications of God's relationship with human beings is to break down the insistence of the rational mind that everything can be explained and grasped. In fact, God does not fit into our categories. Everything in our world and our experience must be one thing or another, but God is both nothing and everything. He is both near and far, both transcendent and immanent, absent and present, both this and not this.

Many Sufis maintain, in fact, that true understanding of God can only be achieved through perplexity and bewilderment. The paradoxical and sometimes scandalous utterances that tend to emerge as a result are simply the outward manifestation of inner awe, wonder, and astonishment, which render the rational mind incapable of employing its usual care and precision. According to some Sufis, bewilderment in face of God's reality is in fact the highest stage of human understanding. One of their favorite expressions of this perplexity in God is an aphorism that goes back to Abu Bakr, the close companion of the Prophet and the first caliph after the Prophet's death. He said, in a concise paradox, "Incapacity to perceive is perception." We perceive the things of this world by perceiving them, but we perceive God by the clear recognition of the impossibility of perceiving Him.

So important is the stress on paradox and bewilderment for Sufi rhetoric that it is easy to classify most Sufi authors on a continuum in keeping with the degree to which it enters their discourse. The Sufis themselves frequently call the two extremes of this continuum "sobriety" and "drunkenness," and it is common for them to discuss their forerunners in terms of stress on one side or the other. This pair of terms coincides with many other pairs that also enter into discussions of the nature of the God–human relationship, such as fear and hope, contraction and expansion, gathering and dispersion.

Drunkenness, expansion, and hope correlate with God's nearness. Drunkenness designates the joy of the seekers in finding the eternal source of all joy within themselves. God's nearness in turn is closely related to those of his names that designate mercy, compassion, love, kindness, gentleness, and so on. In contrast, sobriety, contraction, and fear correlate with God's distance and the clear differentiation of the individual from the source of all good. Sobriety refers to the human response to divine names that designate God's majesty, glory, splendor, magnificence, might, wrath, and vengeance.

These two poles of the experience of God become manifest in human cognition through reason and imagination, which are the "two eyes" with which people see their way to God. The eye of reason knows nothing of God's presence, because its analytical approach can only dissect endlessly and prove that God is nowhere to be found. Soberly, reason talks of God's distance and transcendence, and all of us rational people are quickly convinced by the reasonableness of its arguments. In contrast, the eye of imagination, unveiling, and ma'rifah revels in God's presence and throws away all pretensions to sober judgment and logical precision.

In short, on one extreme we have Sufis whose expressions and discourse can be categorized as intoxicated by the wine of their Beloved's presence, and on the other extreme are Sufis who soberly evaluate the nature of things and explain in clear and reasonable detail the nature of our existential situation in face of God. It is the sober works that also describe in careful detail the provisions and equipage that travelers will need in order to undertake the long journey to God and then, at the end, to find him present in their own souls, where he had been waiting for them the whole time. The provisions and equipage for the road pertain to the three basic dimensions of Islam—practice, understanding, and purity of heart.

Reading the Sufi writings, we quickly see that poetry tends toward intoxication and prose toward sobriety. But even Sufis who never wrote anything can often be classified as sober or drunk because of the accounts of their lives and teachings that have come down to us. Many Sufi authors make use of both modes of expression and try to strike a happy balance between the two. And by and large, Sufi teachers have come out in favor of the superiority of sobriety over drunkenness.

In the frequent Sufi discussions of the relative virtues of these two, we commonly meet the description of three stages on the Sufi path. The first is the initial sobriety that is achieved through repentance and awakening, when the aspiring seekers turn away from the follies of this world and come to their senses after having been drunk and besotted with the trappings and goals of ordinary life.

After long and intense struggle on the path of self-discipline and purification, the travelers are opened up to the effusions of divine love, mercy, and knowledge. They are so overcome by drunkenness that they lose their rational capacity and tend to express themselves in ecstatic and paradoxical language.

But this is not the final stage. Neither the Prophet nor the vast majority of the great Muslims who followed in his footsteps can be said to have been intoxicated. Practically all of them had reached the furthest stage, which is sobriety after drunkenness. This is the return to the world after the journey to God. Through the journey, the seekers undergo total transformation, and now they return to the world with helping hands. They began as stones, they were shattered by the brilliance of the divine light, and now they have been resurrected as fine jewels—beautiful, luminous, and fixed in the divine attributes.

For those who know something about Sufi teachings, it should be clear that the two higher stages of this tripartite scheme—that is, "drunkenness" and "sobriety after drunkenness"—correlate with the famous expressions *fanâ'* and *baqâ'*, or "annihilation" and "subsistence." Through the journey of self-purification and devotion to God, the travelers reach a stage where they become fully open to the divine light, and the brilliance of this light annihilates all the human attributes that had held them back from seeing their true selves and their Lord. This annihilation of obstacles and impediments allows them to see that they in themselves had been nothing and are still nothing, because God alone has true reality. Instead of themselves, who had never had any reality to speak of, they now see what subsists after the annihilation of false selfhood. What remains in the station of subsistence is precisely God in his full glory, and this full glory demands the shining of his light. The travelers find that from the beginning they had never been anything but rays of the divine light. They had never had any reality of their own. In their ignorance and heedlessness, they had thought that they were real and God was real, but now, after the annihilation of these false perceptions, they have found the subsisting truth that God alone is real, that God alone shines in the light of this world's darkness, and that perfected human beings—made and then remade in God's image—are nothing but the full radiance of His shining.

This famous pair of terms (*fanâ'* and *baqâ'*) is derived from the Quranic verse, "Everything on the face of the earth is *annihilated*, and nothing *subsists* but the face of your Lord, Possessor of Majesty and Generous Giving" (55:26). The specific divine name with which this verse ends—"Possessor of Majesty and Generous Giving"—is especially appropriate in the context of the spiritual journey, because it alludes to the two-sided perception of things that needs to be achieved. God is the Possessor of Majesty, because He is Great, Distant, Wrathful, Vengeful, King, and Transcendent. His majesty and splendor are such that they annihilate the reality and existence of everything else; only He is truly worthy to be. But God is also "Possessor of Generous Giving," because He is Loving, Merciful, Compassionate, Gentle, Clement, Kind, and Nurturing, and He does nothing but give generously to His creatures. Although His majestic reality annihilates the creatures, His generous giving bestows upon them reality and subsistence.

It is subsistence that is real, not annihilation, for subsistence is the affirmation of an ancient reality, but annihilation is the negation of something that never truly was. In other words, mercy and compassion are primary in the reality of God, not wrath and severity. Here the Sufis typically cite one of their favorite prophetic sayings, "God's mercy takes precedence over His wrath," which is to say that it is the subsistence of mercy that has the final say, not the annihilation that is brought about by wrath, which is in fact a passing accident.

*
* *

One of the most often cited expressions of the final stages of the approach to God is found in a saying of the Prophet. Before I cite it, however, I need to mention a Quranic verse that situates the saying in its proper context. In the verse, God is addressing Muhammad personally. The verse reads, "Say [O Muhammad!]: 'If you love God, follow me, and then God will love you'" (3:31). There is hardly any verse in the Qur'an more important for specifying the rationale for Islamic praxis than this verse. Why is it that Muslims strive so hard to follow the Prophet's Sunnah? The answer is simply that they love God and that they have been commanded to follow Muhammad so that God will love them.

In a typical Sufi reading of the significance of the verse, love for God drives the seeker to search for the mutuality of the situation, which is to say that the lover wants to be loved by his beloved. No lover is satisfied short of reciprocity. The Qur'an tells us here that the only way to show that you love God is to follow Muhammad, and this means that you must follow his practices, that is, the

Sunnah. If one sincerely follows Muhammad, this makes one worthy to be the object of God's love.

The prophetic saying that I want to cite in this context refers to the nature of the final stages of the approach to God. In it, the Prophet explains what happens when someone reaches the stage of being worthy for God's love. Note that the saying refers to two types of practices, the "obligatory" or incumbent, and the "supererogatory" or voluntary. Both were established by Muhammad himself, and both are necessary in order to achieve the final goal. The saying quotes the words of God himself (and is thus technically known as a *hadîth qudsî*, a "holy saying"): "My servant," God says, "draws near to Me through nothing that I love more than what I have made obligatory for him. My servant never ceases drawing near to Me through supererogatory works until I love him. Then, when I love him, I am his hearing through which he hears, his sight through which he sees, his hand through which he grasps, and his foot through which he walks."

In short, once people love God, they put the necessities of this love into practice by following the Prophet. Then they may come to be loved by God. The result of being loved by God is that God's love intoxicates the lover and "annihilates" all human failings and limitations. It drives away the darkness of temporality and contingency, and it leaves in its place the radiance of God's own eternal being. Note here that the hadith says, "When I love him, *I am* his hearing through which he hears. . . ." As some of the Sufis have pointed out, the words *I am* here alert us to the fact that God is already our hearing through which we hear, our sight through which we see, and so on. The problem is not God's nearness to us, because He is eternally near to us and closer to us than our jugular vein. The problem is our nearness to God, which we cannot see and cannot grasp. We have to achieve the seeing of God's nearness, and the only way to achieve it is to follow the prophetic model as closely as possible.

*
* *

Let me come back to where I began, which is the name and reality of Sufism. When people start naming things, the "reality" that tends to get lost is the presence of God. Naming brings about a certain distance, differentiation, and sobriety. The Qur'an tells us that after God created Adam, "He taught him the names, all of them" (2:31). Naming things is part of human nature, because God taught human beings all the names at the beginning of creation. But naming things pertains to sobriety, to the separation and multiplicity of created things that allows us to experience ourselves separately from others. In relation to this sobriety and differentiation, the uncreated and undifferentiated represents a kind of drunkenness, because in God's unity all multiplicity, separation, and otherness are effaced. On the path of the return to God, people become drunk because all distinctions blur and because they are drowned in the sweet ocean of love's unity, an ocean that knows nothing of created distinctions.

The "names" that God taught to Adam are bodies that God gives to those eternal meanings and realities that give birth to this world, and like all bodies, they pass and perish. Also like all bodies, they have fixed archetypes in the divine itself. In the same way, our own bodies name the divine spirit that has been blown into each of us, but each body provides the spirit with a different name. As human beings, we differentiate things through our own selves, because we are the diverse images of the one God. In the same way, we differentiate things though naming the things outside ourselves because we are Adam's children.

The difficulty of our situation arises from the fact that we have forgotten that God taught us the names at the beginning, and that, in order to know the significance of the names, we have to know them as God taught them. This is achieved by loving God rather than by loving the names and what the names designate, and loving God is put into practice by following Muhammad. Then God will love us and revivify the names, and then we will see that every name designates nothing but a ray of God's effulgent reality.

If Sufism began as a "name without a reality," it was because those Muslims who loved God at the beginning of Islam simply loved God and therefore followed the Prophet, and they in turn were loved by God. They had no need to name what they were doing. They lived in harmony with their Creator by following His designated messenger. But as time passed, people found it more and more difficult to live up to the reality of love, to imitate the Prophet with perfect compliance, and to achieve the state where God was their hearing and their sight, speaking to them about Himself and showing them the signs of His presence in all things. Instead, they spoke more and more about how presence with God was to be achieved, and they named it by a name they devised themselves. The name—whether it be "Sufism" or something else—is perishing and of no real account. The reality, however, is everything, and it is this reality that has been the concern of all Muslims sincere in their love for God from the beginning of Islam.

MERTON'S REFLECTIONS
ON SUFISM

Burton B. Thurston

When Thomas Merton gave a series of lectures on Sufism he began by saying: "Don't let anyone give you a course on Sufism, and I have no right to talk about Sufism. . . . It will be wasting a half hour before Vespers." However he might have meant this comment, we know that there is in Merton that empathy, stressed some years ago by Wilhelm Dilthey in his "Die Entstehung der Hermeneutic," that, unless you can enter the mindset and thought patterns of the author, your understanding will be faulty and wrong. As I followed his correspondence, journals, and lectures which touched on Sufism, my feeling increased that Merton's knowledge of Sufism had reached a point where a non-Muslim could go no further than he had gone.

The key to understanding Merton's reflections on Sufism is a very simple, straightforward statement which he made in his first lecture to the novices at Gethsemani: "The Sufis are seeking to know God and have ways of seeking to know God and this should have some success with us. . . . We should be closer to the Sufis."[1] For the sake of his audience Merton goes into the fundamentals of Islam and its nature as a prophetic religion, but soon moves into the esoteric and mystical enclave of the Sufis.

He is comfortable with the assumed and historical relations between Sufis and Christian mystics. He is strongly tempted from his own experience of praying over the Cautions and Councils of St. John of the Cross to see the presence of Sufi influence through Ibn

Abbad on St. John. He was impressed, but probably not surprised, at Abdul Aziz's interest in John of the Cross.[2]

The Sufi distinction in the two kinds of holy war or *jihâd* became a special emphasis in Merton's treatment of the Sufi "path" (*târiq*). The Sufis see the greatest war, or the *jihâd al-akhbâr*, as the holy war against yourself, which is a lifelong battle. This opening to the means of entering the spiritual life on the part of the Sufis was filled with a variety of possibilities which Merton would explore.

When Sufis enter the "path" and pass through various stages they ultimately face indecision and "bewilderment." This was a live catalyst for Merton in dealing with novices in the monastery. He looked upon the trials of the spiritual life as an essential stage in the development of that life. He found a congenial parallel in the Sufi stage of "bewilderment" (*dahash*). It was not clear in his comment at the end of his third lecture whether he was talking only about Sufis or including all mystics. "We get into total bewilderment, we lose our own hearts. They say we are no longer able to get in contact with the best of our own being." Among the Sufis this was a specific time of development and was the stage just before the final stage. This idea of bewilderment is especially important to some Sufis. Farîd ud-Dîn 'Attâr thought of bewilderment as the stage before the final vale on the path of poverty and annihilation. The earlier stages are search, love, gnosis, independence, *tawhîd*, and bewilderment.[3] 'Attâr gives a sophisticated form of bewilderment. When praising God, the Sufi poets did not express more than their utter bewilderment. One of the mystical poets wrote that he broke his pens in complete bewilderment (*MDI*, 301).

Thomas Merton uses this Sufi bewilderment to open up the question of inner authority. When conflicting directions face one the question arises: "Who am I and where am I going?" Merton's comment is very pointed: "Shut out the world and all that jazz!" One should not lose his/her identity in the mess. He then quotes a Sufi: "In all these classes of men I sought for my aim. I could not find it."[4]

Closely associated with bewilderment in the thought of Thomas Merton was the matter of trials and testing. He related the trials in the monastic community to the Sufi emphasis upon the essentialness of trials. The martyr-mystic al-Hallâj, whom Merton knew through Louis Massignon, has a loaded sentence regarding trials. "Suffering is He himself . . ." (*MDI*, 72). Hallâj explains this by saying the more God loves a person, the more He will test that person. He takes away every trace of earthly consolation so that the lover has only God to rely upon (*MDI*, 136). Merton sees several contacts between the Sufi emphasis on trials and the monastic life. He concentrated the theme by saying: "You can't live for God without trial . . . love and trials are inseparable."[5] This apparently came as a surprise to some of the newcomers he was teaching. He quoted some unidentified third person who said: "I came here for personal fulfillment and what am I getting these trials for?"

Every stage in the Sufi "path" is encompassed with trials. The major one, as stressed by Hujwîrî who tends to systematization, is the struggle with the "soul" (*nafs*). It is the constant battle with the base instincts. Sûrah [Quaranic chapter] 79 (*an-Nâzi'ât*—The Yearners) is a special admonition to those who would face this struggle. In v. 40 they are admonished "to fear to stand before the Lord and restrain (*naha*) *nafs* from lust." The main duty of the pious is to overcome this trial by acting contrary to the appetites of the soul. Merton picked this up as being also a Christian response when he said in his third lecture to the novices: "The reality comes through struggling with this thing and overcoming it, by God's grace." To the Sufi it was the soul or *nafs* which would incite to evil (Sûrah 12.53), but according to Rûmî this can be completely cured by love. Rûmî, who apparently was a special source for Thomas Merton in regard to the spirit of Sufism, had a majestic view of love.

> From Love, bitter things become sweet,
> From Love, copper becomes golden,
> From Love, the dregs become pure,
> From Love, pain becomes medicine,
> From Love, the dead are made alive,
> From Love, Kings are made slaves, (*MDI*, 124)

Merton looked upon the trials as a mark of the friends of God. "If you are a friend of God you are going to get special treatment. You are going to get a hard time but you will also have a good time. . . . There is not any consolation that has not been prepared for by real rugged suffering."

While there are general similarities in stages of development among various mystics such as repentance, renunciation, fasting, poverty, and contemplation, there was the final stage of the "path" which attracted Merton's special attention. The final stage in all Sufi progress is *fanâ'* which is variously translated as "annihilation," "extinction," or "passing away." Merton refers to the technical term but then expresses the culmination or goal of the providential trial. Merton's view of the final stage is that "Man is overwhelmed, he is reduced to nothing, a tested heart, a proved heart is a destroyed heart" (Third Lecture). He sees in this idea a form of exaggeration, such as the Sufi emphasis on love, when it leads to the idea that as a friend of God He will destroy you. Even in mystical metaphor the expression of being killed or destroyed raised serious questions.

In order to reach *fanâ'*, which took on various forms with the Sufis, the destruction or passing of the self was required. Al-Hallâj was executed for heresy when he said *ana al-haqq* (I am the truth) which was taken to mean that he was God, as *al-haqq* was one of the *al-asmâ' al-husnâ* (Beautiful Names of God). Râbi'a lost herself in union with the Divine. Al-Muhâsibî entered into the life of perfect fellowship with God. Dhû'l-Nûn, by gnosis, entered the mystic experience of union (*tawhîd*). Abû Yazîd al-Bistâmî ended personal separate existence and returned into the One.[6]

Following his explanation of the Sufi "path" in his lectures, Merton then concentrated his attention on Sufi worship. This would possibly be a normal or natural counterpart of his expressed views on contemplative prayer. One quotation from his writings had a governing effect on his view of Sufism. He wrote: "Contemplative prayer is the recognition that we are the Sons of God, an experience of Who He is, and of His love for us, flowing from the operation of that love in us. . . . He makes us realize at least obscurely that it is He who is praying in us with a love too deep and too secret for us to comprehend."[7]

This same theme is repeated in his correspondence with Abdul Aziz. On January 30, 1961, he wrote of the value he placed on the prayers for him which were uttered by Aziz and wrote that prayer "represents for us the moment of the nearest presence of God in our lives" (*HGL*, 46). More than two years later he wrote again to Aziz on the subject of prayer and contemplation (*HGL*, 15). He had already begun to work on the similarities between the Sufis and the Oriental Christian mystics. About sixteen months after he wrote to Abdul Aziz asking information, he was giving lectures on the Sufis to the novices at Gethsemani (*HGL*, 41). As time went on and his reading of the Islamic mystics increased, he felt closer to some of them such as Shaikh Ahmad al-'Alawî and al-Junayd. He shared with Aziz in writing his own personal method of worship and prayer, but said that he hesitated to chant the Qur'an because he did not know how to do it correctly (*HGL*, 61–63). He was fascinated by the prayer methods peculiar to the Sufis.

When Merton first took up the study of their prayer method, called *dhikr*, is not clear. While he mentioned it in his Asian journal, that reference is later than his treatment of it in his lectures concerning the Sufis which he gave at Gethsemani at the end of 1965.[8] In his fourth lecture about the holy war against the self, he said: "Now we get to some of their real practices. The one real practice that is really important for them is *dhikr*." It was here that Merton saw the similarity between the Sufi method of prayer and the Eastern monks' hesychastic prayer related to breathing. The Sufis developed *dhikr* (remembrance or recollection) connected with some sort of breath control. One of the Sufis expressed the idea that the breaths are counted, and every time one breathes out in recollecting (*dhikr*) the Lord, the breath is connected with Him. As Merton explained it to the novices, the breathing was related to the recitation of the *shahâdah* or witness that there is no god except God. In one of his humorous notations he suggested that they not invoke aloud the name of *Allah* or he would get fired for having all the novices pray to *Allah*. He said it was perfectly all right to pray the first part of the *shahâdah* as "there is no god except God."

Merton explained to the novices that the method of learning *dhikr* was for the disciple to sit before his Sufi master and then they start breathing rhythmically together. The disciple follows the master and starts saying the *shahâdah* as he exhales: "*Lâ ilâha illa 'Llâh.*" This becomes a total renunciation of everything except God. In this process the disciple concentrates on what is happening. He thinks: "I want nothing, I love nothing, I seek nothing but God." The exhaling breath turns everything out, and then he breathes in love, desire and total concentration on God. The aim is for the whole person to be completely centered on God. Merton commented: "This is actually a beautiful way to pray." He suggests that a Christian could go through the same experience using the Jesus prayer: "Lord Jesus Christ have mercy on me a sinner." To him the breathing and aim were both a help in prayer.

Because of Merton's expressed interest in al-Junayd (d. Baghdad 910), I will close these comments with one of his prayers:

> Turn Thy goodness and mercy toward all faithful men and women who have departed this life in Thy true faith. Be Thou a protector, guardian and defender to them and to us. Forgive the living the evil which they have done and receive their penance. Have mercy upon the transgressors, help the oppressed, heal the sick. Allow us and them to turn to Thee in sincere repentance, such as is pleasing in Thy sight. Be Thou, O God, a protector, guardian, defender and helper to those who fight in Thy holy war, Give them a mighty victory over their enemies. . . . Prosper the rulers and their subjects. To those whom Thou hast set in authority over the faithful give support and lasting joy. Prosper their lives and the lives of those over whom they rule. Show them grace, goodness and mercy and bestow lasting joy upon us and them. Prevent the shedding of blood, let discord and insurrection come to an end and protect us from severe trials. In Thy mercy Thou has promised us this, Thou who art all knowing and all powerful. Grant that we may never see the faithful of Islam draw their swords against one another or any dissension reign among the believers. Instead unite them in obedience to Thee and in all those things which bring them closer to Thee, O God, we pray that Thou wouldst lead us to glory and not to humiliation, that Thou wouldst raise us up and not debase us, that Thou wouldst be for us and not against us. Unify for us the course of things, those matters of the earth which are to be a means for us to fulfill our obedience to Thee, and a help in reaching agreement with Thy will; and those things of the next world which are the highest goal of our desire. In Thy providence send us that which is dearest and most pleasing to Thee, O Thou who hearest the voice of all people and knowest that which is hidden, Thou Lord of the heavens.

NOTES

1. Thomas Merton, "First Lecture on the Sufis: Introduction / Islam and the Sufi Mystics," *The Mystic Life*; The Merton tapes, series II (Chappaqua. New York: Electronic Paperbacks, 1976): tape 1A.

2. Thomas Merton to Abdul Aziz November 17, 1960 In *The Hidden Ground of Love: Letters on Religious Experience and Social Concerns*; ed. William H. Shannon (New York: Farrar, Straus & Giroux, 1985), 44, 53. Hereafter referred to in the text as *HGL*.

3. Annemarie Schimmel, *Mystical Dimensions of Islam* (Chapel Hill: University of North Carolina Press, 1975), 123. Hereafter referred to in the text as *MDI*.

4. Thomas Merton, "The Straight Way," in *The Mystic Life* series.

5. Thomas Merton, "Creative Love and Compassion of God," in *The Mystic Life* series. Hereafter referred to in the text as Third Lecture.

6. See Chapter 10 in Margaret Smith, *The Way of the Mystics: the Early Christian Mystics and the Rise of the Sufis* (London: Sheldon Press, 1976).

7. Thomas Merton, *The Sign of Jonas* (New York: Harcourt Brace & Company, 1953), 291.

8. Thomas Merton, *The Asian Journal of Thomas Merton*; ed. Naomi Burton Stone, Brother Patrick Hart, & James Laughlin (New York: New Directions, 1973), 274.

2

THOMAS MERTON'S INTEREST IN ISLAM: THE EXAMPLE OF *DHIKR*

Bonnie Thurston

Writing to the Pakistani Sufi and mystic Abdul Aziz on December 26, 1962, Thomas Merton remarked, "It seems to me that mutual comprehension between Christians and Moslems is something of very vital importance today, and unfortunately it is rare and uncertain, or else subjected to the vagaries of politics."[1] Thirty years later, alas, the statement is no less true.

Merton is well known as a seminal figure in the Buddhist-Christian Dialogue. His interest in and penetrating insight into Buddhism, especially Zen, awakened a generation of scholars to the study of that subject. Unfortunately, Merton's interest in Islam is less well known, and has been practically ignored by Merton scholarship.[2] One is forced to wonder if this is another manifestation of the general Christian and specifically American unwillingness to learn about and to explore the rich religious and cultural heritage of the youngest of the three great monotheistic religions, Islam. Merton's own study and prayer exhibited no such unwillingness.

The Orientalists who have worked with Merton's Islamic materials have noted not only his great appreciation and understanding of Islam, but its profound influence on him. One scholar noted, "Merton's knowledge of Sufism had reached a point where a non-Muslim could go no further than he had gone."[3] In writing of Merton and Louis Massignon, whose book on the martyred Sufi mystic al-Husayn ibn Mansûr al-Hallâj "was almost single-handedly responsible for arousing scholarly interest in the west in Sufism and Islamic mysticism,"[4] Herbert Mason reports, "Merton told me himself of the far-reaching effect this book had on his life, coming at a particularly critical moment for him, in helping turn his attention toward the East."[5] (Unfortunately neither Merton nor Mason say specifically when this critical moment was or what it entailed.)

In a letter to Abdul Aziz which discusses Martin Lings' book on Ahmad al-'Alawî, Merton remarks, "I speak the same language [as al-'Alawî] and indeed have a great deal more in common with him than I do with the majority of my contemporaries in this country" (HGL, 55). He later asks Aziz when Ramadan will occur in 1965 because "I would like to join spiritually with the Moslem world in this act of love, faith, and obedience toward Him Whose greatness and mercy surround us at all times. . . ." (HGL, 60). In an entry in his journal in 1964 Merton notes ". . . Asia, Zen, Islam, etc., all these things come together in my life. It would be madness for me to attempt to create a monastic life for myself by excluding all these. I would be less a monk."[6] Merton's intense interest in Islam continues to the end of his life and is evident in his last writings preserved in The Asian Journal, especially in Appendix IV, "Monastic Experience and East-West Dialogue," notes for a talk to be given at Calcutta in October, 1968.

In his correspondence in the 1960s Merton makes frequent reference to his studies of Islam, especially Sufism, its mystical tradition. June 28, 1964, he comments that he is writing on "Islamic mysticism for the magazine of our Order" (HGL, 59). December, 1965 he notes, "I will shortly be lecturing on Sufism to the novices and young monks here" (HGL, 41). January 16, 1968, he remarks that he has been giving conferences on Sufism to the monks for about a year, (HGL, 66) and again in April of that year he mentions "weekly talks" (HGL, 66).

Even a cursory glance at the Merton canon reveals the extent of his interest in Islam. Raids on the Unspeakable contains "Readings from Ibn Abbad,"[7] and there are at least four explicitly Islamic poems in The Collected Poems.[8] Conjectures of a Guilty Bystander, A Vow of Conversation and The Asian Journal contain multiple references to Islam. "The Meaning of Malcolm X" in Faith and Violence discusses the Islamic influence on Malcolm X and Arab involvement in the slave trade.[9] A shorter, unpublished writing, "A note on spiritual direction in Sufism" exists.[10] Merton's letters to Reza Arasteh, Abdul Aziz, and Martin Lings in The Hidden Ground of Love all deal with Islam. There are two tapes in The Mystic Life series which record Merton's talks on Sufism. And when he sought to describe the famous experience of March 18, 1958, on the corner of Fourth and Walnut in Louisville, Merton chose a phrase from Massignon's work on al-Hallâj, *"le point vierge."*[11]

Merton's interest in Islam goes beyond scattered references in his talks and writings. Those references represent serious and sustained study. The list of Islamic scholars whose works Merton had read is wide and impressive, and represents the best scholarship of his day.[12] Both Griffith and Mason have noted Merton's extensive knowledge of Louis Massignon, who "was among the twentieth century's most important Orientalists, especially in the area of the study of Islamic mysticism and sociology."[13] A list of the Islamic saints mentioned in Merton's writings reads like a "who's who" of classical Islamic philosophy and Sufi thought. Such a list would include Ibn Abbad, al-Hallâj, Rûmî, Imâm Riza, al-Ghazâlî, Avicenna, Ibn Arabî, al-'Alawî, al-Junayd, al-Hujwîrî, and Averroës.

Why was Merton so interested in Islam, and, specifically, in the Sufi tradition? Several answers come immediately to mind. First, he himself tells us that he held a great many beliefs in common with the Muslim community.

> I can certainly join you with my whole heart in confessing the One God (*tawhîd*) with all my heart and all my soul, for this is the beginning of all faith and the root of our existence. . . . I believe with you also in the angels, in revelation, in the Prophets, the Life to Come, the Law and the Resurrection . . . the differences begin with the question of soteriology (salvation). Personally, in matters where dogmatic beliefs differ, I think that controversy is of little value because it takes us away from the spiritual realities into the realm of words and ideas. . . . But much more important is the sharing of the experience of divine light, and first of all of the light that God gives us even as the Creator and Ruler of the Universe. It is here that the area of fruitful dialogue exists between Christianity and Islam. (*HGL,* 54)

The quotation is helpful not only in outlining Merton's dogmatic kinship with Islam, but in pointing to the root of that kinship which is sunk deep in the soil of spiritual experience. As with his studies of Buddhism, Merton's interest in Islam went beyond the surface facts of history, doctrine or practice, and penetrated to the central spiritual core of the tradition. He refused to be sidetracked by the accidents of history.

For example in tape 1, side B, of the Sufi lectures in *The Mystic Life* series, Merton correctly asserts that "Islam in a nutshell" is that "God wishes to make himself known to his creatures and they know him." Merton continues, "The basic thing in Islam is that man should come to know Allah by his name, not all his names, but by the name he speaks to us under the names of Allah. This is the basic thing in religion, the total response in one's heart and to confess he is our creator."[14] Serious students of Islam will agree with Merton. The basic "facts of the religion," the "sending down" (*tanzil*) of the Holy Qur'an to the Prophet Muhammad, the Five Pillars of Islam, the law (*sharî'ah*), are all gifts of God, ways in which God attempts to make himself known to creation.

Merton's interest in Islam as shown in his writings focused on central Islamic concepts like the unity of God (*tawhîd*) and the revelation of God's word (*tanzil*). But his primary interest was not "the realm of words and ideas," but "spiritual realities." Hence his fascination with the Sufis, with whom he obviously felt a certain "stylistic" affinity. Merton notes that the Sufis "don't have formulas or public answers. . . . They have stories and sayings and hints and proverbs and things like that and you make out the best you can. They just throw all kinds of material around. . . ."[15] As a spiritual writer, Merton was, himself, more a poet and an artist than a systematic theologian, and the Sufi use of story and poem to reveal religious experience was comfortable to him.

Furthermore, in the context of a comment on Ibn 'Arabî and al-Hujwîrî in *Conjectures of a Guilty Bystander* Merton notes the "non-logical logic of mysticism and of direct experience, expressed in statements which do not agree and which nevertheless finally explode into a meaning that can be seized if one has some experience of what is being said." "Sufism is essence without form."[16] Merton found the Sufis' metaphorical and "non-logical" expression of the truths of religious experience congenial.

He also remarked that "One Sufi did everything to be as shocking to the *'ulamâ* as possible. They have a tendency to break all of the laws from A to Z down as a way of hiding their inner life. That is what I have been doing the last 25 years to hide my Sufi experience."[17]

Merton's tone of voice on the tape reveals his wholehearted approval of what he calls the Sufis' "beatnik style." Anyone familiar with Merton will recognize in this statement his awareness and enjoyment of his own unconventionality.

But Merton's interest in Sufism went much beyond the style of presentation of its ideas. He deeply appreciated the Sufi analysis of the human spiritual condition. Burton Thurston's article, "Merton's Reflections on Sufism," describes six areas of interest: the stages of the Sufi path (*tarîq*); the *jihâd al-akhbâr* (the greater *jihâd*, or struggle with the self); the question of inner authority; the matter of trials and testing; the final stage of Sufi progress, *fanâ'* (annihilation, extinction, or passing away); and the prayer method called *dhikr*.[18] It is this final and characteristic Sufi practice to which I wish to devote the rest of this essay.

Dhikr (translated from the Arabic as "remembrance," "recollection," and "invocation") has been called by Islamic scholars the "central means of worshipping God and invoking his presence."[19] Since the names of God form the "cornerstone of Islamic spirituality," *dhikr* is "the very heart of all Islamic spiritual practice."[20] *Dhikr* is a technical term signifying "the glorifying of Allah with certain fixed phrases, repeated in a ritual order, either aloud or in the mind with peculiar breathings and physical movements."[21]

There is both Quranic and traditional support for the practice of *dhikr* in Islam. In the Holy Qur'an, God declares "Remember Me and I shall remember you" (2:235). "'Therefore glorify Me, I will make you eminent, and give thanks to Me and be not ungrateful to Me" (2:152). Prophetic traditions (the hadîth) of Islam report the following statements: "Let thy tongue be forever moistened with the mention of God Most High"; "Be abundant in the mention of God Most High. . . ." The Prophet himself is reported to have quoted God having declared "When my worshipper's thought turns to Me, there I am with him. And when he makes mention of me within himself, I make mention of him within Myself. . . ."[22]

In Islam, *dhikr* is "the means whereby [God] can be known experientially and realized inwardly."[23] While there are different forms of *dhikr*, the practice basically involves the recitation of phrases, coordinated with the breath, centered on the Names of God, of which there are 99 in Islam (divided into the Names of Majesty and the Names of Beauty). *Dhikr* transforms the human psyche. By means of its practice ". . . man first gains an integrated soul—and then in the *dhikr* he offers this soul to God in the supreme form of sacrifice. Finally in annihilation (*fanâ'*) . . . he realizes that he never was separated from God. . . ."[24] According to the renowned scholar of Islamic mysticism, Annemarie Schimmel, not only the tongue and heart are filled with the name of God in the experience of *dhikr*, "but the whole body of the meditating Sufi is permeated so that his blood and each of his limbs is replete with the name of God and practices as it were, its own *dhikr*."[25] *Dhikr*, then, is

> . . . aimed at changing the insinuating self. . . to the state of self at peace. . . . The characteristic of the self at peace is that it merges into the Divine Will and . . . the lover experiences the unveiling of the vision of the Beloved. In that sublime moment, the lover experiences the passing away of the personal self (*fanâ'*) and entrance into eternal life (*baqâ'*), into the Unity of the One Being.[26]

The goal of *dhikr* is that "the invoker (*dhâkir*) becomes the invocation (*dhikr*) and the invocation, the invoked (*madhkur*)."[27]

Merton apparently had spent considerable time in the study of *dhikr*. He mentions it frequently in his letters to Abdul Aziz (*HGL*, 49, 54, 57) and provides the novices with an extended discussion of the practice on side B of tape 2 in *The Mystic Life* series. There Merton calls it "the one real practice that is really important for them," and "a beautiful way to pray" because "what they are aiming at is to try to get the whole man completely centered on God."

He explains "the real way to learn it" as follows

> . . . when the disciple is ready to learn *dhikr*, with abandonment, patience, and the love of God, he sits down in front of the spiritual father and the spiritual father sits there, and they start breathing rhythmically at the same time. The disciple breathes as the spiritual father breathes. The disciple finally takes in the way the spiritual father recites this prayer. He doesn't repeat it; he just listens to it. He breathes in unison with him. He works this way with his spiritual father until he has the spiritual father's rhythm of prayer. The way it normally goes, when breathing out you say, "*Lâ ilâha illa 'Llâh.*" This is the rejection of all that is not God. . . . You breathe out the whole world, and you breathe

in God right into your heart, and you keep on doing it. . . .
Your prayer becomes tied in with this deep breathing. The
idea is that when you are doing this, you are thinking of
your breath being sanctified by God.[28]

Merton was well aware that this Sufi form of prayer was a great
deal like that practiced by the hesychasts in Christianity. He commented to Aziz that *dhikr* "resembles the techniques of the Greek
monks and I am familiar with its use for it brings one close to God"
(*HGL*, 49). Later he noted, "I believe that the 'Jesus Prayer' has parallels with certain Sufist methods of prayer" (*HGL*, 54). And he
calls hesychasm "the point of contact between Christian mysticism
and the Sufis" (*HGL*, 57).

Here Merton has, indeed, isolated a significant point for dialogue
between Christianity and Islam. By hesychasm, Merton does not
mean the hesychast controversy of the mid-fourteenth century. He
is referring to the method of prayer which in the Orthodox tradition
is called the "Jesus Prayer," and which has been associated with the
monks of Mt. Athos. It is the "most classic of all Orthodox
prayers."[29]

A hesychast "is one who in silence devotes himself to inner recollection and private prayer."[30] The founder of this form of prayer,
in which the practitioner regulates the phrase "Lord Jesus Christ,
Son of God, have mercy on me" (some traditions add, "a sinner")
with the breath, is said to be Arsenius the Great (died c. 449), but
its greatest proponents were St. Simeon the New Theologian
(949–1002) and St. Gregory Palamas (1296–1359). The practice
was revived in the Church largely due to the work of St. Nicodemus
of the Holy Mountain, who compiled an anthology on the theory
and practice of the Jesus Prayer called the *Philokalia*, which was published in Venice in 1782 and then issued in an expanded translation
in Russian in five volumes by Theophane the Recluse (1815–94).

The point of the Jesus Prayer is to follow the biblical injunction
to "pray unceasingly" (1 Thes 5:17). "Hesychasm aims at human
integration through constant remembrance of God, which can be
attained by 'guarding' our hearts." Thus the Jesus Prayer is called the
"prayer of the heart."[31] The practitioner bows the head, rests the
chin on the chest, and fixes the eyes on the heart (which is regarded as the focal point of the whole person) as the prayer is repeated.
The prayer of the heart begins with the lips and mind (intellect),

but comes to be "offered spontaneously by the whole being of man."[32] It is reported that for some there comes a time when the Jesus Prayer enters the heart and recites itself spontaneously. For hesychasm the culmination of the prayerful experience is the vision of Divine and Uncreated Light which is thought to be identical with the Uncreated Light seen at Jesus' Transfiguration.[33] Bulgakov, the Orthodox historian and theologian, puts it this way, "Shining through the heart, the light of the Name of Jesus illuminates all the universe."[34]

Notice how much similarity there is between these descriptions of the practice of the prayer of the heart and *dhikr*. In both traditions the practice is learned and practiced under careful spiritual direction. In both the focus is on the Name of God with its inherent holiness and power. In both what begins as a verbal prayer comes to permeate the whole body of the one who prays. In both the one who prays may experience the Divine. In both the goal is human transformation.

Interestingly, when Merton shares with Abdul Aziz what he as a Christian believes in common with Muslims, he uses a phrase from the hesychast tradition. What is important, he says, "is the sharing of the experience of divine light" (*HGL*, 54). Merton had so appropriated both traditions of prayer that he came to use their terminology interchangeably.

Merton's conjunction of *dhikr* and hesychasm is a perfect example of the way he penetrated to the heart of another religious tradition and found the important point of spiritual contact with his own. There are, indeed, in both practice and rationale many similarities between the hesychasts' use of the Jesus Prayer and *dhikr*. But, again, it is not just similarity of practice that Merton points out. He is able to describe the profound religious understanding behind the practice, the meaning of the Name of God.

Many religious traditions place emphasis on the Name (or Names) of God, and Merton knows this. A fragment in *The Asian Journal* records: "[Shaivite] *japa*, [Sufi] *dhikr*, [Zen] *nembutsu*, Jesus prayer."[35] This fact of comparative religions is not the point. What matters for Merton is that the naming of God personalizes religion, establishes relationship between God and human beings.

"Each person knows God by a special name," Merton explained in tape 1, side B of *The Mystic Life* series, "Each one speaks to God with a name that he alone has for God, and God speaks to him with a name God has for him."

> The secret of the life of prayer is to find the name of your Lord, of my Lord, and speak to Him who is your Lord. Don't speak to someone else's God. Someone else's Lord may be Satan to you. You have to be careful. The mercy that some-one else sees in the name of God may be for you destruc-tive. Therefore, one has to be careful not to impose on other people one's own Lord, your own idea of God. The Sufis are very particular about this kind of thing. [36]

According to Merton, our special name for God is tied up with our identity (a subject in which he had much interest and to which he devoted many pages). To use or accept someone else's name for God is to lose our own identity as given to us by God. "To have this name of God by which we know Him, by which he makes himself known to us, is to receive Islam's view of God's mercy."

Would Merton have come to this profound understanding of the relationship between our being named by God and our naming of God had he not studied Islam? No definitive answer can be given. It is certainly true, however, that Islam helped Merton to articulate the point, gave him the vocabulary with which to express and to share his spiritual experience. And the crucial point of contact was, as in his studies of Zen Buddhism, the practice of prayer. Whether it was sitting in the Zen tradition, *dhikr* in Islam, or the Jesus Prayer of Christianity, Merton knew and had the courage to live out the fact that his "own access to God ran through the hearts of other people."[37] For him, "other religions were other people, and not just sets of other doctrines."[38] In Merton, the ecumenist and the person-alizer were united.

He came to understand this impulse for unifying as essential to his vocation, and thus to his identity. "For myself, I am more and more convinced that my job is to clarify something of the tradition that lives in me, and in which I live: the tradition of wisdom and spirit that is found not only in Western Christendom but in Orthodoxy, and also, at least analogously, in Asia and in Islam" (CGB, 194). Merton's motive for this unifying and clarifying was nothing less than the glory of the God Who holds all people in his embrace. He encouraged his friend, Abdul Aziz, "We must strive more and more to be universal in our interests and in our zeal for the glory of the One God, and may His Name be magnified forever in us" (*HGL*, 55).

NOTES

1. Thomas Merton, *The Hidden Ground of Love,* William H. Shannon, ed. (New York: Farrar, 1985), 53. (Hereafter references appear in the text as *HGL*.)

2. At the First General Meeting of The International Thomas Merton Society in Louisville, KY, May, 1989, there was a section of papers on Merton and Islam. Two were subsequently published: Sidney H. Griffith, "Thomas Merton, Louis Massignon, and the Challenge of Islam, *The Merton Annual 3* (1990): 151–72 and Burton B. Thurston, "Merton's Reflections on Sufism," *The Merton Seasonal* 15 (1990): 4–7. [Both are reprinted in this volume.] Also available is Herbert Mason's, "Merton and Massignon," *Muslim World* 59 (1969): 317–18.

3. Thurston, 4.

4. Griffith, 155.

5. Quoted in Griffith, 163

6. Thomas Merton, *A Vow of Conversation* (New York: Farrar, 1988), 62.

7. Thomas Merton, *Raids on the Unspeakable* (New York: New Directions, 1964) 141–51.

8. "The Moslems' Angel of Death," "Song for the Death of Averroës," "The Night of Destiny," and "Tomb Cover of Imam Riza."

9. Thomas Merton, *Faith and Violence* (Notre Dame, Ind.: University of Notre Dame Press, 1968), 182–88.

10. See Item 2.740 in Breit and Daggy, *Thomas Merton: A Comprehensive Bibliography* (New York: Garland, 1986). [Editor's note: "A Note on Spiritual Direction in Sufism" is found among Merton's reading notebooks and is not really an essay, but rather an outline of fragmentary notes.]

11. Griffith, 152, 168.

12. Merton's sources on Islam include Abdeslam (a Sufi master who visited Gethsemani in the fall of 1966), Arberry, Arasteh, Aziz, Burckhardt, Corbin, Foucauld, Iqbal, Lings, Massignon, Nasr, Nwyia, and Schuon.

13. Griffith, 158.

14. Quotations from the tapes are taken from a transcription by Burton B. Thurston.

15. Tape 1, side A.

16. Thomas Merton, *Conjectures of a Guilty Bystander* (New York: Doubleday, 1968). (Hereafter references appear in the text as *CGB*.)

17. Tape 1, side A.

18. See Thurston article, note 2 above.

19. Frederick M. Denny, *An Introduction to Islam* (New York: Macmillan, 1985), 285.

20. Seyyed Hossein Nasr, "God," in *Islamic Spirituality*, ed. S. H. Nasr (New York: Crossroad, 1987), 318.

21. Gibbs and Kramers, eds., *Shorter Encyclopedia of Islam* (Leiden: E. J. Brill, 1953), 75.

22. Constance E. Padwick, *Muslim Devotions* (London: SPCK, 1961), 17, 18.

23. Nasr, 319.

24. Seyyed Hossein Nasr, *Sufi Essays* (Albany: State University of New York Press, 1972), 49–50.

25. Annemarie Schimmel, *As Through a Veil: Mystical Poetry in Islam* (New York: Columbia University Press, 1982), 28.

26. Saadia K. K. Chishti, "Female Spirituality in Islam," in *Islamic Spirituality*, 216.

27. Nasr, "God," 319.

28. Tape 2, side B.

29. Timothy Ware, *The Orthodox Church* (New York: Penguin, 1963/76), 312.

30. Ibid., 73.

31. O'Collins and Garrugia, eds., *Concise Dictionary of Theology* (New York: Paulist, 1991), 91.

32. Ware, 74. For further information on this phenomena, see the classic work, *The Way of A Pilgrim*, and also *The Jesus Prayer* (Crestwood, N.Y.: St. Vladimir's Seminary Press, 1987).

33. Ware, 75.

34. Quoted in Ware, 313.

35. Thomas Merton, *The Asian Journal* (New York: New Directions, 1968), 274.

36. Tape 1, side B.

37. Griffith, 169.

38. Ibid.

3

MERTON, MASSIGNON, AND THE CHALLENGE OF ISLAM

Sidney H. Griffith

Among the books that Thomas Merton was reading on his Asian journey was Louis Massignon's classic study in comparative mysticism, *Essai sur les origines du lexique technique de la mystique musulmane.*[1] It is a book that concentrates on the technical vocabulary of Islamic mysticism in the Arabic language. But along the way the author clarifies the terms he studies by comparing them to earlier Christian usages, and sometimes by putting them side by side with the expressions Hindus and Buddhists use to describe similar mystical phenomena. By 1968 such an approach to the study of Christian religious life was, to say the least, very congenial to Merton. And in *The Asian Journal of Thomas Merton* there are two quotations from Massignon's book that neatly point to the two themes of the present essay.[2]

Merton was struck by the Islamic critique of monasticism, expressed in part in the famous phrase attributed to Muhammad, "There is no monasticism in Islam" (*Essai*, 145–53).[3] Early Muslim mystics had to justify their own behavior in the light of this dictum, and to explain its original import. They advanced in response the notion that what was wrong with Christian mysticism was, as Merton put it, the substitution of "human institutions for divine providence" (*AJ*, 263).

Here is just one example of the insightful challenge to Christian life and thought that one can find abundantly in Islamic texts. Given Merton's concern for the reform of monastic life, it is no wonder that his eye lingered long enough over Massignon's discussion of the issue in the works of early Muslim writers to mark the spot and to highlight a telling phrase or two. The issue reminds the reader of the even more far-reaching critiques of Christianity one can find in Islamic texts. And the Muslim critic sometimes opens a way to a deeper appreciation of truths at the very heart of the Christian's own response to God. We shall explore below another instance in which Merton followed the guidance of Massignon into just such a matter, the mystic center of the human being that Merton, following Massignon, called *"le point vierge."*

Another passage in Massignon's *Essai* that took Merton's attention in 1968 and caused him to reach for pen and notebook is one in which the author explained his approach to the study of the early Muslim mystics. He was after "experiential knowledge," he said, by an "introspective method" that seeks to examine "each conscience 'by transparency.'" The method was to search "beneath outward behavior of the person for a grace which is wholly divine" (*Essai*, 138; *AJ*, 263). Again, this idea struck a responsive chord in Merton. It expressed the sympathy Merton felt for Massignon himself that persisted from their first acquaintance in 1959, through Massignon's death in 1962, right up to Merton's final months in 1968.

The purpose of the present study is twofold: to sketch the outlines of the relationship between Massignon and Merton; and to give an account of the significance of Massignon's phrase, *"le point vierge,"* which Merton found so evocative that he appropriated it for his own purposes. The emphasis here will be on Massignon, whose biography is not so well known to Americans as is Merton's. And while Merton's use of Massignon's pithy phrase *"le point vierge"* has received attention, its origins in the study of the martyr mystic of Islam, al-Husayn ibn Mansûr al-Hallâj (d. 922), has gone unremarked for the most part.[4]

I. MERTON AND MASSIGNON

Thomas Merton was known in the French Catholic intellectual circles in which Louis Massignon was a major figure for almost a decade before they started writing to one another. In the early 1950s Merton published several pieces in the Parisian journal, *Dieu Vivant*, on whose editorial board Massignon served for five of the ten years of the journal's life.[5] And even after his break with Marcel More, *Dieu Vivant*'s moving spirit, Massignon remained friends with many of the magazine's regular contributors. One of these was Jacques

Maritain, whom Merton first met in New York in the spring of 1939 but did not see again until the philosopher visited the monk at Gethsemani in 1966, although the two had by then been in correspondence for years.[6] And it was Maritain who, already in 1952, had urged Massignon to visit Merton when Massignon was on a lecture tour in the United States and Canada.[7] Unfortunately, they never met. But, as we shall see, the writings of Massignon on Islam and other subjects exerted a considerable influence on Merton's thinking in the 1960s. And throughout 1960 they corresponded with one another on an almost monthly basis.

It would be impossible in the small time and space available here to provide even a quick sketch of Professor Louis Massignon (1883–1962) of the Collège de France that could in any way do justice to him. Like Merton, he was a man of many faces, to borrow Glenn Hinson's apt characterization of the numerous roles the monk seemed to assume for the many different people who knew him.[8] And what is more, for all their manifest differences, there are some remarkable parallels in the biographies of Merton and Massignon.[9] This feature of their compatibility would have appealed to Massignon, who was very interested in biography, and liked to plot on the graph of history and current events what he called the "curve of life" of persons whose stories attracted his attention for one reason or another.[10]

A. Massignon's "Curve of Life"[11]

Louis Massignon was the son of a sculptor who was an agnostic, but his mother was a Catholic, and she reared Louis in the pious style conventional among her kind in nineteenth-century France. This is an important item in Massignon's story, one that will have a strong effect at a later turning point in his life. Meanwhile, the father too was a strong influence, playing no small role in encouraging his son's academic career. Furthermore, it was the senior Massignon's network of friends among artists and writers that brought about Louis Massignon's meeting with the Roman Catholic convert and novelist Joris-Karl Huysmans (1848–1907) in 1900. Although the meeting was brief, even fleeting, the young Massignon appealed to the novelist, and the memory and influence of Huysmans remained with Massignon for the rest of his life.[12]

Massignon's first substantive academic project took him to North Africa in 1903 to investigate the terrain in Morocco described by Leo Africanus in the sixteenth century. This enterprise led him to write an appreciative letter, and to send a copy of his thesis on Leo's geographical work to the earlier explorer of the Sahara, Charles de Foucauld, who was then living as a hermit in the desert regions of the southern Sahara.[13] And the hermit became a major formative influence in Massignon's spiritual development.

Difficulties on his North African journey prompted Massignon to master the Arabic language, both the classical tongue and the modern spoken dialects. Eventual success in this purpose led him to Cairo for further studies in 1906. While there he made the acquaintance of yet another spiritual giant. This time the person was long dead, having been executed for blasphemy in the year 922 A.D. He was a Muslim mystic, whose life and teachings it would become Massignon's vocation to explore and to make known not only in the world of Western scholarship, but in the Muslim world as well. His name was al-Husayn ibn Mansûr al-Hallâj (858–922). Eventually Massignon's study of this holy man was published in 1922 as his doctoral dissertation, under the title *La Passion d'al Husayn ibn Mansour al-Hallâj: martyr mystique de l'Islam.*[14] It became a landmark book that was almost singlehandedly responsible for arousing scholarly interest in the West in Sufism and Islamic mysticism. It would be impossible to overstate the book's importance and influence. There were repercussions even in Roman Catholic theology, in that Massignon's advocacy of al-Hallâj's cause raised the question of the recognition of genuine mysticism beyond the Church's formal boundaries.[15]

Long before the publication of *The Passion of al-Hallâj*, there were dramatic changes in Massignon's personal life. While on an archaeological expedition in Iraq in 1908, he became entangled in a skein of dramatic circumstances that disoriented him to the point of attempted suicide. But in these very circumstances, Massignon himself had a mystical experience, an encounter with God, with "the Stranger," as he often said, after the manner of Abraham in the story of the visit of the three angels at Mamre, recounted in Genesis 18. This experience issued in Massignon's conversion from agnosticism, and a certain moral libertinism, to the Catholicism of his upbringing.[16] He attributed his conversion to the intercessory

prayers of his mother, Huysmans, and Foucauld, and to the advocacy of al-Hallâj. Thereafter Massignon lived an intense religious life,
supported by a rather strict Roman Catholic orthodoxy, purified, as
he believed, by the sharp religious challenge of Islam. He recognized
in Islam a genuine heritage from the kindred and ancestral faith of
Abraham. And on this foundation he built his lifelong campaign for
better mutual relationships between Christians and Muslims.[17] The
fruit of his efforts is to be seen in the irenic references to Muslims in
the Vatican II documents, Lumen Gentium and Nostra Aetate, as
well as in the ecumenical efforts of the present-day Secretariat for
Non-Christian Religions and of the Pontifical Institute for Arabic
Studies in Rome.[18]

After his conversion, Massignon continued his scholarly career.
He married in 1914, after some hesitation over the possibility of a
religious vocation. After the First World War, because of his Arabic
skills, Massignon assumed a role in behalf of France comparable to
that of T. E. Lawrence for England in the Sykes-Picot accords in
Syria/Palestine in 1917–19.[19] All the while he continued both his
scholarly and religious interests. In the years 1924–28, he played a
major role in promoting interest in the ideals of Charles de
Foucauld, including the publication of the latter's rule for religious
life, The Directory.[20] In 1931, Massignon became a third-order
Franciscan, and on the occasion of taking the habit, he also assumed
the religious name "Abraham." He professed his private vows in
1932. Meanwhile, in 1931 in Paris Massignon had met Mohandas
Gandhi, in whom he recognized a kindred, genuinely spiritual man.
In the struggles of the Algerian War, Massignon adopted the nonviolent confrontation methods of Gandhi to protest the human
rights violations of Arabs by the French government.[21]

In 1934, Louis Massignon, together with his longtime friend and
associate in Cairo, Mary Kahil, founded a religious movement dedicated to prayer and fasting on the part of Arabophone Christians,
in behalf of the Muslims under whose political control they lived.[22]
The organization was called in Arabic, al-Badaliyyah, a word that in
Massignon's use of it bespeaks a form of mystical substitution of one
person and his merits and prayers for the salvation of someone else.
The doctrine of mystical substitution was very prominent in the
works of later-nineteenth-century French writers, especially
Huysmans, who had a considerable influence on Massignon.[23] What
is more, Massignon found the doctrine in the thought of al-Hallâj.

So it became the focus of his efforts to bring real fasting, prayer, and religious dedication to the joint Christian/Muslim effort to bring about mutual trust and fidelity between Christians and Muslims.[24] In Cairo the *Badaliyyah* movement had a center for its activities run by Kahil, under the name *Dar as-Salam*. There were meetings, prayers, conferences, discussions and fasts held under its auspices. The center also published the bulletin, *al-Badaliya*, as well as a more formal periodical, *Mardis de Dar as-Salam*. In later years Massignon arranged for copies of these publications to be sent to Merton.[25]

The better to align himself with other Arabophone Christians, particularly those living in the Islamic world, Massignon received in 1949 the permission of Pope Pius XII to transfer his allegiance from the Latin rite to the Greek Catholic Melkite rite. In 1950, with the tacit permission of the Vatican and the full cooperation of Patriarch Maximos IV, Massignon was ordained a priest in the Melkite rite. To offer the eucharistic liturgy was for Massignon the perfect way to integrate his personal act of mystical substitution for others with Christ's own gratuitous act of vicarious suffering in substitution for the whole of sinful humanity.

In his scholarly career, Massignon never missed an opportunity to integrate his researches with the aims and purposes of his religious apostolate. A case in point is the work he did to search out all he could discover about the early Christian devotion to the Seven Sleepers of Ephesus. According to their story, they slept concealed in a cave through centuries of the persecution of Christians by the Roman authorities, until the Empire itself became Christian and they awoke to testify to the resurrection of justice. Their cult was popular among Christians in the East from the fifth century onward. What attracted Massignon to their story was the fact that it also appears in the Qur'an, in a chapter (*Sûrah*, 18) that Muslims recite every Friday, the day of their communal assembly. So both Muslims and Christians are devotees of the legend of the Seven Sleepers, and crowds of them come to pay their respects at the shrine of the Sleepers in Ephesus to this very day. Massignon bent every effort to trace the devotion in Christian piety. And in his own native Brittany he found a church dedicated to them at Vieux-Marché near Plouaret, where he often led pilgrimages of Christians and Muslims together, especially in his later years when he was protesting French atrocities in the Algerian War.[26]

From 1953 until his death in 1962, Massignon was engaged in active resistance to the war by every nonviolent means at his disposal, in public and in private. His antiwar activities earned him both respect and obloquy, as one might expect. It is important to observe that for Massignon it was not only pacifism and nonviolence that motivated him. The Algerian War was a conflict between Muslims and Christians, people who are brothers and sisters in the faith of Abraham whom love and hospitality should bring together. Most painful to Massignon was France's own broken word to the Muslims. To resist the war, to give aid to its victims was a religious act for Massignon, and every demonstration or sit-in where he appeared was an occasion to practice the mystical substitution that was at the heart of his devotional life.[27]

Throughout his career Massignon remained very much the French academic, the professor of the Collège de France. His scholarly work was enormously influential. And in this role he was almost another persona. It is no exaggeration to say that he was among the twentieth century's most important Orientalists, especially in the area of the study of Islamic mysticism and sociology.[28] To this day many academics find it almost impossible to reconcile the two sides of the man, the indefatigable researcher and the passionate believer, a confessor of the faith.[29] But they were the same man. Massignon was that rarity in the modern world, a truly saintly scholar.

Massignon's bibliography as a scholar is an impressive one. To read down the list of his publications, books, articles, lectures, and reviews, is to see first-hand how broad his interests were.[30] It would be out of place even to attempt to sketch the profile of his output here. Suffice it to call attention to two collections of articles and essays that, in addition to his scholarly books, present the essential Massignon to the reading public. The first and most important of them is called *Parole donnée*, a collection that Massignon himself supervised, but which appeared only after his death.[31] The pieces included in this volume reflect the whole spectrum of his interests, both religious and scholarly. From the perusal of them one truly gets a sense of the man. What is more, Massignon himself was virtually responsible for the interviews with the author that introduce the book and that are ascribed to the editor, Vincent-Mansour Monteil. So we have for all practical purposes a self-portrait.

There are two other collections of Massignon's essays and articles to mention. The first is the three-volume *Opera Minora* that

Moubarac assembled and published long before Massignon's death.[32] These volumes contain more than two hundred Massignon pieces, many of which are hard to find otherwise since they appeared originally in little known or no longer existent journals. And finally one must mention the recent publication of a selection of Massignon's most important essays in English translation.[33] This volume should go a long way toward bringing the personal side of Massignon more to the attention of Americans than has hitherto been the case. It is somehow not surprising that long before the translations, it was Thomas Merton who knew and spoke of Massignon to the American reading public.

B. *Massignon and Merton in Correspondence*

In the mid-1960s it must have brought a wry smile to Merton's lips to read in his personal copy of *Parole donnée* what Massignon wrote in 1949 about Trappist asceticism. In that year, when *The Seven Storey Mountain* was holding up the Trappist way of life to Americans as a beacon of spiritual health for all, Massignon was maintaining that "in the face of the growing social perversity and the mystery of iniquity at the present time, the ultimate recourse of humanity is right there," in Trappist asceticism (*Parole*, 257). What is more, Massignon went on to say of the Trappists: "When the convents of the strict observance become weak, as we have seen in France prior to 1789 and in Russia prior to 1917, society itself falls into decay" (*Parole*, 259).

In context, Massignon was commending to his readers the purifying prayer and fasting that Trappist monasteries preserved in modern times from the long tradition of Christian asceticism that traced its line of descent in the West from Armand de Rance, St. Bernard, and St. Benedict, all the way back to St. Augustine, St. Basil, and Pachomius. Massignon thought this was a pedigree of sanity for the modern world. He saw its effects in the lives of those who exercised the most spiritual influence on him: Huysmans, Leon Bloy, and Foucauld. So it was perhaps inevitable, given their common friends both ancient and modern, that Merton and Massignon would meet, if only by correspondence.

Maritain had urged Massignon to visit Merton in 1952.[34] But the two men did not in fact meet until the summer of 1959, and then it was only by letter. The person who brought them together was a young American writer, Herbert Mason, who was in Paris for research interests of his own in 1959. He wrote to Merton on May 21, 1959, in connection with his work on St. John of the Cross. And it was not long before Merton and Mason were exchanging letters and poems on a regular basis.[35] In a letter dated August 2, 1959, Mason told Merton about his own enchantment with Massignon and presumably sent him an offprint of one of Massignon's articles on the "Seven Sleepers of Ephesus."[36] For by the end of the month Merton wrote Mason to say: "One of the most fascinating things I have had my hands on in a long time is that offprint of Massignon about the Seven Sleepers" (*Memoir*, 117–18). And in the meantime Merton had sent a reprint of his Boris Pasternak article to Paris. In a letter of August 31, 1959, Mason mentions receiving it and promises to show it to Massignon. By September 3, 1959, Massignon himself is writing to Merton to thank him for the "Pasternak," and with this letter the Merton-Massignon correspondence began.[37]

In the archives of the Thomas Merton Center there are fourteen letters from Massignon to Merton, written in English, and dating from September 3, 1959, to April 26, 1961. They are brief letters for the most part, but they reveal much about the two correspondents. It is clear that they are both searching for holiness, and they are both convinced that their search for it must include some attempt to address themselves to the evils of their own societies. By this time Massignon was actively engaged in his protests against the atrocities of the Algerian War. On August 2, 1960, he explained his ideas about civil disobedience to Merton: "Peace could not be gained by rich means, but through the outlawed, and it was required of us 'to assume their condition' (spiritually I mean), in 'substitution' as our dear Lord did in Gethsemani."[38]

In this brief paragraph Massignon neatly put a practical point on one of his most cherished convictions, the notion of "mystical substitution," an idea that he had spent a good deal of time expounding in his writings over the years. It is not unlikely that Massignon's thinking on this point had an effect on Merton. Already in a letter to Mason, dated September 3, 1959, the same day of Massignon's first Merton letter, Merton wrote: "I want to say how deeply moved I am at this idea of Massignon's that salvation is coming from the most afflicted and despised. This of course is the only idea that makes any sense in our time" (*Memoir*, 122–23).

By spring of the following year, Merton in Gethsemani was fasting in solidarity with Massignon's political actions on behalf of the afflicted and despised North Africans in Paris. On April 21, 1960, Merton wrote to Jean Danielou:

> Louis Massignon strikes me as a grand person. He has been writing about all the causes in which he is interested and I am going to try and do a little praying and fasting in union with him on the 30th of the month when there is to be a demonstration outside Vincennes prison —even Gabriel Marcel participating. This is one way in which I can legitimately unite myself to the témoignage and work of my brothers outside the monastery.[39]

There are other issues in the correspondence that were of more interest to Massignon than they were to Merton. One of them is Massignon's devotion to St. Charles Lwanga and his companions, young Christian men of the royal court of Uganda who in 1886 forfeited their lives rather than renounce Christianity or yield to the sexual requirements of their nominally Muslim ruler.[40] Immoral sexual practices in Christian societies, and even in the priesthood, were of great concern to Massignon. He told Merton in a letter of April 30, 1960, that he had spoken of his concern about these matters to Pope Pius XII in 1946. Now he wanted Merton to help him find out whether or not there was a Trappist monastery in Uganda or neighboring parts of Africa, where prayers and fasting would be offered in solidarity with the sacrifices of Charles Lwanga and his companions.[41] Such an interest was typical of Massignon. It reminds one that for Massignon himself, and for his spiritual friends such as Huysmans, Bloy, and de Foucauld, not to mention Merton, Trappist discipline had been their own means of conversion from lives in which incontinence had been a debilitating factor (*Mésopotamie*, 189).

Merton's letters to Massignon are not nearly so personal, dealing as they do with many of the issues in which both men were passionately interested. But it is clear that Massignon's influence affected Merton deeply. He often spoke to him warmly, in his journals and in letters to others.[42] For example, in a letter to Jacques Maritain dated August 17, 1960, Merton wrote:

> Letters have come to me from Louis Massignon too, his troubles. I have got to be quite close to him with his mystery of suffering Islam, its flint-faced rejection and mad sincerity. I want to understand all the people who suffer and their beliefs and their sorrows. Especially desert people·[43]

One result of the exchange of letters between Merton and Massignon was their widening network of mutual friends. A notable instance is Massignon's encouragement of the Pakistani Abdul Aziz to write to Merton on November 1, 1960. Merton replied on November 17, 1960, and so there began a correspondence that was to continue until 1968, and one in which Merton revealed much of his inner life in contrast to his usual reticence about his personal religious practices (HGL, 43–67). On December 31, 1960, Massignon wrote to Merton to say: "Ch. Abdul 'Aziz (he is the son of a converted Hindoo) wrote me [of his] joy to come in touch with you. He is a *believer* in Abraham's God without restriction."[44]

Merton and Massignon continued to correspond until 1961. And Merton mentioned Massignon with some awe in letters he wrote to other people. But Massignon died on October 31, 1962, thus bringing to an end their correspondence. After hearing of his death, Merton wrote in his journal: "Tomorrow, F. of the Presentation, I will offer Mass for Louis Massignon who died at the end of October. A great man!"[45] Merton then dedicated his own next published book, Life and Holiness, "In Memoriam: Louis Massignon 1883–1962."[46]

Nevertheless, there were still Massignon's numerous articles and books. Merton was reading them up until and even during his journey to the East.[47] They had begun to exchange books and offprints at the very beginning of their acquaintance. At that time Mason was often the go-between. After Massignon's death, he continued to be Merton's contact with the world of Massignon. But already in 1959 Mason was receiving such requests as the following one from Merton: "By the way, I want to put something about Hallâj in the book I am writing, and have nothing at hand. Can you lend or send me anything?" (Memoir, 124).

By the spring of 1960 Merton had received Massignon's *Akhbar al-Hallâj* and *Diwan de al-Hallâj*. On May 12 of that year he wrote to Massignon, "I like al-Hallâj more and more each day."[48] Earlier, on first starting the first book, Merton had written to Massignon: "to read Hallâj makes one lament and beat his breast."[49] In the same letter, Merton had continued:

> How can I begin to write you a letter about the amazing book of the prayers and exhortations of Hallâj? I think it is tremendous. In many ways the rude paradoxes are striking in the same way as Zen. But there is the added depth and fire of knowledge of the one God. There is the inexorable force of sanctity. The sense of the Holy, that lays one low: as in Isaias. . . . may the Lord give me the grace to be worthy of such a book, and to read it with a pure and humble heart, as I hope I have been doing. May I have ears to hear this voice, so alien to our comfortable and complacent piety.[50]

By August of 1960, when Herbert Mason visited Gethsemani, Merton had already read much of the Hallâj material and, as Mason says: "Hallâj and M[assignon] himself struck him deeply as 'knowing the way.' I think Merton sensed M[assignon] was spiritually revolutionary for future Islamic/Christian influences."[51]

It was al-Hallâj, the Muslim mystic, who had fired Massignon's enthusiasm and who played a role in his conversion back to his own ancestral Roman Catholicism. Hallâj the Muslim showed him the way back to God. This was the point that struck Merton: the fact that a compassionate encounter with another, a seeker of the God of Abraham in another tradition, could open a way for one to reach God in one's own heart. The challenge of Islam then meant a challenge to open oneself to the "Other." This was the challenge of *La passion d'al-Hallâj* for Merton, as Herbert Mason reports it: "Merton told me himself of the far-reaching effect this book had on his life, coming at a particularly critical moment for him, in helping turn his attention toward the East."[52]

Merton also had a copy of Massignon's *La parole donnée*, the collection of essays Massignon himself chose to represent the spectrum of his thought, although it was published posthumously. The copy is now in the collection of the Thomas Merton Center at Bellarmine. In certain sections of the book Merton marked passages that particularly appealed to him, especially in the essays on Foucauld, al-Hallâj, and Gandhi, although there are marks scattered through-out the book, indicating a relatively thorough reading. It is clear that reading Massignon did not restrict Merton to Islam. In a letter to James Forest on May 20, 1964, a single sentence makes the point: "I am reading some fantastic stuff on Islam by Louis Massignon, and Buddhist books which I now have to review for [a] magazine of the Order" (HGL, 280).

So it is clear that the Merton/Massignon correspondence was a fruitful one. Each one of them gave his impression of the other man to yet other correspondents. Merton had sent some of his poems to Massignon, who spoke of them to Mason, saying: "[H]e couldn't judge the verses' merit but they showed he was a poet rather than a dry theologian" (Memoir, 143). This was a mark of respect on Massignon's part, who had a dim view of merely academic theologians. As for Merton, he wrote of his respect for Massignon in a let-ter to Abdul Aziz, just about two months after Massignon's death:

> The departure of Louis Massignon is a great and regrettable loss. He was a man of great comprehension and I was happy to have been numbered among his friends, for this meant entering into an almost prophetic world, in which he habit-ually moved. It seems to me that mutual comprehension between Christians and Moslems is something of very vital importance today, and unfortunately it is rare and uncer-tain, or else subjected to the vagaries of politics. I am touched at the deep respect and understanding which so many Moslems had for him, indeed they understood him perhaps better than many Christians. (HGL, 53)[53]

II. LE POINT VIERGE

Conjectures of a Guilty Bystander, published in 1966, is the book in which one finds the most explicit published trace of Merton's collo-quy with Massignon. This is not surprising since he compiled Conjectures from notes, correspondence, and readings from the pre-vious decade (Mott, 429, 631, n. 470).[54] He had been in correspon-dence with Massignon throughout 1960, and he was reading and marking books by Massignon well into 1964, as we have seen. And in *Conjectures* the passage that most commentators cite as evidence of Merton's debt to Massignon is the following one:

> Massignon has some deeply moving pages in the *Mardis de Dar-es-Salam*: about the desert, the tears of Agar [Hagar], the Muslims, the *"point vierge"* of the spirit, the center of our nothingness where, in apparent despair, one meets God—and is found completely in His mercy. (CGB, 151)

One must hasten to point out that contrary to what one sometimes reads, *Les Mardis de Dar-es-Salam* is not the title of a book by Massignon, but the name of the periodical edited by him and published in Paris and Cairo under the auspices of the *Badaliyyah* movement.[55] In 1960, Massignon arranged for copies of the journal to be sent to Merton.[56] And in the volume for 1958–59, there is an article by Massignon on the subjects Merton mentions in the quotation from *Conjectures*.[57] The phrase, *"le point vierge,"* duly appears in the article, but Massignon uses it only in passing here, and one must look elsewhere in his writings to learn what it really means.[58] Clearly, the phrase caught Merton's fancy when he had read it in this place and elsewhere in pieces by Massignon.[59] The vague reference to *Mardis de Dar-es-Salam* must then have been simply the closest reference to hand when Merton made the note that appears in *Conjectures*. For he clearly understood the deeper significance of the phrase, and it will repay one to see how Massignon himself used it before returning to Merton's appropriation of it for his own purposes.

In the sense in which Massignon employed the phrase *le point vierge*, it has its roots in the mystical psychology of Islam, especially as one finds it in the thought of al-Hallâj. Massignon was fond of quoting a saying of al-Hallâj to the effect that "our hearts are a virgin that God's truth alone opens."[60] To understand the saying, one must know how al-Hallâj thought of the mysticism of the heart. Massignon offered the following explanation:

> Hallâjian psychology . . . allows man the guiding rule and basic unity of an immaterial principle: *qalb*, heart, or *ruh*, spirit. How does man bring about the purification of his heart? Hallâj retains the vocabulary of previous mystics who, preoccupied with their asceticism, subdivided and parceled out the heart into successive "boxes," running the risk of confounding it and destroying it with its "veils" out

of desire to reach beyond it to God. Hallâj retains and expands the Quranic notion that the heart is the organ prepared by God for contemplation. The function cannot be exercised without the organ. Thus, if he mentions the successive coverings of the heart, he does so without stopping at them. . . . At the end, he declares mystical union to be real; far from being the total disappearance of the heart, . . . it is its sanctifying resurrection. . . . The final covering of the heart . . . is the *sirr*, the latent personality, the implicit consciousness, the deep subconscious, the secret cell walled up [and hidden] to every creature, the "inviolate virgin." The latent personality of man remains unformed until God visits the *sirr*, and as long as neither angel nor man divines it. (*Passion*, vol. 3, 17–19).

This long quotation from *La passion d'al-Hallâj* has been necessary for it to become clear that for al-Hallâj and for Massignon, "the virgin" is the innermost, secret heart (*as-sirr*)—the deep subconscious of a person. It is to this heart that the saying of al-Hallâj applies: "Our hearts, in their secrecy, are a virgin alone, where no dreamer's dream penetrates . . . the heart where the presence of the Lord alone penetrates, there to be conceived."[61]

If the innermost heart is "the virgin," the other term in the phrase we are investigating, "the point," puts one in mind of "the primordial point" (*an-nuqtah al-asliyyah*) of which al-Hallâj and other Muslim mystics often speak. It is the apophatic point of the mystic's deep knowledge of God.[62] So the "virgin point," *le point vierge*, in Massignon's parlance, is by analogy the last, irreducible, secret center of the heart. The phrase used in this way begins to appear in Massignon's writing in the 1940s, where he uses it even to express a profoundly Christian sentiment. For example, at Christmas 1948, he wrote to Mary Kahil:

The return to our origin, to the beginning of our adoption —by reentering our Mother's womb, as our Lord told Nicodemus, to be born again—by finding again at the bottom of our heart, the virgin point (*le point vierge*) of our election to Christianity and the action of God's will in us. (*L'Hospitalité*, 257)

Perhaps the clearest expression Massignon was to give to what he meant by the phrase *le point vierge* came in an essay he published in 1957, in comparing Muslim and Christian mysticism in the Middle Ages. He wrote:

> The "science of hearts," the early nucleus of the method-
> ological traits of mysticism in Islam, began with the identi-
> fying of anomalies in the spiritual life of the believer who
> prays, who must be simple and naked; the early technical
> terms served to designate the errors of judgment, the men-
> tal pretences, the hypocrisies. . . . The "heart" designates
> the incessant oscillation of the human will which beats like
> the pulse under the impulse of various passions, an impulse
> which must be stabilized by the Essential Desire, one single
> God. Introspection must guide us to tear through the con-
> centric "veils" which ensheathe the heart, and hide from us
> the virginal point (*le point vierge*), the secret (*sirr*), wherein
> God manifests Himself.[63]

Having found this felicitous phrase well apt to evoke al-Hallâj's thoughts about the meeting place of God and man in the human heart, Massignon used it often in other contexts. Presuming its pri-mary sense in al-Hallâj's mystical psychology, Massignon then bor-rowed the phrase, so to speak, to give sharper focus to the discussion of other issues. For example, he spoke of the faith of Abraham as the very axis of Islamic teaching, the "true virgin point (*point vierge*) that is found at its center, that makes it live and by which all the rest is sustained invisibly and mysteriously."[64] And in the passage to which Merton referred in the article in *Les Mardis de Dar-es-Salam*, the "virgin point" is the manly honor of the Muslims, expressed in the rules of sacred hospitality, that by 1960 Massignon was prepared to say he and Foucauld had raped by their "rage laïque de compren-dre, de conquerir, de posseder" before the First World War (*L'Hospitalité*, 155, n. 73).

In a letter to Massignon about this article, dated July 20, 1960, Merton recorded his first impression of the arresting phrase. He wrote:

> Louis, one thing strikes me and moves me most of all. It is
> the idea of the "*point vierge, où le désespoir accule le coeur de
> l'excommuné.*"[65] What a very fine analysis and how true. We

in our turn have to reach that same "*point vierge*" in a kind
of despair at the hypocrisy of our own world.[66]

Massignon's friends also adopted the phrase. In a letter to
Merton, Herbert Mason wrote: "More and more I understand the
visiting of prisons; for once the soul has been dragged out to its vir-
ginal point by the sharpest sin, as a friend here said," grace may
enter in.[67] The friend was most probably Massignon himself. And it
was in offering praise to Massignon's memory that Fr. Georges
Anawati, O.P., used the phrase in a way that recalls its true mystical meaning. He spoke of Massignon's own personal ability to discern the problems of other people, "to touch within them," he said,
the virgin point where the conscience is affected and disarmed
before the living God."[68]

Merton too found the phrase both apt and untranslatable. In
view of its mystical sense, it is noteworthy that Merton chose it to
help express what he had experienced on March 18, 1958, on the
famous occasion of his sudden "realization" at the corner of 4th and
Walnut in Louisville. He later wrote of this event in *Conjectures*,
describing how he realized that "I loved all those people" crowding
the center of the shopping district. And toward the end of the
account he wrote:

> Then it was as if I suddenly saw the secret beauty of their
> hearts, the depths of their hearts where neither sin nor
> desire nor self-knowledge can reach, the core of their real-
> ity, the person that each one is in God's eyes. . . . Again,
> that expression, *le point vierge*, (I cannot translate it) comes
> in here. At the center of our being is a point of nothingness
> which is untouched by sin and by illusion, a point of pure
> truth, a point or spark which belongs entirely to God. . . .
> This little point . . . is the pure glory of God in us. . . . It is
> like a pure diamond, blazing with the invisible light of
> heaven. It is in every body. (CGB, 156–58)

Reading this passage it is not surprising to learn that Merton was
composing this section of *Conjectures* in 1965 by which time he was
already steeped in Massignon's thought and had already adopted the
phrase "*le point vierge*" as his own (*Mott*, 310–11). He used it in
another place in *Conjectures* in a way one cannot quite imagine

finding it in something Massignon would have written, but it is true to al-Hallâj's thought. Merton wrote:

> The first chirps of the waking day birds mark the "*point vierge*" of the dawn under a sky as yet without real light, a moment of awe and inexpressible innocence, when the Father in perfect silence opens their eyes. They begin to speak to Him, not with fluent song, but with an awakening question that is their dawn state, their state at the "*point vierge*." Their condition asks if it is time for them to "be." He answers "yes." Then, they one by one wake up, and become birds. (CGB, 131).

The phrase lingered in Merton's thoughts and appeared later in another published piece as a theme in variation. In *The Asian Journal* one finds the following statement about the contemplative life:

> It should create a new experience of time, not as stopgap, stillness, but as "*temps vierge*"—not a blank to be filled or an untouched space to be conquered and violated, but a space which can enjoy its own potentialities and hopes — and its own presence to itself. One's own time. (AJ, 117).

To follow the trail of a single catchy phrase in Merton's work shows the searcher how inventive a writer he was. It is clear that he met and communicated well with such an idiosyncratic thinker as was Massignon. But Massignon was only one of many persons whose works Merton read, with whom he corresponded, and whose happier phrases he made his own. He was truly a man of many faces. But Massignon was not wrong to have thought "he was a poet rather than a dry theologian."

III. The Challenge of Islam

One thing Massignon and Merton surely had in common was an interest in other people, both in the present and in the historical past. Both of them conducted a vast correspondence with likeminded persons around the world, and both of them spent an enormous amount of their time in research in works written by scholars and saints, not only from the past, but from several religious traditions, not to mention numerous language communities. What is more, this interest in persons, in biography one might say, was not just a passing fancy, for both Merton and Massignon understood that their own access to God ran through the hearts of other people. In the first place, of course, there is the heart of the incarnate son of God to lead one into the depths of the divine. But for both Merton and Massignon, in addition to their faith in Jesus Christ, their encounters with other people who had met God were also of great moment. And nowhere was this more the case than in their encounters with people of other religions. For both of them, other religions were other people, and not just sets of doctrines.

It was through Massignon initially that Merton came to know Muslims, Islam, and something of the Sufi mystical tradtiion. Massignon put Merton into touch with Abdul Aziz, the Pakistani scholar of Islamic mysticism, who was the person who elicited from Merton the clearest description we have of his own prayer practices (*HGL*, 63–64). But it was not Islam that was the other religion which most enticed Merton. Taoism and Zen Buddhism probably enchanted him more. But he did give lectures to the monks at Gethsemani on Sufism,[69] and at a retreat for contemplative women given at Gethsemai in May 1968, he declared, "I'm deeply impregnated with Sufism."[70] In addition, there are those who believe that it was Massignon's relationship with al-Hallâj and his evocation of the Muslim's life of holiness that helped Merton to see the powerful force of the "other," the religious stranger, as one who can kindle one's own fires anew (*Mason*, 317).

Massignon was fond of saying in so many words that it was not he who possessed al-Hallâj, but al-Hallâj who had co-opted him. The Muslim mystic captured his fancy when he was a young man still living a life of incontinence, and still an unbeliever. Al-Hallâj was present to him at his conversion, and remained the focus of his life work in the scholarly world. In his religious life he wrestled not only with questions of vocation and holiness, but with how to find a place for al-Hallâj with him in his Catholic life.[71] On his death bed he was still exhorting his friends to do whatever they could do to make al-Hallâj better known in the world.[72]

Massignon's personal relationship with al-Hallâj brought him to the very heart, one might say *le point vierge*, of the Muslim world. With al-Hallâj he encountered Muhammad, who was caught up with a word of God he was compelled to recite. The Qur'an, coming to the Arabic-speaking world by way of Muhammad's experience of God, brings one face to face with Abraham, his concubine Hagar, his son Ishmael, who were also recipients of God's blessing and promise. Massignon had the sense of a deep personal relationship with Abraham and, as we have seen, took his name when he became a third-order Franciscan. He informed Merton of this fact in his second letter to him, dated September 9, 1959.[73] Of Massignon's relationship with Abraham, one modern historian of religion has written: "In short, it seems to us that for him the religion of Abraham was the 'natural religion,' or the nature of religion; mysticism is its essence, and sacrifice is its end."[74]

Massignon brought all of his personal relationships somehow back to Abraham: al-Hallâj, Muhammad, the Seven Sleepers, St. Francis, Huysmans, Bloy, de Foucauld, Gandhi.[75] And it is in this context too that one sees how the religious values of "substitution" and "compassion" functioned for him.[76] "Substitution" is personal. It requires meeting another person in what Catholics would call the communion of saints. It involves carrying one another's burdens, putting oneself in another's place, accepting another's help. Within the embrace of the immortal communion of the saints, such a personal encounter is a mystical experience. One might say the same thing for "compassion." For Massignon, "compassion" meant getting it right, feeling the other person's predicament to the point that it provokes oneself to action. Massignon's own action in the last years of his life consisted in prayer, fasting, public demonstrations, and civil disobedience in behalf of the victims of the Algerian War. The supreme model for Massignon, the one to whom Abraham points, is, of course, Jesus the Christ, God Incarnate.

It is at this point that Massignon meets the challenge of Islam. In a letter to Merton, Mason once wrote that Massignon used to say that communism is a "cross examination of Christianity."[77] One can say much the same for Islam on the religious level, especially in refrence to the testimony of the truth about Jesus Christ. For Muhammad and in the Qur'an, Jesus, Mary's son, is but a man, a messenger of God. In terms of Massignon's thought, it is instructive to observe the role he sees for al-Hallâj in this regard: "Muhammad halted at the threshold of the divine fire, not daring 'to become' the Burning Bush of Moses; Hallâj took his place out of love."[78]

But Islam's challenge to Christians still stands. In this regard Massignon was struck by what happened on one occasion when a body of Christians came from the old Arabian city of Najran to meet Muhammad at Medinah. The Qur'an only alludes to that event, but Islamic tradition has it that on that occasion Muhammad proposed an ordeal by fire to test who was telling the truth about God and Jesus the Christ, with the Christians themselves and Muhammad and his family ready to be holocaust victims. The Christians withdrew from the challenge on that occasion (*Parole*, 147–67). But for Massignon the challenge still stands. He noted that in November 1219 at Damietta, St. Francis of Assisi stood to the challenge on the Christians' behalf once again, in the presence of the Muslim Sultan. They let him go, and he returned to Italy to receive the stigmata. But in our own day, the same challenge is still before us.[79]

Massignon, together with his friend Mary Kahil, formed the *Badaliyyah* as a way in which Arabophone Christians might themselves accept the Islamic challenge—to put oneself in the place of the other and to take the consequences. He once tried to explain his actions in one of his letters to Merton:

> My case is not to be imitated; I made a duel with our Lord, and having been an outlaw (against nature in love), against Law (substituted to Moslems), and Hierarchy . . . (leaving my native proud Latin community for a despised, bribed and insignificant Greek Catholic Melkite church), I die lonely in my family, for whom I am a bore. . . . I am a gloomy scoundrel.[80]

This is not a statement of despair, but a summary statement of his own situation, as Massignon saw himself. It was all part of the price of putting himself in the other's place, following al-Hallâj, Huysmans—Jesus Himself. It was his way of facing the challenge of Islam.

As for doctrine, Massignon was convinced that contrary to much Christian polemic against the Muslims, Muhammad was a prophet, a negative prophet he used to say, summoned to challenge the Christians and other religious people to the truth of the natural religion of Abraham, and to warn them away from their moral errors. As for the Qur'an, it points to Christ for Massignon. But it is a revealed scripture only in terms of the truth it contains. He called it "an Arabic edition of the Bible with a conditional authority"— conditional because in the end it excludes the full revelation of Jesus the Christ in the Gospel and in the Church.[81]

From Massignon's perspective, Islam and Islamic mysticism, encountering the God of Abraham, pose a challenge for purity of heart to Christians. In concrete terms, Sufism poses this challenge to Christian monasticism. Perhaps that is why in Merton's case he began, in 1967 and 1968, reading steadily in Islamic literature and giving lectures to the monks at Gethsemani on Sufism (*HGL*, 97). And it is why he was still reading Massignon and wondering about the Islamic view of Christian monasticism on his Asian journey. Merton finally thought he understood it this way:

> The Moslem interpretation of this: that Allah did not prescribe the monastic life but some disciples of Jesus invented it, with its obligations, and once they accepted its obligations they were bound to them in His sight. The moral being: how much more will He require others to keep what He has prescribed. (*AJ*, 264).

This is the point at which we began to follow the course of the Merton/Massignon correspondence. It is a good point at which to bring it to a close. Their dialogue was a fruitful one. It continued past the point of no return for both of them.

NOTES

1. Louis Massignon, *Essai sur les origines du lexique technique de la mystique musulmane* (Paris: J. Vrin, 1964). Hereafter referred to in the text as *Essai*. This text has now been translated into English by Benjamin Clark as *Essays on the Origins of Islamic Mysticism* (Notre Dame, Ind.: Notre Dame University Press, 1998).

2. Thomas Merton, *The Asian Journal of Thomas Merton*; ed. Naomi Burton Stone, James Laughlin & Brother Patrick Hart (New York: New Directions, 1973), 263–64. Hereafter referred to in the text as *AJ*.

3. See also, for a different view, Paul Nwyia, *Exégèse coranique et langage mystique: nouvel essai sur le lexique technique des mystiques musulmans* (Beirut: Dar el-Machreq, 1970), 55–56.

4. See M. Madeline Abdelnour, S.C.N., "*Le Point Vierge* in Thomas Merton," *Cistercian Studies* 6 (1971), 153–71; Donald Grayston, *Thomas Merton: The Development of a Spiritual Theologian*; Toronto Studies in Theology,

vol. 20 (New York & Toronto: Edwin Mellen Press, 1985), 9; Anne E. Carr, *A Search for Wisdom and Spirit: Thomas Merton's Theology of the Self* (Notre Dame, Ind.: University of Notre Dame Press, 1988), 69, 157.

5. See Thomas Merton, "Le moine et le chasseur," *Dieu Vivant* 17 (1950): 95–98; "Le sacrement de l'avent dans la spiritualité de saint Bernard," *Dieu Vivant* 23 (1953): 23–43. See also E. Fouilloux, "Une vision eschatologique du christianisme: *Dieu Vivant* (1945–1955)," *Revue d'Histoire de l'Eglise de France* 57 (1971): 47–72.

6. Michael Mott, *The Seven Mountains of Thomas Merton* (Boston: Houghton Mifflin, 1984), 121–22, 461. Hereafter referred to in the text as *Mott*.

7. Letter of Massignon to Merton, September 3, 1959, Thomas Merton Center, Bellarmine College, Louisville, Kentucky. Hereafter referred to as *TMC*. The Massignon letters have now been published in *Witness to Freedom: Letters in Times of Crisis*, edited by William Shannon (New York: Farrar, Straus & Giroux, 1994), hereafter referred to as *WTF*.

8. See E. Glenn Hinson, "Merton's Many Faces," *Religion in Life* 42 (1973): 153–67.

9. A. H. Cutler called attention to the parallels in an appendix to his English translation of Giulio Basetti-Sani, *Louis Massignon (1883–1962): Prophet of Inter-Religious Reconciliation* (Chicago: Franciscan Herald Press, 1974), 170–77.

10. Massignon discussed his idea of the "curve of life" in the context of other major premises of his work in the preface to the new edition of his major life's work that was published only after his death. See Louis Massignon, *La passion de Husayn ibn Mansûr Hallâj* (Paris: Gallimard, 1975) I: 26–31.

11. Among the available biographies of Louis Massignon one might note the following: Jean Morillon, *Massignon* (Paris: Éditions Classiques du XXe siècle, 1964); *Masssignon* (ed. By J.-F. Six), Cahier de l'Herne (Paris: l'Herne, 1970); Vincent Monteil, *Le Linceul de feu* (Paris: Vega, 1987)—hereafter referred to in the text as *Monteil*. In English there are available the book by Basetti-Sani cited in n. 9 above, as well as *Louis Massignon: The Crucible of Compassion* by Mary Louise Gude (Notre Dame Ind.: University of Notre Dame Press, 1996). The best biographical sketch of Massignon in English is by Herbert Mason in the "Foreword" to his translation of *La passion de Hallâj: Louis Massignon, The Passion of al-Hallâj: Mystic and Martyr of Islam* (Princeton: Princeton University Press, 1982), I: xix–xliii—hereafter referred to in the text as *Passion*.

12. See Robert Baldrick, *The Life of J.-K. Huysmans* (Oxford: Clarendon Press, 1955), 286–87. See also B. Beaumont, *The Road from Decadence: From Brothel to Cloister, Selected Letters of J.-K. Huysmans* (Columbus: Ohio State University Press, 1989).

13. For an orientation to the life and work of Charles de Foucauld, see R. Aubert, "Charles de Foucauld," in the *Dictionnaire d'Histoire et de Géographie Écclésiastique* (Paris: Letouzey et Ané, 1971), XVIII: cols. 1394–402. See also D. Massignon, "La Rencontre de Charles de Foucauld et de Louis Massignon

d'après leur correspondance," and J.-F. Six, "Massignon et Foucauld," in *Presence de Louis Massignon: hommages et témoignages*; ed. By D. Massignon (Paris: Maisonneuve et Larose, 1987), 183–91, 201–6.

14. Louis Massignon, *La Passion d'al-Hosayn-ibn Mansour al-Hallâj, martyr mystique de l'islam* (Paris: Geuthner, 1922), 2 volumes. Massignon continued to work on a new edition of this book until he died *in medias res* in 1962. After his death, the new edition was assembled by a group of scholars working together with Massignon family members and friends. Louis Massignon, *La Passion de Husayn ibn Mansûr Hallâj, martyr mystique de l'islam*; 2d ed. (Paris: Gallimard, 1975) 4 volumes. The new edition was translated into English by Herbert Mason: Louis Massignon, *The Passion of al-Hallâj: Mystic and Martyr of Islam* (Princeton: Princeton University Press, 1982), 4 volumes.

15. Massignon was pleased by the judgments expressed by J. Maréchal, *Étude sur la psychologie des mystiques* (Paris: Desclée de Brouwer, 1937), II: 487–531. See also L. Massignon, "Mystique musulmane et mystique chrétienne au moyen age," *Opera Minora*, II: 470–84.

16. See the discussion by Daniel Massignon, "Le Voyage en Mésopotamie et la conversion de Louis Massignon en 1908," *Islamochristiana* 13 (1988), 127–99. Hereafter referred to in the text as *Mésopotamie*.

17. See the authoritative study of Massignon's religious thought in Guy Harpigny, *Islam et christianisme selon Louis Massignon*; *Homo Religiosus*, 6 (Louvain-la-Neuve: Centre d'Histoire des Religions, 1981). See also Maurice Borrmans, "Louis Massignon, témoin du dialogue islamo-chrétien," *Euntes Docete* 37 (1984): 383–401.

18. See Robet Caspar, "La vision de l'islam chez L. Massignon et son influence sur l'église," in *Massignon*; ed. By J.-F. Six (Paris: Cahier de l'Herne, 1970), 126–47.

19. See Albert Hourani, "T. E. Lawrence and Louis Massignon," *Times Literary Supplement* 188 (July 8, 1983): 733–34.

20. See D. Massignon, "La rencontre de Charles de Foucauld," 191.

21. See Camille Drevet, *Massignon et Gandhi, la contagion de la verité* (Paris: Le Cerf, 1967).

22. See Louis Massignon, *L'Hospitalité sacrée*; ed. By Jacques Keryell (Paris: Nouvelle Cité, 1987). This volume includes selections from the letters of Massignon to Mary Kahil, along with many documents from the foundation of the *Badaliyyah*. Hereafter referred to in the text as *L'Hospitalité*.

23. See the relevant chapter in Richard Griffiths, *The Reactionary Revolution: The Catholic Revival in French Literature* (London: Constable, 1966), 149–222. It is noteworthy that Louis Massignon is one of the three people to whose memory the author dedicates his work.

24. See Guy Harpigny, "Louis Massignon, l'hospitalité et la visitation de l'étranger," *Recherches de Science Religieuse* 75 (1987): 39–64. See also his *Islam et christianisme*, 161–91.

25. Merton to Massignon, September 4, 1960; *WTF*, 279.

26. See L. Massignon, "Les 'Sept Dormants', apocalypse de l'islam," and "Le culte liturgique et populaire des VII dormants martyrs d'Ephese (*ahl al-kahf*):

trait d'union orient-occident entre l'islam et la chrétienté," in L. Massignon, *Opera Minora* (Beyrouth: Dar al-Maaref, 1963), III: 104–80. In the latter article Massignon collected, among many other items, prayers from the liturgies of the "Seven Sleepers." Thomas Merton called his attention to prayers composed by St. Peter Damian. See "Le culte liturgique," 180. Massignon asked Merton for this information in his letter of May 16, 1960, TMC.

27. See especially the relevant chapters in Monteil, *Le Linceul de feu.*

28. See Jean-Jacques Waardenburg, *L'Islam dans le miroir de l'occident* (Paris: Mouton, 1963). Massignon is one of the major figures to the study of whose scholarship this book is devoted. See also J.-J. Waardenburg, "L. Massignon's Study of Religion and Islam: An Essay à propos of his *Opera Minora*," *Oriens* 21–22 (1968–69): 135–58.

29. See Edward W. Said, "Islam, the Philological Vocation, and French Culture: Renan and Massignon," in *Islamic Studies: A Tradition and Its Problems*; ed. By M. H. Kerr (Malibu, Calif.: Undena, 1980), 53–72; Julian Baldick, "Massignon: Man of Opposites," *Religious Studies* 23 (1987): 29–39.

30. See Youakim Moubarac, *L'Oeuvre de Louis Massignon; Pentalogie Islamo-Chrétienne* I (Beyrouth: Éditions du Cenacle Libanais, 1972–73). It is interesting to note that in an epilogue to this volume, Moubarac has published the original English and a French translation of Thomas Merton's poem, "The Night of Destiny," 204–7 (the poem is included in this volume, 313).

31. Louis Massignon, *Parole donnée: précédé d'entretiens avec Vincent-Mansour Monteil* (Paris: Julliard, 1962). The book has appeared in two subsequent publications: Paris: Coll. De Poche 10/18, 1970; and Paris: Le Seuil, 1983. Hereafter referred to in the text as *Parole.*

32. Louis Massignon, *Opera Minora*; ed. Y. Moubarac (Beyrouth: Dar al-Maaraef, 1963; Paris: Presses Universitaires de France, 1969).

33. *Testimonies and Reflections: Essays of Louis Massignon*; ed. By Herbert Mason (Notre Dame, Ind.: University of Notre Dame Press, 1989). Hereafter *Testimonies.*

34. Masignon to Merton, September 3, 1959, TMC.

35. See Herbert Mason, *Memoir of a Friend: Louis Massignon* (Notre Dame, Ind.: University of Notre Dame Press, 1988), 62–63. Hereafter referred to in the text as *Memoir.*

36. Mason's letters to Merton are in the archives of the TMC and have also been published in *WTF,* 261–74.

37. Merton wrote two pieces on Pasternak in 1959. See *The Literary Essays of Thomas Merton*; ed. Brother Patrick Hart (New York: New Directions, 1981), 37–83.

38. Massignon to Merton, August 2, 1960, TMC.

39. Thomas Merton, *The Hidden Ground of Love: Letters on Religious Experience and Social Concerns*; ed. William H. Shannon (New York: Farrar, Straus & Giroux, 1985), 134. Hereafter referred to in the text as *HGL.*

40. On Charles Lwanga and his companion martyrs, see the documents in the *Acta Apostolicae Sedis* 56 (1964): 901–12.

41. Massignon to Merton, April 30, 1960; July 1960. On April 3, Massignon sent Merton a prayer card dedicated to Charles Lwanga and companions. On

June 3, 1960, Merton said Mass "for Louis Massignon and for his project for African boys, under the patronage of Blessed Charles Lwanga. I happened in a curious and almost arbitrary manner to pick June 3d, and only today did I discover by accident that June 3d is the Feast of the Uganda Martyrs." Thomas Merton, *Conjectures of a Guilty Bystander* (Garden City, N.Y.: Doubleday/Image Books, 1968), 144; hereafter referred to in the text as *CGB*. We know the date from Merton's letter to Mason on June 1, 1960 (*Memoir*, 158).

42. Merton's letters to Herbert Mason are, of course, full of references to Massignon. See, *WTF*, 261–74.

43. Merton, *The Courage for Truth*, 32.

44. Massignon to Merton, December 31, 1960, *TMC*.

45. Merton, *Turning toward the World*, entry for November 20, 1962.

46. Thomas Merton, *Life and Holiness* (New York: Herder & Herder, 1963).

47. See the various references in *AJ*.

48. *WTF*, 277.

49. Ibid., 276

50. Ibid.

51. Herbert Mason to Sidney H. Griffith, October 21, 1988.

52. Herbert Mason, "Merton and Massignon," *Muslim World* 59 (1969): 317. Hereafter referred to in the text as *Mason*.

53. Merton himself published this letter in "Letters in a Time of Crisis," *Seeds of Destruction* (New York: Farrar, Straus & Cudahy, 1964), no. 27, "To a Moslem," 300–302.

54. William H. Shannon, "Thomas Merton and the Living Tradition of Faith," in *The Merton Annual* 1; ed. R. E. Daggy et al. (New York: AMS Press, 1988), 90–93. Hereafter referred to in the text as *Shannon*.

55. See the citations in n. 4 above.

56. Massignon to Merton, August 2, 1960, *TMC*.

57. Louis Massignon, "Foucauld au desert: devant le Dieu d'Abraham, Agar et Ismael," *Les Mardis de Dar-es-Salam* (1958–59), 57–71. The article is reprinted in *Opera Minora*, III: 722–84 and appears in English in *Testimonies*, 21–31.

58. In context, Massignon is speaking of the training both he and Foucauld had received to gather intelligence in North Africa for the sake of the government's military purpose there, a purpose that Massignon now said he thought of "comme d'un 'viol du point vierge des Musulmans." Massignon, " Foucauld au desert," 59, *Opera Minora*, III: 774; *Testimonies*, 30.

59. Merton marked and underlined the phrase when he read it in his copy of Massignon's essay on Gandhi in *Parole*, 132.

60. He quotes it in this form in a letter to Mary Kahil, March 26, 1948, *L'Hospitalité*, letter 134, 249. As we shall see below, Massignon quotes this saying in several forms.

61. For this form of al-Hallâj's saying, see Louis Massignon, "Le 'coeur' (*al-qalb*) dans la prière et la méditation musulmanes," in *Le Coeur; les études carmelitaines* (Paris: Desclée de Brouwer, 1950), 97. Massignon's article is reprinted in *Opera Minora*, II: 428–33.

62. Louis Massignon, *Kitab al-Tawasîn par abou al-Moghith al-Husayn ibn Mansour al-Hallâj* (Paris: Paul Geuthner, 1913), 196–97.

63. Herbert Mason, *Testimonies and Reflections*, 127. For the original see Louis Massignon, "Mystique musulmane et mystique chrétienne au moyen age," in *Oriente e Occidente nel Medioevo* (Rome: Accademia Nazionale, 1957), 20–35. The piece is reprinted in *Opera Minora*, II: 470–84.

64. Louis Massignon to Robert Caspar, November 12, 1955, quoted in Caspar, "La vision de l'islam chez L. Massignon," 132.

65. Massignon, "Foucault au desert," 67.

66. Merton, *WTF*, 278.

67. Undated letter from Herbert Mason to Thomas Merton, TMC. The letter must date from the second half of 1959 or the first half of 1960, when Mason was still in France.

68. Quoted by Jacques Jomier, "Le centenaire de la naissance du professeur Louis Massignon, sa célébration au Caire (October 11–12, 1983)," *Islamochristiana* 10 (1984): 43.

69. In his last letter to Abdul Aziz (April 24, 1968), Merton wrote, "For more than a year now I have been giving weekly talks on Sufism to the monks here." Shannon, *HGL*, 66–67. See also William H. Shannon, *Silent Lamp: The Thomas Merton Story* (New York: Crossroad, 1992). See also Burton B. Thuston, "Merton's Reflections on Sufism," *The Merton Seasonal* 15 (1990): 4–7; Bonnie Thurston, "Thomas Merton's Interest in Islam: The Example of *Dhikr*," *The American Benedictine Review* 45:2 (June 1994): 131–41 [both included in this volume]. Two tapes containing some of Merton's conferences on Sufism have been released, "Sufism: Knowledge of God" and "Sufism: The Desire for God" (Credence Cassettes, Kansas City, Mo.: National Catholic Reporter Publishing Co., 1988). More tapes, plus Merton's notes on this readings in Sufi sources are available in the collections of the Thomas Merton Center, Bellarmine College, Louisville, Kentucky.

70. Thomas Merton, *The Springs of Contemplation: A Retreat at the Abbey of Gethsemani* (New York: Farrar, Straus & Giroux, 1992), 266.

71. See the very revealing letters in *Paul Claudel/Louis Massignon (1908–1914)*; ed. by Michel Malicet; Les grandes correspondences (Paris: Desclée de Brouwer, 1973).

72. See Louis Gardet, "Esquisse de quelques thèmes majeurs," in *Massignon*; ed. Six, 78.

73. Louis Massignon to Thomas Merton, September 9, 1959, TMC.

74. Jacques Waardenburg, "Régards de phénomenologie réligieuse," in *Massignon*; ed. Six, 148.

75. See especially Louis Massignon, "Les trois prières d'Abraham, Père de tous les croyants," *Parole*, 257–72; English translation in Mason, *Testimonies and Reflections*, 3–20.

76. On these themes see especially J.-F. Six, "De la prière et de la substitution à la compassion et l'action," in *Presence de Louis Massignon*; ed. D. Massignon, 155–66.

77. Herbert Mason to Thomas Merton, no date, TMC.

78. Quoted in Six, "De la prière," 156.

79. See Louis Massignon, "Mystique musulmane et mystique chrétienne," *Opera Minora*, II: 483–84.

80. Louis Massignon to Thomas Merton, December 31, 1960, *TMC*.

81. See M. Hayek, "Louis Massignon face à l'islam," in *Massignon*; ed. Six, 188–99; Martin Sabanegh, "Le cheminement exemplaire d'un savant et d'un chrétien à la rencontre de l'islam," in *Presence de Louis Massignon*; ed. D. Massignon, 113–28. On these subjects, see some of the ideas of Massignon in Giulio Basetti-Sani, *The Koran in the Light of Christ: An Interpretation of the Sacred Book of Islam* (Chicago: Franciscan Herald Press, 1977).

4

A TREATISE ON THE HEART

Muhammad ibn 'Ali al-Hakîm al-Tirmidhî

translated by Nicholas Heer

(A translation of the Bayân al-Farq bayn al-Sadr wa al-Qalb wa al-
Fu'ad wa al-Lubb[1] of Abû 'Abd Allâh Muhammad ibn 'Ali al-Hakîm al-
Tirmidhî (d. ca. 932). This appeared in four issues of the Hartford
Seminary Foundation's The Muslim World in 1961, which Merton kept
among his miscellaneous papers now at the Thomas Merton Center at
Bellarmine. The following selection includes the translator's introduction
and Part I of the whole six-part treatise, which will be brought out in a
new edition by Fons Vitae. Perhaps Merton found further elucidation on
"le point vierge" in the metaphors put forward within this work.)

Al-Hakîm al-Tirmidhî, the author of the treatise presented here
in translation, flourished in Khurasan and Transoxiana during
the third century of the Muslim calender. He is mentioned in most
of the Arabic and Persian biographical sources, but these contain
little information concerning his life other than the names of his
teachers and disciples and some of his more important works. No
date is given for his birth, and various dates ranging from 255 to 320
A.H. are given for his death. His autobiography,[2] which is a rather
curious work concerned principally with the dreams of his wife,
gives us only scanty information, mainly on the early years of his
life. From it we learn that he began his studies when he was eight
years old and that these studies included the science of traditions
('ilm al-âthar) and the science of opinion ('ilm al-ra'y). At the age of
twenty-seven he made the pilgrimage to Mecca and on the way
spent some time in Iraq gathering traditions.

Al-Tirmidhî was a prolific writer and some sixty titles are ascribed
to him. Most of these have survived as manuscripts to the present

day, but very few have as yet been edited and printed. Detailed information on his life and works can be found in my article "Some Biographical and Bibliographical Notes on al-Hakîm al-Tirmidhî" in *The World of Islam, Studies in Honour of Philip K. Hitti*, edited by James Kritzeck and R. Bayly Winder, London 1959, 121–34; and in the article of Othman Yahya, "L'Oeuvre de Tirmidi" in *Mélanges Louis Massignon*, vol. III, Damascus 1957, 411–50.

Al-Tirmidhî's psychological system, as given in the *Bayân al-Farq*, is primarily concerned with a description of the heart (*qalb*) and the self (*nafs*). The basic elements of the system and the vocabulary used are all derived from the Qur'an and the hadith. Their arrangement into a fairly coherent system, however, is the result of al-Tirmidhî's own creative thought.

Al-Tirmidhî divides the heart into four parts or, as he calls them, stations (*maqâmat*). These are the breast (*sadr*), the heart proper (*qalb*), the inner heart (*fu'ad*), and the intellect (*lubb*). They are arranged in concentric spheres, the breast being the outermost sphere followed on the inside by the heart, the inner heart, and finally the intellect. Within the intellect are yet other stations which, however, are too subtle to be described by words.

Each of these stations of the heart has its own characteristics and functions. Thus the breast is the abode (*ma'din*) of the light of Islam (*nûr al-islâm*). Al-Tirmidhî uses Islam here in a restricted sense to mean the physical acts performed in obedience to God's commandments such as prayer, fasting, etc. The breast is thus also the repository of that type of knowledge (*'ilm*) which, enables one to perform these acts, such as knowledge of the *sharî'ah* (Islamic law). This knowledge is gained through listening to a teacher or through reading and may be lost through forgetfulness

The heart proper, which is within the breast, is the abode of the light of faith (*nûr al-îmân*). By faith is meant the acceptance by the heart of the truth of God's revelation. The light of faith is constant and neither increases nor decreases. It is thus different from the light of Islam, which, increases and decreases in accordance with one's works and one's acts of obedience or disobedience. The heart is also the abode of what al-Tirmidhî calls the valuable or useful knowledge (*al-'ilm al-nâfi'*). This is an interior knowledge of reality granted by God. It cannot be learned from books or from a teacher as can that type of knowledge associated with the breast.

The inner heart is the abode of the light of gnosis (*nûr al-ma'rifah*). It is associated with the vision (*ru'yah*) of reality. Whereas the heart has mere knowledge of reality, the inner heart actually sees reality.

The intellect, the innermost sphere of the heart, is the abode of the light of unification (*nûr al-tawhîd*). It is the basis of the three outer spheres and is the recipient of God's grace and bounty.

Each of these four stations of the heart is associated with one of the four spiritual ranks of the Sufi. Thus the breast and the the light of Islam within it correspond to the first rank, that of the *muslim*. The light of faith in the heart corresponds to the believer (*mu'min*), the light of gnosis in the inner heart to the gnostic (*'ârif*), and the light of unification in the intellect to the highest rank, that of the unifier (*muwahhid*).

The self (*nafs*), on the other hand, it not a part of the heart but a separate entity in the stomach. It is like a hot smoke and is the source of evil desires and passions. When these passions are not kept in check through spiritual disciplines, they escape from the self and enter into the breast filling it with smoke. The light of the heart within the breast is thus obscured by this smoke and can no longer illuminate the breast. The breast, in turn, being deprived of this illumination is no longer able to perform its proper functions but becomes subject to the authority of the self. The self, however, is powerless to affect the heart, and the light of faith within it remains firm and constant even when obscured by the dark passions which have entered into the breast.

Through discipline (*riyâdah*), however, the self may be brought under control and made to pass through four stages of development corresponding to the four stages of the spiritual development of the Sufi. Thus the self which exhorts to evil (*al-nafs al-ammârah bi'l-sû'*) is the yet undisciplined self and belongs to the rank of the *muslim*. The inspired self (*al-nafs al-mulhamah*) is somewhat less evil and corresponds to the rank of the believer (*mu'min*). The blaming self (*al-nafs al-lawwâmah*) is the self of the gnostic (*'arif*) and the peaceful self (*al-nafs al-mutma'innah*) that of the unifier (*muwahhid*).

The main elements of al-Tirmidhî's system are summarized in the chart on the following page.

The only manuscript of al-Tirmidhî's *Bayân al-Farq* known to exist is that of Dâr al-Kutub al-Misrîyah in Cairo listed under tasawwuf

BREAST (sadr)	HEART (qalb)	INNER HEART (fu'ad)	INTELLECT (lubb)
light of Islam (nûr al-islâm)	light of faith (nûr al-îmân)	light of gnosis (nûr al-ma'rifah)	light of unification (nûr at-tawhîd)
muslim	believer (mu'min)	gnostic ('arif)	unifier (muwahhid)
knowledge of shari'ah, etc.	interior knowledge from God	vision (ru'yah)	God's grace and bounty
self which exhorts to evil (al-nafs al-ammârah bi'l-sû')	inspired self (al-nafs al-mulhamah)	blaming self (al-nafs al-lawwâmah)	peaceful self (al-nafs al-mutma'innah)

367. This manuscript was edited by myself and published in Cairo in 1958, and the present translation has been prepared from it. The manuscript itself is carelessly written and contains a number of errors and corrupt passages. Although it was possible to correct and reconstruct many of these passages in the printed edition, the meaning of some of them remains unclear and can only be conjectured from the context. Such passages have been indicated in the notes.

Brackets have been placed around all words and phrases not found in the Arabic text but which have been added in the translation to clarify the meaning.

Translations of verses from the Qur'an are based on the translation of Mohammed Marmaduke Pickthall.[3] In the notes, however, the numbers of the verses are those of the standard Egyptian edition of the Qur'an.[4]

Translation

In the Name of God, the Merciful and the Compassionate. O my Lord, give ease and help.

Abû 'Abd Allâh Muhammad ibn 'Ali al-Tirmidhî said: One of the people of learning and understanding has asked me to explain the difference between the breast (*sadr*), the heart (*qalb*), the inner heart (*fu'ad*), and the intellect (*lubb*), as well as what is beyond them, such as the depths of the heart (*shaghâf*), and the places of knowledge. I should like to explain [this] to him with the help of God, for He makes easy all that is difficult, and I therefore ask His help.

[Part One: the Stations of the Heart]

Know then, may God increase your understanding in religion, that the word "heart" (*qalb*) is comprehensive and includes [in its meaning] all the interior stations (*maqâmât al-bâtin*), for in the interior [of man] there are places that are outside the heart and others that are within it. The word "heart" is similar to the word "eye," since "eye" includes [in its meaning] that which lies between the two eyelashes, such as the black and white parts of the eye, the pupil, and the light within the pupil. Each of these parts has its own nature and a meaning different from that of the others. Nevertheless, they act in concert and the functions of each are connected with those of the others. Moreover, each part which is on the outside is the basis of that which follows it on the inside. Thus the subsistence of the light [of the pupil] depends on the subsistence of the other [part of the eye].

Similarly the word "homestead" (*dâr*) is a term which includes everything contained within its walls, such as the gate, the corridor, the court surrounded by its houses, and such things as the closet and storeroom. Every place and position in it has its own characteristic different from that of its neighbor.

Likewise the word *haram* is a term which includes the sacred area around Mecca, as well as the city, the mosque, and the Ka'bah; and each of these areas contains a different station [of the pilgrimage].

Again, the word *qindîl* is a comprehensive term for the [various parts of the] lamp. In the lamp the position of the water is different from that of the wick, and the position of the wick is different from that of the water, since the former is within the position of the water. Moreover, it is the wick which contains the light, and in the position of the wick is the oil, which has no water in it. Thus the fitness of the lamp depends on the fitness of all its parts, for if one of these is deficient, the others become useless.

Similarly the word "almond" is a term which includes the outer covering which surrounds the hard shell, the inner shell itself, which is like bone, as well as the nut or kernel within this shell, and the oil which is in the kernel.

Know, may God increase your understanding in religion, that there are marks and degrees in this religion, that its people are in various classes, and that the people of learning in it are in various ranks. God said: *And we have raised some of them above others in rank*[5]. He also said: *And over every lord of knowledge there is one more knowing.*[6] Thus as a science is more elevated, its position in the heart is more secret, more special, more protected, more concealed, and more veiled. Nevertheless, among common people, mention of the word "heart" takes the place of the mention of all its stations.

The breast, in the heart, is the station that corresponds to the white of the eye, to the court of the homestead, to the area that surrounds Mecca, to the place of the water in the lamp, or to the outer covering of the almond out of which the almond itself emerges if it dries on the tree.

The breast is the place where evil whispering (*waswâs*) and misfortunes enter, just as the white of the eye is subject to the misfortune of pimples, inflammation of the veins, amid many other diseases of the eye. In like manner, wood and refuse are put in the court of the homestead, and all sorts of strangers sometimes enter it, just as wild animals and beasts enter into the court of the *haram*, or just as moths and other insects fall into the water of the lamp, for the oil is above the water, and the water constitutes its lowest part. Similarly maggots, gnats, and flies crawl into the outer covering of the almond if it splits open until even small worms enter into it.

That which enters into the breast is seldom felt at that time. It is the place of entry of rancor, desires, passions, and needs. At times it contracts and at other times it expands. It is also the area in which the self which exhorts to evil (*al-nafs al-ammârah bi'l-sû'*) exercises its authority, for it has an entry into the breast where it takes charge of things, becoming proud and pretending to possess power of itself.

The breast is also the seat of the light of Islam (*nûr al-islâm*), as well as the place in which knowledge that is heard (*al-'ilm al-masmû'*) is retained. [This type of knowledge must] be learned and includes the laws and traditions and all that which can be expressed with the tongue, the principal means of one's attaining to it being study and listening [to a teacher].

The breast was so named because it is the first part (*sadr*) of the heart and its first station, just as the *sadr* of the day is its beginning or as the court is the first place in the homestead. Into the breast from the self emerge whispering desires and distracting thoughts, and these emerge from it into the heart also if they become established over a long period.

The heart proper (*qalb*) is the second station. It is within the breast and corresponds to the black of the eye, whereas the breast corresponds to the white. It also corresponds to the city of Mecca inside the *haram*, to the place of the wick in the lamp, as well as to the house within the homestead, and the almond within the outer covering.

The heart is the abode (*ma'din*) of the light of faith (*nûr al-îmân*) and the lights of submissiveness (*khushu'*), piety (*taqwâ*), love (*mahabbah*), consent (*ridâ'*), certainty (*yaqîn*), fear (*khawf*), hope (*rajâ'*), patience (*sabr*), and contentment (*qana'ah*). It is the abode of the principles of knowledge (*usûl al-'ilm*), for it is like a spring of water, the breast being its pool, so that just as the water flows out of the spring into the pool, so also knowledge emerges from the heart into the breast. Knowledge, however, also enters the breast by means of its being heard. From the heart emerge certainty (*yaqîn*), knowledge (*'ilm*), and intention (*nîyah*), which then enter into the breast, for the heart is the root and the breast is the branch. Moreover, the branch is only made firm by the root.

The Apostle of God said: "Works are only according to intentions," and explained that the value of an action performed by the self is dependent only upon the intention of the heart. Thus the good deed increases in value in accordance with the intention. Action is a faculty of the self; and the limit of the authority of the self over the breast depends upon the intention of the heart and its authority. The heart, due to God's mercy, however, is not under the authority of the self, for the heart is like a king and the self is its kingdom. The Apostle of God said: "The hand is a wing, the two feet are a post-horse, the two eyes are a means of good, the two ears are a funnel, the liver is mercy, the spleen is laughter, the two kidneys are deceit and the lung is breath. Thus if the king is sound, his troops are also sound, and if the king is corrupt, so also are his troops corrupt." The Apostle of God thus explained that the heart is a king, and that the breast is to the heart as the square (maydân) to the horseman.

He also pointed out that the soundness of the members of the body depends on the soundness of the heart and that their corruption depends on the corruption of the heart. The heart is like a wick, and the soundness of the wick is judged according to its light, which, in the case of the heart, is the light of piety and firm belief, for if the heart lacked this light it would be as a lamp) the light of whose wick has gone out. All the deeds which originate in the self, exclusive of the heart, are not taken into account in the last judgement, nor is the doer of such deeds taken to task should they be acts of disobedience, or rewarded should they be acts of obedience. God said: *But He will take you to task for that which your hearts have garnered.*[7]

The inner heart (fu'ad), within the heart proper, is the third station, and it corresponds to the pupil in the black part of the eye, to the mosque in Mecca, to the closet or storeroom in the house, to the wick in its position in the middle of the lamp, and to the kernel within the almond. This inner heart is the seat of gnosis (ma'rifah), spiritual thoughts (khawâtir), and vision (ru'yah). Whenever a man profits, his inner heart profits first, then the heart. The inner heart is in the middle of the heart proper, which, in turn, is in the middle of the breast, just as the pearl is within the oyster shell.

The intellect (lubb), which is within the inner heart, corresponds to the light of seeing in the eye, to the light of the wick in the lamp, and to the hidden fat in the kernel of the almond. Each one of these exterior parts [of the heart] is a shield or curtain for that which follows it on the inside. Each is similar to the others, for they act in concert and are close in meaning, agreeing with one another and not differing. They are the lights of religion, for religion is one, even though the ranks of its people are different and varied.

The intellect is the seat of the light of unification (nûr al-tawhîd) and the light of uniqueness (nûr al-tafrîd). It is the most perfect light and the greatest power.

Beyond this there are other subtle stations, noble places, and elegant subtleties. The basis of them all, however, is the light of unification, for unification is a mystery *(sirr)* and gnosis is a bounty *(birr)*. Faith is the preservation of the mystery and the contemplation of the bounty. Islam in giving thanks for the bounty and surrendering the heart to the mystery, for unification is a mystery which God makes manifest to His servant *('abd)* and to which He directs him, since he could not comprehend it with his reason *('aql)* were it not for God's supporting and guiding him.

Gnosis is a bounty which God gives to His servant when He opens for him the door of favor and grace, beginning without the servant's being worthy of that and then granting him guidance until he believes that this is all from God, given to him as a favor from Him Whom he is unable to thank except through His assistance. And this, again, is yet another favor from God.

Thus he contemplates the bounty of God and preserves His mystery, for He is the bestower of success, and the mode of being of His lordship is not comprehended. [The servant of God] knows that He is one and avoids making Him similar to anything else *(tashbîh)*, denying His attributes *(ta'tîl)*, giving Him form *(takyîf)*, or making Him unjust *(tajnîf)*. This, then, is faith, which contemplates God's bounty and preserves His mystery.

Islam, however, is the use of the self *(nafs)* for the sake of God through obedience to Him with thanksgiving and righteousness. It is the surrender of lordship to Him and abstaining from the comprehension of the mystery; the acceptance of servitude, and persistence in that which brings one closer to Him.

Islam is practised only through the self, and the self is blind to the comprehension of the truth *(haqq)* and the contemplation of it. Moreover, it is not required of [the self] that it comprehend truths. Do you not see that the servant of God was commanded to have faith through the heart but was not required to comprehend that in which he believes from the standpoint of its real nature *(kayfîyah)*? His is only to follow and to avoid innovation. Surrender is all that is required of the self.

The ineffable stations, which lie beyond those already mentioned, are perceived only by the servant of God who has succeeded, with God's help, in understanding those stations [which we have] described with these well-known analogies, for God helps His servant and assists him in understanding them. These stations, which are beyond those already mentioned, are like the increased purity of water should it remain for a period in the jar. By such analogies is the way of the ineffable mystery comprehended.

NOTES

1. *The Elucidation of the Difference between the Breast, the Heart, the Inner Heart, and the Intellect.*

2. *Bad' Sha'n Abî 'Abd Allâh*, manuscript, Isma'il Sa'ib 1571, 9.

3. Mohammed Marmaduke Pickthall, *The Meaning of the Glorious Koran*, New York, Mentor Books, 1953.

4. Second edition, *Maslahat al-Masâhah and Dâr al-Kutub al-Misrîîyah*, 1371/1952.

5. Qur'an, 43:32.

6. Qur'an, 12:76.

7. Qur'an, 2:225.

5

ISLAMIC THEMES IN
MERTON'S POETRY

Erlinda G. Paguio

Many themes related to Islam may be found in the essays, conferences, and especially the poems of Thomas Merton. In *Love and Living* he referred to the soul as the true Self, the mature personal identity, which is found only after one has discarded what is false and artificial in oneself. In explaining the paradox of the self—which attains its true nature when it ceases to seek, grows still, and *is* what it has become, or *always was*—Merton used the term *ridâ* (satisfaction/contentment), which is the goal of the spiritual journey in Sufism.[1] He spoke about this with greater clarity in his conference on "Satisfaction, the End of the Ascetic Life" on July 3, 1967.[2]

Merton stated that it is insufficient to build one's security outside of oneself. Man must stop worrying, because worry includes self-love. In the Sufi state of "satisfaction," one has peace and contentment of heart. God is satisfied with the person who is completely satisfied with Him.

Above photo: tomb cover of the Muslim saint Imam Riza (see page 90).

Merton correlated this state of satisfaction with Cassian's goal of attaining purity of heart, where desire can no longer divert one from God. A person's will is in accordance with His will. One is united with God, and has freedom from the domination of outside forces. Merton stressed that it is possible to attain this state through both an act of faith and by one's determination to work at it. It is something, he says, we all can do, and something God is asking us to do.[3]

On October 27, 1960, while visiting the Cincinnati Art Museum, Merton came across a beautifully designed silk cloth, which was used as a cover spread over the tomb of Imam Riza. So moved was he by this sacred cloth that two days later he wrote about it to Louis Massignon:

> I was utterly stunned by the magnificent tomb cover of a Moslem saint, Imam Riza, once seen by thousands of pilgrims, now ignored by tourists. It had on it a wonderful Sufi poem, translated for those who were interested. This encounter had a deep effect on me, as also my seeing everywhere faces of saints, angels, liberated ones from France, Catalonia, Persia, India, Cambodia. All of them innocent, silent, enigmatic, smiling in their humble understanding and acceptance of their position: they are at home everywhere, and we who think we are at home are, among them, aliens.[4]

Merton also described Imam Riza's tomb cover to Massignon's friend, Abdul Aziz. He expressed profound gratitude to God for having come in contact with Imam Riza's great spirit through the tomb cover. He greatly regretted, however, that such a holy object should be viewed as a mere "work of art," unappreciated for its spiritual significance.[5]

Abdul Aziz informed Merton that Imam Riza (Persian for *ridâ*) was the 8th Imam of the Shî'ites. He was known to be a man of great tenderness, humility, charity and generosity. He was also revered for his piety and learning.[6]

Merton's poem, "Tomb Cover for Imam Riza," is his own version of the poem embroidered in calligraphy on the tomb covering itself. His interpretation is derived from the English translation made by the Islamic scholar, Arthur J. Arberry, and from the subsequent reformulation made by the art expert, Phyllis Ackerman. Merton's version is faithful to the thoughts expressed in these two translations.

Although Merton's is much easier to read than the other two, one error is obvious in comparison. *Kawthar*, the River of Abundance in the Islamic Paradise, is misspelled in Merton's poem as "Kanthar."[7]

The poem brings out clearly the important role of the Imam in Islam. The Shî'ites believe that the Imam is the true leader of the faithful and that he is the true interpreter of Islam. According to Shî'a doctrine, Muhammad passed on his power of spiritual direction and initiation to his son-in-law, 'Ali. Designated descendants of 'Ali inherited this function. The Imam is the preserver of a "primordial light" or a "luminous divine substance, which enables him to know divine mysteries. To be attached to the Imam, therefore, is to be attached to this light because the Imam is the mediator between God and man.[8] Imam Riza, also known as 'Ali Rida, is called the "Imam of Initiation." Many Persians, who seek a spiritual master and who wish to be initiated into Sufism, go to his tomb in Mashhad, Iran, to seek his assistance. Pilgrimage to this tomb of Imam Riza is the central subject of the poem Merton interpreted. The tomb is the threshold of holiness and all who go there are rewarded. The last stanza states:

> Without weariness of the road they reach the fountain of life
> And leave to Alexander for his portion the realms of darkness
> Greater joy than the water of life is their pleasure
> Who give their hearts to the winebearer of Kanthar. [sic][9]

In Sufism, a most important communication of spiritual truths lies in the personal contact between the disciple and his spiritual master, who is called *shaikh* (elder). The *shaikh*, who may often have reached a state of sainthood, supervises the spiritual development of the disciple by entrusting to him certain formulae of the *dhikr*, or the remembrance of God, through the repetition of His Name. He determines which prayer is appropriate for the disciple's spiritual level and aptitude, and he sends him into *khalwah*, a spiritual retreat that could last for up to forty days. Basic to Sufi life is obedience to the master. It is thought that a person who has no spiritual guidance has Satan for his master.[10] The disciple, who is connected to such a spiritual master, is given guidance concerning the illusions and distractions encountered on the spiritual path.

Merton's appreciation for the role of the spiritual master in Sufism is evident in his meditative and poetic work, "Readings from

Ibn Abbad." He found a "mordant, realistic and human quality" in the life of Ibn Abbad, and was truly touched by his zeal.[11]

Ibn Abbad of Ronda (1332–90) was the main preacher at the Karawiyyin mosque in Fez, Morocco, and a well-known director of souls. Merton's verses point out Ibn Abbad's compassionate and detached character. Merton describes him as "a recollected man in whom renunciation and great kindness are one. . . . For above all things he prizes peace and tranquillity of soul."[12] Ibn Abbad was a friend to shoemakers, who adopted him as their patron because he prayed for them and with them at the mosque. His writing on desolation resonates with St. John of the Cross's dark night of the soul. Some writers believe there is evidence of Ibn Abbad's influence on St. John of the Cross. Merton, however, captures Ibn Abbad's teaching that it is in the times of darkness and in emptiness that God seizes the soul to Himself.

> To belong to Allah
> Is to see your own existence . . .
> To see your being in His Being,
> Your subsistence in His Subsistence
> Your strength in His Strength.
> Thus you will recognize in yourself
> His title to possession of you
> As Lord,
> And your own title as servant,
> Which is nothingness. [13]

Abdul Aziz, who sent Merton many books on Islam and Sufism and who faithfully corresponded with him from Pakistan, was delighted to read "Readings from Ibn Abbad." He considered it an excellent work but recommended that Ibn Abbad's teachings on the contemplation of divine unity, good conduct, and gratitude be included in the selection.[14] Annemarie Schimmel, a well-known Islamic scholar, says that the concept of gratitude has particular relevance to modern man: There is always a reason and a way to thank God for something. The more this constant gratitude grows, the more it becomes a habit of the soul, and man is able to leave unnecessary worry because he feels like a child in God's lap.[15]

In volume 18 of Merton's reading notebooks he states that a Sufi can teach only what he has learned from his own master. In "Readings from Ibn Abbad" he shows both the Sufi master's severe criticism of the disciple who abandons the spiritual way and his openness to the erring person who returns to Allah: "As for me, I can help only by prayer. But what help is that, if you do not help me by a sincere return?"[16]

Throughout the 1960s, Merton's understanding of Islam and Sufism deepened through his own intensive study, and his correspondence with Sufis and scholars of Islam like Louis Massignon, Abdul Aziz, and Reza Arasteh. He also enjoyed a profound encounter with Sidi Abdeslam, a Sufi master from Algeria, who visited Gethsemani in 1966.

In his January 14, 1961 letter to his friend Herbert Mason, Merton referred to his own poem, "The Moslems' Angel of Death." He sent a copy of the poem to Mason with a note mentioning that had he sent it to Massignon, the latter might think that Merton was prophesying about his death since Massignon had been in poor health at that time.[17]

In volume 4 of Merton's journals, he noted that he was reading [Frithjof] Schuon on Moslem angels on January 8, 1961. The editor's footnote originally indicated that Merton may be referring to the works of Gershom Scholem, but this was corrected in the paperback edition.[18]

Merton also sent a copy of this poem to Ernesto Cardenal in Nicaragua. He wrote on September 11, 1961 that it was based on an Islamic text which he found dazzling. In the same letter he mentioned his correspondence with Abdul Aziz and Massignon.[19]

"The Moslems' Angel of Death (Algeria 1961)"[20] has a parenthetical reference to Algeria, which evokes the fierceness of the conflicts between the Algerians and the French during the Algerian war for independence. The last two lines of the poem suggest the end of the war, yet the destruction of many lives.

Azrael is the name of the angel of death. His appearance is of cosmic magnitude: he has four faces and four thousand wings; his whole body consists of eyes and tongues, the number of which corresponds to that of the living. It is said of him that if the water of all the seas and rivers were poured onto his head, not a drop would reach the earth. His seat of light is in the fourth or seventh heaven, on which one of his feet rests. His other foot stands between paradise and hell.[21] Because of his ferocity and strength, Allah appointed him angel and master of death. Although he keeps a directory of mankind, he does not know the date of death of the individuals. He does know who is damned and who is blessed. The names of the blessed are surrounded by a bright circle while those of the damned are darkened.

Merton compares the Muslim angel of death to a jeweled peacock, who stirs the world with fireflies, and takes pleasure in lights. He is also a "great honeycomb of shining bees, with a million fueled eyes, exploring life." He is like a miser, who clutches his money between his fingers. The Muslim angel of death puts the golden lights in his pocket. No one can escape him.

Merton's study of Islam led him to the writings of the great Spanish mystic Ibn 'Arabî (1165–1240) and the Persian poet Rûmî (1202–73). His poems "Song for the Death of Averroës" and "Lubnan" have been inspired by his reading Ibn 'Arabî. In *Conjectures of a Guilty Bystander*, he speaks of the anguish which St. Thomas Aquinas sensed in the life of Averroës (Ibn Rushd) and Aristotle. Although endowed with brilliant minds, they failed to grasp what Sufi mystics like Ibn 'Arabî experienced. Merton's rendering of "Song for the Death of Averroës" pictures Ibn 'Arabî recalling Averroës' tendency toward the rational. Ibn 'Arabî had the impression that although he understood Averroës, the latter could not understand him. Averroës arrived at the truth by reasoning alone, whereas Ibn 'Arabî experienced direct revelation from God. Averroës' deep thinking was the veil which prevented his seeing what the mystics have seen.

According to Merton's poetic interpretation, Ibn 'Arabî was struck by the sight of a mule carrying Averroës' coffin when his body was returned to Spain. Serving as counterweight to the coffin on the other side of the mule were all the books that Averroës had written. Ibn 'Arabî wondered whether if in death the desire of Averroës to know God had been fulfilled. Merton commented that in mysticism and direct experience, there is a "non-logical" logic, in which meaning is not immediately intelligible. If one has direct experience of it, however, the meaning is imparted.[22] Merton writes in his reading notebooks that for Ibn 'Arabî, "the true knower is not a servant of reasoning but a servant of the Lord."[23] He also notes that according to Ibn 'Arabî, the highest level of *dhikr*, or remembrance of God, is a complete awareness of his union with God. Total "remembering" means that one is identified with God, and there is no further distinction between subject and object.[24]

Union with God is well explained by this often quoted saying: "He who adores Me never ceases to approach Me until I love him, and when I love him, I am the hearing by which he hears, the sight by which he sees, the hand by which he grasps, and the foot by which he walks."[25] Ibn 'Arabî's spiritual guide, a ninety-year-old holy woman named Fatimah, expressed her admiration for Ibn 'Arabî as one who approached her with a wholeness and a presence that she did not find in others. She said that he was a great consolation to her because "when he rises up it is with all of himself and when he sits it is with his whole self, leaving nothing of himself elsewhere."[26]

One of Ibn 'Arabî's most important works on mysticism is the *Fusus al-Hikam* or *The Bezels of Wisdom*. Merton's acquaintance with this book is indicated in a letter to the poet, Louis Zukofsky: ". . . I read a Sufi, Ibn al-'Arabî, just getting into him, who says remarkable things about the imagination . . ."[27] He had also read Toshihiko Izutsu's *A Comparative Study of the Key Philosophical Concepts of Sufism and Taoism* (1966–67), which is a penetrating analysis of Ibn 'Arabî's *The Bezels of Wisdom*. So moved was Merton by Ibn 'Arabî's thought on the inner transformation of man as symbolized in the names *Idrîs* (Enoch) and *Ilyâs* (Elias) that he composed the poem, "Lubnan." *Idrîs* (Enoch) is one of the patriarchs, who lived before Noah. It is written that he walked with God and disappeared because God took him. In the Qur'an, he is considered a "true man," a prophet, whom God elevated to the heart of celestial bodies because of his patience and righteousness. *Ilyâs* (Elias), on the other hand, is mentioned in the Second Book of Kings. While walking with Elisha, a fiery chariot with a horse of fire came between them, and Elias was taken up to heaven in a whirlwind.[28]

In the *Bezels of Wisdom*, Ibn 'Arabî writes that Idris and Ilyas were two names assumed by one and the same person. Idris, who was in a high state of being, was sent down to Baalbek and given the name Ilyas. He had a vision in which he saw Lubnan, or Mt. Lebanon, splitting open. From it sprang out a fiery horse and a harness of fire. Ilyas rode the fiery horse, and immediately all lusts left him. He became pure intellect. By attaching himself to the fiery horse, he became completely free from whatever connected him to his physicality.[29]

Merton's poem begins with these two symbolic names:

> Idris-Ilyas: Two names
> One star, one prophet

> Throned in the Sun (Idris)
> And coming down
> The ladder of alchemy and metals
> To Baalbeck. [30]

He captures the bursting of Mt. Lebanon in these words:

> One day the stonewall mountain
> Cracked the blue dome
> Let out a horse harnessed in flame
> A car of fire
> Which Ilyas happened to notice.[31]

Ibn 'Arabî teaches that in order for man to overcome his worldly state of being and enter into a spiritual state, he must go through the transformation that Idris and Ilyas endured. Ilyas pushed his earthly state to the extreme limit and became almost like an animal, even unable to speak. In this state his knowledge of God was still imperfect. Merton expressed Ibn 'Arabî's thought in this way:

> He [Ilyas] did not stop halfway
> To rutting Bedlam
> Tried out all the dreams
> Wasted his demon machine
> In a university of lepers
> And lost the faculty of speech.
>
> Idris-Ilyas one interpreter
> May be back tomorrow morning
> When the vision
> Will be total.[32]

Toshihiko Izutsu writes that the person who desires to re-experience the life of Idris-Ilyas must thoroughly actualize his animality before a kind of "unveiling," which is natural to wild animals, is given him.[33] Ibn 'Arabî writes that when he realized this state in his own life, he had visions, which he wanted to talk about, but could not. He adds that if a person continues his spiritual exercise, his intuition will be such that he will see things as they *are*. He will have attained the state of being loved by God in which God will be his hearing, his seeing, his grasping, and his walking.[34]

Fritz Meier, in his article "The Transformation of Man in Mystical Islam," explains that in the training of a Sufi disciple, the emphasis is on lowering the function of sensation so that the intuitive faculties may be heightened.[35]

Reza Arasteh, whose books on Rûmî and final integration impressed Merton very much, interprets this in terms of the experience of removing the "I." It is the experience of *fanâ'* in which those experiences, which obstruct the revealing of the real Self, are annihilated. He writes: "In essence, the Sufi's task is to break the idol of the phenomenal self, which is the mother idol; having achieved this aim his search ends. Empty-handed, empty-minded and desire-less, he is and he is not. He has and he has not the feeling of existence. He knows nothing, he understands nothing. He is in love, but with whom he is not aware of. His heart is at the same time both full and empty of love. . . ."[36] He passes into the stage of *baqâ'*, in which he functions with complete spontaneity and expressiveness. He is no longer an observer of life, but he is life itself.

In the poem "The Night of Destiny," Merton attempts to describe the manifestation of this "life" during the Muslims' month-long fast in Ramadan, which commemorates the revelation of the Qur'an to Muhammad. He finds in "The Night of Destiny" something of the spirit of Christmas. In both events, the heavens opened and the Word came to the world.

The poem, which begins and ends with "In my ending is my meaning," suggests that transforming union takes place when the false self disappears and the true Self becomes one with the Beloved. In silence and solitude the Word descends upon the heart, and the "tongue of flame," the spirit, speaks in the heart. The Word, "the red and sable letters on the solemn page," is revealed in the heart. The "homeless light" finds its room and home in the heart. Love that is made visible in darkness and silence is exquisitely expressed in these verses:

> See! See!
> My love is darkness!
> Only in the Void
> Are all ways one:
> Only in the night
> Are all the lost found.[37]

Merton wrote this poem in the winter of 1966 before the community retreat at Gethsemani. On January 18, 1966, he wrote in his journal: "Evening. Beginning of retreat. Since it is the Night of Destiny (27 Ramadan) I stayed up late. Like Christmas, The Night of Destiny is perhaps a Moslem 'Christmas'—heaven opens to earth—the angels and 'The Spirit' come down, all the prayers of the faithful are answered. Night of joy and peace! I shared the joys of the Moslems and prayed for them and for my own needs, and for peace."[38]

In Sufism, the inner reality of man as he is known by God is centered in the "heart." Merton found this so fascinating that he spoke of it in his Alaskan conference on "The Life That Unifies." The word "yes" contains the secret affirmation God places in a person's heart, which is his "yes" to God. Merton reminded his audience that every person's destiny in life is to uncover this "yes" to God. This complete assent to God in the heart is the most profound meaning of every person's being.[39] Merton related this secret "yes" to the writings of Meister Eckhart and the Hasidic writers on the "spark" of the soul. Merton wrote that all we need to do is to turn towards this spark and allow it to become a flame.[40]

NOTES

1. Thomas Merton, *Love and Living*. (New York: Harvest/HBJ Book, 1985), 4–5.

2. A tape of this conference is in the Thomas Merton Center, Bellarmine College (referred to as TMC after this) Tape 257, Side B is entitled "Satisfaction, the End of the Ascetic Life." This is Tape #3, Side B, in the Credence Cassette series, and is entitled "The Goal of the Ascetic Life."

3. Ibid.

4. Thomas Merton's letter to Louis Massignon, October 29, 1960 in *Witness To Freedom*, selected and edited by William Shannon (New York: Farrar, Straus, Giroux, 1994), 279–80.

5. Thomas Merton's letter to Abdul Aziz, November 17, 1960 in *The Hidden Ground of Love*, selected and edited by William Shannon (New York: Farrar, Straus, Giroux, 1985), 45. See also Michael Mott's *The Seven Mountains of Thomas Merton* (Boston: Houghton Mifflin, 1984), 352, 619.

6. Letter of Abdul Aziz to Thomas Merton, December 2, 1960 in the TMC.

7. Letter of Glen Markoe to Erlinda G. Paguio, April 20, 1995. Mr Markoe, who is the Curator of Classical and Near Eastern Art at the Cincinnati Art Museum, sent the author a picture of Imam Riza's tomb cover, the text of the poem in calligraphy, Arberry's translation, and Ackerman's reformulation of the Arberry translation.

8. Seyyed Hossein Nasr, *Sufi Essays* (New York: Schocken Books, 1977), 107–11. See also Annemarie Schimmel's *Islam An Introduction* (New York: SUNY Press, 1992), 91.

9. *The Collected Poems of Thomas Merton* (New York: New Directions, 1977), 985–86. [Full text of all of Merton's Sufi poems are also included in this volume, 297–315.] See *also Islamic Spirituality*, ed. Seyyed Hossein Nasr (New York: Crossroad Press, 1991), 160–78; *Shiism, Doctrines, Thought and Spirituality*, also ed. Seyyed Hossein Nasr (New York: SUNY Press, 168), 123–26; and Annemarie Schimmel's *Deciphering the Signs of God: A Phenomenological Approach to Islam* (New York: SUNY Press, 1994), 7.

10. Schimmel, *Islam An Introduction*, 110–11, 122.

11. Merton, "Readings from Ibn Abbad" in *Raids on the Unspeakable* (New York: New Directions, 1966), 141.

12. Ibid., 142–43.

13. Ibid., 146.

14. Letter of Abdul Aziz to Thomas Merton, Dec. 1, 1965 in TMC.

15. Schimmel, " Preface" to Ibn Abbad of Ronda, *Letters on the Sufi Path*, trans. John Renard , S.J. (New York: Paulist Press, 1986), xiii.

16. Merton, *Raids on the Unspeakable*, 151.

17. *Witness to Freedom*, 269

18. *Turning Toward the World, the Journals of Thomas Merton*, vol. 4, ed. Victor Kramer (New York: HarperSanFrancisco, 1997), 86. Schuon's widow, Catherine, thinks it is almost certain that this must have been Schuon's essay entitled "An-Nur," which had appeared first in French as part of *L'Oeil du couer*, then in his second book to appear in English, *Dimensions of Islam*.

19. *The Courage for Truth*, ed. Christine Bochen (New York: A Harvest Book, 1994,c1993), 127.

20. *The Collected Poems of Thomas Merton*, 307–8.

21. *Encyclopedia of Islam*, ed. E. Van Donzl, et al. (Leiden: E. J. Brill, 1971), v. 4 , 294.

22. Merton, *Conjectures of a Guilty Bystander* (New York: Doubleday/Image Books, 1968), 208, 210–11.

23. Merton's reading notebook, no. 18 , 1966–67 at TMC.

24. Ibid.

25. Titus Burkhardt, *An Introduction to Sufi Doctrine*, trans. D. M. Matheson (Lahore, Pakistan: Ashaf Press, 1958), 92.

26. *The Sufis of Andalusia. Ruh al -quds and al-Durral a-Fakhirah* by Ibn 'Arabî., trans. R. W. Austen (Berkeley and Los Angeles: University of California Press, 1972), 143.

27. Letter of Thomas Merton to Louis Zukofsky, April 15, 1967 in *The Courage for Truth*, 292.

28. *The Jerusalem Bible* (New York: Doubleday, 1968), 394. (See also *Encyclopedia of Islam*, v. 3, 1156.)

29. Ibn 'Arabî, *The Bezels of Wisdom*, translation and introduction by R. W. Austen. Preface by Titus Burckhardt (New York: Paulist Press, 1980), 229–30. See also Toshihiko Izutsu's *Sufism and Taoism* (Berkeley and Los Angeles: University of California Press, 1984), 15–17.

30. *The Collected Poems of Thomas Merton*, 614.

31. Ibid.

32. Ibid.

33. Izutsu, *Sufism and Taoism*, 16–17.

34. Ibn 'Arabî, *The Bezels of Wisdom*, 235.

35. Fritz Meier, "The Transformation of Man in Mystical Islam" in *Bollingen Series*, no. 30, v. 5 (1964), 37–68. [See also Merton's review of this essay in this volume, 320.]

36. Reza Arasteh, "The Art of Rebirth" in *Monks Pond. Thomas Merton's Little Magazine*, ed. Robert E. Daggy (Lexington: University Press of Kentucky, 1988), 146.

37. *The Collected Poems of Thomas Merton*, 634–35.

38. *Learning To Love. The Journals of Thomas Merton*, vol. 6 ed. Christine Bochen (New York:HarperSanFrancisco, 1997), 9

39. Merton, "The Life That Unifies" in *Thomas Merton in Alaska. The Alaskan Conferences, Journals and Letters* (New York: New Directions, 1988), 153–54.

40. Ibid.

6

"AS ONE SPIRITUAL
MAN TO ANOTHER"*
THE MERTON–ABDUL AZIZ CORRESPONDENCE

Sidney H. Griffith

I. THE BEGINNING OF THE CORRESPONDENCE

In December 1951, a young Pakistani Muslim assistant collector of customs in the Karachi Custom House, named Abdul Aziz, asked his boss, the collector of customs, one A. E. Wright, who happened to be a Catholic, to recommend to him a good book on Christian mysticism. Wright suggested a book by Thomas Merton called *The Ascent to Truth*, which had just been published that same year.[1] Through the good offices of a British airlines pilot, Abdul Aziz acquired the book from London in February 1952. Not so long afterwards, Abdul Aziz began a correspondence with the eminent French Orientalist, Louis Massignon (1883–1962), a well-known Catholic scholar of Islamic mysticism, who had a personal devotion to the Sufi saint, Husayn ibn Mansûr al-Hallâj (857–922). In one of his letters Abdul Aziz mentioned that he had purchased and read Merton's book. In reply, Massignon advised him to write to Merton, citing Merton's interest in al-Hallâj.[2] Then in 1959, when Massignon visited Karachi, Abdul Aziz met him in person and in the course of conversation asked him for "the name and address of some genuine Christian saint, contemplative mystic, so that I may correspond with him in respect of Christian mysticism."[3] It was on this occasion that Massignon gave him the American Trappist's address. Massignon himself had just begun his own exchange of letters with Merton in that same year.[4] Abdul Aziz then wrote to Merton on November 1, 1960, and thus began a correspondence that was to last until Merton's death in 1968 and was one of the most interesting epistolary exchanges between a Muslim and a Christian in the twentieth century.

When Abdul Aziz first wrote to Merton on November 1, 1960, he was just making contact. He addressed him as "Dear Father Louis Thomas Merton," revealing that Massignon must have informed him that Thomas Merton was known in religion as Father Louis, O.C.S.O. Nevertheless, thereafter in the correspondence the two men customarily addressed one another as "My Very Good Friend."

In this very first letter there are several features which recur in all the subsequent letters. The most prominent of them is book talk. Abdul Aziz tells Merton of the books he is searching for on the theme of Christian mysticism, suggests to Merton books on Islamic mysticism which he thinks are worthwhile, and gives Merton a list of the books he has in his own library on the subject of Christian mysticism. Sometimes the major part of a letter is taken up with bibliographical details of this sort. Abdul Aziz tells Merton of his interest in St. John of the Cross, and how helpful in this regard it had been for him to read *The Ascent to Truth*. This interest had been kindled, Abdul Aziz said, by an article he read by Paul Nwyia comparing the thought of John of the Cross with that of the Spanish Sufi master Ibn 'Abbâd de Ronda (1333–90).[5]

Merton responded to Abdul Aziz' first letter on November 17, 1960. He enthusiastically joined in the book talk, recommending titles and authors, and promising to send copies of his own books, even offering his services as something of a book agent for Abdul Aziz in America. But there was one of his books which Abdul Aziz had requested that Merton refused to send. It was *Seeds of Contemplation*.[6] Merton said, "The book was written when I was much younger and contains many foolish statements, but one of the most foolish reflects an altogether stupid ignorance of Sufism."[7] In the letter, Merton does not say what the foolish statement is, but William H. Shannon, the general editor of Merton's published letters, notes that in *Seeds of Contemplation* Merton had spoken of "the sensual dreams of the Sufis as a poor substitute for the true contemplation that is found only in the Church."[8] Now, just over a decade later, Merton was prepared to say to Abdul Aziz:

> As one spiritual man to another (if I may so speak in all humility), I speak to you from my heart of our obligation to study the truth in deep prayer and meditation, and bear

witness to the light that comes from the All-Holy God into this world of darkness where He is not known and not remembered. . . . May your work on the Sufi mystics make His name known and remembered, and open the eyes of men to the light of His truth.[9]

Throughout the 1960s, up to Merton's death in 1968, Merton and Abdul Aziz carried on their correspondence. A measure of Merton's enthusiasm for it may be seen in the journal entry he wrote on January 3, 1961, after he received Abdul Aziz' second letter, dated December 20, 1960. He wrote: "The chief joy of the Christmas season was the warm and cordial letter from Abdul Aziz, Moslem scholar, student of mysticism, at Karachi."[10] In the end, there are some seventeen Merton letters that survived, fifteen of which have been published.[11] Sixteen of Abdul Aziz' letters are extant, but none of them are yet published. One hopes in the near future to bring out an edition of the full correspondence between Merton and Abdul Aziz, with an appropriate introduction and commentary. In the meantime, it will have to suffice to take advantage of the present opportunity to review the highlights of the thoughts the two men exchanged.

These letters are rare in that they contain a correspondence between a notable Christian and a practicing Muslim in religious dialogue in modern times. Of course, Merton had long been writing letters to other scholars of Islam, some of them Muslims. But the letters to Abdul Aziz are uniquely personal and religious. Indeed one has the impression that Abdul Aziz pushed Merton, sometimes quite persistently, to express himself on themes which he would not otherwise willingly have addressed. The result is that Merton was compelled to state his position on matters of interreligious dialogue, and other topics, in ways which other Catholic writers and scholars have adopted in print only in recent years. As for Abdul Aziz, it is clear that the correspondence was deeply important for him as well. Many years later he wrote,

My correspondence with Thomas Merton was based on "poverty in spirit," being humble to learn from each other, without display of any scholarship or erudition. . . . Such correspondence, apart from revealing true feelings, also exudes spiritual fragrance, especially as the holy names of various blessed saints and mystics of Islam and Christianity and their essential teachings have been touched upon therein, apart from the Most Holy Name of Almighty God.[12]

So strongly was Abdul Aziz affected by his experience with Merton that in another letter he wrote to William H. Shannon he said, "I am of the view that each and every word written by Thomas Merton should be made public."[13] This advice came as a result of the observation that in the published letters some incidential phrases and postscripts had been omitted.

For the present purpose it seems best to review the prominent themes in the correspondence, rather than to attempt to give an account of each and every letter. Accordingly, in what follows we shall track the exchange of ideas on the following topics: personal observations; the phenomenon of secularization in the modern world; Sufism; spiritual masters; and interreligious dialogue.

II. ONE SPIRITUAL MAN TO ANOTHER

On December 30, 1960, Louis Massignon had written to Merton to tell him, among other things, that Abdul Aziz was the son of a converted Hindu, and that "he is a believer in Abraham's God without restriction."[14] But this was not enough for Merton. At the end of his letter to Abdul Aziz on May 13, 1961, he asked, "Would you tell me something about yourself? Are you a university professor? Or a theological student? What do you do?"[15] Abdul Aziz answered on November 18, 1961:

> I am a senior high official of the Government of Pakistan (Pakistan Customs Service) posted as Secretary, Central Board of Revenue. Since my youth I have been interested in spiritual matters because I believe that the highest ideal is to make contact with one's Creator. I am in the 46th year of my life and still unmarried. I have also occasionally associated with a true Muslim saint of a high order (he passed away in 1951)[16] and contacted other pious men but I find that most of them are formalists.[17]

Louis Massignon had also written to Abdul Aziz about Merton. He said of Merton, as Abdul Aziz later reported it to the monk, "you are pure but you are a 'simurgh' (a very rare bird) among your order."[18] This was not enough for Abdul Aziz, any more than what

Massignon had said about Abdul Aziz had been enough information to satisfy Merton's curiosity. In response to his correspondent's persistent inquiry, Merton finally wrote the following paragraph about himself on April 4, 1962:

> We are about the same age, perhaps almost exactly the same age. I am now forty-seven. I was born in France, educated in France, England, and America. My outlook is not purely American and I feel sometimes disturbed by the lack of balance in the powerful civilization of this country. It is technologically very strong, spiritually superficial and weak. . . . [I entered the monastery twenty years ago, and am the novice master here.] I believe my vocation is essentially that of a pilgrim and an exile in life, that I have no proper place in this world but that for that reason I am in some sense to be the friend and brother of people everywhere, especially those who are exiles and pilgrims like myself. [I cannot get along with formalists, I am alien to them and they to me.] My life is in many ways simple, but it is also a mystery which I do not attempt to really understand, as though I were led by the hand in a night where I see nothing, but can fully depend on the Love and Protection of Him who guides me.[19]

Very early in their correspondence Merton and Abdul Aziz adopted the practice of praying for one another at dawn of each day. It was Abdul Aziz who first mentioned it. When he received Merton's first letter, he wrote back to say, "I have been greatly moved by the hearty sentiments expressed in your letter, so much so that involuntarily I had to pray for your long life and prosperity and advancement in spiritual illumination at dawn the very next day."[20] Merton liked this idea, and in a letter of January 30, 1961 he spoke of the hour of dawn as the time "when the world is silent and the new light is most pure, symbolizing the dawning of divine light in the stillness of our hearts."[21] He went on to say that it is the time when he usually said Mass in a remote part of the monastery. Abdul Aziz repeatedly told Merton that he prayed for him especially during the month of Ramadan and on the "Night of Power/Destiny" (*laylat al-qadr*). And Merton adopted this practice too. For example, at the conclusion of a letter on January 2, 1966, he wrote, "I am united with you in prayer during this month of Ramadan and will remember you on the Night of Destiny."[22] Merton also prayed for Abdul Aziz in a special way on the feast of Pentecost. As he said in a letter of May 13, 1961, it is the feast on which "we celebrate the descent of the Holy Ghost into the hearts and souls of men that they may be wise with the Spirit of God."[23]

It is a measure of the close spiritual friendship and trust that developed between Merton and Abdul Aziz that it is from a letter to Abdul Aziz that we learn of Merton's daily *horarium* in the hermitage on the Gethsemani property to which he moved full time in late 1964. More importantly, in the same letter he took the, for him, hitherto unprecedented step of sharing with his Muslim friend a description of his personal method of meditative prayer. In closing the account he wrote, "I do not ordinarily write about such things and I ask you therefore to be discreet about it. But I write this as a testimony of confidence and friendship. It will show you how much I appreciate the tradition of Sufism."[24]

III. This World of Darkness

A constant theme in Merton's letters to Abdul Aziz, from the very beginning, was a concern for the dark state of the world. In the very first letter, on November 17, 1960, Merton wrote:

> The world we live in has become an awful void, a desecrated sanctuary, reflecting outwardly the emptiness and blindness of the hearts of men who have gone crazy with their love for money and power and with pride in their technology. May your work on the Sufi mystics make His Name known and remembered, and open the eyes of men to the light of His truth.[25]

Merton often returned to this theme in his letters. On May 13, 1961, he said to Abdul Aziz, "We live in dreadful times, and we must be brothers in prayer and worship no matter what may be the doctrinal differences that separate our minds."[26] While Abdul Aziz did not have much explicitly to say about this theme, he did respond to Merton's preoccupation with it. A concrete case in point was furnished in 1961 in connection with Merton's "A Letter to Pablo Antonio Cuadra Concerning Giants."[27] It is really a sermon, maybe even a desperate plea, in the form of a mimeographed public letter addressed to Cuadra, and widely circulated among Merton's friends in Latin America, in which the monk voices his fears about a coming nuclear holocaust, precipitated by the spiritual aridity of the two super powers, the United States of America and the Soviet Union, symbolized in the letter by the apocalyptical characters Gog and Magog from the Bible. Merton says that "Gog is a lover of power, Magog is absorbed in the cult of money."[28]

On September 24, 1961, Merton wrote to Abdul Aziz to say that he was sending him a copy of the mimeographed, "A Letter to Pablo Antonio Cuadra Concerning Giants." He went on to say, "It is my belief that all those in the world who have kept some vestige of sanity and spirituality should unite in firm resistance to the movements of power politicians and the monster nations."[29] He wanted to know what Abdul Aziz thought of this idea, and what people in Pakistan generally thought about the cold war. Abdul Aziz answered on November 18, 1961:

> As regards your open letter to Cuadra, it has correctly surveyed the miserable international conditions prevailing in the world and your description of the U.S.A. and Russia as Gog and Magog is very apt. You would probably be surprised to know that the Holy Quran has twice mentioned about Gog and Magog and that their "opening" would herald Dooms-day.[30] I admire your efforts in writing such thought-provoking articles and books to bring back the insane world to the path of sanity and morality. Pakistan being based on Islamic ideology shares, in substance, the thoughts expressed in your open letter. The President of Pakistan has prayed that the East–West conflict may be averted so that humanity may be saved from unimaginable destruction by thermo-nuclear warfare.[31]

It is in the "Letter to Cuadra" that Merton voices some of his most fundamental ideas about interreligious dialogue, in the context of his meditation on the earlier missionary activity of the Church. He wrote:

> One of the great tragedies of the Christian West is the fact that for all the good will of the missionaries and colonizers . . . they could not recognize that *the races they conquered*

were essentially equal to themselves and in some ways superior [Merton's italics]. . . . The preachers of the Gospel to newly discovered continents became preachers and disseminators of European culture and power. They did not enter into dialogue with ancient civilizations: they imposed upon them their own monologue and in preaching Christ they also preached themselves.[32]

Just previous to this observation, citing the implications of the Christian mystery of the Incarnation, Merton wrote, "Since the Word was made Flesh, God is in man. God is in *all men*. All men are to be seen and treated as Christ" [italics Merton's].[33] Consequently, Merton said,

It is my belief that we should not be too sure of having found Christ in ourselves until we have found him also in the part of humanity that is most remote from our own. . . . If I insist on giving you my truth, and never stop to receive your truth in return, then there can be no truth between us. . . . God speaks, and God is to be heard, not only on Sinai, not only in my own heart, but in the *voice of the stranger* [italics Merton's].[34]

Having shared these thoughts with Abdul Aziz, it is no surprise to find in the correspondence between the Pakistani student of mysticism and the American monk an ongoing Christian/Muslim dialogue, as well as a meeting of minds and hearts. In a letter to Abdul Aziz on December 26, 1962, Merton wrote, "It seems to me that mutual comprehension between Christians and Moslems is something of very vital importance today, and unfortunately it is rare and uncertain, or else subjected to the vagaries of politics."[35]

IV. MUTUAL COMPREHENSION

From the beginning of their exchange of letters Merton and Abdul Aziz would regularly explain to one another whatever obscure points in Christian or Islamic faith and practice that came to their attention. Eventually the principal doctrines called for some attention. On December 26, 1962, Merton asked about the concept of faith in the two religions, where he supposed "a deep divergence may be found"[36] between Islam and Christianity. Abdul Aziz answered on April 4, 1963, as follows:

Perhaps you might be aware that Islam is very simple and practicable being based on the truths which could be deduced from the laws of nature; it is indeed a natural theology. Islam believes that man's salvation lies in faith (right beliefs) and righteous actions including good morals. Now, faith according to the Quranic conception consists of as follows. It is our knowledge of certain truths, with convictions strong enough to convert them into action or fulfill their requirements. These are the 7 articles of our faith:

i) God, as the Source of Law — i.e., belief in the Monotheism of God (*tawhîd*), i.e., oneness of God.

ii) Angels — the functionaries of Law.

iii) The Revealed Books — the records of Law

iv) The Prophets, i.e., the messengers of God — being the intermediate persons who receive the first message from the Lord.

v) The Hereafter.

vi) The Law, and

vii) The Resurrection.

Islam inculcates individual responsibility for one's action and does not subscribe to the doctrine of atonement or theory of redemption. The Muslims believe that this was the common faith of all the true messengers of God right from Adam down to the last Holy Prophet of Islam, including great patriarchs like Noah, Abraham, Isaac, Jacob, Joseph, Moses, David, Solomon and Jesus Christ. It is obvious that "faith" cannot change with the different epochs.[37]

Merton responded to Abdul Aziz' sketch of Islamic faith on June 2, 1963. Although the passage is long, it is worth quoting in full. He said:

Thank you for your brief outline of the Moslem faith. I can certainly join you with my whole heart in confessing the One God (*tawhîd*) with all my heart and all my soul, for this is the beginning of all faith and the root of our existence. Without this faith we are in deep night and do not know where we are going, and this precisely is the source of all the evils in the world. I believe with you also in the angels, in revelation, in the Prophets, the Life to Come, the Law and the Resurrection.

As you say, the differences begin with the question of soteriology (salvation). Personally, in matters where dogmatic beliefs differ, I think that controversy is of little value because it takes us away from the spiritual realities into the realm of words and ideas. In the realm of realities we may have a great deal in common, whereas in words there are apt to be infinite complexities and subtleties which are beyond resolution. It is, however, important, I think, to try to understand the beliefs of other religions. But much more important is the sharing of the experience of divine light, and first of all of the light that God gives us even as the Creator and Ruler of the Universe. It is here that the area of fruitful dialogue exists between Christianity and Islam. I love the passages of the Quran which speak of the manifestations of the Creator in His Creation.[38]

On August 2, 1963, Abdul Aziz responded to these observations with some more questions, and with some further remarks of his own. He wrote:

I am specially interested to know as to why the belief in the Sonship/Divinity of Christ, Doctrine of Trinity, Doctrine of Redemption is essential for Salvation, when the Prophets prior to Christ did not hold any such belief. How to reconcile the belief in one God (*tawhîd*) with the Doctrines of Sonship and Trinity and how to reconcile the Doctrine of the personal responsibility with that of the theory of Redemption?

I am glad to know that you have appreciated the passages of the Holy Quran which speak of the manifestations of the Creator in His Creation. From the Muslim point of view, the excellence of this last "Word of God" lies in the fact of its being a complete Code for all the problems of life, social, economic, political, moral and spiritual etc. It is a book of Divine Wisdom par excellence, and I think its proper study lies in one's pondering over its message for mankind.[39]

Merton responded to Abdul Aziz' further questions about Christian beliefs in a letter dated October 18, 1963. First of all, he wrote, "I find it difficult to reply to questions about Christian belief in such a way as to be able to present the ideas comprehensibly. . . . Like so many other Christians, I am perhaps not equal to the task of making clear what I believe in such a way as to satisfy one of another religion."[40] This said, further on in the letter Merton addresses himself to the issues of the doctrines of the Trinity and the Incarnation. The passage is a long one, but again it is worth quoting in full because it allows one to see how Merton thought about the most important doctrinal issues dividing Muslims and Christians. He wrote:

> Just as you (and I too) speak with reverence of Allah Rahman and Rahim,[41] so I think you can see that speaking of Father, Son and Holy Ghost does not imply three numerically separate beings. The chief thing that is to be stressed before all else is the transcendent UNITY of God. Now as this unity is beyond all number, it is a unity in which "one" and "three" are not numerically different. Just as Allah remains "one" while being compassionate and merciful, and His compassion and mercy represent Him in different *relations* to the world, so the Father and Son and Holy Spirit are perfectly One, yet represent different relations.
>
> But there is of course a distinction: Rahman and Rahim are "attributes" and "names" of God, but not subsisting *persons*. Here the trouble comes in the definition of person. The idea of "person" in God is by no means the same as the current and colloquial idea of "person" among men: where the "person" is equivalent to the separate individual man in his separateness. This is of course where the confusion comes, in speaking of the "Three Persons" in God. This naturally conjures up an image of three separate beings, three *individuals*. The idea of Person must not be equated with that of individual. And, once again, "three" is not to be taken numerically.[42]
>
> The one thing which we must absolutely confess without any hesitation is the supreme transcendent Unity of God, and the fact that there is no other with Him or beside Him. He has "no helper." The work of creation and of the salvation of man is entirely His work alone. The manner in

which Christianity preaches salvation in and through Christ must not obscure this fact which is basic to the Christian faith, as it is to Islam. The fact is that we believe, as you know, that Christ is not a being outside of God who is His helper. It is God in Christ who does the work of salvation. But here we come to the enormous difficulty of stating in technical terms the Incarnation without making Christ something separate from God, when in fact the humanity of Christ is "an individual" human nature. This is beyond me for the moment, but I will try to think about it in terms that would be meaningful to you. . . . There seems to be much in common between our idea of the working of God in and through Christ and your idea of God manifesting Himself to the world in and through the Prophet. I must leave this to future consideration. The one technical difference of a doctrine of the incarnation is of course enormous.[43]

Merton addressed one other doctrinal point in this same letter, regarding the Christian idea that salvation is to be achieved by faith in Christ. Abdul Aziz had raised the issue of salvation in connection with a quotation he found in a book by Martin Lings on the life and teachings of the North African Sufi saint, Shaikh Ahmad al-'Alawî (d. 1934). In a footnote, Lings had quoted a remark made by Pope Pius XI (1857–1939) to Cardinal Facchinetti, whom he was sending as Apostolic Delegate to Libya. The Pope said to him, "Do not think that you are going among infidels. Moslems attain to salvation. The ways of Providence are infinite."[44] Abdul Aziz shared this quotation with Merton and wanted to know what he thought about it. In reply Merton said:

I perfectly agree that any man who in his heart sincerely believes in God and acts according to his conscience, with all rectitude, will certainly be saved and will come to the vision of God. I have no doubt in my mind whatever that a sincere Muslim will be saved and brought to heaven, even though for some reason he may not subjectively be able to accept all that the Church teaches about Christ. There may be many extrinsic reasons which make it impossible for him to understand what the Church means. I think that all men who believe in One God Who is the Father of all and Who wills all to be saved, will certainly be saved if they do His Will. This is certainly the teaching of the Catholic Church, and this is being brought out clearly now, in connection with the Council. But it was also brought out a hundred years ago at the time of the First Vatican Council.[45]

Merton returned to this issue in a letter to Abdul Aziz almost a year later, on June 28, 1964. He repeated in substance the ideas he had mentioned earlier, but then he added the following observation:

How can one be in contact with the great thinkers and men of prayer of the various religions without recognizing that these men have known God and have loved Him because they recognized themselves loved by Him? It is true that there are different ways to Him and some are more perfect and more complete than others. It is true that the revelation given to the "People of the Book," Christians, Jews and Muslims, is more detailed and more perfect than that given through natural means only to the other religions.[46]

Speaking of the Muslim concept "People of the Book," it is interesting to know that in 1965 Abdul Aziz sent Merton a copy of A. J. Arberry's interpretation of the Qur'an.[47] Apparently he had proposed earlier that Merton take up the habit of chanting passages from the Islamic scripture daily.[48] In the letter in which he acknowledged the receipt of the Arberry translation, Merton explained:

It would not be right for me to chant the Koran daily, as I do not know how this ought to be done properly, and I would not want to simply go in for improvisation in so serious a matter. It seems to me that here again, my task is rather to chant the sacred books of my own tradition, the Psalms, the Prophets, etc., since I know the proper way of doing this. But on the other hand I read the Koran with deep attention and reverence.[49]

On December 1, 1965, Abdul Aziz, for his part, explained why he had suggested the chanting of the Qur'an in the first place. He wrote:

I had suggested the chanting of the rhymed translation of the Holy Quran in the normal sense of recitation of good verses especially as you are gifted with poetical talents and I thought that such recitation would give more relish and pleasure to you than the mere prosaic reading. I knew that as part of your religious duty you have to chant the Psalms etc. but I did not know such chanting had a special technique but I learnt on receipt of your letter that such chanting is being done by Christians in the technique laid down by Gregory[50] and hence I understood your scruples for 'improvisation' in this respect.[51]

There were other occasions when Abdul Aziz had advice for Merton in the conduct of his life of prayer. In a letter of January 2, 1966, Merton had described his method of meditation to Abdul Aziz. He wrote:

I have a very simple way of prayer. It is centered entirely on attention to the presence of God and to His will and His love. . . . One might say this gives my meditation the character described by the Prophet [Mohammad] as "being before God as if you saw Him." Yet it does not mean imagining anything or conceiving a precise image of God, for to my mind this would be a kind of idolatry.[52]

Abdul Aziz was afraid that Merton may have misunderstood the phrase attributed to the Prophet, "being before God as if you saw Him." Particularly, he thought that Merton might have interpreted the sense of the phrase as commending a kind of idolatry. He wrote back on January 26, 1966, to say:

I hope that such is not your inference from, or your interpretation of the saying. What it means is only this, that one should worship God *as if* one saw Him because if man is unable to see Him, He sees man. The idea behind this precept is the same as practicing the Presence of God and not that a Muslim has to imagine anything or conceive a precise image of God as Islam is iconoclastic par excellence. In the Holy Qur'an it has been stated that God is so Transcendent that "nothing is like Him";[53] rather "nothing is like even His Similitude." Of all the various types of religious worships and its liturgy, Islamic worship is the most simple and untrammelled, without any external aid or symbol; it has a direct approach to God. However, I find that your method of meditation is on the correct lines especially conforming to the Sufi mode which says, "you should not exist at all — that is perfection," i.e., self-effacement before one's Creator.[54]

In his next letter, Merton registered his full agreement with this line of thinking. He said:

Of course when I spoke in my letter of not making mental images of God, I fully realized that this is one of the great virtues of Islam: the deep respect for the purity of the divine Oneness which is beyond any possible representation. I meant only to say that in this above all I was in profound agreement.[55]

In the last two letters he wrote to Abdul Aziz, on January 16, 1968, and again on April 24, 1968, Merton told his friend about the conferences on Sufism he had been giving to the monks at Gethsemani for more than a year. On both occasions he remarked that he was able to do this because of the many books and articles Abdul Aziz had sent him over the years of their correspondence.[56] In fact, the whole exchange between Merton and Abdul Aziz in the ensemble can be read as a long dialogue on Sufism and Christian mysticism, often consisting almost entirely of the exchange of bibliographical information and commentary on spiritual writers and their works.

V. MYSTICS AND SUFI MASTERS

In his letters Abdul Aziz revealed himself to be a man profoundly interested in mystics both Christian and Muslim. He and Merton both had a voracious appetite for books on the subject and they reached around the world in their endless search for more of them. They read the books, marked their favorite passages, wrote marginal comments, and constantly sent copies of them back and forth to one another.[57] What is more, they were both in constant correspondence with other people of similar interests, and they wrote to one another about their other friends and interlocutors on this all-consuming subject. Indeed the Merton–Abdul Aziz correspondence itself began because the Pakistani Sufi adept wanted someone with spiritual experience in the Christian world to talk to about mysticism. As we have seen, Abdul Aziz had become aware of the comparability of the thought of Ibn 'Abbâd de Ronda and St. John of the Cross; he read Merton's book on the Spanish mystic's teaching, *The Ascent to Truth*, and through the good offices of Louis Massignon, who gave him the address, he wrote to Merton. Abdul Aziz was precise in the statement of his main interest in his very first letter. He wrote to Merton,

> I request you to suggest to me really useful books on practical mysticism dealing with the path leading to spiritual illumination, esp. mortification of inordinate desires, which is the main teaching of the Holy Quran and Sufis like Tirmizi, Muhâsibî, & Junayd. If any useful book on Christian monastic life could also be suggested, I shall be grateful. I am not interested in speculative aspects of mysticism.[58]

At the beginning of their correspondence Merton evinces an interest in Sufism; in his first letter he mentions the names of al-Hallâj, about whom he learned from Massignon, and Jalâl ad-Dîn al-Rûmî (1207–73), "who is to my mind," Merton wrote to Abdul Aziz, "one of the greatest poets and mystics, and I find his words inspiring and filled with the fire of divine love."[59] But it was with his reading of a book on Sufism by Titus Burckhardt,[60] which Abdul Aziz had sent him, that Merton became truly excited. He wrote to Abdul Aziz on May 13, 1961, to say, "It is one of the most stimulating books I have read for a long time. . . . In a sense it is one of those books that open up new horizions that I have been waiting for."[61] Toward the end of the letter he wrote, "One of the chapters I like best in Burckhardt is that on the renewal of creation at each instant, and also that on the *dhikr* which resembles the techniques of the Greek monks, and I am familiar with its use, for it brings one close to God."[62]

Reading Burckhardt's book prompted Merton further to declare:

> I am tremendously impressed with the solidity and intellectual sureness of Sufism. There is no question but that here is a living and convincing truth, a deep mystical experience of the mystery of God our Creator Who watches over us at every moment with infinite love and mercy. I am stirred to the depths of my heart by the intensity of Moslem piety

toward His names, and the reverence with which He is invoked as the "Compassionate and the Merciful." May He be praised and adored everywhere forever.[63]

Reading the many books and articles Abdul Aziz sent him over a year or more led Merton to write on April 4, 1962, that "there is much in common, on the level of experience, between Sufism and Christian mysticism."[64] As if in testimony to this observation, a constant point of reference in the letters of both men is the teaching of St. John of the Cross. Abdul Aziz was so taken by the comparability of his doctrine with that of the Sufis that he once wrote to Merton about the Spanish mystic to say, "He has appealed to me as his teachings greatly resemble, in certain parts, those of Hakim at-Tirmizi [al-Tirmîdhi].[65] My view is that his Ascent and Dark Night are indispensable for every student (practical or academic) of Mysticism as he has gone to its substantial roots."[66] Once too in this connection Abdul Aziz wrote to Merton quoting a favorite passage from the Trappist's own book on the doctrine of John of the Cross and asking for clarification. He said, "I have been greatly impressed by one sentence: 'And desire is the movement of the soul seeking joy; therefore, the secret of ascetic liberation is the 'darkening' of all desire.'"[67] On December 26, 1962 Merton responded to this observation with a long comment on the subject, ending with the expression of his opinion that the purpose of asceticism is the increase of faith. He went on to say, "I think here the important point is now to discuss the relation between the concept of faith for a Christian and a corresponding concept for a Moslem. This is probably where a deep divergence may be found, though perhaps not as deep as I anticipate."[68] In fact, Abdul Aziz and Merton did go on from this point to discuss the differences between Christian and Islamic faith, as we have seen above.

Merton's study of Sufism, progressing somewhat under the tutelage of Abdul Aziz, took a decisive step forward in 1963 when he received from his Pakistani friend a copy of Martin Lings' book on the Algerian Sufi master, Shaikh Ahmad al-'Alawî of Mostaganem (1869–1934), then entitled *A Moslem Saint of the Twentieth Century.*[69] Abdul Aziz mailed the book to Merton on July 29, 1963, as he mentioned in a letter on August 2 of the same year. He also included in the same mailing a copy of his own enthusiastic review of Lings' work.[70] In the subsequent letter, Abdul Aziz went on to mention to Merton that he was himself in correspondence with Martin Lings and that the latter had recommended to him the works of the Swiss thinker and Muslim convert, Frithjof Schuon (1907–98), who had had connections with Shaikh al-'Alawî; Abdul Aziz included a list of some titles in English translation. In due course Merton would himself become much involved with the friends and disciples of Schuon, principal among them being Marco Pallis (1895–1989), with whom he was engaged in correspondence from the summer of 1963 until 1966.[71] In the meantime, Merton wrote to Abdul Aziz on October 18, 1963, to tell of his own reaction to Lings' book on al-'Alawî. He said he was moved and impressed by the book and was looking forward to reading it a second time. Then he said,

> With Shaikh Ahmad, I speak the same language and indeed have a great deal more in common than I do with the majority of my contemporaries in this country. In listening to him I seem to be hearing a familiar voice from my "own country" so to speak. I regret that the Muslim world is so distant from where I am, and wish I had more contact with people who think along these lines.[72]

When Abdul Aziz wrote to Merton again, on December 19, 1963, he told him that by the good offices of a pilot friend of his, Merton's remarks on Shaikh al-'Alawî had been shown to Martin Lings in London. Abdul Aziz reported that "Dr Lings was quite pleased and surprised to read your appreciative remarks about his book." Six months later, on June 28, 1964, Merton wrote back to say that he was planning to review the book.[73]

In 1966 Merton made direct contact with someone in the spiritual lineage of Shaikh al-'Alawî in the person of an Algerian Sufi master named Sidi Abdeslam. Although he spoke only Arabic, the man from Algeria came to Gethsemani with some friends from Temple University, one of whom could serve as interpreter.[74]

On December 28, 1966, Merton wrote excitedly to Abdul Aziz about Abdeslam's visit, saying, "We had a very pleasant conversation through his interpreter and I feel he is a true friend."[75] As Michael Mott has put it, "Merton sensed that he and Sidi Abdeslam were able to communicate beyond the translated words."[76] And the thought which Abdeslam communicated to Merton disturbed him. The fall of 1966 was already a troubled time for the monk; he was wrestling with the pains of a human love recently experienced.[77] Nevertheless, the visiting Sufi, whom Merton recognized as a genuine mystic, "left him with the message that he [i.e. Merton] was very close to a mystical union and that the slightest thing could bring that union about."[78] Then, on the February 14, 1967, Sidi Abdeslam wrote Merton a letter in which he asked him if he "had yet set aside the distractions of words, his own words and those of others, in order to realize the mystical union."[79] Abdeslam left Merton with this cryptic phrase to ponder: "What is best is what is not said."[80]

But Merton was always busy with what to say. In 1965 Abdul Aziz had sent him a book on the life and works of the Spanish Sufi master Ibn 'Abbâd de Ronda (1333–90), containing French versions of the Sufi's Arabic poems.[81] Merton told Abdul Aziz in a letter of November 7, 1965, that he was "very much impressed" with them and that he "even did some adapted versions of his thought, in semi-poetic fashion, based of course on the French version. These will be published next year in a book with other things of mine."[82] The texts did appear in Merton's Raids on the Unspeakable, where Ibn 'Abbâd's thoughts and words spoke through Merton's meditative translations.[83] He used the method he had employed in the composition of The Way of Chuang Tzu, a project he had been working on in the spring and summer of 1965, at the same time when he was reading so extensively about Islam and Sufism.[84] He read translated texts of poems from the tradition he was studying and mastered them by recasting them in verses of his own making. This is what Merton meant when he said that he had "adapted" versions of Ibn 'Abbâd's thought "in semi-poetic fashion."[85] For his part, Abdul Aziz was delighted with the results and he wrote to Merton on December 1, 1965, to say so:

> I am glad that you have done excellent renderings from Ibn Abbad (actually when I read your poetic notations I made the remark "good renderings done" but on second thoughts I found that the word "good" should be replaced by "excellent," so much I was pleased with your verses) and I showed it to Dr. Peter Fernandez, who also greatly admired the smooth flow of your versions.[86]

Meanwhile, Abdul Aziz continued to guide Merton in his search for the classic writers of Sufi texts. For example, when in 1965

Merton heard of the publication of 'Azîz an-Nasafî's treatise on *The Perfect Man*[87] he thought Abdul Aziz could acquire a copy for him.[88] But his Pakistani friend wrote back to say that, contrary to Merton's expectations, only fifty some pages of the six-hundred page book were in French; the rest were in Persian, and so not of much use to Merton.[89] On the other hand, Abdul Aziz had an important book by A. H. Abdul Kader on Abû'l-Qâsim Muhammad al-Junayd (d. 910) to recommend to Merton in his letter of January 26, 1966.[90] He said of this Sufi author that he "was the greatest exponent of the 'sober' school of Sufism and elaborated a theosophical doctrine which determined the whole course of orthodox mysticism in Islam." He went on to say that the Abdel Kader book is "worth re-reading." But he had a caveat about a chapter on "Plotinus and Junayd." Abdul Aziz disapproved of what he referred to as the author's "unwarranted 'findings' about the influence of the former on the latter." He attributes this suggestion to two factors: the circumstance that Abdel Kader was a student of A. J. Arberry, "who believes in the Neo-Platonic influence on Sufism;" and that "being Egyptian, [Abdel Kader] has been carried away by the modern wave of patriotic nationalism to establish the Egyptian cultural and spiritual influence on persons of other nationalities." Abdul Aziz went on to say, "This tendency is very regrettable and I feel that he has done great injustice to the soul of al-Junayd."[91] Abdul Aziz was always on the lookout to protect the Sufi authors from what he regarded as misrepresentations by western scholars.

In addition to recommending books to Merton, Abdul Aziz also had some definite ideas about a book Merton should write. He first raised the matter in his letter of December 2, 1965. He suggested that Merton "plan a book on 'How to Know God' on a psychological, moral and spiritual basis." He went on to say:

> The book should deal with the fundamental principles which are essential to be followed by a seeker after truth to attain his moral and spiritual perfection with a view to attaining contemplation of God and communion with Him and the mystic vision of God with the eye of the heart in this very life. . . . In writing the book much material is already available i.e., the writings of the great Saints and Mystics of Islam and Christianity but this should be coupled with the modern principles of psychoanalysis as applied to ethics.[92]

The interreligious character of Abdul Aziz' suggestion is immediately apparent. He wrote again on December 20, 1965, to press
Merton further on the matter, making sure that he understood there
should be chapters on practical matters such as detachment and mortification of desires. When Merton answered on January 2, 1966, he
did not reject the idea out of hand, and he even said "I hope that I
will be able to do this." But he mentioned the numerous difficulties
and he noted that he had written about such things in the past, and
he even proposed to send some of them to Abdul Aziz, including the
mimeographed notes he used to teach ascetical and mystical theology in the monastery.[93] But what Abdul Aziz wanted was an essay that
would draw on the riches of both the Islamic and the Christian traditions under the same rubrics. Regrettably, Merton never produced
it. Perhaps he came closest to doing so in the last two years of his life,
in the conferences he gave on Sufism to the monks of Gethsemani
who were interested in the subject. Here he drew freely from both
the Islamic and the Christian mystical traditions.

The tapes of Merton's so-called Sufi conferences remain for the
most part unpublished, and even unstudied.[94] At one time there was
a project to transcribe the tapes and to publish them in hard copy.
But in the end it was thought best to leave them in oral form.[95]
Merton speaks quite casually on the tapes, sometimes in a mean-
dering way, a style that can be quite disconcerting to the unwary listener, unacquainted with the informal ways of an afternoon talk in
a monastic setting. When through the kindness of his correspondent Willie Yaryan, Abdul Aziz finally heard the tapes in 1986, he
was startled by this informal style and he wrote to Msgr. William H.
Shannon to say:

> I have been simply shocked and disappointed about
> Merton's burlesque/parody of Sufism in a garbled, hotch-
> potch version. If I were to make critical comments it would
> take a number of pages.[96]

But it was from just such raw material as one finds on Merton's
Sufi tapes that he was in the habit of producing his more publish-
able prose. After listening to them for a while, and being frustrated
by the seeming stream-of-consciousness style of his speaking, one
finally realizes that Merton had indeed gotten the point of much
Sufi teaching. Had he lived to do it, he may well have produced

from this matrix the book Abdul Aziz requested. By this time he was writing to his friends to say such things as, "I am the biggest Sufi in Kentucky though I admit there is not much competition."[97] And in a retreat conference to contemplative women given at Gethsemani in May 1968 he declared, "I'm deeply impregnated with Sufism."[98]

As was his habit, Merton was in correspondence with a number of other people about Islam and Sufism, in addition to Abdul Aziz, but there can be no doubt that his exchange with his Pakistani friend was of particular importance.[99] Even now, thirty some years after the two men exchanged letters with one another, the vibrancy of their spiritual friendship still radiates from the pages they wrote. And from the perspective of interreligious dialogue on an experiential basis, particularly between a Muslim and a Christian, the Merton/Abdul Aziz correspondence is still unique.

NOTES

* Thomas Merton to Abdul Aziz, November 17, 1960, in Thomas Merton, *The Hidden Ground of Love* (ed. William H. Shannon; New York: Farrar, Straus, Giroux, 1985), 45 (Hereafter *HGL*).

1. Thomas Merton, *The Ascent to Truth* (New York: Harcourt, Brace & Co., 1951).

2. Abdul Aziz to Merton, November 1, 1960. Abdul Aziz' letters to Merton are unpublished; they are kept in the archives of the Thomas Merton Center, Bellarmine College, Louisville, Kentucky (Hereafter *TMC*).

3. Abdul Aziz to William H. Shannon, December 21, 1982. I am grateful to Msgr. Shannon for allowing me access to his correspondence with Abdul Aziz, which began in September 1982, when Shannon was working on the publication of Merton's letters, of which he was general editor. His own correspondence with Abdul Aziz continued until the beginning of 1990.

4. See Sidney H. Griffith, "Thomas Merton, Louis Massignon, and the Challenge of Islam," *The Merton Annual* 3 (1990), 151–72 [included in this volume, 51–78]; *idem*, " 'A Discourse on All Things Human and Divine': the Correspondence of Louis Massignon and Thomas Merton," to appear in the published proceedings of the international conference, "Louis Massignon; the Vocation of a Scholar," University of Notre Dame, Notre Dame, Indiana, October 2–5, 1997. Merton's side of the Merton/Massignon correspondence is published in Thomas Merton, *Witness to Freedom; the Letters of Thomas Merton in Times of Crisis* (ed. William H. Shannon; New York: Farrar, Straus, Giroux, 1994), 275–81 (Hereafter *WTF*).

5. The article was, in all probability, Paul Nwyia, "Ibn 'Abbâd de Ronda et Jean de la Croix; à propos d'une hypothèse d'Asin Palacios," *Al-Andalus* 22 (1957), 113–30. Later Abdul Aziz sent the article to Merton, who did not like it. He wrote to Abdul Aziz on May 13, 1961 to say of it, "Only the little article

of your Syrian friend about St John of the Cross and the Moroccan mystic was a distinct disappointment to me. It really said nothing at all. In any case this western habit of seeking causal relationships and 'influences' everywhere is largely an illusion. How much better it would have been to make a positive comparison of the inner riches of the two great mystics." These sentences are omitted in the published letter in *HGL*, 49.

6. Thomas Merton, *Seeds of Contemplation* (New York: New Directions, 1949).

7. Merton to Abdul Aziz, November 17, 1960, in Merton, *HGL*, 44.

8. Ibid., 44, asterisk note.

9. Ibid., 45–46.

10. Thomas Merton, *Turning toward the World; the Pivotal Years* (*The Journals of Thomas Merton*, vol. 4, Victor A. Kramer, ed. (San Francisco: HarperSan Francisco, 1996), 85.

11. Merton, *HGL*, 43–67. The two additional letters came to light after the publication of *HGL*, when Abdul Aziz had received the volume and compared the contents with the letters in his possession. Subsequently he sent copies of seven Merton letters to William H. Shannon, including the two missing ones. They are now in the collections of The Merton Room in the Lorrette Wilmot Learning Resources Center, Nazareth College of Rochester, Rochester, N.Y.

12. Abdul Aziz to William H. Shannon, April 14, 1983.

13. Ibid., December 14, 1984.

14. Massignon to Merton, December 30, 1960. Louis Massignon's letters to Thomas Merton remain unpublished. *TMC*.

15. Merton, *HGL*, 50.

16. This Muslim saint was no doubt Malik Barkat Ali of Arup, Pakistan. In a later letter to Merton, dated January 26, 1966, Abdul Aziz spoke of him as "one of the greatest modern Muslim saints . . . with whom I had the good fortune of associating ocassionally; he passed away in August 1951 and I may write to you about him some time later."

17. Abdul Aziz to Merton, November 18, 1961.

18. Ibid., March 8, 1961. The *simurgh* is a mythical bird in ancient Persian literature; in later Islamic mystical texts it figured in an elaborate allegory for the relationship between a worshipper and God. See F. C. de Blois, "Simurgh," *EI*, 2nd ed., *s.v.*, vol. VI, 615.

19. Merton, *HGL*, 51–52. The passages in brackets are omitted in the published form of the letter.

20. Abdul Aziz to Merton, December 20, 1960.

21. Merton, *HGL*, 46.

22. Ibid., 64. About this time Merton wrote the poem titled, "The Night of Destiny." See Thomas Merton, *The Collected Poems of Thomas Merton* (New York: New Directions, 1977), 634–35; the poem is also included here, 313–14.

23. Merton, *HGL*, 49.

24. Ibid., 64.

25. Ibid., 45–46.

26. Ibid., 49.

27. Published originally in Thomas Merton, *Emblems of a Season of Fury* (New York: New Directions, 1963), 70–89, and reprinted in Thomas Merton, *The Collected Poems of Thomas Merton* (New York: New Directions, 1977), 372–91. Pablo Antonio Cuadra is a poet of Nicaragua, with whom Merton was also in correspondence. See Thomas Merton, *The Courage for Truth: The Letters of Thomas Merton to Writers* (Christine M. Bochen, ed.; New York: Farrar, Straus, Giroux, 1993), 178–95. Merton speaks of the "letter" in question in a private letter to Cuadra of September 16, 1961, 188–90. It is interesting to note in passing, that Merton had written to Cuadra on January 4, 1961, "I have been in contact with a Moslem scholar in Pakistan [Abdul Aziz], a student of Islamic mysticism, and this is very interesting and inspiring," 188. This letter must have been written in 1961, and not in 1960, as printed in *Courage for Truth*; Merton's first letter to Abdul Aziz was November 17, 1960. Either Merton himself wrote the wrong year, or a mistake was made in the editing process.

28. Merton, *Collected Poems*, 375.

29. Merton, *HGL*, 50.

30. The Qur'an passages are XVIII *al-Kahf* 94 and XXI *al-Anbiyâ'* 96. It is the latter passage that refers to letting loose Gog and Magog, their "being opened" from behind their wall, to presage the fulfillment of God's promise.

31. Abdul Aziz to Merton, November 18, 1961.

32. Merton, *Collected Poems*, 381–82.

33. Ibid., 380.

34. Ibid., 382–84.

35. Merton, *HGL*, 53.

36. Ibid., 54.

37. Abdul Aziz to Merton, April 4, 1963.

38. Merton, *HGL*, 54.

39. Abul Aziz to Merton, August 2, 1963.

40. Merton, *HGL*, 55.

41. The reference here is to the Islamic *Basmalah*, the Arabic formula found at the beginning of every *sûrah* in the Qur'an except one, and often used by Muslims as an invocation of God at the beginning of any activity: *bismi-Llâhi-r-Ra'mâni-r-Ra'îm*; "In the Name of God, the Merciful, the Compassionate." It is likely that Merton was influenced here by Frithjof Schuon, *Comprendre l'Islam* (Paris: Gallimard, 1961). In this same letter he told Abdul Aziz he had just finished reading the book and "I like his exegesis of the Basmalah." See Merton, *HGL*, 56, where this particular phrase was omitted by the editor.

42. In an earlier letter to Abdul Aziz, dated May 13, 1961, Merton had written: "The question of *tawhîd* is of course central and I think that the closest to Islam among the Christian mystics on this point are the Rhenish and Flemish mystics of the fourteenth century, including Meister Eckhart, who was greatly influenced by Avicenna. The culmination of their mysticism is in the 'Godhead' beyond 'God' (a distinction which caused trouble to many theologians in the Middle Ages and is not accepted without qualifications) but at any rate it is an ascent to perfect and ultimate unity beyond the triad in unity

of the Persons. This is a subtle and difficult theology and I don't venture into it without necessity." Merton, *HGL*, 49.

43. Ibid., 56–57.

44. Martin Lings, *A Moslem Saint of the Twentieth Century: Shaikh Ahmad al-'Alawî, his Spiritual Heritage and Legacy* (Berkeley & Los Angeles: University of California Press, 1973), 81, n. 1. Lings cites as his source for this remark a publication called *L'Ultima*, Anno VIII, 75–76, 261 (Florence, 1954). I have not independently yet been able to verify it.

45. Merton, *HGL*, 57. The second session of the Second Vatican Council began on September 29, 1963. The First Vatican Council met from December 1869 to October 1870.

46. Ibid., 58.

47. Arthur J. Arberry, *The Koran Interpreted* (Oxford: Oxford University Press, 1964).

48. The letter in which Abdul Aziz gave this advice has apparently not survived. We know of it only from Merton's response.

49. Merton, *HGL*, 61.

50. Apparently Abdul Aziz means Pope Gregory the Great (c. 540–604), after whose name the traditional music of the Latin rite of the Christian liturgy is known as "Gregorian Chant."

51. Abdul Aziz to Merton, December 1, 1965.

52. Merton, *HGL*, 63–64.

53. The reference is to the Qur'an's phrase: *laysa kamithlihi shay'un*, "Nothing is like unto Him." *ash-Shûrâ* 42:11.

54. Abdul Aziz to Merton, January 26, 1966.

55. Merton to Abdul Aziz, March 23, 1966. This letter is unpublished and is kept in the collections of The Merton Room at the Lorette Wilmot Learning Resources Center, Nazareth College, Rochester, N.Y.

56. See Merton, *HGL*, 66–67.

57. In this connection it is interesting to note that toward the end of their correspondence, after almost a decade of book talk between them, and when Merton had taken up life in the hermitage, Abdul Aziz wrote to say, "Reading interferes with solitude as a person in solitary retreat may be away from the company of men but if he is engrossed in reading and writing he cannot get interior detachment. A famous Muslim Saint Hakim Tirmizi has mentioned in one of his books on spiritual discipline that association with one's brethren and reading are means of attachment and joys for the carnal self and therefore, they should be avoided in preliminary spiritual discipline." Abdul Aziz to Merton, December 18, 1967. Merton replied on January 16, 1968. Among other things he said: "There are times when it is necessary to read, and even to read quite a lot, in order to store up material and get new perspectives. . . . In the solitary life, however, though one has a lot of time for reading, it becomes difficult to read a great deal. One finds that in a couple of hours he reads only a few pages. . . . Someone in solitude who would read voraciously all the time might perhaps be considered in the wrong place." Merton, *HGL*, 66. Having said this, Merton went on at the beginning of a new paragraph in

the same letter, omitted in the published text, to say, "I am always very interested in receiving and reading Sufi texts."

58. Abdul Aziz to Merton, November 1, 1960.

59. Merton, HGL, 44.

60. Titus Burckhardt, Introduction to Sufi Doctrine (Lahore, 1959).

61. Merton, HGL, 48.

62. Ibid., 49. In this connection see Bonnie Thurston, "Thomas Merton's Interest in Islam: the Example of Dhikr," The American Benedictine Review 45 (1994), 131–41 [included in this volume, 40–50].

63. Merton, HGL, 48.

64. Ibid., 51.

65. This is the early Sufi writer, Abû 'Abdullâh Muhammad ibn 'Ali al-Hakîm al-Tirmidhî, who flourished in the second half of the ninth Christian century. See Nicholas L. Heer, "Some Biographical and Bibliographical Notes on al-Hakîm al-Tirmidhi," in James Kritzeck & R. Bayly Winder (eds.), The World of Islam; Studies in Honour of Philip K. Hitti (London: Macmillan, 1960), 121–34. On December 19, 1963, Abdul Aziz asked Merton in a letter to help him find an American Orientalist to translate a work of al-Tirmidhî into English, the Kitâb al-Riyâdah wa Adab al-Nafs, a title which Abdul Aziz translated as, "Book of Mortification & Discipline of the Carnal Self." Merton answered on June 28, 1964, explaining that he had no real contacts in the academic world and, in a passage not published in HGL, 59, he wrote, "The scholars are like Chinese Mandarins, and they are occupied in rising in the academic hierarchy before all else."

66. Abdul Aziz to Merton, June 21, 1962.

67. Ibid., December 18, 1962. See Thomas Merton, The Ascent to Truth (First Harvest/HBJ ed.; San Diego: Harcourt, Brace, Jovanovich, 1981), 54. In his letter Abdul Aziz refers to p. 41 of the original, 1951 edition of Merton's book.

68. Merton, HGL, 53–54. Merton published an extract from this letter under the heading, "To a Moslem," in his Seeds of Destruction (New York: Farrar, Straus and Giroux, 1964), 300–302. He alerted Abdul Aziz to it in a letter of December 9, 1964, where he also mentioned that he was sending him a copy of the book. See Merton, HGL, 60.

69. Martin Lings, A Moslem Saint of the Twentieth Century: Shaikh Ahmad al-'Alawî; his Spiritual Heritage and Legacy (London: George Allen & Unwin, 1961). This book was re-published in a second edition in 1971 under the title: A Sufi Saint of the Twentieth Century. In 1973 it was published in a paperback edition by the University of California Press, Berkeley.

70. Abdul Aziz, "[Review of] A Moslem Saint of the Twentieth Century," Islamic Studies 1 (1962), 153–57. Abdul Aziz was not totally uncritical. He objected to Lings' view that whereas love predominates in Christian mysticism, knowledge predominates in Sufism. And he discerned "the author's strange Christian predilection" in a footnote about Christ's last words on the cross.

71. See Merton, HGL, 463–77 and "Merton, Marco Pallis, and the Traditionalists" in this volume, 203–75.

72. Thomas Merton, Dancing in the Water of Life: Seeking Peace in the Hermitage (The Journals of Thomas Merton, vol. 5, ed. Robert E. Daggy; San Francisco: HarperSanFrancisco, 1997), 20–21.

73. The review appeared the next year as, "[Review of] A *Moslem Saint of the Twentieth Century, Shaikh Ahmad al-'Alawî* by Martin Lings," *Collectanea Cisterciensia* 27 (1965), 81–82 [in French]. Translation in this volume, 318–19.

74. Nicole Abadie (Khadidja Benaissa), who has contributed a chapter, "Sidi Abdeslam's Visit to Gethsemani," in this volume, 192–202.

75. Merton, *HGL*, 65.

76. Michael Mott, *The Seven Mountains of Thomas Merton* (Boston: Houghton Mifflin, 1984), 462.

77. See Merton, *Learning to Love, passim*. See also John Howard Griffin, *Follow the Ecstasy; Thomas Merton, the Hermitage Years, 1965–1968* (Fort Worth, Tex.: JHG Editions/Latitudes Press, 1983), 77–131.

78. Mott, *The Seven Mountains*, 462. One recent commentator has suggested that Merton's experience of human love in 1966 was a precipitating factor for the spiritual breakthrough which the visiting Sufi master recognized. See Terry Graham, "The 'Strange Subject': Thomas Merton's Views on Sufism," *Sufi* 30 (1996), 36–37.

79. Mott, *The Seven Mountains*, p. 468.

80. Ibid.

81. Paul Nwyia, *Ibn Abbad de Ronda* (Beyrouth: Impr. Catholique, 1961). See also Paul Nwyia, *Lettres de direction spirituelle (ar-rasâ'il as-Sughrâ) par Ibn 'Abbâd de Ronda* (Lettres Orientales de Beyrouth, 7; Beyrouth: Impr. Catholique, 1958).

82. Merton, *HGL*, 61. In an earlier, unpublished letter of November 2. 1965, a copy of which is now in the collections of the Merton Room in the Lorette Wilmot Learning Resources Center at Nazareth College, Rochester, N.Y., Merton mentions that he sent a copy of his adaptations to Abdul Aziz. He wrote, "Also you might like these poor efforts to render some of the ideas of Ibn Abbad which you will instantly recognize as coming from one of the books you sent. I have simply put them from French into English with a little editing to make them attractive to readers here. In some small way they may make the name of Ibn Abbad known. He is a very great mystic and I am grateful to have come to know him."

83. Thomas Merton, *Raids on the Unspeakable* (New York: New Directions, 1966), 141–51.

84. See Thomas Merton, *The Way of Chuang Tzu* (New York: New Directions, 1965).

85. Merton was somewhat frustrated by his lack of mastery in the original languages of Sufi writers. He wrote to Herbert Mason on August 24, 1959 that "I have wanted for ten minutes to learn some Oriental languages," and again on January 14, 1961 he wrote that "several times I have fought the temptation to start on Arabic and then Persian, but for me this is nonsense, I think." Merton, *Witness to Freedom*, 262, 270. He wrote in the same vein to James Laughlin, this time invoking the influence of Abdul Aziz. He wrote on January 4, 1961 to say, "Have also an awful urge to study Sanskrit and then Persian . . . . Yah, it is probably crazy. I will never have the time. But I do have an interesting contact in Pakistan, a Moslem scholar with a lot of interesting information

about Sufis, and he says he prays for me in his morning prayer." Again, on February 3, 1965, Merton returned to the theme, writing, "A friend [Abdul Aziz] (Moslem) is trying to urge me to learn Arabic, but I am wary of that, at least when there is no instructor in the picture. I know how much time one can waste trying to get Russian by oneself (I soon gave that one up after I had got as far as ["] Ivan working like the devil in his factory["]). I probably will not start Arabic." David D. Cooper (ed.), *Thomas Merton and James Laughlin: Selected Letters* (New York: W. W. Norton, 1997), 164, 258.

86. Abdul Aziz to Merton, December 1, 1965. Abdul Aziz went on to encourage Merton to include in his forthcoming publication of the verses two important letters of the Spanish Sufi, because he, Abdul Aziz, thought that "without the inclusion of these two masterpieces, the ideas conveyed of his teachings may be deficient." Merton in fact did not follow this advice.

87. Marijan Molé (ed.), *'Azîz an-Nasafî, Le livre de l'homme parfait* (Teheran: Institut France Iranien, 1962).

88. This portion of Merton's letter of November 7, 1965, was omitted in Merton, *HGL*, 62.

89. Abdul Aziz to Merton December 1, 1965. Abdul Aziz went on to tell Merton of the editor, Marijan Molé's tragic death by suicide. On January 2, 1966, Merton responded, "I am sorry to hear the tragic story of Molé. Unfortunately the state of Western society is now so chaotic morally that all sorts of things like this happen frequently. It is very sad indeed." This section of the letter is omitted in Merton, *HGL*, 62.

90. A. H. Abdel Kader, *The Life, Personality and Writings of al-Junayd* (Gibb Memorial Series, n.s., 22; London: Luzac, 1962).

91. Abdul Aziz to Merton January 2, 1966. The point here is that the Neo-Platonic philosopher Plotinus (205–70), who was born in Lycopolis, studied in Alexandria, Egypt, before going to Rome to found his philosophical school.

92. Abdul Aziz to Merton, December 2, 1965.

93. See Merton, *HGL*, 62. It is surprising to note that one of the books Merton here proposes to send is *Ascent to Truth*, the very text that introduced Abdul Aziz to Merton when he purchased it back in 1952!

94. Two tapes containing some of Merton's conferences on Sufism have been released: "Sufism: Knowledge of God," and "Sufism: the Desire for God," (Credence Cassettes; Kansas City, Mo.: National Catholic Reporter Publishing Co., 1988). Six sets of tapes, under the general title, "The Mystic Life," plus Merton's notes on his readings in Sufi sources are available in the collections of the Thomas Merton Center, Bellarmine College, Louisville, Kentucky. See Burton B. Thurston, "Merton's Reflections on Sufism," *The Merton Seasonal* 15 (Summer, 1990), 4–7 [included in this volume, 33–39]; Graham, "The 'Strange Subject,'" esp. 38–40.

95. The project had been undertaken by Willie Yaryan, who corresponded with Abdul Aziz about it, who in turn explained it all to William H. Shannon in a letter dated May 10, 1986. See Willie Yaryan's own interaction with Merton's thought in his article, "Seeing Through Language: Thomas Merton's Contemplation of Hidden Wholeness with a Perspective from Ludwig

Wittgenstein," *The Merton Seasonal* 11 (Autumn, 1986), 2–9. Bernadette Dieker's "Merton's Lectures to the Novices," which follows immediately in this volume is the first lengthy transcript of the taped Sufi lectures ever published.

96. Abdul Aziz to William H. Shannon, May 10, 1986.

97. Merton to Ad Reinhardt, October 31, 1963, in Thomas Merton, *The Road to Joy; the Letters of Thomas Merton to New and Old Friends* (ed. Robert E. Daggy; New York: Farrar, Straus, Giroux, 1989), 281.

98. Thomas Merton, *The Springs of Contemplation; a Retreat at the Abbey of Gethsemani* (New York: Farrar, Straus, Giroux, 1992), 266.

99. Merton also corresponded with the Iranian Muslim, Reza Arasteh. See Merton, *HGL*, 40–43. This was also an important contact; Merton wrote his essay, "Final Integration: Toward a 'Monastic Therapy,'" in dialogue with Arasteh's book, *Final Integration in the Adult Personality* (Leiden: E. J. Brill, 1965). See Thomas Merton, *Contemplation in a World of Action* (New York: Doubleday, 1971), 219–31. And at Merton's invitation Arasteh contributed an article to the literary journal Merton founded, "The Art of Rebirth; Patterns and Process of Self-Liberation in Near Eastern Sufism," *Monks Pond* 2 (Summer, 1968), as re-published in Robert E. Daggy, *Monks Pond; Thomas Merton's Little Magazine* (Lexington: The University Press of Kentucky, 1989), 89–93. Merton's essay is included in this volume.

7

MERTON'S SUFI LECTURES TO CISTERCIAN NOVICES, 1966–68

Bernadette Dieker

Thomas Merton used the conferences before Vespers to teach his fellow monks at Gethsemani about Christianity and life as a monk. Along with lecturing on the monastic life, Merton also offered his knowledge of other religions to assist the monks in their quest for God. In the late 1960's, Merton lectured on Sufism, the mystical dimension of Islam with which he felt a special connection. Merton's understanding and knowledge of Islam was basic, yet his lectures witness that he realized the deep and significant relationships between Islam and Christianity, and specifically for him, between Sufism and his own contemplative life.

Merton is candid and entertaining as he helps the novices understand the essential points in Sufism. At times, Merton seems irreverent, as he often was in his interactions as a teacher, but his love for God and the knowledge of God is in no way diminished by his personality. Merton can especially be appreciated through his lectures for his humanity, as well as for his serious spiritual scholarship.

Merton instructed monks from various educational and cultural backgrounds. He understood these differences among his brothers, and thus gave concrete examples and stories to exemplify the sometimes highly abstract and metaphysical ideas of the Sufi masters he presented. Due to the straightforward nature of his lectures, they remain one of the most accessible teachings of mystical life, a spiritual life seemingly inaccessible to many people. Merton's lectures are simple and profound, and they are a powerful beginning for one interested in learning more of Sufism, mysticism, and the monastic life.

In the first lectures in his series on Sufism, Merton admits that he knows little of Islam—his point in broaching the subject is simply to create a sense of background before moving on to Sufism, the dimension of Islam most closely associated with the contemplative life. Due to this objective, Merton refers constantly to Christian beliefs in relation to other faiths, for he is interested in the monks deepening their spiritual lives through lessons from other tradi-tions. Without Merton's references, a listener may not be able to discern the particular religion he discusses, which is precisely Merton's goal—to illuminate by revealing the similarities of the world's great spiritual traditions.

Some novices who studied under Merton have stated that for some time they did not know that their Father Louis was *the* Thomas Merton, and the lectures are proof of Merton's two separate public roles, that of the joking though brilliant monk and that of the thoughtful and usually sober scholar and writer. In his lectures, Merton teaches the profundity he finds in the various religions clear-ly and simply, often straying from his main point in an effort to main-tain his audience's interest. At times a listener may think that the academic or spiritual nature of a lecture is lost. But when one listens to the lectures in their entirety, one understands that Merton loved humor, and he relished his position as a kind of elder in the monastic community. He enjoyed the freedom to teach as he desired, using examples he created in an effort to provide greater clarity. He also encouraged laughter, which helped the novices understand his points without being intimidated by the lectures' serious nature.

In addition to his taped lectures, Merton's style of teaching is appar-ent by reading his working notebooks. Merton's teaching notes are as thorough and scholarly as his published writings. What differentiates his lectures from his published work is the presence of Merton himself delivering his message: his love of mischievousness, even silliness. At the same time, he never loses the critical nature of his lessons—he impresses upon the monks the urgency of a life of prayer and faith.

Merton ends each lecture abruptly, when the bell tolls, thus he often repeats the same points in various lectures. The repetition allows for an even greater understanding, for he connects the topics in a manner which facilitates a more complete view of Islam and Sufism. He does not separate any particular topic or argue the most important points, for he knows all are necessary if the novices are to learn a basic knowledge of this other religious tradition and to apply the lessons to their own practices.

The following excerpts from the taped lectures are arranged according to subject and not as Merton delivered them. They are focused on the essential points he presented—essential in the sense that these points expose the goal in Sufism, and again in the sense that one can gain a further knowledge of God through reading them. The excerpts are edited for easier reading. Merton is completely understandable in his lectures, but he is very informal and conversational, thus the exact transcriptions would be filled with typical Merton sayings such as, "Well," "I mean," "kind of," "sort of," along with many stuttered beginnings of sentences. This is not meant as criticism: Merton simply did not lecture in the style with which he wrote. An example of Merton's published writings which is close to his style of lecturing is his book *New Seeds of Contemplation*. This book is carefully composed, but he uses second person references and a very informal tone.

The excerpts offered here are simply essential points for the understanding of Sufism as presented, analyzed, and understood by Merton. The reader is encouraged to listen to the actual taped lectures to gain a complete understanding of Merton the teacher.

Union of God and Man

So the basic idea of Islam . . . is this union of God and man, God manifesting Himself in the world created by Him, and man in the world as the one who has the job of knowing that God is manifesting His love in him and in the world, and [of] responding [to that knowledge]. And man is granted the gifts of intelligence and freedom and speech in order to respond to Allah's love, and of course, what is the great way to respond?

Well, the basic thing about Islam is that man should come to know Allah by His Name—by all His Names if possible—but . . . especially by the Name by which He really speaks to us, and to utter these Names of Allah from one's heart. What is this? This is the basic thing in religion, the total response of one's heart to God, known and recognized and confessed as the Source of all good. As our Creator, as He loves us, as He redeems us, as He saves us and so forth. And of course, there are two standard ways of doing this, one is in public canonical prayer, the prayer [where] they all go down [while facing] towards Mecca . . . and the other is in *dhikr*, which is your private, constant crying out to Allah in your heart. It's all built on names, on the Name of Allah, not on big long petitions and that sort of thing, but crying out to God, total response to Him.

Before you get any further into Sufism you've got to have the basic truths of Islam. . . . The whole religion of Islam is extremely simple. And it's all contained in one or two basic formulas, real basic formulas. And the most basic one is a thing called the *shahâdah*—*La ilâha illa 'Llâh*—*Muhammadun Rasûlû 'Llâh*—which is the famous statement, "There is no god but God, (there is no god but Allah) and (Muhammad is the one who is really sent), Muhammad is His Prophet." The way this is usually translated is "There is no god but Allah and Muhammad is His Prophet." Now, of course the way that is usually interpreted is in terms of a kind of orthodoxy, but that's not the way the Sufis look at it. . . . It is not confined to that . . . if that was all they were saying, they wouldn't have got so far. . . .

Actually, what you've got in the two parts of the *shahâdah*, you've got *tanzîh* and *tashbîh*. The first part is *tanzîh* and the second part is *tashbîh*. The first part . . . begins, as some of these Sufi commentators say, with a denial. The first part says "There is no god." It starts with that, "There is no god," and then it says, "but there is, and He is Allah." So what this statement is, then, is a negative and then an assertion. That there is no god and it also means there is no reality, so what this is saying is nothing is real . . . except Allah. He alone is Real.

And then, and this is your *tanzîh* statement, there is this infinite hidden reality, and this is The Reality, but then comes up the question, What about everything else? God alone is Real—*tanzîh*. What about everything else? Well, it's real too, insofar as it comes from Him. . . . How do you get that out of "Muhammad is His Prophet?" Well, [as] the Sufis interpret this, the first part is about God, the second part is about the world. And the world is that which has come forth from God . . . and into which He has sent the prophets, and especially Muhammad, the Prophet who comes with the last word of God, so to speak. Muhammad doesn't just simply mean this one

particular prophet. He stands in a certain sense for man, insofar as he is considered by the Muslims the perfect man.
Muhammad was the one who "made it." Everybody else should
seek to some extent to approach the knowledge of God which
Muhammad had. Everybody should try to be to some extent a
kind of prophet. And so, Muhammad came into the world as a
representative of what man ought to be, and what man ought
to be is [a person] who knows that Allah is the One Reality,
and that everything else is a manifestation of God.

And so what every man has then is this job to do on earth, a
job of being, so to speak, a witness of God's love, a witness of
what is. This is the way things are.

What we [Christians] are saying is that all comes from God
and that all Creation is a manifestation of God, and it is all
summed up in Christ. . . . Muhammad is for them only a man,
only a prophet, and in our Christology, Christ is the son of
God . . . but the basic idea is structurally the same kind of thing.
The idea of God's manifestation of Himself in creation and
man's office as witness to proclaim this, to acknowledge this,
and to thank God for this and to turn to God with thanksgiving and so forth. . . .

You've got time and eternity in there . . . this idea of movement in the world, you've got the stillness of eternity and the
abyss of His Infinitely Hidden Being, and then you've got the
movement of time into which a prophet is sent, which is the
realm of *tashbîh* . . . and then once again, this idea that everything is governed by God's love.

KNOWLEDGE OF GOD

In discussing the knowledge of God, Merton explains that God, in
essence, is unknowable. The point of the monastic life, as he
explains through Sufic terms, is believing in and having faith in the
presence of God in all things:

We're working on this idea of Sufism and the basic thing that
we're considering is the idea of religious knowledge, the knowledge of God. How do you know God? And this is a very
important idea . . . for us. Basically, it is something we tend

to . . . talk about everything else but. But it's one of the things that we are here for. So, it's a . . . very worthwhile thing to talk about: . . . the knowledge of God as the idea is approached by these people of another religion and who are nevertheless not that far away from us really, and see how they approach it.

Because after all that's a great question. And you don't know God the way you know anything else. See, that's the first thing about it. Your knowledge of God is not like the knowledge of any object. And above all, your knowledge of God is not arrived at merely by logic. . . . You prove the existence of God—you know nothing. You can prove the existence of God until you are blue in the face, and you have no knowledge. There's no question of any religious knowledge of God involved in this. That's not what we're here for, and neither are the Sufis interested in that.

Now what tends to happen around in this kind of life we're living, in which the big issue really is knowing and loving and serving God (of course that's the big issue in the Christian life), is you tend to get away from it in one way or another. Well, you say "You can't know Him," and really, you can't know Him, and you can know about Him. And we become content with a certain amount of ideas about God. We fill in the void with ideas about God which are not knowledge of God, and we talk an awful lot about God, "God this," "God that," "God's will," all that. The big thing is to be here with a certain number of ideas about God in your head and then be with God. See, do what you're supposed to do, behave yourself. It is not a very satisfactory form of life.

Nor is the knowledge of God the reward of finding some special magic gimmick. . . . You get the feeling in a place like this, that everybody is convinced that there is some hidden trick to it somewhere. Probably nobody around here has got it, but in the old days, some monk or other had that sort of an ace up his sleeve somewhere, and if we only could find it. Maybe if we stumble around enough . . . we'll fall over this by accident one of these days, we'll find this special gimmick which will enable us to suddenly be enlightened. Or . . . it's a reward for being beaten over the head continually. . . . I mean if you just let yourself be totally beaten to a pulp, maybe as a reward you will get the knowledge of God.

Well, I don't know, I think that the thing that we have to do is really to know what is involved and work at it, and do a little something about what we are here for. You are here to seek God. And any ordinary monk can deepen his knowledge of God by living the monastic life. This is assumed in these talks, so get rid of your despair which you have been nourishing now for some time. Get rid of it and stir up your hope. . . . God isn't all that hidden. He didn't bring us here out of a kind of a trick. He didn't lure us in here and get us in this box in order to . . . torture us for the rest of our lives. He brought us here for real, and He wills that we know Him.

TANZÎH AND TASHBÎH—GOD MANIFEST

Merton explains through the Islamic concepts of *tanzîh* and *tashbîh* the concept of God as Being and the presence of God in the world:

I was talking last time about the two ideas, the two approaches to the knowledge of God in Islam, which are called *tanzîh* and *tashbîh*. *Tanzîh* is the knowledge of God as invisible and as, so to speak, beyond knowledge. And there are ways of arriving at that by logic, and if you arrive at it by logic, you exclude everything else, and you've got a completely unknown God.

Tashbîh is the knowledge of God as manifested and evident in everything, just the opposite—the other end of the thing. And this also can be pushed to an extreme which excludes *tanzîh*, excludes the unknown God, and then you get . . . idolatry. You get God, so to speak, made too concrete, exclusively concrete and tangible. . . . Real religious knowledge is a unity of both these apparently contradictory kinds of knowledge of God. He is both visible and invisible. He is invisible in Himself and visible because He has willed to make Himself visible. And to know Him then is to be aware of how He makes Himself visible to us, which He does all the time. He is hidden and yet manifest.

A simple concrete example is: you see light coming through a green glass, a green window pane, and you say what you see— this is an illustration . . . of *tanzîh* and *tashbîh*, and its quite clear what the two things are. The light coming through the green window pane is green. That's *tashbîh*. As you experience it, you experience it as green. But also it is not green. Because it's made green by the window pane and in itself it is not green, and you know that too, and that's *tanzih*. . . . When you become aware of these—this is God and creatures—God as He appears to us in created being . . . His being appears to us in a being which is not His. But it appears to us and He appears to us in His creatures—He makes Himself known in His creatures. Not merely by argument from cause to effect; the Islam people are very definite about the fact that every creature manifests God's love. It doesn't manifest God's *essence*, but manifests His love, is a manifestation of love.

Everything manifests love, everything comes from love and is a manifestation of love. But it is obviously not a manifestation of God as He is in Himself, it is the light turned green by passing through creatures—creatures give it another color. . . . St. John of the Cross puts it in another way: the light of the sun coming into a room, you don't see the actual ray of the sun but you see it by virtue of the dust motes which are floating in it. And so therefore, all creatures are the locus, the place, of the manifestation of God. God shows Himself in His creatures, but, you have to see Him there.

Now, the difference between *tanzih* and *tashbih*—there's also a question of affirmation and denial, because the creature is not God, and you have to say this. The creature is a manifestation of it, but definitely is not God. The worst thing that a Muslim could possibly do is to point to a creature and say "That is God." That would be utter blasphemy . . . but nevertheless, it is God Who manifests Himself in the creature—His Love manifests itself through the creature. And so to say when a creature is there, the creature is, in a certain sense, a denial of God, and yet at the same time a manifestation of God. And then the Infinite Perfection of God is a certain denial of the reality of anything else, and yet it is manifest in everything else.

PERPLEXITY TO PERFECTION—MERCY

The beginning of the real deep spiritual life for a Muslim is the perplexity which is set up by this apparent contradiction, and where we start is with this sense of perplexity, this inability to come to grips with the fact that God is manifest in creatures which are nevertheless not God, and that He is beyond them and yet He is there. He is present. And this is the complete opposite of this whole idea "God is dead" pitch. The . . . "God is dead" pitch, which has its own value, too, in another sphere, is that anybody who says that he has any knowledge of God whatever is just kidding. It is . . . grabbing onto *tanzîh* without any possibility of *tashbîh*. Just one end, and you've got to have them both. Whereas here, God is manifest in everything, but you have to be able to see it. How do you come to see this? Well, Islam, the whole idea of Islam, is seeing this by total consecration of oneself to God and carrying out God's will, and then God is manifest. If you are with Him, you see Him. If you are against Him, you don't see Him.

The person who arrives at spiritual perfection in this is beyond this contradiction, beyond this perplexity, in a certain sense even beyond good and evil. Sees God in good, sees God even in what appears to be evil. Sees God in everything. Of course this can be pushed too far, naturally. And . . . this . . . has come through to a great extent in some of the Christian mystics . . . because I think it is common to all mysticism actually. It does come through into the Christian mystics—you get things like this in St. John of the Cross, you get things like this in the Rhenish mystics. So that is why it is important to know that God Who is Manifest in creatures is manifest primarily as Mercy.

The Muslims place an enormous amount of importance to the Names of God. See they've got the idea that these Names are in God clamoring to the invisible, unknown, absolute abyss of God for manifestation. And God breathes on them and they are manifested in creatures. All creatures are not manifestations of the Hidden Essence of God, they are manifestations of Names of God. And the Name of God which is the top of the pyramid [other than Allah] and which includes every other Name is Merciful. God the Merciful. Allah the Merciful. And therefore one seeks to ascend to the knowledge of God as Merciful in everything. The Mercy of God in everything. And of course one of the chief Christian Sufis of the last hundred years is Saint Thérèse. The Little Way of St. Thérèse is Sufism. It's a form of Christian sufism, and it is based on this particular attitude toward God, this idea of God.

THE NAMES OF GOD

Merton emphasizes the validity of knowing God by a Name particular to each individual person:

> Here's an idea that I think is valuable for the life of prayer for everybody. Each person knows God by a special name. Now that doesn't mean a special word that you get out of a book somewhere—it is [that] each one speaks to God by a Name which strictly speaking he alone has for God. And God speaks to him by a name which God has for him. And the name by which I speak to God is the Name under which He is really my God and my Lord. Of course . . . this has to be seen within the framework of an intensely communal Islam[ic] spirit—. . . there is a great communality and a great sense of unity in Islam. And you should see them all, I mean they all get down and start bowing down towards Mecca as soon as they get the word. You know at certain times of the day, wham! down they go—great unanimity in prayer.
>
> But nevertheless, one of the secrets in the life of prayer is to find the name of your Lord, of *my* Lord, and speak to Him who is your Lord. I must speak to Him who is My Lord. Don't speak to somebody else's God, because somebody else's Lord may be Satan for you if you don't look out. You have to be careful, you may not understand the goodness and the love and so forth that somebody else sees in his name of God. It may be for you intensely destructive. Therefore, one has to be terribly careful not to impose upon other people one's own Lord, one's own idea of God. . . .
>
> They make a great point of this—the Sufis do—now the other Muslims don't go worry about distinctions like this, but the Sufis are very particular about this kind of thing. You have to know Your God, and of course that doesn't mean that there is a different God for every person, on the contrary, there is One God for all, but each person knows God by a special name.
>
> What is His Name? What is your name? Who are you? This depends. Actually this is all tied up with your own identity. To have somebody else's God is to lose one's own identity. To have somebody else's God is to have an idol, because it's not really God for you. . . . To be in contact with this Name of God which

is His Name by which we know Him, by which He makes Himself known to us, is to receive into oneself the breathing of God's Mercy. But of course all these Names go back to Mercy, even if you have some real kooky special name for God, in the end you don't get out of the common business of it really being a name for Mercy. If it's not a name for Mercy then you are not in His love and then you've had it, it's not the one God, it's an idol. But, for you mercy may mean all sorts of things. And of course this gets the Muslims into strange predicaments, I mean people think, "Well, these Muslims, they can do anything they want . . . they don't give a hoot about anything. They just justify it as the will of Allah." . . . Well, behind it is the idea . . . you don't know why He is doing this or why He is doing that, or what's behind Him, it's His business. Islam is . . . they are very fussy about a lot of things, but also they are very liberal about a lot of things, and a great deal of it, especially in Sufism, is everybody minding his own business. And yet nevertheless a great deal of fraternity, a great brotherhood, because Sufism is synonymous with a kind of brotherhood in Islam. It is not individualistic, not strictly individualistic.

So, a saying of the Prophet [relating God's words]: "I was a Hidden Treasure," he says, "and I loved to be known, I desired to be known." The word for "loved to be known" / "desired to be known" here is the same kind of word that our Lord uses in the Gospel, "with desire have I desired to eat this Pasch with you," this sort of a thing, this intense desire of God to make Himself known as He is to His creatures, as Merciful to His creatures. And the duration of Mercy is an intensely personal relationship. "Accordingly I created the creatures, and thereby made Myself known to them, and they did come to know Me. I was a hidden treasure (tanzîh) and I loved to be known. Accordingly I created the creatures (tashbîh) and made Myself known to them and they did come to know Me."

That's Islam in a nutshell. God wishing to make Himself known to His creatures and He makes creatures that they may know Him, and they know Him. And who knows Him? Islam. It's the idea that Islam is the way of those to whom God is fully manifest. They are the ones who know.

LOVE AND MERCY

Ibn 'Arabî says: "If it were not for this love, the world would never have appeared in its concrete existence." In this sense, the movement of the world toward existence was a movement of love which brought it into existence. And not only the movement of the world into existence, the coming of everything into existence is an act of love, the development of everything is an act of love. Everything that happens is love and is mercy. Not that it always appears to be that way, very often it appears to be just the opposite. But everything that happens is love. And of course the ones in Islam who emphasize this the most are the Sufis, because the great thing in Sufism is Love.

When this Sufi [Sidi Abdeslam] was here, we were up in the cow barn. And you know how cows are, cows are very intimate, warm and affectionate, and that sort of thing. So a cow is leaning over and licking [his] hand, and the Sufi monk says, *mahabbah*, which means love. I suppose our reaction would be, well, "dirty old cow, better go wash your hands, you might get a disease." His main idea is: in all things, of all things, is manifested love if you know how to see it. The Mercy of God in everything, but you have to know how to see it.

THE STRAIGHT WAY

Merton explains the Fâtihah, the opening prayer of the Qur'an, in an effort to describe the belief that God is the ground of everything:

> This opening [phrase] of the Qur'an, . . . is kind of a fundamental prayer which they say all of the time, which sort of contains everything. So I'll just read that, "In the Name of God the Merciful, the Compassionate." That phrase there is what they call the *Basmalah*, that's a phrase with which they open everything and which sort of includes the reminder of everything to do with God, the Merciful and the Compassionate. (. . . God as Merciful or *rahman*, is the basic mercy in which everything is grounded; God Himself as the ground of all being is Mercy itself. And then the Compassion of God is in events. It shows itself in His intervention in particular events here and there, over and above the other. . . .)

"In the Name of God the Merciful and the Compassionate, Praise belongs to God, the Lord of all Being, the All Merciful, the All Compassionate" (again you got that same distinction) . . . "the Master of the Day of Doom [Judgment/Accountability]." (That is to say He is at the end of the line . . . we foresee our total extinction in Him, and after the Day of Doom we live only in Him. You see, after the Day of Doom, the realm of Mercy as ground persists and the ground of Compassion and events ceases, but the Eternal Mercy goes on.) "Thee only we serve, to thee alone we pray for help. Guide us on a Straight Path, the path of those whom Thou hast blessed, not of those against whom Thou art wrathful, nor of those who go astray." . . .

The Straight Path is the . . . path of Islam. . . . What is the straight path? How do you know where the straight path is? For Islam it is very simple. The straight path is purely and simply What Is. Everything that is is willed by Allah, and whatever is, that's it, that's the straight path.

Well, if that's the case, how can you get off it? From a certain point of view, everything is on the straight path whether it wants to be or not, it's all going where God wants. . . . Basically you get this in Christianity too, but we're just not quite so strong on it as they are. And of course, there are certain problems involved in this . . . the problem of evil, the problem of a lot of things we don't want to have happen comes up . . . but basically they say simply What Is is the straight path, we're *on* it. One of the Muslim mystics says, "Verily God's is the straight way, the way is there exposed to sight everywhere. (It's right in front of you.) It is to be perceived in great things and in small, and [in] those who are ignorant of the truth, as well as those who know it well."

This is why it is said that His Mercy covers everything. Everybody walking on earth is on the straight way of the Lord, but the trouble is that a lot of them don't want to be. Where the problem comes in is not in what is going on, in what is willed by God, but the problem comes—we are all on the straight way, but we don't want to be. And from the moment that I prefer something else than What Is, then I am on the straight way as far as everything goes, [but] I am not on it as far as my will goes. . . . This is typical of Muslims, this is the way the Muslims look at it, that's not the way we look at it. They've got their own concept of freedom . . . which is built into this kind of concept.

This is the sort of thing which works beautifully if you're a mystic. But short of mysticism, it can get you in plenty of trouble. If a person starts rationalizing about the thing, starts figuring it out wrong . . . starts saying things about it that are . . . produced by those that do not come from total submission to this thing in a completely spiritual way, then we . . . can find [ourselves] rationalizing all kinds of things that shouldn't be. But basically, What Is is God's will, and to have no preference but for What Is is to be on the straight way.

The only problem comes in where we do things that are dictated from a source that is not in accord with the will of God but is in accord with some preference of our own in which we attempt to substitute something else for God's way. The more that we do it, it becomes God's way, it is incorporated in the straight way, but it is something which we have put into it, in a perverse way out of our own preference trying to improve on God's way. And so while He incorporates it into His will, it nevertheless works against us.

If it were possible for a person to simply, purely, completely accept What Is and go along with it, life would be extremely simple. . . . On the other hand this does not necessarily mean total blank passivity; now that of course is another whole problem.

"To love the true good in everything without personal preference is to be on the right way of Allah, to be like Muhammad, to be under Mercy, and to manifest Mercy."

And so the great sign of Mercy is that a person is able to see the good in everything that is and go along with it. . . . To see that in Everything That Is is the Mercy of God, and therefore to prefer nothing, not to improve on it in any way, this is the approach.

The average person, who stands outside the will of God . . . and looks in, . . . he does not understand that really everything is willed by God and he makes choices, and . . . he makes his own plans, and he submits them to God. His idea of the Mercy of God is that, he makes his plans, and then God being merciful to him helps him so that it pans out the way he wants. It doesn't take Muslims to do that, that's kind of a common thing. . . .

The only basic thing that the Sufis say about it is that a man who lives in that realm doesn't really know what's cooking. He has the wrong idea of how things are set up. In other words, he thinks that he is able to stand outside of all this, and make plans, and size things up, and then submit them to Allah, and then he and God are going to work things out on basis of appeal, but . . . this is not the way it is.

Ibn 'Arabî says, "Those who are veiled from the truth ask the Absolute to show mercy upon them each in his own particular way."

[This veiling is] the underlying of a basically insufficient concept of who we are and of how we function in relation to God, and this insufficient concept is the concept that we all have, it is the basic assumption that we all start from. That we are somehow or other completely a little world by ourselves and in the center of this little world of our own is our own mind down in there figuring things out. And if you stop and think, we consider ourselves more or less like sort of a turtle in a shell . . . there's your turtle and inside this little shell, this little metaphysical shell, which is the self, inside there is the living being, hidden from everything, figuring things out. And we think that this living center, which is within the center of ourselves, is kind of walled off from everything else. And here we are, because this is what we experience, this is the only thing that we experience directly as reality, and we take this to be reality. We take the turtle inside our shell, which is there, the self, which is down in there, we experience this as reality and we start from there. And we judge everything in reference to that, and everything that we see that we experience through the senses, immediately, . . . is the outside, and then way up behind the whole thing somewhere is God. And we say, "Now look God, here's me and here's them, now fix it so that everything works out." But that's not the way it is. It isn't like that. It's quite a different proposition, and this is something that you see in many of the higher religions, it works out the same way.

Actually, the ground of everything is within me and it is God, and it's within everybody too. And there's one ground for everybody, and this ground in the Divine Mercy. . . . The people of the unveiling, that is to say the Sufis, ask the Mercy of

God to subsist in them. These are the ones who ask in the Name of God and He shows Mercy upon them only by making the Mercy subsist in them. This is a totally different outlook. It is the outlook whereby the Mercy of God is not arranged on the outside in events for me—in good and bad events—but it is subsisting in me all the time. Therefore what happens is that if the Mercy of God is subsisting in me—and that goes to say if I am united with the will of God— . . . if I am completely united with the will of God in love, it doesn't matter what happens outside, because everything that is going on outside that makes any sense is grounded in the same ground in which I am grounded. The opposition between me and everything else ceases, and what remains in terms of opposition is purely accidental and it doesn't matter. And this is . . . a basic perspective in all . . . the highest religions. You ought to get down to this, you get down to it in Christianity, you get down to it in Buddhism, you get down to it in Hinduism, and so forth. It is arriving at a unity in which the superficial differences don't matter. It doesn't mean that they're not real, it doesn't mean that they're not there. They still subsist. . . .

All of these we've said are these basic perspectives which are absolutely fundamental for all religious depth, and incidentally, these are the kind of perspectives that today are not very much in fashion. This isn't the sort of stuff that people are getting wildly excited about, but it's something fundamental. If a person has a grasp of this kind of thing, he has the sort of thing that religions exist to give to man and the sort of thing that we ask from religion, because it gives a man an inner strength which nothing can assail, a strength which is not based on some gimmick or other, it is based on God. It helps the person to break through to the realm in which he is in fact immediately united with God. And in which he is directly supported by God, I mean, in which God cannot fail him.

The Sufis are the fellows who try to get down to this real basic level, and one of the things that they claim about themselves is that they are seeking purity of heart . . . but purity of heart has to be understood in the way I just said . . . the purity of heart of a Sufi is non-preference, not preferring anything to What Is, taking What Is straight, without adding onto it any other preference, without substituting something for it, without trying to make it better.

People are feeling [and] experiencing today a great need for the direct acceptance of simply What Is without piling a lot of explanations on top of it. Take it straight, and if you don't know how it's explained, don't try to explain it, just do it. And don't add a huge amount of justifications for it.

"'The true Sufi is he that lives in purity behind and in purity itself." He does not put any self-interpretation on the thing, he takes it straight. "Purity is characteristic of lovers of God who are suns without a cloud." "The perfect Sufi is lost in God. He that is absorbed in the Beloved and has abandoned all else is a Sufi." This is standard in all the great religions.

Searching for God

In the following section. Merton describes the futility of most explanation in the spiritual life and the necessity of realizing the self as an obstacle to God.

[We must] . . . wake up and realize that we are not doing the thing that we are supposed to be doing, and this is one of the basic ways in which God speaks to us. And this is constant.

In the life of the spirit you are constantly running up against these absolutely fundamental things, which you can't define, you can't explain, you can't account for, and you know what's around and they're universal. There is something in man that God has put there . . . there's something there that is there. There is something about man that when he is not doing what he was made for, he knows it, and he knows it in a very deep way, and it becomes very important to him to change things.

There is the possibility of not knowing this, and when you reflect deeply on religious things, it's one of the worst things that can happen, to be in a position where one doesn't know something as important as this . . . from the moment that a person recognizes these basic truths and accepts them, he knows that he is right, he knows he is on the way.

How do you explain these things? The thing is not to explain them, the thing is to deepen them, the thing is to live them, and instead of getting by the thing with explanations and forgetting about it, it is much better not to and to get deeply into it. And that's what the monastic life is about. The monastic life is given to us for one reason only, it's to really deepen this dimension of religious reality.

You come to a monastery because you are looking for something, and you stay here because you keep looking for it, and the whole thing about it is that you believe that there is a point to this search and when you get away from this search . . . you begin to hear the voice, "This isn't the job you're supposed to be doing. Get back on the track of what you are looking for. Do the thing you're supposed to be doing." . . . Once a person has received from God the charge to seek what he has to seek, then he puts everything else aside and seeks it.

On the basis of truth like this, accepted and lived, you get a Sufi and you get a monk.

The beginning of the spiritual life: "I need God desperately and I am blocking him from helping me because I am getting in His way. I am doing my will not His, and I don't really know quite what to do about it."

Do It Yourself

In two of the lectures, Merton reveals that he has struggled with some of the changes of Vatican II. But he clearly accepts the new emphasis on individual seeking, in the sense that no monk can get away with simply following the rules of monastic life. He focuses on the necessity of acceptance of change with the understanding that human nature leads to changes in traditions. Besides accepting change, Merton also emphasizes the necessity of a spiritual director to assist one through the independent spiritual life. He uses examples from Sufism, for without a master, the Sufi disciple is bound for self-destruction. The disciple cannot reach illumination without a master:

Since we're living in a time of crisis, well, what's a time of crisis? It's a time of insecurity. Don't give in to your own insecurity, learn how to master it by yourself. Nobody's going to help you, you've got to do it yourself. . . . It isn't a question of being propped up by somebody else, nobody's going to prop you up. Prop yourself up or else! . . . It is . . . no longer possible at all to function around here on somebody else's reasons. A person now who hasn't got reasons of his own is finished. . . . You have to have your own reasons which are independent of external changes.

That's one of the things that Sufism does. . . . I am not promising you . . . any kind of illumination from this study of Sufism. But Sufism does aim to make the person completely independent of external circumstances. You can't be so independent of external circumstances that nothing ever matters, but to be able to handle external circumstances in such a way that you can work with almost anything. And that is what we are going to have to do. Now there's nothing wrong with that, the only thing is that it's kind of new. . . .

Traditionally we have always assumed that this was the kind of a place where everything was unchangeably strict and that no matter what happened . . . you could bank on it being tough . . . having a certain kind of pattern and having . . . certain limitations. Well, it isn't necessarily like that, apparently. . . .

And that is what the Sufis have always done . . . they have nothing really like monastic[ism]. . . . Sufis have always functioned in the world. . . . Sufis live their deep spiritual life in the world, but independent of the world, and not . . . dominated by external circumstances.

I would say that around here that's what we're going to have to do . . . nobody else is going to live your spiritual life for you. You have to live it yourself, and if you're [going to] live it yourself, you have to know how, and if you're [going to] know how, you need a director. If you've never been through the mill, well, you need somebody to take you through the mill. . . .

If you haven't started now, get busy at once, because there is no time to lose.

DISSOLUTION OF SELF

In Sufism . . . they are after what we're after: The dissolution of one's present status to be reintegrated on a new level. Dissolution, rebirth. Death, rebirth. Death, resurrection. It's the same thing for us. . . . God speaks to the faithful saying, "Unless you are first disintegrated, how can I reintegrate you again?" . . .

What is this disintegration, what is this reintegration? You can't learn it from a book, you've got to learn it by experience. And if you're learning it by experience, you need somebody else who's been through the mill to tell you what's happening to you . . . what is going on. And that is what Sufism is for, is to provide the situation where there is somebody around who knows the score and who can tell you. . . . Sufism does not aim to provide you ideal external circumstances.

Merton repeats many times the necessity for humility and the emptying of the ego in the monastic life, if one is to receive knowledge of God. Besides the importance of the death of the self, one must also forget that one is attempting to cultivate a ground for the gift of mystical graces from God. This understanding is necessary, for as Merton says, "God gives mystical graces to whomever He pleases, and He doesn't choose those people who work solely, in a sense, to receive them."

One of the central things in the monastic life is you really die. When you enter the monastery, you die to the world. . . . When you take on the monastic life, you change your mind about the way you've been living and you embrace a new idea about life, a whole new conclusion of what life is for . . . and you lay down your life for Christ in this particular way, and this presupposes some sort of a sense that you have . . . [as in] Sufism, of this disintegration and reintegration.

First I'll take a few sentences that express this idea of Sufism, of this disintegration and reintegration, called *fanâ'* and *baqâ'*, but *fanâ'* is the disintegration part. For example, "it is a process wherein," says one author, "the soul is stripped of all its desires, affections, and interests so that in ceasing to will for itself it becomes an object of the Divine Will, that is the Beloved of God, and that which loves it and which it loves is now its inward and real Self, not the self that has passed away." Of course that's a very deep statement . . . it . . . coincides with a kind of complete purity of heart . . . this death is the death to all our own individual desires of a superficial nature—to die to these superficial desires and to attain a purity of love in which our love is not directed by our own will. . . .

And this is fundamental to Christianity. It is fundamental to our monastic vocation. To reach a state in which we are not guided by our own will. Now, this is one of the truths that I think is rapidly getting lost, it is not exactly the most popular one in the new theology or the new spirituality. But it is a basic truth that [underlies] what we are striving for [that is] if we are striving for a liberation or [for] a freedom in which we are liberated from our own will. . . .

We are seeking a kind of life in which we are transformed interiorly and not guided by our own will but moved by the will of God. So you can say that with another author, "The Sufi is he that is dead to self and living by the Truth." To be moved directly by the will of God is to be moved by Truth. To be moved by God's love is to be moved by Truth. . . .

But that's what the Sufis do . . . they have a man around to tell them, okay, here is what is happening to you, here is how you fit this into the circumstances where you live. That's what spiritual direction is, and that's what the spiritual life depends on: having somebody to tell you that in the beginning. After awhile you can tell yourself. . . .

In Sufism direction is very important.

STATES AND STATIONS

Merton explains the differences between Sufi "states" and "stations," in order to help the monks appreciate grace in their own spiritual lives. The Sufi designations of states and stations are arranged, "to objectively state what the roadsigns are and what they mean and how to interpret them. How to find your way in this spiritual life."

[There is a] distinction between what they call "states" and what they call "stations." Actually it is only a distinction between the ascetic life and the mystical life. The stations along the way are areas which you cover by your own efforts. For example, one of the stations is repentance . . . you start out [on] the ascetic life, you repent . . . the beginning of the dissolution of one's present status is that you realize that there is something wrong with it. You ask yourself what has gone wrong? . . .

What the Sufis tell you is [that] when you enter this particular station of the way, this is what you should do. . . . We
say, "We'll go to confession and forget about it, read another
book and then tomorrow another state, another station. . . ."
What the Sufis do is say, "Okay you are in the station of
repentance, get stabilized there, get into it, get with it so that
you understand it, so that you have really lived your repentance. Then from repentance you may pass onto some next
station. . . ." But you pass onto the next one in such a way
that you also get more aligned than the one you were just in.
And you are more stabilized in the one you just left when you
pass on to the next one.

It really builds, and so that when you have moved on . . . you
have really got it and it's going to be there for the rest of your
life. You've earned your station, you're there.

The states are gifts of God. And they sort of flow in and you
can't make them happen. . . .

One of the great problems in mystical theology: to what
extent do you get deep enough into a certain kind of state for it
to remain? . . . Do the mystics get into certain states and stay
there for keeps? . . . It is more practical from a certain point of
view to think not. . . . Is this a permanent acquisition? . . .

Things are set up so that a person really understands where
he is and what it's about and what he has to do so that he gets
stabilized and really gets the fruit out of it, and that's the thing
that Sufism has.

After explaining the Sufi states and stations, Merton returns to
his point that people must become free from external circumstances
if they are to truly reach peace with God.

One of the troubles with modern man is his feeling that there
is a great deal going on and he's not with it. And this is true of
us, too, we feel that there's probably a lot going on and we're
missing it. Perhaps one of the things God is teaching us in our
crisis is that you don't get anywhere if you take concepts like
[monastic] orders . . . if you take that too seriously, sooner or
later you've been had, so don't take that too seriously. . . . Don't
build your life on something external.

The Sufis don't do that . . . [Sufism] is not institutionalized. They don't have an institutional setup at all except the very minimum. And it is not caught in this business where you have to worry when the thing changes because they understand that they are going to change. It is understood with them that it is going to evolve in any way that suits the generation that is in the thing. It is for the use of the fellows that are trying to do this particular work, and you adapt it to the people that are there.

One author [says, on] the nature of Sufism being evolutionary, "It is by definition impossible for a Sufi body to take any rigid permanent form. Schools appear and carry out an activity designed to further the human need for completion of the individual."

"The extent to which the Sufi adheres to these forms is determined by his need for them as prescribed by his master."

If you have a flexible situation, then you make use of what helps you most.

COMMUNITY FOLLOWING A LEADER—WITH GRACE (THE SHAIKH)

The essential thing in monasticism . . . is a community of people who are drawn together around the master who is going to teach them the way of prayer, whom they obey, whom they follow, and with whom they worship, and the community of worship. . . . The basic thing about monasticism is coming together where you are going to learn the ropes of a different way of life from what's lived in the world, although you may stay in the world, you may live in the world. But you come together to deepen your experience, to find out who you are, to find out what it's all about, and where are we going . . . this is what we always have to keep in mind because that's the grace that God puts in a monastic community, the grace for this to happen. And remember when that grace is present, it doesn't take necessarily exceptionally gifted people. The grace works—if people are faithful to the situation and want what's there and open themselves up to it, grace will see to it that the thing happens right.

It would really be quite silly if we let ourselves really bother about all the things that are happening that may disturb us. As if that could stop God doing what He wants to develop us. Nothing can stop Him. Only our own lack of correspondence and courage and willingness to let Him do with us what He wants, that's the only thing that can stop Him. . . . If we let Him act, and if we really seek and follow the grace that has been given to us, we can't miss. And it does not depend on what's going on around us outside, it comes from within. . . .

They [Sufis] really insist on getting in contact with a real traditional experience of the spiritual life that has been handed down from master to master and is practiced seriously by people who really want to get into this and who really are interested in helping one another . . . that's what the monastic life is about, and the Sufis want that and we want that, and so let's not be afraid to learn from the Sufis [or] . . . how they look at this thing. . . . But on the other hand, you don't get attached to this institution, you don't even get attached to the master.

At this pont, Merton gives a Sufi example (which is greeted with uproarious laughter) to help the monks understand the natural function of the master and of ritual, while also emphasizing the need for reliance on the internal spiritual life.

"If the scissors are not used daily on the beard, it will not be long before the beard is by its luxuriant growth pretending to be the head" (Jami). It's the accidental to the essential . . . the beard is the external structure, the observance and all the things that you do and all the ritual . . . , so you use the scissors on the beard in the sense of not getting too attached to that aspect of it, and then you stick to the real basic thing which is the internal and the spiritual.

It is a very personalized thing, it is in terms of the individual needs of the people that they're here and now seeking to live a life of prayer.

EXTINCTION OF SELF

Merton returns to the death of the self and the ego, to emphasize one's total dependence on God's Mercy:

The real purpose of this whole Sufi life is a kind of extinction of the self, and that is interesting. Of course they emphasize this much more than we do, but nevertheless it is important for us too because we come here to, in a certain sense, lose ourselves, and to find ourselves by losing ourselves. . . .

And of course, what does this mean? . . . It is a very deep concept, it's a very difficult concept, really, and yet in a certain sense we do in our hearts all know to some extent what it's about, because most of us in one way or another are called to this kind of thing. . . .

It's not self-extinction in order to become lost. This is a highly dialectical business, and it is losing oneself in order to find oneself. According to the Gospel concept, "He that would lose his life for My sake shall find it." It's this ultimate losing and ultimate finding. This is the point, this is what we are here for, and this is what we are looking for, and this is what life is really about. We are seeking union with God.

PERMANENT CRISIS OF THE PERSON

Using a Hasidic metaphor, Merton describes the urgency of the spiritual life, and he then goes on to state that this is the image to keep in mind with the lectures on Sufism—the search for God is critical:

"Let everyone cry out to God and lift his heart up to God, as if he were . . . (this is how to pray . . .) hanging by a hair and a tempest were raging to the very heart of heaven and he were at a loss for what to do and there were hardly time to cry out. It is a time when no counsel indeed can help a man and he has no refuge save to remain in his loneliness and lift his eyes and his heart up to God and cry out to Him. And this should be done at all times for in the world a man is in great danger."

When the life of prayer really begins to get somewhere . . . you feel this, you realize . . . personally and existentially, the tremendous seriousness of [your] life of prayer, not as an obligation, not as a duty, but it is the seriousness of breathing when you're drowning.

In prayer, nobody else is going to do it for you, you've got to do it yourself. And you might as well do it now, and no counsel is going to do it.

He is in great hazard, he doesn't know what to do, things are not peaceful, things are not well-ordered, things are not calm, things are not encouraging, things are not looking real good, they are looking bad . . . he has no refuge save [God] . . . and ultimately, this is the spirituality of the Psalms.

The jolt comes in the last line [of the above quote] . . . you're in a crisis all of the time. . . . "In the world a man is in great danger.". . . From a certain point we could lose everything.

We tend to think . . . you do something very generous and you get a flood of consolation. And that's the way the life works, and you press the right button every Monday morning . . . and you swim through the week on a tide of consolation and then start over again the next weekend. . . . But it isn't like that. When the spiritual life is going well is very often when a person realizes what a mess he's in, and the thing is not going well, and then you cry out to God, and then crying out to God with this sense of things not being so wonderful, you find that they are good . . . that is the dialectical thing . . . of realizing I could lose everything, and I cry out to God and then I realize that He is sustaining me and this is consolation, comfort, and so forth.

Every step is important.

One of the most important things in the spiritual life and in the life of prayer is to let a great deal go on without knowing quite what is going on, and without messing with it, without interfering with it.

You can't be helped in the best parts of the spiritual life. If you could be helped it wouldn't be worth it. There is a great deal of the spiritual life where God alone helps you, and you don't know that He's helping you and you can't tell that He's helping you . . . but you have to believe this. Learning to trust when you don't see what's happening.

You make a breakthrough, and what you do is you break through into a deeper level of yourself. . . . You find a deeper truth that's really there, in you, but it's not yours, it's God's, and it's not something that you have accounted for, it's something that He has accounted for. . . . You have to take this into account, you have to realize that that's the way human nature, helped by grace, works.

Humility

In this section, Merton describes the human need, the "terrible obsession," to see the self developing, to see God working within the self. He understands that almost everyone experiences this need, but states that the need must be forgotten if one is to truly seek God.

> The thing that has to happen in all this is exactly the opposite. This self that we wish to get rid of . . . we can't get rid of ourselves by ourselves. . . . The best thing to do . . . is to forget about it altogether . . . and not think about it, and in a certain sense not desire it . . . and then go and sweep the floor or whatever. . . .
>
> It's somewhere in between the two, it's not the business that "I've got to make it in three years . . ." and it's not this thing, "Oh, forget about it altogether." There is a way, but you've got to find the right way. And the great thing is knowing the way. It is a question of self-transcendence and breaking through into a different realm by working through into it.
>
> What we have to do is to work very hard to work through something that we have fairly recently found out. Because what we do is we neglect to work through the truth that we know. Instead of working through something . . . you see the whole thing kind of clearer for a moment, and you get a new perspective. This is very satisfying, and it's pleasant, and we think that when we've seen something like that, that that's it. But when you see it, that means you've got to travel it. And we don't do that. . . .
>
> Instead of working through something that we really have sort of got hold of for the first time just a little bit, we transfer over into the daydream bit, and we daydream about the things that we would like to have and the other things that we would like to see.
>
> But it isn't that kind of a thing, it is much more humdrum kind of work. . . .
>
> This interior working through is really deepening one's experience of this truth and deepening one's grasp of this truth and one's understanding of it from different angles. And that means to say, several things are involved in this. One of them means

exposure to new possibilities which have been opened up by this kind of thing, unexpected possibilities. . . . The work that is involved all along, this is just simply meeting a new possibility head-on, and suffering the shock, maybe, of its newness, and just being hit by it for awhile. One of the reasons why we neglect this is that we don't realize how good it is, and we don't realize the greatness of it.

Don't try to see that it's the whole thing, but believe that it is. Underlying all of this is faith.

If I do the thing that I have to do now, everything else is taken care of, and I'm believing that I don't have to see. . . . Realizing that you don't have to see is seeing in the realm of faith. And it can become very clear seeing. A deep awareness and conviction of the fact that you don't need to see can be a very clear form of sight, and this is of the nature of a high kind of grace, but these things you must not reflect on.

Go ahead and do what you are doing, but with the realization of the depth and the dimension of what you're doing, but this realization has to be from faith.

This is the way we really grow, and the thing that we have to do is grow, because this is an imperative obligation in the spiritual life, this is the great demand. . . . When something new opens up like that, it is a new self that opens up, if it is significant enough. . . . A new level of being opens up to us which has to be accepted, and the acceptance means work . . . it is not enough to accept up here [meaning "in the head"], you have to accept in practice by doing the work that the acceptance implies, whatever it is in each particular case. It may mean sacrificing something that you realize now you no longer need, and I don't mean by that some material thing, I mean much more, some interior attitude. . . . This working through is to a great extent abandoning interior attitudes, abandoning ways of thinking that you don't need anymore. You no longer have to spend time thinking about certain aspects of the spiritual life, thinking about certain problems that you're finished with. That's another way which we don't work through these jobs that we need to work through—we cling to problems that are no longer significant in our life.

If we do not work through these things, we enter a real acute conflict, and of course that's healthy too, that's a good thing, but acute conflict can arise where there is a perception of a new opening up, without any corresponding work. This is one of the great sources of painful conflict in our life here.

It is good to feel this kind of thing, but the trouble is we don't know how to identify this, and we identify it wrong.

Very often we open up to a new state of being and we don't take the necessary step to move into it, we don't do the necessary work to move into it, and then we are in trouble, and conflict and anguish and so forth, and we don't know why. And it would be very nice if we had somebody to tell us why, but we don't, that's one of the big problems. It would be very nice if there were more people around who could give you a push at the right time in these particular things. That is one of the things that we most need in the monastic life—people who experience this and who can give you the right push at the right time and save you from hurting unnecessarily. . . .

Most of the time it's a do-it-yourself project. . . .

PEACE

The idea of the ascetic life, which is the idea of the monastic life . . . is to bring a person to a state of complete peace. . . .

In times of constant change, people get upset and worried and all that sort of thing, and what one has to get out of the ascetic life is a deeper outlook on things, so that we are in a state where we are not buffeted around by changes that are taking place on a more surface level. Let these changes take place, and we take our part in them, but our real life is actually going on on a much deeper level than that, in which there can be a profound peace which is terribly important. And this kind of stability—this inner stability ties into our relations with other people . . . and it's a very deep thing. . . .

THE MYSTICAL LIFE IN SUFISM

In Sufism . . . they've got a different approach, they're very practical about it. This is all based on intensive study of experience and intensive practical work with a director . . . because the relation of the disciple and the guide is absolutely decisive in Sufism. It's the real heart of it.

The difference between the ascetic life and the mystical life is that . . . in the mystical life, the whole work is God's work. Now of course for the Sufis, everything is God's work anyway, this is the central thing with them. . . . Sufism . . . starts with the assumption that God alone acts, and that nothing else is, and that only God is. . . . And you might say that the task of the Sufi is to gradually realize this, until it not only takes complete possession of him but he is no longer there, and what he realizes is realized in the fact [that] God Alone is and there's no longer any Sufi around. . . . And the person has to be completely stripped of all self-seeking. . . .

Mystical graces are not necessarily reserved for saints . . . there's no timetable on these things.

Mystical graces are deep experiences which are the result of direct gifts of God's grace and nothing to do with our own effort.

These things have to be said, but they are not supposed to be concentrated on. For example, if I say the justification of this kind of life is that it creates an atmosphere in which God can give mystical graces, and then if you go to the evening meditation and break your head and think, "Give me one now, otherwise I'll leave," forget it. The whole thing . . . if there's a literal approach to it . . . well that's the wrong way.

If you are busy thinking about the mystical graces, get busy on the degrees of humility. Stop thinking about the mystical graces and start being humble.

[God] wants to give [people] the fullness of life and light, to which we all aspire. As Christians, we aspire to know God. . . . None of us . . . is . . . going to be content to spend the rest of his life in this place just knowing about God, hearing about God remotely. . . . That's not it. We come to know God as our Friend, with the direct intimate knowledge that a friend has of a friend. That doesn't have to be mystical. . . .

Cross off the idea of mystical and throw it over your shoulder and forget it, and you will be nearer the Truth. The beginning of the mystical life for the Sufi is . . . a living awareness of God. . . . This does not have to be mystical. . . .

Mystical experience is, as it were, hearing the harmony of everything on a very high sort of spiritual, musical level . . . St. Bernard talks about it in that kind of way. . . . And you have a Sufi mystic . . . called Rûmî—he explains it this way, "We are all parts of Adam and in Adam we heard the melodies of Paradise.'

The basic thing in Sufism then is . . . the awakening to total awareness and to a real deep sense of the Reality of God. Not . . . a sense of God as object, not a sense of God as thing . . . not that we see God over there or out there or up there . . . and it is even to a great extent beyond this I/Thou dichotomy, because I would say that one of the characteristic things that affects mystical awareness of God is that it is somehow subjective. That is to say, an awareness of God as Subject, an awareness that God is within my own subjectivity, that He is the root of my own personality so that I do not see Him as somebody else entirely, and yet He is Totally Other.

The Sufis approach it . . . by talking about the awareness that one is totally penetrated by God's knowledge of us. This is their first approach to it . . . a sense not only that God is listening when we pray but that we are known and seen through and through by Him and penetrated by Him . . . which is not necessarily coming from out there but from within us.

So that for St. Benedict, [similar in a way to] the Sufis, [what is] basic in the monastic life is . . . to try to cultivate the kind of awareness, the kind of attitude toward life which will enable one to naturally and spontaneously at many times during one's life feel oneself completely penetrated by God's Knowledge of us, God as our Father, as our Creator, loving us, redeeming us. . . . To feel oneself completely possessed and penetrated by this loving knowledge that God has for us which is at once the Source of our Being and is a redemptive knowledge (in theological, not mystical terms). Everything in the Rule of St. Benedict is meant to favor this kind of awareness.

The intense respect which St. Benedict inculcates about every little thing, this attitude of respectfulness is one way of cultivating this constant attention.

How does it happen that man can suddenly be possessed with a longing for God? Such as . . . in Psalm 41? One of the great

reasons we are here is we have realized this. . . . The great thing
in life is this desire for God . . . this thirst for God.

[In Sufism, this "thirst" is described as passion.] A passion of
love arising out of a supreme intuition . . . yet somewhere there
is an intuition that sparks this whole thing. . . .

The sense that God is everything, that He is the Beginning
and the End . . . and that His love is the Source and the
Beginning and the End and the All of Everything. Especially in
Sufism, there is this idea that we come from God, that's why we
desire to return to Him, because God is where we belong. It's in
Him that we are Real and that away from Him we are not real,
and that His Reality is The Reality and any other reality is only
a sham and any other thing is only a lie. And this runs through
the Bible. And basically, this is why the great sin, the sin of all
sins, is idolatry. It is placing some other thing, some object, in
the place of the Supreme Love; it is frustrating this Supreme
Love by diverting it to some object which is only partial, which
is not our Real Love.

One of the Sufis says this: "This borrowed life of mine, handed over to me by the Friend, I shall hand back to Him when at
last I see His Face." . . . The fact that we belong to Him . . .
that's the reason we desire Him.

And another saying . . . "Before all men were made, God
spoke to them in Adam and He said to them, 'Am I not your
[Lord],' and in Adam, they all answered 'Yes.'" And therefore in
this answer of "Yes" which Adam gave to God's question "Am I
not your [Lord]?" there was a pact made for all creatures, and in
Adam, all admitted that they belonged to God.[1]

The desire of God is tied up in our hearts with this deep
sense, the deepest thing in our nature, not that He is a god, not
that He is God or the Supreme Being, but that he is Our God,
that He is My God. When our Lord says on the cross, "My God
why hast thou forsaken me?" It isn't just God, it is "My God."

Sufism is a particular way of realizing that "Yes" in a total
love, a total surrender of ourselves to God.

"Those who once knew God as their Supreme Love, when
He manifested Himself to them in this light . . . they suddenly
become beside themselves and intoxicated with ecstatic love
for they know the scent of the wine, they have drunk it before."

When we come in any way whatever close to God, whom we love above all, the recognition of closeness to Him is . . . a recognition of where we belong. It's as though we have been there before. . . . Paradoxically it can be said that the dis-covery of God, the true deep discovery of the Reality of God as Our God, is a discovery not always of something strange but of something intimate and close and real to us, because He is more intimate to us than we are to ourselves. So that the discovery of God, this true recognition of God as Our God, is the recognition of that which is deepest and most intimate to ourselves.

As revealed in the Qur'an: "then He will be thy Hearing and thy Sight, and when He is thy Hearing and thy Sight, then will thou hear only Him and see only Him, for thou wilt be seeing Him with His Sight and hearing Him with His Hearing." (Martin Lings, A *Moslem Saint of the 20th Century*, 139.)

All quotes transcribed from tapes made of these lectures, available from Credence Cassettes P.O. Box 22582, Kansas City, MO 64141; these transcriptions have been verified and clarified by consulting Merton's reading notebooks, especially number 18, which contains his working notes for these lectures. Permission to quote from the tapes has been granted by The Merton Legacy Trust.

NOTES
1. The Qur'an adds that they were made to testify, "Lest ye should say on the Day of the Resurrection: Verily, of this we were unaware." From Martin Lings, *The Eleventh Hour* (Cambridge: Quinta Essentia, 1987).

8

THOMAS MERTON
AND A SUFI SAINT

Gray Henry

One of the volumes to be found in Merton's personal library is entitled *A Moslem Saint of the Twentieth Century* by Martin Lings.[1] It is heavily underlined throughout. Often in the margins, Merton marked material with several bold vertical lines or with asterisks next to the text. As these highlighted passages must represent what Merton felt best elucidated Islamic mysticism, or were ideas he may have agreed with or found to be useful for his own spiritual growth or understanding, a small selection of these are presented here in order to illustrate some of the concepts and ideas to which Merton was attracted. At the same time, it is hoped that this selection will further inform the reader about the nature and depth of Sufism.

Martin Lings, formerly Keeper of Oriental Manuscripts in the British Museum and in the British Library, and author of many important works on Islam and Sufism, opens this wonderful volume with a chapter "Seen from Outside," which presents the impressions of Dr. Marcel Carret, who tended the Algerian saint Ahmad al-'Alawî (1869–1934) in his final years. Dr. Carret's initial impression of Shaikh al-'Alawî is as follows:

> The first thing that struck me was his likeness to the usual representation of Christ. His clothes, so nearly if not exactly the same as those which Jesus must have worn, the fine lawn head-cloth which framed his face, his whole attitude—everything conspired to reinforce the likeness. It occurred to me that such must have been the appearance of Christ when he received his disciples at the time when he was staying with Martha and Mary.

Dr. Carret later recalled:

> Fairly often while I was talking quietly with the Shaikh, the Name Allah had come to us from some remote corner of the *zâwiyah*, uttered on one long drawn out vibrant note:

> "A . . . l . . . la . . . h!"

> It was like a cry of despair, a distraught supplication, and it came from some solitary cell-bound disciple, bent on meditation. The cry was usually repeated several times, and then all was silence once more.

> "Out of the depths have I cried unto Thee, O Lord."

> "From the end of the earth will I cry unto Thee, when my heart is overwhelmed; lead me to the rock that is higher than I."

> These verses from the Psalms came to my mind. The supplication was really just the same, the supreme cry to God of a soul in distress.

> I was not wrong, for later, when I asked the Shaikh what was the meaning of the cry which we had just heard, he answered:

> "It is a disciple asking God to help him in his meditation."

> "May I ask what is the purpose of his meditation?"

> "To achieve self-realization in God."

> "Do all the disciples succeed in doing this?"

> "No, it is seldom that anyone does. It is only possible for a very few."

> "Then what happens to those who do not? Are they not desperate?"

> "No: they always rise high enough to have at least inward Peace."

> Inward Peace. That was the point he came back to most often, and there lay, no doubt, the reason for his great

influence. For what man does not aspire, in some way or other, to inward Peace?

In the chapter "The Reality of Sufism," found in "Part One: The Path and the Order," Merton marked lines to do with spiritual aspiration. For the most part, the passages he noted (indented below) are the exact words of the saint himself. Often Shaikh al-'Alawî cites passages from the Qur'an, hadith—or sayings of the Prophet Muhammad—and from the writings of many of Islam's great saints and mystics of previous centuries. Dr. Lings, for the most part "allows the Sufis . . . to speak for themselves in a series of texts mainly translated from the Arabic."

> The aspiration "to let one's Spirit (that is, as here meant, one's centre of consciousness) rise above oneself" presupposes at the very least some remote awareness of the existence of the Heart, which is the point where the human self ends and the Transcendent Self begins. If the clouds in the night of the soul are so thick as to prevent the moon of the Heart from showing the slightest sign of its presence, there can be no such aspiration. [page 40]

In a hadith (saying of the Prophet), God states:

> "My slave ceaseth not to draw nigh unto Me with devotions of his free will until I love him; and when I love him, I am the Hearing wherewith he heareth, and the Sight wherewith he seeth, and the Hand wherewith he smiteth, and the Foot wherewith on he walketh." (Bukhari)[37]

> The Qur'an insists without respite on remembrance of God, dhikr Allah, and this insistence holds the place in Islam that is held in Christianity by the first of Christ's two commandments. It is the Quranic use of the cognitive term "remembrance" rather than "love" which has, perhaps more than anything else, imposed on Islamic mysticism its special characteristics. [45]

Many passages which interested Merton seemed to validate the aims and nature of monastic life. The first one of many such passages marked by Merton are lines from the early eighth-century saint Hasan al-Basrî:

"He that knoweth God loveth Him, and he that knoweth the world abstaineth from it," and the saying of another early Sufi: "Intimacy (*uns*) with God is finer and sweeter than longing." [46]

From "The Spiritual Master," there is more on what would have appealed to a monk who made a hermitage in the forest, as did Merton, in the following paragraphs, which Merton marked, some written by Dr. Lings and some directly quoting Shaikh al-'Alawî.

One of his motives for taking this step [for adding his own name 'Alawî to distinguish his particular branch of the Darqâwî tarîqah] was that he felt the need to introduce, as part of his method, the practice of *khalwah*, that is, spiritual retreat in the solitude of an isolated cell or small hermitage. There was nothing very drastic in this, for if remembrance of God be the positive or heavenly aspect of all mysticism, its negative or earthly aspect is retreat or drawing away from other than God. The Tradition "Be in this world as a stranger, or as a passer-by" has already been quoted, and one of the most powerful aids to achieving this permanent inward spiritual retreat is bodily withdrawal which, in some form or another, perpetual or temporary, is a feature of almost all contemplative orders. In some Sufic brotherhoods—the Khalwatî Tarîqah, for example—it was tradition to make retreat in a special hermitage. But in the Shâdhilî Tarîqah and its branches, the spiritual retreat had usually taken the form of withdrawal to the solitudes of nature, after the pattern of the Prophet's retreats in the cave on Mount Hira, and though inevitably the *khalwah* must have been used on some occasion, to introduce it as a regular methodic practice was something of an innovation for the descendants of Abû 'l-Hasan ash-Shâdhilî. However, the Shaikh no doubt found this form of retreat more practicable than any other in view of the conditions in which most of his disciples lived. We have already seen that he himself had suffered for want of a definite place where he could be alone, and that it was part of his method to supervise at times very closely the invocation of his disciples, which presupposed that the disciple in question would be within easy reach of him.

'Abd al-Karîm Jossot quotes the Shaikh as having said to him:

"The *khalwah* is a cell in which I put a novice after he has sworn to me not to leave it for forty days if need be. In this oratory he must do nothing but repeat ceaselessly, day and night, the Divine Name (Allah), drawing out at each invocation the syllable *âh* until he has no more breath left. . . .

"During the *khalwah* he fasts strictly by day, only breaking his fast between sunset and dawn. . . . Some *fuqarâ*² obtain the sudden illumination after a few minutes, some only after several days, and some only after several weeks. I know one *faqîr* who waited eight months. Each morning he would say to me: 'My heart is still too hard,' and would continue his *khalwah*. In the end his efforts were rewarded." [84–85]

It interested Merton that the spiritual retreat demanded by the Shaikh al-'Alawî for his disciples was very difficult for most to endure:

But what might have been intolerable in other circumstances was made relatively easy because the Shaikh knew how to provoke "a state of spiritual concentration." None the less, some of the *fuqarâ* would come out of the *khalwah* almost in a state of collapse, dazed in both body and soul, but the Shaikh was indifferent to this provided that some degree of direct knowledge had been achieved. [105]

Other ideas which would also have been of relevance to a monk are:

Let him examine himself: if what his heart hides is more precious than what his tongue tells of, then he is *one whom his Lord hath made certain* (Qur'an, XI, 17), but if not, then he has missed far more than he has gained. . . . The Prophet said: "Knowledge of the inward is one of the Secrets of God. It is wisdom from the treasury of His Wisdom which He casteth into the heart of whomsoe'er He will of His slaves" and "Knowledge is of two kinds, knowledge in the Heart which is the knowledge that availeth, and knowledge upon the tongue which is God's evidence against His slave." This shows that secret knowledge is different from the knowledge that is bandied about. [89–90]

The Prophet said, "The earth shall never be found lacking in forty men whose Hearts are as the Heart of the Friend [Abraham] of the All-Merciful." . . . and where else is this body of men to be found save amongst the Rememberers, who are marked out for having devoted their lives to God?

"From men *whose sides shrink away from beds*." (Qur'an XXXII, 16.)

"To *men whom neither bartering nor selling diverteth from the remembrance of God*." (Qur'an, XXIV, 36)

In addition to the Sufi practice of using the rosary, reciting the litanies, and remembering God (*dhikr*) through the invocation of His Holy Name, occasionally members of some orders participate in certain movements which have been called a "sacred dance." Merton highlighted the following:

None the less, the subjection of the body to a rhythmic motion is never, for the Sufis, any more than an auxiliary; its purpose is simply to facilitate *dhikr* in the fullest sense of remembrance, that is, the concentration of all the faculties of the soul upon the Divine Truth represented by the Supreme Name or some other formula which is uttered aloud or silently by the dancers. It was explained to me by one of the Shaikh's disciples that just as a sacred number such as three, seven or nine, for example, acts as a bridge between multiplicity and Unity, so rhythm is a bridge between agitation and Repose, motion and Motionlessness, fluctuation and Immutability. Fluctuation, like multiplicity, cannot be transcended in this world of perpetual motion but only in the Peace of Divine Unity; and to partake of this Peace in some degree is in fact that very concentration which the *dhikr* aims at. . . .

If the grace of ecstasy is beyond you, it is not beyond you to believe that others may enjoy it. . . . None the less I do not say that dancing and manifestations of ecstasy are among the essentials of Sufism. But they are outward signs which come from submersion in remembrance. Let him who doubts try for himself, for hearsay is not the same as direct experience. [95]

God commended the people of the Book [Jews and Christians] for their rapture, mentioning one of its aspects with the highest praise: *When they hear what hath been revealed unto the Prophet, thou seest their eyes overflow with tears from their recognition of the Truth.* (Qur'an V, 83) [93]

The Prophet said: "The solitary ones take precedence, they who are utterly addicted to the remembrance of God." [94]

Thus when the Prophet was asked what spiritual strivers would receive the greatest reward, he replied: "Those who remembered God most." Then when questioned as to what fasters would be most rewarded he said: "Those who remembered God most," and when the prayer and the almsgiving and the pilgrimage and charitable donations were mentioned, he said of each: "The richest in remembrance of God is the richest in reward." [97]

When Dr. Lings explains that the "litany comes as it were from midway between the Heart and the head," Merton boldly marks a following sentence, "Beyond litany is invocation in the sense of the word *dhikr*. This is a cry from the Heart, or from near to the Heart." [111]

A few pages ahead, Merton noted that another form of the invocation is found in groaning: "The Prophet said, 'Let him groan, for groaning is one of the Names of God in which the sick man may find relief.'" [113]

The first chapter in "Part Two: The Doctrine," is entitled "Oneness of Being." In the fulfillment of the Gnostics' ascent, "They see directly face to face that there is naught in existence save only God and that *everything perisheth but His face*, not simply that it perisheth at any given time but that it hath never not perished. . . . Each thing hath two faces, a face of its own, and a face of its Lord; in respect of its own face it is nothingness, and in respect of the Face of God it is Being. Thus there is nothing in existence save only God and His face, for *everything perisheth but His Face*, always and forever." [123]

What a spiritual novice must unlearn struck Merton:

> One of the first things that a novice has to do in the 'Alawî
> Tarîqah—and the same must be true of other paths of mysti-
> cism—is to unlearn much of the agility of "profane intelli-
> gence" which an al-'Alawî *faqîr* once likened, for my benefit,
> to the "antics of a monkey that is chained to its post," and to
> acquire an agility of a different order, comparable to that of
> a bird which continually changes the level of its flight. The
> Qur'an and secondarily the Traditions of the Prophet are the
> great prototypes in Islam of this versatility. [124]

Regarding the three levels of recitation said upon the rosary, Dr.
Lings explains:

> What might be called the normal level of psychic percep-
> tion, is concerned with the ego as such. This is the phase of
> purification. From the second standpoint this fragmentary
> ego has ceased to exist, for it has been absorbed into the per-
> son of the Prophet who represents a hierarchy of different
> plenitudes of which the lowest is integral human perfection
> and the highest is Universal Man (*al-Insân al-Kâmil*), who
> personifies the whole created universe and who thus antici-
> pates, as it were, the Infinite, of which he is the highest sym-
> bol. The disciple aims at concentrating on perfection at one
> of these levels. From the third point of view the Prophet
> himself has ceased to exist, for this formula is concerned
> with nothing but the Divine Oneness. [125]

After Dr. Lings explains that "The soul is not merely immortal
but Eternal, not in its psychism but in virtue of the Divine Spark
that is in it," Merton boldly marked one line from a poem by Shaikh
al-'Alawî:

> Thou seest not who thou art, for thou art, yet art not
> "thou." [127]

Merton then highlights the words quoted of al-Ghazâlî (d. 1111):

> There is no he but He, for "he" expresseth that unto which
> reference is made, and there can be no reference at all save
> only unto Him, for whenever thou makest a reference, that

reference is unto Him even though thou knewest it not through thine ignorance of the Truth of Truths. . . . Thus "there is no god but God" is the generality's proclamation of Unity, and "there is no he but He" is that of the elect, for the former is more general, whereas the latter is more elect, more all-embracing, truer, more exact, and more operative in bringing him who useth it into the Presence of Unalloyed Singleness and Pure Oneness. [127–28]

I have never looked at a single thing without God being nearer to me than it. (Abû 'Ubaidah, d. 639) [128]

In concluding "Oneness of Being," Lings mentions that "the highest saints are referred to as the *Near*," and that what the Qur'an means by "nearness" is defined by the words:

We are nearer to him than his jugular vein and *God cometh in between a man and his own heart* (Qur'an VIII, 24). [129]

Thomas Merton marked many paragraphs as important in "The Three Worlds." The chapter begins with the words of the Moroccan Shaikh ad-Darqâwî:

I was in a state of remembrance and my eyes were lowered and I heard a voice say: *He is the first and the Last and the Outwardly Manifest and the Inwardly Hidden.* I remained silent, and the voice repeated it a second time, and then a third, whereupon I said: "As to *the First*, I understand, and as to *the Last*, I understand, and as to *the Inwardly Hidden*, I understand, but as to *the Outwardly Manifest*, I see nothing but created things." Then the voice said: "If there were any outwardly manifest other than Himself I should have told thee." In that moment I realized the whole hierarchy of Absolute Being. [131]

So realize, my brother, thine own attributes and look with the eye of the Heart at the beginning of thine existence when it came forth from nothingness; for when thou hast truly real-ized thine attributes, He will increase thee with His. [137]

One of thine attributes is pure nothingness, which belongeth unto thee and unto the world in its entirety. If thou acknowledge thy nothingness, He will increase thee with His Being. . . .

Extinction also is one of thine attributes. Thou art already extinct, my brother, before thou art extinguished and naught before thou art annihilated. Thou art an illusion and a nothingness in a nothingness. When hadst thou Existence that thou mightest be extinguished? Thou art *as a mirage in the desert that the thirsty man taketh to be water until he cometh unto it and findeth it to be nothing, and where he thought it to be, there findeth he God.* Even so, if thou wert to examine thyself, thou wouldst find God instead of finding thyself, and there would be naught left of thee but a name without a form. Being in itself is God's, not thine; if thou shouldest come to realize the truth of the matter, and to understand what is God's through stripping thyself of all that is not thine, then wouldest thou find thyself to be as the core of an onion. If thou wouldst peel it, thou would peelest off the first skin, and then the second, and then the third, and so on, until there is nothing left of the onion. Even so is the slave with regard to the Being of the Truth.

It is said that Râbi'ah al-'Adawiyyah met one of the Gnostics and asked him of his state, and he replied: "I have trod the path of obedience and have not sinned since God created me," whereupon she said: "Alas, my son, thine existence is a sin wherewith no other sin may be compared." [137]

The text then refers to what must necessarily be attributed to God as follows: "Being, Beginninglessness, Endlessness, Absolute Independence, Incomparability, Oneness of Essence, of Quality and of Action, Power, Will, Knowledge, Life, Hearing, Speech, Sight." Merton was interested in the comments of Shaikh al-'Alawî:

Here he explaineth what belongeth unto God. See therefore, O Slave, what belongeth unto thee, for if thou shouldst qualify thyself with any of these qualities, thou wilt be contending with thy Lord. [131]

Such a statement reminds a seeker of his own essential emptiness, which were he to realize, he would gain the Divine Presence, for which he yearns. One can imagine why Merton would have been drawn to the passages above which encourage the spiritual aspirant to recall his own "nothingness," for

> then He will be thy Hearing and thy Sight, and when He is thy Hearing and thy Sight, then wilt thou hear only Him and see only Him, for thou wilt be seeing Him with his Sight and hearing Him with His Hearing. [139]

> *Wheresoe'er ye turn, there is the Face of God.* Things lie hidden in their opposites, and but for the existence of opposites, the Opposer would have no manifestation. [140]

Merton was concerned with many of the passages which remind man to accept both the blessings and trials of life with an equal heart and to love God's will for us whether it brings ease or contraction into our lives:

> The Outwardly Manifest is veiled by naught but the strength of the manifestations, so be present with Him, nor be veiled from Him by that which hath no being apart from Him. Stop short at the illusion of forms, nor have regard unto the outward appearance of receptacles. Do not know Him only in His beauty, denying that cometh unto thee from His Majesty, but be deeply grounded in all the states, and consider Him well in opposites. Do not know Him in expansion only when He vouchsafeth, denying Him when He witholdeth, for such knowledge is but a veneer. It is not knowledge born of realization. [142–43]

> Be turned unto God, welcoming all that cometh unto thee from Him. Busy thyself with naught but let everything busy itself with thee, and do thou busy thyself with proclaiming the Infinite and saying there is no god but God, utterly independent therein of all things, until thou comest to be the same in either state. . . . [144–45]

In "The Symbolism of the Letters of the Alphabet," Merton was particularly interested in the writings of Shaikh al-'Alawî with regard to the metaphysics of the manifested world and the nature of the Godhead, whose Essence is to be found in Qualities.

In "The Great Peace," Dr. Lings explains:

> The rhythm to which the breathing is subjected is the rhythm of creation and dissolution, of Beauty and Majesty. Breathing in represents creation, that is, the Outward Manifestation of the Divine Qualities . . . breathing out represents the "return" of the Qualities to the Essence, the next intake of breath is a new creation, and so on. The final expiring symbolizes the realization of the Immutability which underlies the illusory vicissitudes of creation and dissolution, the realization of the truth that "God was and there was naught else beside Him, He is now even as He was. . . ." [159]

> The fullest attainment of inward Peace means the shifting of the consciousness from a secondary or illusory centre to the One True Centre, where the subject is . . . no longer created being but the Creator. This is in fact what is meant by 'concentration'; it follows therefore that for one who is truly concentrated, the symbolism of breathing is necessarily inverted: breathing in becomes absorption of all in the Oneness of the Essence, and breathing out is the Manifestation of the Divine Names and Qualities. [159]

> To say that beyond his created plenitude Universal Man has an aspect of total extinction means that beyond this extinction he has an aspect of Absolute Plenitude, for his extinction is simply the measure of his capacity to receive. [160]

According to Shaikh al-'Alawî:

> [A] Gnostic may be dead unto himself and unto the whole world, and resurrected in his Lord, so that if thou shouldest ask him of his existence he would not answer thee inasmuch as he hath lost sight of his own individuality. Abû Yazîd al-Bistâmî was asked about himself and he said, "Abû Yazîd is dead—May God not have mercy on him!" This is the real death; but if on the Day of Resurrection thou shouldest ask one who hath died only the general death "Who art thou?" he would answer "I am so-and-so," for his life hath never ceased and he hath never sensed the perfume of death, but hath simply passed on from world to

world, and none graspeth the meaning of the real death save him who hath died it. Thus have the Sufis a reckoning before the Day of Reckoning, even as the Prophet said: "Call yourselves to account before ye be called to account." They laboured in calling themselves to account until they were free to contemplate their Lord, and theirs is a resurrection before the Resurrection. [161]

Extinction and submersion and annihilation come suddenly upon the Gnostic, so that he goeth out from the sphere of sense and loseth all consciousness of himself, leaving behind all his perceptions, nay, his very existence. Now this annihilation is in the Essence of Truth, for there floweth down over him from the Holiness of the Divinity a flood which compelleth him to see himself as the Truth's Very Self in virtue of his effacement and annihilation therein. [163]

Regarding extinction from oneself and subsistence in God, the great Andalusian saint, whose tomb has become the spiritual center of Alexandria in Egypt, :

Abû'l 'Abbas al-Mursî used to pray, "O Lord, open our inward eyes and illumine our secret parts, and extinguish us from ourselves, and give us subsistence in Thee, not in ourselves." [167]

The point is made that even though someone be blessed with Union with God, this in no way absolves him from following the revealed law. To be fully mature in the spiritual life

one should combine outward stability with inward o'erwhelmedness, so that one is outwardly spiritual effort and inwardly contemplation, outwardly obedient to God's command and inwardly submissive (mustaslim) to His Utter Compulsion and that the Supreme State belongs to those "who combine sobriety (sahw) with uprootedness (istilam)" . . . so that outwardly they are among creatures and inwardly with the Truth, integrating two opposite states and combining the wisdom of each. [168]

In the same vein, Merton marked passages which discussed the true cause of the great sadness Jacob felt at the loss of Joseph. A disciple of Shaikh al-'Alawî had inquired of his master how the "beauty of Joseph could have diverted [Jacob's] attention from the beauty of the Truth," and the Shaikh explained:

> Jacob's exceeding sorrow was not for the person of Joseph but because Joseph was for him a place of the Manifestation of the Truth, so that when Joseph was by, Jacob's own presence with God was increased in intensity. [164]

> Therefore the Truth trieth those whom He loveth by the sudden disappearance of the form, so that their vision may be deflected from the part unto the whole, as He did with Jacob. [165]

Merton also highlighted a magnificent line from al-Ghazâlî (d. 1111), which refers to this meeting of the finite with the Infinite:

> Each thing hath two faces, a face of its own and a face of its Lord; in respect of its own face it is nothingness, and in respect of the Face of God it is Being. [169]

Among the many ideas which attracted Merton in "Gnosis," is one regarding sight:

> But the Shaikh affirms that it is none the less possible for the outward eye, while still "in this world," to see the Truth, provided that it can first achieve a perfect co-ordination with the inward eye. [Footnote by Dr. Lings: During this life, the Saint's "resurrection in God" is a resurrection of the soul, not yet of the body. But through the coordination just referred to, he may also have foretaste of the resurrection of the body.] [172]

> The outward eye is the ray of the inward eye and the *faqîr* should not open his outward eye (in the hope of seeing Reality) until the connection hath been established between it and his inward eye. When, in virtue of this connection, his outward eye hath become pure inward vision, then he will see the Lord of the verse *Naught is like unto Him* with all his faculties, just as he will also hear Him with all his faculties. . . . [172]

The sight cannot attach itself unto nothing, and that therefore no object of sight can be void of the outward manifestation of the Truth, for things in themselves are naught. [174]

Merton was interested in the meaning and inner purposes of the ritual ablution before prayer in Islam, and the symbolism of water. In respect that everything returns to the Archetype, the world is compared to an iceberg and man, to the water flowing from its sides, melting back to Essence. Among the paragraphs which Merton singled out is:

The purpose of the ablution in Islam is the removal of inward impurity symbolized by various modes of outward impurity. . . . The meaning of defilement (hadath), continues the Shaikh, is ephemeral existence (hudûth), that is, the existence of other than God. This is not ousted from the heart of the Gnostic, and its film is not removed from his inward eye to be replaced in his sight by Eternity, save through his finding the Water and his Purification therewith. Except he be purified by It, he is far from the Presence of his Lord, unfit to enter It, let alone to sit therein. Likewise the slave will not cease to suppose the existence of defilement in all creatures until he have poured this Absolute Water over their outward appearance. Without It he will not cease to condemn them, and how should his verdict be revoked when he seeth their defilement with his eyes, and when his Heart believeth in the independent existence of creation? [182–83]

In "The Ritual Prayer," Merton is seen to have taken a special interest in the deepest significance of the positions in Muslim prayer. Shaikh al-'Alawî explains that after the worshipper begins his prayer by raising his hands and proclaiming "God is Most Great," or Allâhu Akbar, he begins gradually to draw himself in more and more as he approaches the Divine. The extremity of Nearness is attained by the state of prostration.

The Prophet said: "The slave is nearest his Lord when in prostration." At his prostration he descendeth from the stature of existence into the fold of nothingness, and the more his body is folded up, the more his existence is folded up. . . . [187–88]

Before his prostration the Gnostic had the upright stature of existence, but after his prostration he hath become extinct, a thing lost, effaced in himself and Eternal in his Lord. . . . [188]

When the worshipper hath obtained the degree of prostration and hath been extinguished from existence, he prostrateth himself a second time that he may be extinguished from that extinction. Thus is his (second) prostration identical with his rising up from (the first) prostration, which rising signifieth subsistence. [188]

He is prostrate with regard unto the truth, upright with regard unto creation, extinct (even as a Divine Quality is extinct) in the Transcendent Oneness, subsistent in the Immanent Oneness. Thus is the prostration of the Gnostics uninterrupted, and their union knoweth no separation. The Truth hath slain them with a death that knoweth no resurrection. Then He hath given them Life, Endless Life, that knoweth no death. [189]

After the final prostration before the end of the prayer, the worshipper resumes the sitting position from which, after expressions of devotion to God and invocations of Peace on the Prophet, himself and all the faithful, he seals the prayer by turning his head to the right with the words As-Salâmu 'alaikum—Peace be on you! [190]

Of this final sitting position the Shaikh says: He must take a middle course when he returneth unto creation, that is, he must be seated, which is midway between prostration and standing, that he may make good his intercourse with creation. For if he went out unto creatures in a state of being prostrate, that is, in a state of extinction and obliteration, he could take no notice of them. Nor must he go out unto creation standing, that is, far from the Truth as he used to be before his extinction, for thus would he go out unto creation as one created and there would be no good in him and none would profit from his return. Even so he must take a middle course, and "midmost is best in all things." It is said: "Long live the man who knoweth his own worth and taketh his seat beneath it!" Now a man gaineth knowledge of his worth only at his obliteration. Thus is a sitting position required of him after his obliteration. [190]

On the subject of meditation, the Algerian master wrote:

> Meditation may be on things that are made, but not on the Essence, even as the Prophet said: "Meditate upon all things, but meditate not on the Essence lest ye perish." Thought is only used with regard unto what is made, but when the Gnostic hath attained unto the Maker, then is his thought changed to wonderment. Thus is wonderment the fruit of thought, and once it hath been achieved the Gnostic must not swerve from it nor change it for that which is its inferior. Nor can he ever have enough of wonderment at God, and indeed the Prophet would say: "O Lord, increase me in marveling at Thee." Meditation is demanded of the *faqir* whilst he be on his journey. One meditateth on the absent: but when He that was sought is Present in Person, then is meditation changed into wonderment. [190–91]

Merton also underlined these words regarding the wasting of one's time:

> Trifling, for the Gnostic, is being busied with that which concerneth him not, once he hath realized the degree of Perfection; and everything except being busied with God is such frivolity and trifling as justifieth neither a turn of the head thereunto nor the waste of a moment of time thereon. [191]

In the section on the funeral prayer, parallels between the spiritual and physical death struck Merton. As one will be passive in the hands of whoever washes one's body at death, so should the disciple be in the hands of his master "lest he be left with all his impurities upon him by reason of his stubbornness and willfulness and want of passivity." Merton must have wrestled with the fame which came in conjunction with his writings. Perhaps this was one of the reasons he highlighted the following:

"Bury thine existence in the earth of obscurity, for if a seed be not buried it bringeth not forth in fullness." (Ibn Ata Allah d. 1309)

[The Shaykh says:] "Indeed, there is nothing better for the disciple than obscurity after attainment, and no harm is greater for him than fame at that moment, that is, at the moment of his entry unto God, not afterwards, for after his burial in the earth of obscurity there is no harm in the spreading of his fame inasmuch as the growth hath come after the roots were firm, not before, so that there is no doubt that he will bring forth in fullness." [193–94]

Analogously, by a symbolism parallel to this last, the realization of Supreme Sainthood is mirrored in the funeral prayer. Just as the body yields up the soul at death, so the soul, at spiritual death, yields up the Spirit. The Shaikh says: "Bodily death taketh not place without the Angel of Death, and even so spiritual death taketh not place save through the intermediary of a Master who knoweth how to grasp the Spirits of his disciples."

"The soul is precious, yet for Thee will I exchange it,
And being slain is bitter, yet in Thy Good Pleasure is it sweet." [194]

In the funeral prayer itself, the four affirmations of the greatness of God are recited so that the one who has died may be reminded of the four Aspects of Being, the Firstness and Lastness, and Outward Manifestation and Inward Hiddenness. Then this soul can find no outlet: "His spirit departeth and his body goeth to nothing, inasmuch as the directions of space exist no longer for him through his finding not even so much as the breadth of a fingertip left vacant by these four Aspects, whithersoever he turneth. Even if he turn unto himself, he findeth that he himself is one of the Aspects, and so it is wherever else he turn, according to His Words *Wheresoe'er ye turn, there is the Face of God*. Thus when the rapt one turneth his face unto himself [he] seeth in the mirror of his existence the Face of God.

Thus in the service itself, the seeker has a final reminder of his essential nothingness before God—which indeed would seem to be the goal of Realization.

The final phrase of this work which Merton noted was a Prophetic saying revealed by God in His Words. One cannot help but imagine that Merton's writings and efforts were intended to please his Lord and draw men to His Remembrance and His worship. [195]

> The dearest of men unto Me is he who maketh Me dear unto men, and maketh men dear unto me.

NOTES

1. The most recent edition is entitled *A Sufi Saint of the Twentieth Century, Shaikh Ahmad Al-'Alawî, His Spiritual Heritage and Legacy* (Cambridge, England: The Islamic Texts Society, 1993). It contains two new chapters which Dr. Lings now feels would have been of great interest to Merton.

2. *Faqîr*, pl. *fuqarâ*—this term refers to someone who becomes a disciple of a master with the intention of emptying himself for God. The root "f-q-r" means "poverty" or "emptiness." A spiritual martyr is someone who has achieved this emptiness and can be said to have achieved what Saint John of the Cross meant by "Die before you die." Humility is a form of this effort.

9

THE VISIT OF SIDI ABDESLAM
TO GETHSEMANI

Nicole Abadie [Khadidja Benaissa]

N.B. *The French system of spelling has been kept for the purpose of retaining the flavor of Madame Abadie's account.*

Thomas Merton and Sidi Abdeslam met at Gethsemani in the fall of 1966. Although it is known Merton was interested in Sufism and had read extensively about it, it seems to have been his first face-to-face encounter with a follower of the Sufi path. The meeting was arranged by Dr. Bernard Phillips of the Department of Religion at Temple University. Dr. Phillips had met Sidi Abdeslam Talidi (1900?–1980) in 1964 in the course of a trip to North Africa when he visited the *zâwiyah*[1] Allaouia in Mostaganem, Algeria, after reading Martin Lings' book about Cheikh El Allaoui, the founder of the *zâwiyah*. It was on this occasion that my husband and I were introduced to Dr. Phillips, who consequently came to the farm where we lived, near Oran, some eighty kilometers from Mostaganem. Being the only present member of the Allaoui *tarîqah* at that time who spoke fluent English, I had the good fortune to act as an interpreter between Sidi Abdeslam, my husband, and Dr. Phillips. Little did I know at the time that this would evolve into our trip to the United States.

PERSONAL DISCOVERY OF SUFISM

I had been prompted to visit the *zâwiyah* after reading Dr. Carret's booklet about Cheikh El Allaoui, which Martin Lings included in his own book *A Moslem Saint of the Twentieth Century*. I had known Dr. Carret personally since I was a child, as he was a friend of my father, who was also a physician, and was a frequent visitor to our house. He was a very cultivated and interesting man, with an original mind, and I remember being fascinated by his memories recalling his travels to distant lands. In fact, I thought his way of life was an ideal one: he would work for a few years, living frugally without taking any time off, and then close shop for a couple of years and travel with his wife around the world, in the days when a trip around the world was still an adventure. Dr. and Madame Carret would choose a shipping line and then stay in a country without deciding beforehand for how long, rent a place to live so as to mix with the locals, and when they were ready to explore new horizons, inquire about the arrival of the next ship and board it for their next destination.

However, neither then nor later, when I was a student at the university, do I remember the doctor mentioning Cheikh El Allaoui or his book; it is all the more surprising that I spent some five months with Dr. Carret when he accompanied my father as his secretary—myself, again as interpreter—during an official mission to the United States and Canada in 1944.

But to be honest, even if it had come about in the course of our daily conversations, I had other things on my mind at the beginning of my active life and did not yet have the ears to hear about it. It is only when I came back to Algeria from Paris where I was studying at the Sorbonne, at the time my father died, and while sorting out his library that I found the book which was just what I was looking for.

For a few months before, I had become a Muslima at the Grand Mosquée in Paris. My parents, like Dr. Carret, were agnostics—belonging to a generation which believed Science either explained or would explain everything—and we were raised without a religion but with a respect for all religions. (My brother remains an agnostic, my sister became a devout Catholic.) Islam however was probably the one I knew least about, as was frequently the case with Europeans living in a colonial setting.

Strangely enough, it was while studying the life of the French Romantic poet Gérard de Nerval, who had lived for awhile in Muslim countries and was the subject of the thesis I was then working on, that I was drawn to the esoteric aspects of Islam. I had in fact been looking for some time for a spiritual path, reading about Buddhism, Hinduism, the Orthodox tradition. This can prove dangerous, for it seems to create a magnetic field around a person which attracts all sorts of persuasive groups or individuals. I am forever grateful to René Guénon who, in one of his books, wrote that whoever proclaims to follow the Way must belong to and practice a revealed religion—a criterion which enables one to eliminate many dubious interferences.

When I returned—temporarily, I thought—to Algeria, I found myself in a predicament. My mother had just suffered the loss of her husband and although it might now seem difficult to understand without the knowledge of what the political situation was at the period, I could not ask her to bear the brunt of public opinion by overtly declaring myself to be a Muslim at a time when the war of independence was just beginning.

But as soon as I could, after discovering Dr. Carret's book, I drove to the *zâwiyah*, where I was to return more and more often, and where I spent the month of Ramadan 1954. I will always cherish the memories of these days punctuated by the call to prayer, and the warm welcome I always enjoyed, then and later, on the part of Lalla Kheira, wife of Cheikh Hadj[2] Adda (the successor to Cheikh El Allaoui in the Mostaganem tarîqah) and mother of his successor, Cheikh Hadj El Mehdi. She had a forceful personality and was highly respected by all the members of the extended household, which she ruled with the energy necessary to cater to the daily needs of the numerous *fuqarâ* and *faqirat*[3] living permanently in the *zâwiyah*, whose numbers could be multiplied by the arrival of visitors of all kinds, often unannounced.

Cheikh Hadj El Mehdi introduced me to Sidi Abdeslam, with whom I was to have many long conversations (a fact I still marvel at, as my Arabic at the time, although fast improving, was somewhat rudimentary). He had come from Morocco and received his initiation from Cheikh El Allaoui and remained at the *zâwiyah* as a *mujarred* (a *faqir* who forsakes any worldly pursuits in order to live in the *zâwiyah* in whatever capacity he is assigned by his master). At that time, it meant living in utter poverty: I remember his telling us that they never had enough to eat, often when they had just finished their meal. After Cheikh El Allaoui's death, he was to become a constant companion of Cheikh Hadj Adda, who entrusted him with his eldest son—and future successor as the head of the *tarîqah*[4]—to whom he was to teach the Qur'an. He also performed the function of *imam*[5] of the *zâwiyah* for more that thirty years. He therefore enjoyed a somewhat privileged position, while remaining very independent, surrounded by a small number of disciples particularly devoted to him.

In the summer of 1955, I married one of the disciples, who had received his initiation from Cheikh Hadj Adda. From then on, Sidi Abdeslam was a frequent visitor to our home and the three of us became quite close. In fact, we were to go on the hâjj[6] together in 1964.

TRIPS TO MECCA AND JERUSALEM

It started with a not-out-of-character phone call. Out of the blue Sidi asked me, "Why don't you sell that donkey in the yard and come to Mecca with me?" I can still visualize the place and time; it was as if I had been struck by lightning. We operated a dairy farm; it was therefore difficult to leave for a long period of time. However, not seizing this opportunity to go on the hâjj with Sidi Abdeslam was something we felt we would regret for the rest of our lives. Furthermore, we did not have enough money available. And last but not least, my husband did not have a passport and obtaining one was no easy matter at the time. But by the grace of Allah, we were able to arrange for his brother to take over while we would be away, and another disciple of Cheikh Hadj Adda, Sidi Abderrahman, who was also close to Sidi Abdeslam, lent us some of the money we needed. The question of the passport was to be resolved in Algiers, from where we would first fly to Lebanon, where Sidi Abdeslam was expected. Or so we thought. In fact, we were to be stranded in Algiers for nearly two weeks, facing the prospect of having to go back home without having accomplished what we set out to do. I remember Sidi Abdeslam, when we were nearly losing hope, quoting a Sufi saying that the believer has to endure trials, but not a catastrophe. At the last minute, the passport appeared, as if by a miracle, and we were on our way.

We first stayed in Beyrouth (Beirut) at the home of friends of Sidi Abdeslam for some time before leaving for Djeddah (Jeddah). In 1964, the hâjj was, I believe, in May. When we arrived at the airport in Djeddah, around midnight, and the doors of the air-conditioned plane were opened, it was like stepping into an oven, even at night. This was long before the construction of the new airport. The existing one was crowded beyond belief. The only people who seemed to take everything in stride were the pilgrims from sub-Saharan Africa, good humoredly camping on the floor of the main hall, which was surrounded by the shops of the money-changers with abaci as computers. Things were not so organized as we understand they are today. No air-conditioned hotels or eateries. We arrived in Medina (where the Prophet is buried) at night, where people who rented lodgings were anxiously awaiting the harvest of pilgrims, and we ended up in a kind of underground pit, fortunately located not far from the Grand Mosque. It was so hot we could only absorb liquids. In Mecca, an Algerian friend had introduced us to a *mutawwuf*[7] who assigned us a room with just mats. We finally secured some sheets, using our bags as pillows. But we were so enthralled at finally being in Mecca that we didn't really care. Like everyone, I expect, the first vision of the Ka'ba surrounded by all the pilgrims in a cosmic movement, like planets orbiting around the sun, remains forever engraved in my mind. I was afraid I wouldn't be able to perform the *tawwaf al ousoul*[8] however, as I had been very sick the last two days in Medina and could scarcely walk. But there again, I performed the ritual by the grace of Allah and from then on I recovered. We also met some disciples of the *tarîqah* from North Africa and elsewhere, notably from Al Quds [Jerusalem] and from Syria.

We were taken to Arafat[9] by bus and stayed overnight in tents. But the next day, when we were to leave for Mina[10], in the crush following the ritual[11] at Arafat, Sidi Abdeslam was separated from us. We assumed he was in one of the next buses, but at Mina, he was nowhere to be found. We were terribly worried and spent our time searching for him, going to the police stations, the center where lost people were kept, and even to the hospitals, without success. But returning to our tent we finally found him; he had gotten lost in the jostle, and had not been taken by another bus; he had no money as my husband was our treasurer, and he had walked all the way to Mecca where someone fortunately recognized him and brought him to Mina.

We stayed a few more days in Mecca where he rested a little and then it was time to think about going back. Again no easy matter. First you had to recover the passports, which were all handled in one place in total confusion. My husband's height enabled him to go over some heads and to finally grasp them. Then, back to Djeddah, with a taxi whose driver we kept talking to all the way for he was sleeping

at the wheel. The reservations, although bearing an OK, were totally meaningless and every half hour, you had to implore the counter
personnel of Middle East Airlines, to no avail. So to make sure we
wouldn't lose a chance to embark, we slept the last night on the floor
in front of their agents, on a piece of cardboard, until one of them
finally took pity on us and we were able to leave.

Beyrouth was a welcome respite after our tribulations. But Sidi
Abdeslam's intention was to pray at the Dome of the Rock in Al
Quds, which was still partitioned in two (it was before the 1967
war) and could only be reached by way of Syria and Jordan as no
one with an Arab passport could enter Israel. So after a few days, we
left for Damascus where we visited the Mosque[12] and other holy
places, among them the one dedicated to Ahl al Kaf,[13] before con-
tinuing our journey to Al Quds. I will never forget the golden light
bathing the road when we arrived from the Dead Sea to this beautiful city. We stayed in a hotel just next to the entrance to the Old
City and prayed in the mosque at the Dome of the Rock and in the
Al Aqsa Mosque. We also visited Bethlehem, the Mount of Olives,
and the house where Rabiya[14] al Adawiya is said to have lived. Back
in Beyrouth, we had tickets to go to Egypt, but were discouraged by
our friends. Nikita Krushchev, the Soviet premiere, was there on
official visit with crowds everywhere—and the heat had taken its
toll on us, so we returned to Algeria after a wonderful if somewhat
taxing voyage.

It was in the following summer that Dr. Phillips met Sidi
Abdeslam. Shortly afterwards, however, Sidi Abdeslam decided to
return to Morocco, and we drove him to Tetuan, where he had some
relatives. From there we went to France by way of Spain, and visited him on the way back. He had then settled in a small apartment
in the house of his niece. We were to make the trip from Oran to
Tetuan many times after that—as often as we could steal even a
couple of days from our chores.

We returned to the hâjj in 1966. Sidi Abdeslam had then
returned to Lebanon where he had been staying for some time and
we joined him in Beyrouth, accompanied by Sidi Abderrahman, his
friend who had so kindly helped us on our first hâjj. From there the
four of us followed an itinerary identical to the first, with a pilgrimage to Al Quds following Mecca. We had planned to also visit Iraq,
but the political situation there was in constant flux and again our

plans were regretfully thwarted, so we stopped in Istanbul for a few days instead. I remember at our first hâjj being surprised to read in the paper which was issued at the end of the pilgrimage that the largest number of pilgrims that year came from Turkey, as I had pre-conceived that Kemal Ataturk had all but laicized the country. This was partly true in the big cities like Istanbul and Ankara, but certainly not elsewhere. And even in Istanbul, we could not under-stand why people were staring at us as we were wearing *djellabas*, not being aware that for the Turks, it was forbidden to don traditional Muslim clothes. Most of the men were wearing caps, like in a scene from a Russian movie of the 1930s. But in some of the mosques, people were coming to embrace us.

THE MEETING WITH MERTON AT GETHSEMANI

Dr. Phillips had visited Sidi Abdeslam again in Morocco and was intent on having him come to the United States. It was however quite evident that Sidi Abdeslam would not travel alone to such alien surroundings and so it was decided that my husband would accompany him and I would come along as an interpreter.

We arrived in the fall of 1966 and were guests of Dr. Phillips in Philadelphia, and later of Mr. and Mrs. Chester Carlson, in Rochester, who had paid for our trip in conjunction with Temple University. Mr. Carlson was the inventor of the Xerox process. He and his wife were very spiritually minded and interested in the inner dimension of all religions, and were themselves practicing Hindus. They had financed the installation of a Zen Buddhist cen-ter in Rochester, and a conference with a Zen master in New York and later traveled as far as the West Coast where they attended a lecture by Krishnamurti. "We were all unimpressed by the man, by what he had to say, and by his manner of saying it and so we didn't seek a private audience" (Letter from Dr. Phillips to T. Merton of November 19, 1966).

While in Philadelphia, Sidi Abdeslam also met with students at Swarthmore College, but the highlight of his trip was his meeting with Thomas Merton at Gethsemani. My husband and Dr. Phillips stayed the night, along with Sidi Abdeslam, at the abbey; I in the guest house. I think one of the brothers had some knowledge of Arabic, but not of the North African dialect, and the next day, the

five of us took a stroll in the countryside so that Sidi Abdeslam
could converse more easily with Merton. I do not remember exactly what was said at their meeting, except that they got along and
understood each other very well.[15] It is that meeting that Sidi
Abdeslam referred to when he asked a friend to reply to a letter
from Merton:

> Dear Father Merton,
>   Sidi Abdeslam hasn't forgotten your meeting, the
> moments on the hill and all that remained untold rather
> than what we did tell each other. If it is true that sometimes
> there is a danger of a tree hiding the forest; the risk is not
> as serious as when the forest prevents us from seeing a tree.
> Life is unique and too precious to be sold off for the writ-
> ings of others or the shadows of our own mind.
>
> Where are you and where did you reach of yourself?
>
> The Prophets of the Book were illiterate: they *were* the
> Book that others believed they were writing.

It is worth quoting from a letter by Dr. Phillips, answering
Merton who in 1967 was considering a trip to North Africa and
mentioned that "in addition to Sidi Abdeslam, I would like to have
a list of several other possibilities—people worth seeing and talking
to, who can help me get in contact with the most authentic Sufi tradition and with Islam in a general way." Dr. Phillips answered:

> As to your question of other Sufi centers and teachers, I vis-
> ited several other such . . . it is my impression that except
> from the standpoint of satisfying one's curiosity, there is
> nothing to be gained from such visits. There are eminent
> scholars in Tangiers, Fez, Rabat and elsewhere and I can give
> you names later on. Sidi Abdeslam himself has visited Syria.
> Lebanon, Iraq, Saudi Arabia, Egypt, and I think Tunisia as a
> Diogenes in quest of an honest Sufi and he hasn't come up
> with any. I once asked him, "Do you mean to say that in the
> whole world the truth is to be found nowhere except in the
> company of Sidi Abdeslam and his four or five disciples?" He
> gave me a marvelous answer: "Where do you expect to get
> by that question?" And so I would ask you—where do you
> expect to get by window shopping for Sufis? If I may give you

some advice you haven't asked for—the more time you can spend in daily encounter with Sidi Abdeslam, the more you will enter into the truth and depth of Islam, of Sufis, and more importantly, of yourself. Window shopping is lots of fun, but it is ultimately irresponsible and it avoids the ultimate confrontation. Being with Sidi Abdeslam (after you get beyond the initial stages of exchanging honeyed words) is the most delightful, the most excruciating and the most fruitful thing I've ever done. I would urge you to put all your eggs in this one basket even at the risk of having them all cracked at once.[16]

THE ENSUING CORRESPONDENCE

Sidi Abdeslam and Thomas Merton exchanged several letters following their encounter at Gethsemani, even despite the difficulty of finding someone who could translate to Sidi Abdeslam the letters of Merton. In one of his, Sidi Abdeslam wrote: "Each word has an interior meaning, which comes from the heart, and an exterior one, which anyone can understand. . . . Jesus and the prophets brought with them a secret which it is our obligation to know 'for whoever knows it will know the secret of the world and of all that surrounds us.'" And in another letter:

> You spoke to me about the true Love. Toward what, or whom do you want to direct this true Love? As to the existence of the "ego," Moses asked God: "Where shall I find you?" to which God answered, "Abandon your ego (*nafs*), you will then find Me." On the other hand, a disciple of a Sufi master complained to him that his *nafs* was causing him trouble, "My son," answered the master, "to me she has done a lot of good." My own master, Cheikh Hadj Adda, has said in one of his poems: "I sat in [the] company of my *nafs*, hoping to see her, she was, and I wasn't, her meeting is priceless." Another Sufi has said: "If it were not for the battlefield of the *nafs*, those who search would not find true guidance in their search."

In another letter, about the difficulty for Merton to obtain an authorization to go abroad, "churches, like mosques, are the fruit of an understanding between spiritual people and politicians. People work and show what they do, while our teachings are a deep secret and few are those interested in them. Even those who start practicing them doubt their truthfulness, for they represent real and deep metaphysics."

We have only one letter from Merton—the ones which were in the possession of Sidi Abdeslam were lost—in which he writes:

> You ask me is there a purpose or an object of Love? It seems to me that the true Love is The One (God) who loves in me. Love must use me to love. To love oneself, to love all that exists, to return to the source of all love and all existence. A saint of our monastic order, St. Bernard, said, "I love because I love." For Love to be true, it seems to me I must love the will of The One who loves in me and creates me at all times. But I love more my own will and my passions and we come to what you call "the battlefield of the nafs." It is that I am ignorant and stupid. So the Light of God cannot shine as it should in my nafs because I am too opaque, too resistant. This is a tragedy.

ASSESSING A MASTER

It is very difficult, nearly impossible, to characterize Sidi Abdeslam, his total independence of spirit, his deep understanding of the working of people's minds, his curiosity and wide acceptance of a world foreign to him for so long. He devoted his entire life to the *tarîqah*, but no master is identical to another.

There is this wonderful story of a *faqîr* who wanted to try the patience of two well-known Sufis, one of whom was selling watermelons, the other china. So he went to the first one and asked him to open a watermelon for him, then another, then another, and in the end did not buy anything, all without the vendor ever complaining. Quite impressed, he went to the shop of the second one and seized a cup and saucer, intending to break them on the floor. But the shopkeeper stopped him in his tracks saying: "Make no mistake, you pay for whatever you break. I am not like the man selling the watermelons" (which incidentally also showed he was aware of what had happened).

Sidi Abdeslam's mood would change easily, but always in accordance with the pursuit of the Truth to which he had dedicated his life. Whenever you were with him, your own life acquired a special intensity. His only interest was in raising your level of consciousness and he seemed to read your mind. He also had a wonderful sense of humor, but you always had to remain alert and follow the compass of that truth which was never far from his thoughts. He quoted his cheikh as saying, "with a scholar, watch your words; with a Sufi, watch your heart." May Allah bless his memory and help us along the path he so assiduously followed. Amin[15].

NOTES

1. *Zâwiyah*—literally "corner," a Sufi dwelling or place of convening, or special place reserved for the Remembrance or worship.

2. *Hadj*—when included in a person's title, indicates he or she has performed the hâjj or pilgrimage to Mecca.

3. *Fuqara/faqirat*—men and women disciples. The root (f-q-r) of this word means emptiness or poverty. The spiritual aspirant must be empty for the presence of God to enter therein, as in "Die before you die," of St. John of the Cross.

4. *Tarîqah*—literally "path" which leads to the encounter with God. Here it refers to a Sufi order.

5. *Imam*—leader; person who leads the prayer when Muslims pray together.

6. *Hâjj*—The pilgrimage to Mecca required of all Muslims at least once during life, if the means are available; one of the Five Pillars of Islam.

7. *Mutawwuf*—a person able to guide pilgrims through the various sacred rites and assist them with other needs, such as accommodations.

8. *Tawwaf*—the circumambulation of the Ka'ba.

9. *Arafat*—a plain on which stands the Mount of Mercy, from which the Prophet Muhammad delivered his final sermon. During the time of the pilgrimage, Muslims spend the day here asking God's forgiveness.

10. *Mina*—the area where pilgrims camp in tents.

11. This refers to a ritual commemorating Abraham's willingness to sacrifice his son.

12. The Great Mosque of Damascus where the head of St. John the Baptist is enshrined.

13. *Ahl al Kaf*—The "Companions of the Cave," The Sleepers of Ephesus.

14. *Rabiya*—a female saint of Basra (Iraq), d. 801.

15. Merton himself called the visit "momentous" in his journal. His full account is quoted in this volume in Rob Baker's article on "Merton, Marco Pallis, and the Traditionalists," which follows in this volume.

16. These letters between Merton and Abdeslam and between Merton and Bernard Phillips are in the collection at the Thomas Merton Center, Bellarmine College, Louisville, Kentucky.

17. *Amin* (ah-meen)—Arabic for "Amen." This word derives from the root a-m-n, which indicates truth and honesty.

10

MERTON, MARCO PALLIS, AND THE TRADITIONALISTS

Rob Baker

When writer, recorder and harpsichord player, mountain climber, and Tibetan scholar Marco Pallis sends his first letter to Thomas Merton at Gethsemani on June 25, 1963, he politely hopes Merton will not be offended at "receiving a letter from a stranger."[1] As it turns out, Pallis was not a stranger to Merton after all: the monk knew his name from having read Pallis's classic study of the mountains and religion of Tibet, *Peaks and Lamas*, a few years previously.[2] Merton seems to have answered Pallis rather promptly (for Pallis writes to him again on July 16), apologizing for using a typewriter (since Pallis's own letter had been so beautifully hand-written): "First of all, I hope you forgive the typewriter. I do not type well, but my writing is worse, and I am used to the machine, much as I regret to confess it to the author of *Peaks and Lamas*."[3] Thus, from the first sentence of what is to be a lively and literate correspondence between the two, Merton acknowledges that he knows and respects some of the basic principles of the school of thought that Pallis represents, one generally known as the traditionalist or *sophia perennis* (perennial wisdom) school based on the writings of René Guénon, Ananda Coomaraswamy, and Frithjof Schuon, all adamant foes of "the machine" and other modernist and technological tendencies in contemporary life and thought—the kind of materialistic and secular humanism that they feel has virtually eliminated any sense of the sacred in today's world by wiping out all respect for religious and cultural traditions of the past.

Merton and Pallis correspond enthusiastically and rather frequently over the next few years on like topics—traditionalist ideas in general, but especially those related to Islam (the path which many of the traditionalists followed), Tibetan Buddhism, and Roman Catholicism. At least the first part of this correspondence has been preserved in the archives of the Thomas Merton Center at Bellarmine College in Louisville, Kentucky; these letters are—in addition to their fascinating content—glorious examples in their own right of the lost art of letter-writing (certainly itself a threatened tradition). Somewhat mysteriously, there is an abrupt break in the correspondence—at least in that which is on record—at the end of 1966. The letters seem to stop some two years before Merton's death, except for a brief postcard from Pallis the summer before Merton's fateful Asian journey in late 1968 (though that postcard itself makes reference to a letter not in the collection). There are, morever, quotes from Pallis letters—letters that are not in the Bellarmine collection—which are cited in the editorial footnotes to *The Asian Journal of Thomas Merton*, which further deepens the mystery.[4]

What is particularly frustrating is that the letters break off immediately after Pallis issues an invitation for Merton to become more directly involved in the Sufi-based traditionalist school which he himself espoused. Merton responded that "any relationship" he might have with the school would have to be "not only highly informal in itself but subject to this kind of control—which could even be arbitrary," referring to the standard monastic principle of censorship of mail by the abbot of the monastery: "Correspondence is inspected, contacts which seem valuable are liable to be abruptly cut off without my knowledge."[5] At the end of May, Merton writes again (after apparently not having heard from Pallis in the meantime):

> I have not ceased to think from time to time of your proposal. I remember that my letter was inconclusive but remained open. The chief obstacle to a more or less full participation seemed to me then to be the fact that letters here are subject to complete control. However, as you see by this one, there is a way in which one is permitted to consult other masters without the censorship of the local Superior. You note that I simply put the letter in a sealed envelope which is within another envelope handed open to the Superior. The sealed envelope is marked "Conscience matter." A letter coming in would be the same: the outer envelope would be opened by the Superior but the inner one, properly marked, would be respected.[6]

According to an entry in Merton's private journals, we know at least one such "conscience matter" letter was delivered, either from Frithjof Schuon himself or one of his representatives (perhaps Pallis himself), in early June (see below, at the end of Section III). The letter does not seem to have survived, nor does any reply from Merton. Indeed, the Merton-Pallis correspondence appears virtually to end at this time. Evidently one of three things occurred: (1) The correspondence continued *sub rosa*, or at least under the aegis of "conscience matter" letters, and was destroyed by one or both correspondents; (2) Pallis backed off from his offer of divulging more information to Merton, perhaps fearing his letters concerning matters of confidence would be intercepted; (3) Merton himself got cold feet about the arrangement and so informed Pallis, in a letter which presumably has not survived.[7]

When William Shannon, editor of the Merton letters to Pallis in *Hidden Ground of Love*, visited Pallis in London on September 28, 1983, Pallis told him that he had no letters from Merton to add to the collection of carbons which Merton had kept at Gethsemani because he (Pallis) never kept letters, but always burned them;[8] this is somewhat at odds with several references in the correspondence about how Merton's letters to Pallis were shown to and shared with other members of the traditionalist school. But Pallis's implications were clear: there were certain things about his correspondence with Merton which he felt should not be made public.

To understand this attitude of strict privacy, one must know something of the nature of the traditionalist school and Sufism in general. This information can then, in turn, be examined in relation to (1) the correspondence between Merton and Pallis; (2) Merton's letters to other members of the traditionalist school; and (3) Merton's private journals, his marginalia in the various Sufi and traditionalist books he read, and the notebooks he kept of his impressions of such readings. Merton's private journey into Sufi and traditional thought is an extraordinary and essential tangent on his overall metaphysical journey, as the following pages will attempt to show, without presuming to overemphasize its significance in his spiritual growth as a whole.

I. The Secret and the Open Among the Traditionalists

Sufism, as the inner or esoteric dimension of Islam, has been treated with distrust by certain fundamentalist and even mainstream members of the Muslim community who consider it as potentially heretical. There has been a certain amount of persecution, including even the execution of the Persian Sufi teacher al-Hallâj (857?–922), the figure who so fascinated Merton's correspondent, the French scholar Louis Massignon.[9] As a result, Sufism has often cloaked itself in a degree of secrecy, for its own survival if nothing else, as have similar esoteric or mystical schools within other traditional religions, such as Judaism, Catholicism, or Hinduism. What the fundamentalists decry as heresy in such cases is usually instead an intense inner interpretation of the faith, but one still grounded firmly in a strict orthodoxy. Such was certainly the case with the kind of Sufi traditionalism discussed by Merton and Pallis in their correspondence.

Pallis, though a practicing Buddhist (as he chronicles so vividly in *Peaks and Lamas*), was also a close follower of the spiritual teacher

Frithjof Schuon (1907–98),[10] a Swiss seeker who became a disciple of the Algerian Sufi shaikh, Ahmad al-'Alawî (1869–1934)[11] and carried on his spiritual order or *tarîqah* in the West.[12] Al-'Alawî in turn was a descendant of a long line of Sufi teachers who trace their lineage back to the Prophet Muhammad. But Schuon's studies and teachings encompassed other esoteric ways as well: while remaining firmly grounded in Islam, he was also a leading scholar of other faiths, especially Hindu Vedanta, Buddhism, Christianity, and Native American religions. He wrote extensively on these subjects, as well as about philosophy and aesthetics. Seyyed Hossein Nasr has summed up his opus as follows:

> As far as metaphysics and the spiritual life are concerned, he left few questions unanswered. He created a vast corpus of writings which are the most complete and profound exposition of the *sophia perennis* in our age, a corpus which includes works on individual religions unparalleled in their depth among writings in European languages. One such work is *Understanding Islam*, which has not only helped Westerners to gain an in-depth understanding of the Islamic tradition, but has also guided many born Muslims to the discovery of the deeper dimensions of their own religion. Furthermore, he was unrivaled in his ability to cross religious frontiers and to compare and relate in depth the various elements of diverse religions, revealing their inner unity while fully respecting their formal diversity. He was in fact the champion par excellence of orthodoxy combined with universality, of unity from above or within as opposed to reductionist uniformity so prevalent in so-called ecumenical discussions today.[13]

Schuon is considered a major force in the development of the traditionalist school of thought, which also derived from the ideas and writings of Ananda Coomaraswamy (1877–1947), the Sri Lankan-born scholar of Oriental art and metaphysics (his books include *The Transformation of Nature in Art, The Christian and Oriental Philosophy of Art* and the anti-modernist tract, *The Bugbear of Literacy*), and René Guénon (1886–1951), a French metaphysician who converted to Islam and who wrote several key works of traditionalist thought (including *The Crisis of the Modern World*, *The Reign of Quantity and Signs of the Times*, and *Man and His Becoming According to Vedanta*). Other scholars later associated with the traditionalist school—and with Schuon in particular, visiting him either in Switzerland or in the United States, where he moved in 1981— include Titus Burckhardt (1908–84), Leo Schaya (1916–86), Martin Lings, Whitall Perry, Huston Smith, Joseph Epes Brown, William Stoddart, Seyyed Hossein Nasr, and Pallis.[14]

In his first letter to Merton, Pallis mentions Schuon: "I wonder if you also[15] know the writings of Frithjof Schuon, some of which I have translated? . . . His book *Les Stations de la Sagesse* (which also exists in English as John Murray published a translation) seems to me one of the most outstanding contributions of recent years."[16] He continues to speak of Schuon throughout their correspondence, though it is only in the final letters in the collection that he gives Merton details of Schuon's association with Islam and the Sufi school of thought. But in that first letter, Pallis also whets Merton's curiosity about a British publication called *Tomorrow*, which had just changed hands from being about "ghosts, witches and queer phenomena of all kinds" to becoming a journal of serious religious ideas (it later changed its name to *Studies in Comparative Religion*, and, as such, became the leading traditionalist journal of its day, from 1967 to the mid-'80s).

Once such seeds are sown, Pallis waits to see if Merton is open to such ideas as these, and his patience is rewarded: Merton indeed seems to be a kindred spirit to esoteric and traditionalist concepts, though he himself (and many of his followers and commentators in the three decades since his death who have co-opted him as a liberal or a humanist) would probably never have chosen to classify his thinking with that of a school that some opponents have labelled elitist and conservative, if not reactionary.

It all comes back, in a sense, to the term "esoteric," which has been widely misrepresented and misunderstood. The concept is a keystone of Schuon's thought (and appears in the title of one of his chief studies, *Esoterism as Principle and as Way*). Using the symbol of a circle and its center—a formulation that Schuon also employs in his writings—another leading traditionalist author, Martin Lings, has described how esoterism is actually the link between world religions:

My intelligence had never been able to accept the exclusivist idea that there is only one valid religion. But now it had learned and most readily accepted the truth that the great religions of the world, all of them equally Heaven-sent in accordance with the various needs of different sectors of humanity, can be graphically represented by points on the circumference of a circle, each point being connected with the center, that is, with God, by a radius. The points stand for the outward aspects of the religions, whereas each radius is the esoteric path which the religion in question offers to those who seek a direct way to God in this life, and who are capable of compliance with the demands of that way of sanctification, demands far more rigorous and exacting than those of the exoteric way of salvation.[17]

The secret (or inner) does not negate or deny the open (or outer), which can at times even be said to surround it, contain it, protect it, albeit perhaps unwittingly. In specifically Islamic terms, the *tarîqah* (Arabic for path or Way) does not replace the *sharî'ah* (the law, the highly developed code of rules and regulations that constitutes Islam); both start with the same foundational guidelines. But at the same time, since the esoteric path is one where movement takes place *inside* the circle, its progress may not always be discernible to those on the circumference.

The secret is furthermore not clandestine out of paranoia or some perverse predilection for elitist exclusivism, but because exposure and publicity always crudely compromise the message being preserved. As with the meaning of a fairy tale, any attempt to expose the esoteric to the light of rational analysis spoils it forever, robs it of all its magical meaning: truth vanishes in a puff of smoke under such circumstances. Ripping the veil off a hidden or sacred symbol reveals nothing of the inner clarity of the representation in question, but only the naked hollowness of the vision of the viewer.[18]

The straight path—spoken of as "*al-Sirât al-Mustaqîm*" in the *fâtihah*, the all-embracing opening verses of the Qur'an—of true Sufism thus never really strays outside the circumference of the circle, nor does it meander in and out of it. It heads steadily (and usually with great difficulty) toward the center. As with a traditional craftsman, a painter, or a pianist, years of training in technique are required before the seeker is allowed the grace of improvisation—usually only when the center is within reach.

This demanding or rigorous path is never easy or comfortable, nor is it egalitarian or democratic, accessible to all. It is an initiatic way, the traditionalists insist, one of direct experience which cannot be spoken of to outsiders, not because the listener "should not" be told about it, but because they would and could not recognize the vocabulary, and the very attempt to verbalize it would do far more harm than good for the cause of understanding.

II. Basic Elements of Traditionalist Thought

What then are the basic concepts of the traditionalist school of thought that Pallis and Merton were to discuss over the next few years, and which Merton was to raise with other correspondents and to indicate in his journals, marginalia, and reading notebooks?

The following are key elements of traditionism in general:

(1) Belief in what Schuon spoke of as "the transcendant **unity** of religions," that is, that all schools of traditional religious thought have an inner dimension that is essentially the same, though external doctrines may differ considerably. Rather than trying to water down those external doctrines to make them conform to each other (which they can never be made to do anyway), the traditionalists suggest true dialogue must take place on the esoteric level, the only place where a real common bond can be established. All attempts at ecumenical compromise and syncretism are frowned upon as counterproductive to all the traditions involved.

(2) Emphasis on the significance of **symbol** and **ritual** as the proper language and action for spiritual search, so that objects and tasks take on a meaning and significance beyond that of mundane generalities, signifying something higher and worthier. Herein lies most of the secret, about both meaning and method. Lings has quoted Schuon as saying, "Every sacred symbol is an enlightening form which invites us to a liberating rite."[19]

(3) Significance of **craft** as a discipline: Far from being the quaint pastime it has become in most of the modern Western world, craft or craftsmanship forms an essential building block in traditional societies—a way of living and working where the spiritual remains united

with the utilitarian aspect of daily living; where fathers and mothers pass on skills to sons and daughters; where each element of the social structure serves its purpose and can take pride in its doing and making; where apprenticeship to work is also apprenticeship to life; where guilds of like-minded persons support, aid, and encourage each other, rather than struggling and competing for advantage and material superiority.

(4) Maintaining a traditional **environment**: avoiding the vulgar, the fashionable, the unorthodox, the "modern" in **decor**, **dress**, and **behavior**. Clothes, perhaps, do sometimes make the man (or woman), or at least unmake him (or her). The furnishings of one's home—the things and objects that one is surrounded by—have a deep impact on inner being. One's choice of associates, language, even posture can affect everything one does or is.

(5) Distrust of **modernism**: the theory that newer is always preferable, that more is better, that quantity is superior to quality. The modern world is one in which secular and materialistic priorities abound; a world of technology run amok (the absurdity of a society so dependent on machines that Y2K panic could be anything other than a riduculous joke), science as God, money as God, efficiency and productivity as God; a world without respect for rules and traditions, without hierarchy, without discrimination (the word itself being turned into a pale and inaccurate synonym for prejudice); a world of stock markets and lotteries and "insurances" (themselves lotteries on human life or divine will); a world whose traditional educational system is in a shambles, whose moral values have collapsed, whose art, music, literature, and architecture have lost all sense of objective order and beauty and are governed instead by the lowest common denominators of chaos, ugliness, and egoism.

(6) Rejection of **secular humanism**: placing human values—or as humanists would have it, "social values" or "the common good"—or selfish individualism above spiritual demands. In Islam: making anything an idol, a partner (or equal) of Allah. Compartmentalizing life, rather than looking for its unity. Scientism. Psychiatry. Evolutionism. Teilhard de Chardin.

(7) Insistence instead on **quality of spirit**: the movement "from the divine to the human" (title of another book by Schuon), or, as Martin Lings so delightfully puts it, "Let us mention in passing what a blessed antidote this last title is to one of the twentieth century's slogans in praise of itself, 'from the subhuman to the human.'"[20]

(8) Dedication to an **initiatic path**, requiring the presence of a spiritual **master** and a period of **submission** (the literal meaning of the word "Islam") in order to move toward a place where the beginning of knowledge is possible. Observance of rules, participation in rituals; no free-form eclectic jumble of ways and influences. The straight path.

(9) The **intelligence of the heart**: the core concept, from which all the others spring: the heart, where transcendence meets immanence, where truth resonates, reachable only through the endless stages of self-testing and self-recognition like peeling the layers of an onion. As a popular hadîth (or saying of the Prophet Muhammad) describes the "from the divine to the human" concept: "I was a hidden treasure longing to be known, so I created the world." The Divine Name waiting to be invoked.

*
* *

III THE MERTON-PALLIS LETTERS

In the first letter he wrote to Thomas Merton in the summer of 1963, Marco Pallis wonders if Merton might help him place an article he has written "in some American periodical, preferably one enjoying a fairly wide circulation among serious and intelligent Christians, and especially Catholics."[21] The order is a rather tall one—and one that apparently proves fruitless, though Merton offers several suggestions over the next few months—but it establishs the nature of their correspondence, which is always to be about writing, publishing, and the discussion of "serious and intelligent" spiritual ideas.

Over the next three-and-a-half years, Pallis writes Merton at least fifteen more letters; Merton sends at least thirteen letters in return. They also exchange books and articles of interest on several occasions, and a bond seems to be established almost immediately. Pallis writes on a postcard on August 8, 1963: "The things [books and articles] you sent have arrived and have brought much joy as well as profit. To read something written in a language one also uses is always a great consolation."[22] On the other side of the postcard is a picture of Norwich Cathedral, which Pallis indicates is "one of the two or three in this country" where "one feels a spiritual message coming out of every stone."

The correspondence soon touches on the nature of letter-writing itself. Referring to his own burdensome list of pen-pals, Merton laments that sometimes "'the reign of quantity' takes over, and one must move mountains of mail for little real purpose"[23]—making a play on words on the title of a book by René Guénon, *The Reign of Quantity*. Pallis responds:

> As you said, one tends, despite oneself, to be continually involved in correspondence, much of it useless, yet not altogether unavoidable under the circumstances. What would the world be like if one spoke only when something needed to be said and read and wrote likewise? Surely your monastic silence is an expression of such an intention, though its effective realisation is another thing. One of the things that I loved the Tibetans for was their economy of words, so different from 'le moulin' [French for "millwheel"] to which one is accustomed at home, especially when one belongs, as I do, to a Mediterranean race [i.e., his Greek ancestry]. Fortunately my own parents were not of the ultra-talkative kind, and my father, who was a gifted poet and writer, instilled in his children the hatred of verbiage; he used to get in a rage over a superfluous comma, in one of my letters!

> Between us two there need be no wasted words, I am sure such is your wish too, and such economy can only make communication all the closer.[24]

In the same letter, Pallis indicates his practice of sometimes sharing Merton's letters with others:

> Now that I have answered your letter I intend to send it to one who is both a close friend of mine, and, especially, a spiritual companion in the deepest sense. he is a Scot (William Stoddart is his name) who came to the Catholic Church many years ago and lives his Christian life with rare intelligence as well as piety and virtue. The example of such a person is a precious gift. I thought you should be glad to know of this connection.

This sharing of ideas between like minds dominates the correspondence: it took place as much by exchanges of books as of letters. Merton writes Pallis on October 4, 1963:

I want to thank you especially for the books you so kindly sent. First of all, your own *The Way and the Mountain*. Your essay on the "Active Life" belongs precisely to a tradition that I recognize and live in, and it is very well done. The one on Sikkim Buddhism is perhaps the one that moved me most. Can we hope for a revival of these values? As you say, it is really the cross of our time to see so much that is really valuable being destroyed or discarded in the most irresponsible sort of way. Even efforts to preserve the best things seem at times fated to be foolish and destructive. I wish the Church were more sensitive on this point. There is a glimmering of a beginning now, but perhaps too late, with the formation of a secretariat for relations with non-Christian religions, and with some beginning of understanding of primitive cultures on the part of people in the missions. Too few of them, I'm afraid. . . . [Your essay on clothes is very wise. I have tried to get (Eric) Gill's little book on that subject but it seems unobtainable.] The essay "The Way and the Mountain" is the one I liked best. It is very fine indeed, and as a matter of fact the night after I read it, I dreamed about a "way," high on a cliff yet somehow secure. The Chinese painting of the "way" reproduced in the book is magnificent. I will send you my little book on Direction [*Spiritual Direction and Meditation*], which has many points in common with your essay.[25]

Merton's copy of *The Way and the Mountain* is now in the library at the Abbey of Gethsemani and contains extensive markings (see section V below). Another book which he received from Pallis is Martin Lings' account of the life and teachings of Shaikh al-'Alawî (the Algerian shaikh who was Schuon's master), *A Moslem Saint of the Twentieth Century*:

And now above all, thank you for the superb book on Ahmad al-'Alawî, superb because of its subject and because of the excerpts from his writings. I am immensely impressed by him, and by the purity of the Sufi tradition as represented in him. I am surprised Louis Massignon did not know him better or appreciate him more. I intend to reread the book meditatively; it is one of the richest things of its kind I have found lately. Surely the deepest expression of this kind of mysticism in our time.

Merton kept his copy of A Moslem Saint, which is in the collection of his personal books preserved at the Merton Center at Bellarmine. Like The Way and the Mountain, Ling's book is filled with underlinings and marginal annotations,[26] and Merton did a short review of the book, along with several other titles related to Sufism, for the French monastic publication, Collectanea Cisterciensia two years later, in 1965.[27] Merton went on in the letter to mention the third book Pallis had sent (and another book that he was later to underline and annotate profusely), the original French edition of Frithjof Schuon's highly influential study, Understanding Islam:

> I have not yet got into Schuon's book on Islam, but I will do so immediately. I do as a matter of fact know him and Guénon, though not well enough yet.[28] [I wrote a poem about the Moslem Angel of Death[29] after reading something in a book of Schuon, it must have been L'Oeil du Couer (Eye of the Heart)].

> Perhaps you would like a large omnibus book of my things. It is a bit pretentious but I think it says most of the things I am trying to say, or perhaps not quite. It does not say enough about my growing interest in Islam and Buddhism. I know I am going to profit very much by Schuon, and will perhaps have more to say when I have read a great deal more on these things.[30]

The following summer, Pallis alerts Merton to the fact that his musical group, the Early Music Consort of Viols, will be playing two concerts in Kentucky (in Louisville and Berea) while on tour of the United States; the music, Pallis writes, "though not exactly definable as 'sacred' (seeing it was designed for domestic use), has a character which I would readily denote as 'non-profane.' It is imbued with the Christian sense of things, this is evident to one 'who has ears to hear.'"[31] Pallis wonders if it might be possible to visit Merton at Gethsemani: "It would be a great joy to meet you in the flesh now, after reading several of your books that you kindly sent me. They provide a certain background to your personality, whereby a number of superficial questions do not need to be put at all." Merton replies enthusiastically, inviting the musicians to play for the monks (not realizing there were women in the consort, which precludes the concert in the long run). Pallis writes back to him just before leaving for the United States: "Apart from the music, I hope for a quiet hour with yourself, one to be shared with Richard Nicholson, who has been my comrade in the way since many years, in Tibet and elsewhere. He has read your books and shares whatever I already share with you."[32] The meeting takes place on October 24 at Gethsemani, and Pallis writes quickly to Merton on his return to London, saying that already "it seems a long time since we walked together round the outer court of the abbey and sat under the great tree there."[33] He also indicates that he is sending Merton more of "Frithjof Schuon's most central works" and urges Merton himself to contribute to the traditionalist journal, *Tomorrow*.

Merton writes back less than a week later, returning to Pallis an article by Schuon on monasticism[34] which Pallis either sent him previously (possibly when he sent him the books mentioned above) or left with him during his visit to Gethsemani:

> . . . I have been wanting to write and return M. Schuon's really remarkable essay on monasticism. I like it very much, and like the whole tone of it from beginning to end. It is a much saner and more realistic approach to the question of "the monk and the world" than is being taken at times by some of the monks. The same problem we spoke of in connection with Tibetans. They do not want to be left out of the world!!
>
> It is really remarkable that with all the unrest and perplexity about getting in touch with the world and engaging in "meaningful activity" (the word "meaningful" has come to take on an aura of magic in American religious circles), monks do not realize that they are manifesting a kind of despair, a kind of blind grasping and clinging to the evanescent aspects of life. The old structures, manifestly inadequate in some ways, are being taken away, and instead of being spiritually liberated, Christians are rushing to submit

to much more tyrannical structures: the *absolute* dominion of technology-politics-business (or state capital). I think M. Schuon has exactly the right view, and I am pleased that he remarks in passing on the naïve infatuation with Teilhard de Chardin (though I think there is much that is good in Chardin, along with some grave illusions).[35]

Pallis must have been pleased to hear Merton voicing opinions so compatible with those of the traditionalists. The question of monasticism had come up once before, in Merton's first letter to Pallis, where he wrote: "Though there is such a thing as an 'American' monasticism, which is in its way fairly genuine, we must remember that this country lives by everything that is hostile to a truly monastic life, and even its most cordial embraces tend to prove deadly in the long run."[36] In response, Pallis wrote back at that time:

What you wrote about the state of American monasticism is coming to apply more and more to the rest of the world. An obsessive valuation of life in terms of purely worldly "welfare" provides an ungrateful background for the contemplative ideal; in this respect materialism and the now fashionable "psychologism" work hand in hand. To resist this process, a high degree of intellectual discernment is called for; to watch it with open eyes is the particular cross laid on our generation, our particular form of ascesis; to watch it, without wallowing in the prospect, and still give thanks to God is not always easy, and yet, *mutatis mutandis*, this same problem has always been with man, even if now it seems more actual than ever. Certainly the only hope of facing it successfully is to steer clear of optimistic and pessimistic interpretations alike. "Allah est plus savant" [God is more knowing, or, simply, Allah knows better], as the Muslims say.[37]

The traditionalist dialogue continues the following week in 1964, when Pallis sends Merton a copy of a book by a British member of the Schuon circle, Lord Northbourne. He describes the book's purpose in the letter as

intended to meet the need of the many who, while not altogether biased against religion or even still loosely attached to it, think that "the Church has failed" or who do not see why religion need include dogmas, tradition, authority, etc. It is an attempt to meet some, at least, of these difficulties in a simple clear manner and in terms that remain orthodox in their basis and metaphysically sound while being expressed in language that an average person today can easily grasp.[38]

Pallis goes on to say that the author is "a man of deep piety and much personal virtue" and that he was moved to write the book when two young relatives of his "had been led by their own doubts to embrace one of the many pseudo-Oriental cults of the day—two different ones, in this case, neither of which, however, is of the 'Zen' type."

Merton does not write back to acknowledge the Lord Northbourne book until the following Easter, when he writes:

I am very impressed with the book of Lord Northbourne and have written to him about it. I read it very slowly and carefully and found it to be very clear, solid, and helpful. Actually it clears up for me things that I do not quite get from Schuon. . . . One thing Lord Northbourne's book made very clear and satisfying was that those who think along the lines of Schuon, Guénon, and so on are *not* at all preaching an amalgamation of eastern and western traditions.[39]

Merton's copy, signed by Lord Northbourne, is in the Gethesemani Abbey library (it has no underlinings or annotations), and the two were to begin a correspondence the following spring.

Pallis then writes Merton a monumental 26-page letter, dated January 23, 1965; the length is perhaps due to the fact that Pallis is in the hospital recovering from an operation. He begins wryly by quoting a travel feature from a London newspaper that makes reference to "seeing the Orient before sophistication spoils it all for us." As Pallis comments, "Talk of fatalism, not to say cynicism."[40] He compliments Merton on his essay "Rain and the Rhinoceros,"[41] a meditation on the theme of the Eugène Ionesco play, *Rhinoceros*, about the horrors of modernism (which had been interpreted by most American drama critics as a merely secular political attack on fascism), contrasted to the virtues of the solitude and the monastic life (the rain). Pallis then goes on to broach a wide range of subjects including overpopulation, nuclear destruction, racism, caste, Gandhi, the papal encyclical "Pacem in Terris," and the Islamic concept of *jihâd*, or holy war. But these themes almost always come back to the traditionalist perspective, an all-embracing *Weltanschauung* for Pallis. For example, regarding overpopulation and nuclear war, he writes:

> Mass proliferation of the "human animal," of man so regarded, calls forth the possibility of no less indiscriminate destruction, the one is not worse than the other in the long run, the two things belong together and should not, cannot be regarded apart. Also what does existence itself amount to, in a world where solitude and silence are fast becoming virtual impossibilities? What becomes of the manifested word, when the very possibility of non-manifestation it affirms and whence it derives all its own power, has been abolished? Is a vast suburbia a fitting scene for human existence as such? In facing all these questions, whether globally or separately, the human will (though it has its place obviously) becomes a relatively minor factor.

Pallis continues to challenge an approach to modern problems that is merely humanitarian or secular. The Pope's encyclical, as he sees it, offers little hope: "Does it touch the root of the problem, despite the obviously just things it says about particular aspects of the matter?" And again, he laments there is "little there to cause discomfort to any average humanitarian-minded person, whose premises are not apparently called in question." Regarding Gandhi's theory of peaceful resistance, he notes, "Above all, the method cannot be practiced apart from a profound faith in God (Gandhi always said this), it really excludes the profanely humanitarian approach by definition, despite some superficial resemblances."

Pallis likewise stresses there can be no simplistic answers to the questions of social and racial injustice that Merton raises in *Seeds of Destruction*:

> . . . a wish to keep two races apart can have a motive behind it that not merely does not spring from racial arrogance in oneself but actually springs from the contrary motive, namely respect for a racial quality different from one's own,

which one would fain see preserved for its own sake: in present circumstances this solution may in practice have become impossible, in which case merging (and a consequent general blurring of the outlines) may have become unavoidable, but it could still be a matter of regret, for black and white alike. True equality (one that is spiritually valid and not merely a quantitative one) implies the maximum of differentation in the objects (or persons) compared, it is those who are most themselves, in a qualitative sense, who are able to meet others, different in their qualities, on equal terms: in that case, a solution by mere blending could be an evasion of human equality, a fogging of the issue.

Pallis goes on to point out that the caste system in India—long denounced in the West as non-egalitarian—has actually made it "possible for small immigrant groups like the Parsees and the Chaldean Christians and others too to remain happily separate even to this day," adding "these quite small groups preserved their ethnic and cultural identity without any question of superiority or inferiority ever being raised at all by either party."

Pallis appears somewhat skeptical of Merton's assessment that the white Christian must "accept his own liberation at the hands of the Negro": "By my reading, I have not quite been able to gather the kind of action you have in mind," he writes. Such an action would require an attitude that "has to be whole-heartedly repentant, it must hold nothing back to suit its own convenience"—an attitude that differs considerably from "more or less comforting half-measures such as have prevailed hitherto." He then adds:

> It is a case of wanting a *wisdom*, a right intention founded on full awareness, to be matched by its appropriate *means*, with a view to its immediate realisation: it is a principle of *Mahayana* Buddhism that these two things have to keep in step, otherwise the result will be stillborn, that is why Wisdom and method are always symbolised as copartners, who cannot for a moment be divorced.

The long letter breaks in the middle, and the second half, dated February 2, 1965, starts out as a bit of an apologia; Pallis has perhaps just reread what he's written so far and wants to defend or at least clarify his critical approach:

I hope I judged rightly in supposing that you would wish me to include these [criticisms] in the discussion, in fact I am sure such would be your own wish; you want an all-over honest impression, and even if you were to disagree with what is said, it would at least have called attention to certain passages and this, in itself, might be useful.

Pallis then launches into a list of specific objections to sections of *Seeds of Destruction*, ranging from spelling corrections (Pallis was ever a stickler for details) to a major dissent on Merton's concluding section to "Letters to a White Liberal," where he uses an anecdote about Muhammad and Muslim *jihâd* to symbolize the black struggle. Pallis' objection is not to the comparison, but because what Merton says might be misconstrued regarding an aspect of Islam already widely misunderstood:

There is danger of the concluding sentence ["It was a truth of stark and dreadful simplicity—to be proved by the sword."] being read in the sense of implying that Islam was propagated by the sword, chiefly or entirely. Admittedly the lesser *jihâd*, the "lesser holy war," is built into the exoteric structure of Islam, though far more carefully safeguarded than the Christian "Crusade," which was something of an improvisation and correspondingly chaotic in practice. (The *jihâd al akbar*, the "greater holy war," is the spiritual life, the "unseen warfare," in the deepest sense.) But though the warlike *élan* of the Arabs carried the Islamic influence far and wide in the first eighty years, the general adoption of Islam in many of the countries overrun had other and more essential causes: Islam, for these populations, filled a great need, in an intellectual and moral sense. It is important to note that "religious persecution" in the sense given to that expression in the Christian world has not been a feature in Islam; forcible conversion has been comparatively rare there and it does not accord with the spirit, or even the letter, of Islamic law. Given the much prejudice, coupled with ignorance, affecting Islamic matters in the West (it is the least known of all "foreign" traditions) I would myself feel happier if the whole pasage IV were omitted—it does not seem to add anything to the general argument of the book, and if anything, it is likely to mislead rather than to contribute.

Merton later assured Pallis that the questionable passage would be removed in future editions;[42] though this never occurred, whether through oversight or intention.

Pallis goes on to object to Merton's reference to Thomas Aquinas and the Scholastics drawing upon the "best of the Arab philosophers," maintaining Aquinas simply used what "suited his purposes" and that most Arab philosophy "would in fact have remained totally inaccessible to the Scholastics" since it had not even been translated. He also questions Merton's deeming the religions of Asia "natural preparations for the coming of Christ": "Either the spirituality of India, China, Tibet, etc. must be judged at its face value or else it is better ignored." Regarding Father Bede Griffiths, a Christian monk who embraced Hinduism, Pallis categorizes him as "one whom I do not regard as among those able to build a bridge of true understanding between East and West; despite certain good intentions, or rather certain blurred intentions, I do not think his vocation lay in this field. The wish to engage in it did not include a readiness to pay the price of true qualification." He again credits Gandhi: "His conviction that political action *could not not* be an expression of religion, of faith in God, places him far above the other 'great men' of our time, almost in a class apart." In the final pages of the letter, he launches into a long, four-page defense of vegetarianism (from the Budhhist perspective) and then discusses the effects and implications of war, returning to traditionalist phraseology once more:"One can also ask oneself whether a civilization that is predominantly conditioned by quantity, by mass production of men, of things, by the very idea of men as 'the masses,' can really hope to escape mass reactions in the field of human strife and the pursuit of conflicting interests?"

Part of Merton's March 10 reply to Pallis's 26-page letter (which had been mailed in early February) has been lost; in the page that is preserved, he replies systematically, in a numbered list, to five of Pallis's key points. He agrees with most of Pallis's theorizing, but is a bit more circumspect about the specific criticisms to *Seeds of Destruction*, stating, for example, that one objection about Roman

Catholic vs. Eastern Orthodox doctrine "will obviously be seen from various viewpoints."[43] He writes Pallis again on Easter Sunday, to tell him more books by the traditionalists have arrived:

> Yesterday two more books arived, Schuon on *The [Language of the] Self* and Guénon on *The Crisis of the Modern World*. I want to thank you for them. . . . I am coming to the conclusion that I find Schuon hard going a great deal of the time, as his perspective is somewhat unfamiliar to me. In reading Schuon I have the impression that I am perhaps going along parallel to him, and once in a while I will get a glimpse of what he means in terms of my own tradition and experience. I liked very much his essay on prayer, for instance. But on gnosis I find it harder to follow him, I am not in tune with his conceptions, and it is hard to say whether I agree or not. I simply don't know.[44]

Merton was not alone in finding Schuon difficult to follow. In his 1984 introduction to the revised edition of Schuon's classic *The Transcendent Unity of Religions* (first published in French in 1948 and in English in Britain and America in the 1950s), religious historian Huston Smith states: "I was myself baffled by the book on first round, with the consequence that it sat half-read on my shelves for a decade."[45] But, like Smith, Merton was drawn back to Schuon's texts and ideas over the years, including the key concept of orthodoxy:

> I agree entirely that one must cling to one tradition and to its orthodoxy, at the risk of not understanding any tradition. One cannot supplement his own tradition with little borrowings here and there from other traditions. On the other hand, if one is genuinely living his own tradition, he is capable of seeing where other traditions say and attain the same thing, and where they are different. The differences must be respected, not brushed aside, even and especially where they are irreconcilable with one's own view.[46]

Merton then comes back to the question of the efficacy of Eastern religions and how they have been regarded rather condescendingly by some Christians as having a "natural" (read: worldly or profane) rather than a divine origin:

Of all the questions that I treated in my last letter to you[47] (not nearly all those which you yourself raised), the one that still bothers me is that division "natural–supernatural" in religion and mysticism. I see more and more that it is misleading and unsatisfactory, and I also think that there is every solid reason even within the framework of Catholic orthodoxy to say that all the genuine living religious traditions can and must be said to originate in God and to be revelations of Him, some more, some less. And that it makes no sense to classify some of them as "natural." There is no merely natural "revelation" of God, and there is no merely natural mysticism (a contradiction in terms). However, this whole business of natural and supernatural requires a great deal of study. The terms are not clear or unambiguous even within the Catholic tradition, always. And outside it there is a great deal of confusion as far as I can see.

Pallis writes back in June, saying that he has been to Lausanne to visit Schuon "and saw there your letter to Lord Northbourne.[48] Your observations on both 'liberals' and 'conservatives' in the Church have been much appreciated by our friends."[49] The fellowship of kindred spirits is seen as an important bulwark against "the present scene":

> . . . about everything one hears about anywhere these days seems to echo the same challenge to one's faith and resolution—and to one's love and compassion—so that, while going through this daily experience, it is a great consolation to remember some whom one knows to be responding to this spirit. It is true that one who has God for company ought never for a moment to feel lonely; nevertheless, the presence of some human comrades in the way is one of the special consolations God grants in times of spiritual crisis; their existence is His message to our fainting hearts.

Pallis goes on to ask Merton if he has ever written on the nature of petitionary prayer, which he is concerned may be becoming increasingly difficult for some to experience in the contemporary world (the profane realm which Merton had once likened to the "diaspora"[50] of spirituality: a dispersion that implied dilution and de-sanctification as well):

> So long as faith was general (if often shallow) and tradi-
> tional values could be taken for granted, prayer and its nat-
> ural counterpart in an anticipated resignation to God's will
> went in together; more or less naïve and even incongruous
> expressions of a prayerful attitude caused practically no dis-
> comfort, starting with prayer as taught to the child and
> continuing through life to the end. But this is no longer the
> case—the "diaspora" mentality more or less excludes it. As
> I said before, this is not a question which has troubled me
> personally—cases of abusive examples of prayer were appar-
> ent enough, but one could take these in one's stride, like
> many other things—but it does trouble many today and if
> these people bring their troubles in our direction, as they
> are liable to do, we must be prepared, not with mere "argu-
> ments" which are bound to be unconvincing in most cases,
> but with a dialectic that will enable a troubled mind to see
> these things in proportion. . . . I am thinking chiefly of the
> average person and his difficulties (but how variously felt
> and put!) and how these can best be met, both compas-
> sionately and truthfully.

Pallis then indicates that he and his friend Richard Nicholson are off for a holiday in the Alps: "I feel a great need to be close to Nature for a little time; so probably a wander (with some camping on the spur of the moment) may be a good thing now." (Pallis was seventy at the time and the ensuing backpacking trip lasted for five weeks. He later writes that such "a proper holiday, close to nature was a necessity, therefore a duty" and adds: "We crossed a large num-ber of passes, between wild valleys, and saw many wonders in the flower, bird and insect line, and relatively few men. It was a great refreshment, as well as stimulation, for both body and mind.")[51]

Merton writes on June 17 that he has read the Schuon and Guénon books Pallis has sent (both of which Pallis had helped to translate into English):

> I have been wanting to tell you how much I have benefit-
> ed by your translations of Guénon and Schuon. Not only

the material, but also your own translations, which, I think, contribute much clarity to the originals. I meant to write you after Easter when I had finished the Guénon book on *Crisis*. Now I do so when I am in the middle of Schuon on the *Language of the Self*. The Guénon book is certainly a classic, and I appreciate Schuon more and more. The essay on Buddhism, for example, is most excellent. I am at one with him in his deep reverence for the spirituality of the North American Indian. . . . One feels that there is still, among some of them, a deep consciousness of the real calling, and a hidden hope.[52]

Merton has evidently not given up on trying to understand Schuon and his ideas; he goes as far as to say: "The one thing I do want to say most of all is this: I am most grateful for the chance to be in contact with people like yourself, Lord Northbourne, Schuon and so on."[53] This gratitude is compounded even further over the next few months, as Pallis and Merton both become much more personal in their exchanges, culminating in an extraordinary gift sent by Pallis to Merton in October.

Prior to that, however, there is a letter from Pallis dated August 13, 1965, the first to be addressed "My dear Father Thomas" (all previous correspondence has been simply and formally "Dear Father Merton"), announcing a visit to London by Father Aelred Graham (1907–84), a Benedictine monk from Rhode Island who had once written a negative review of Merton's *The Seven Storey Mountain* but later became a friendly correspondent with whom Merton shared an enthusiasm for Eastern religions. Again the theme of spiritual comradeship arises as Pallis writes:

Father Aelred is very much a "companion in the way" which, as the Buddha said, is the greatest blessing one can expect here on this earth. To know that one is not alone, at the human level, is a great consolation, as I'm sure you'll agree. . . . What especially strikes one, with him, is his complete absence of panic in the face of dangers and evils that he discerns only too clearly. The quality of his contemplation enables him to view these things outside time and circumstances—terrible though they are, their ephemeral nature is nevertheless apparent to him, hence they cannot disturb his poise.[54]

Pallis is helping Father Aelred plan a spiritual pilgrimage to Asia:

> He wished me to give him introductions in the Buddhist and Hindu worlds, which I was able to do; but to this I have added Islam, and Sufism, which also means a stopping off in Iran where I have a friend, Seyyed Hossein Nasr, whose book on *Three Islamic Sages* I intended to send to you, but I cannot quite remember if I did so or not?[55] He is a man of great spiritual qualification, a soul after your own heart. He sometimes is called to Harvard to lecture (being an alumnus thereof) and if I am ever able to send him as far as Gethsemani do please regard him as our brother in every sense of the word.

Again at the end of the August 13 letter, there's a note of personal warmth: "Richard and I are continually speaking about you: our prayers are with you and for your intention, at all times."

Then, on October 14, 1965, Pallis sends off a letter announcing a gift that denotes the pinnacle of their friendship:

> Herewith is a small token of my love: this ikon (Greek, probably Macedonian in origin, of the date c. 1700). It came to me in an unexpected way; as soon as this happened, I thought of you. Your *karma* evidently wished you to receive it. Of the four saints in attendance on the Mother of God, one (St. Charalambos) is only known to me by name, perhaps you know him better, otherwise we can find out; St. Nicholas, St. George and St. Demetrius . . . evidently call for no comment. Byzantine painting, which avoided luxurious additions and never sacrificed its essentially contemplative viewpoint to the love of anecdote, seems well-fitted to make its home in a Cistercian setting. May this ikon be to you a support of deepened realisation, according to its purpose.[56]

The ikon of the Virgin (reproduced on page 193) was an exceptional choice for several reasons: it reflected Pallis's own heredity (the Greek Orthodox tradition); it corresponded to Merton's own deep veneration of the Virgin Mary (his prose poem, "Hagia Sophia," was inspired by another ikon of the Virgin painted by

Merton's friend Victor Hammer; Merton had sent a copy of the poem to Lord Northbourne); and the Virgin is also greatly revered in Islam, especially by Schuon, who made many paintings of the Virgin and named the subdivision of the al-'Alawîyyah *tarîqah* that he headed *Maryamiyyah*).[57] When the ikon arrives in December, Merton gives it a special place of honor in the new hermitage he is occupying at Gethsemani: it seems to come—like all such karmic coincidences—just in time to help him celebrate an important new phase in his own spiritual journey. He writes to Pallis immediately:

> Where shall I begin? I have never received such a precious and magnificent gift from anyone in my life. I have no words to express how deeply moved I was to come face to face with this sacred and beautiful presence granted to me in the coming of the ikon to my most unworthy person. At first I could hardly believe it. And yet perhaps your intuition about my karma is right, since in a strange way the ikon of the Holy Mother came as a messenger at a precise moment when a message was needed, and her presence before me has been an incalculable aid in resolving a difficult problem.

> I do not know if I told you I had received permission to move out to a hermitage in the woods. I have been here going on four months, about three and a half to be exact, and the adaptation is proceeding well, but there have been things to be peeled off, contacts and implications in the world, especialy a difficult one I was caught in with the peace movement. . . .

> But . . . let me return to the holy ikon. Certainly it is a perfect act of timeless worship, a great help. I never tire of gazing at it. There is a spiritual presence and reality about it, a true spiritual "Thaboric" light, which seems unaccountably to proceed from the Heart of the Virgin and Child as if they had One heart, and which goes out to the whole universe. It is unutterably splendid. And silent. It imposes a silence on the whole hermitage. . . .

> Thank you, dear friend, for such a generous and noble gift. It will surely remind me often to pray for you and Richard

to go deeper into your own truth as, I hope, I will go deeper into that which is granted to me to live. I see how important it is to live in silence, in isolation, in unknowing. There is an enormous battle with illusion going on everywhere, and how should we not be in it ourselves? [Except that so many religious people, terribly, seem to rush to line themselves up under the flags of illusion itself, against the silence and loneliness where unity is found. Hence all the cries and curses of divided people and parties, even those who claim to seek God divided against each other by stupid slogans.][58]

Pallis seems to have been similarly moved by Merton's response, and in February he writes his most personal letter to Merton, giving details of his own spiritual search and his association with Schuon, as well as the latter's own deep involvement in Islam and the teaching of the Algerian Shaikh al-'Alawî:

I think all I had told you was that he is attached to the Islamic tradition and that his friends avoid mentioning this fact publicly for a number of reasons, one of which is his wish to avoid being regarded as an agent of some kind of religious propaganda or as the propagator of an exotic cult under an Oriental name; this, and kindred reasons have imposed a certain discretion; but in your case, we all feel you should be fully in the know about what M. Schuon stands for, over and above his published writings.[59]

Though many of those associated with Schuon are also Muslims and participants in his Sufi *tarîqah*, Pallis goes on to say, there are also others: "a small number of adherents of other traditions" who continue to strictly and faithfully follow their own religions (including "some Catholics and also some Orthodox, using the 'Prayer of Jesus' as their chief means of concentration"):

I think I have told you enough on the subject to enable you to form some picture of what "Lausanne" represents for us. It also will have explained what your own call into a more intensive life of contemplation has meant to us all here. This is the great need of the Church, indeed of the whole

world, namely a reawakening, be it in a few, of the contemplative spirit: your own allusion to "actionless activity,"
quoting the Taoists, echos what [Schuon] is always telling
us, namely that though we must be able to exercise a
rigourous discernment in regard to happenings in the
world, we must [not] be worried by them or distracted by
them from the pursuit of the "one thing needful."[60] That
"the world" regards that thing as useless, impractical is not
something to be surprised at: "When the worldly man hears
of *Tao* he laughs, it would not be *Tao* if he did not laugh."
When one has reached a certain degree of intellectual
development it is not difficult to understand this, what is
not easy, however, is to live it oneself, without pride on the
one hand and without bitterness on the other.

The letter reverberates with an acknowledgment that an understanding is possible between two separate paths, both heading
toward the same center:"I need not tell you that you are not forgotten here, just as I know that we are not forgotten either; our mutual prayers, from their respective directions, form a cross."

This convergence brings us to the point of departure with which
this essay began: Merton has, in a sense, been invited to participate
in the circle around Schuon—not formally, for both he and they
know this is impossible, given his monastic vows, but informally,
perhaps, in whatever way he can. His next two letters indicate how
seriously he considers attempting such an involvement, at least by
letter. Then comes the missing "conscience matter" letter of early
June, either from Schuon or one of his associates. Merton writes in
his journal on June 16, 1966:

> Another letter, and an important one, came: a message from
> a Moslem Shaikh (Spiritual Master)—actually a European,
> but formed by one of the great Moslem saints and mystics of
> the age (Ahmad al-'Alawî). That I can be accepted in a per-
> sonal and confidential relationship, not exactly as a disciple
> but at any rate as one of those who are entitled to consult
> him directly and personally. This is a matter of great impor-
> tance to me, because in the light of their traditional ideas it
> puts me in contact with the spirit and teaching of Ahmad

al-'Alawî in a way that is inaccessible just to the scholar or the student. It means I have a living place in a living and sacred tradition. It can have tremendous effects. I see that already. Here again, the Shaikh attaches considerable importance to my life in solitude.[61]

Merton appears never to have replied directly to Schuon, and no such consultation, "directly and personally" seems to have occurred—at least not face-to-face, or letter-to-letter. But Merton on March 11, had written even before the formal invitation:

Now that I know more about your group I will feel closer to you and will, of course, keep you in my prayers, relying also on your intercession in my behalf. I am glad you consider me a fellow traveler on the way, and I am happy that the mysterious ways of Providence have brought us together in this capacity. Nor do I doubt that we can all help one another in many simple and effective ways. I am especially grateful for M. Schuon's kind message.[62] I hope you will thank him for me and assure him of my deep respect and friendship, indeed of my reverence now that I know him in a new capacity.[63]

Merton then cleverly shifts the subject slightly to indicate his own dilemma somewhat obliquely (but unmistakably):

I did of course know of [Schuon's] visits to the Indians and his deep interest in them. This is one side of his work that has most impressed me. I regret very much that I cannot have any contact with the Indians myself, here, but it is one of the drawbacks of my particular situation. I realize that there are many things I would like to do which, though very good in themselves, are unfortunately prohibited me here, and I must make the best of that, recognizing and accepting the fact that one cannot try to do everything and that I must work within the sphere which God has placed me.

In solitude I have seen more and more that everything depends on obedience to God's will and the submission of a total and uncompromising faith. This for me at the moment comes down to the full acceptance of and adjustment to the particular situation He has willed for me here. I think that I am learning not to chafe at limitations that could objectively seem quite unreasonable, but which certainly have a purpose in my life. Spiritually I am much more free in the solitary life, but materially the limitations remain. . . .

Near the end of the letter, he returns to the question of contact with Schuon:

One thing I can certainly profit by in my contacts with you and with M. Schuon will be an occasional reminder of the real nature of the work that is expected of me. Needless to say I will always be glad of general hints as to how to go about it better. I realize of course that an authentic spritual guidance is not a matter of letters. Hence I would stress the informality of the situation, believing that precisely this would leave a certain openness for the Holy Spirit to bridge the gap between two distinct traditions. On the other hand it is a wonderful thing to be immediately in contact with Shaikh Ahmad al-'Alawî and I deeply appreciate this.

So even though no formal communication ever seems to have occurred,[64] the link of hearts and minds is clearly growing. As Merton wrote to Pallis on the Vigil of Pentecost (May 28, 1966), before their correspondence comes to a mysterious, or at least apparent, end (and still before the June journal entry):

I do think it is important to enter into contact with a source of guidance like that of Shaikh Ahmad al-'Alawî and this is possible through M. Schuon. I believe this can be done without irresponsible confusions of one tradition with another, and without creating other worse diversions by involvement in a complex new set of practices, observances, techniques and whatnot. I do not know if this represents the right sort of attitude, but I mention it as my attitude now.[65]

The collected correspondence at the Merton Center contains only a few more brief exchanges between Pallis and Merton. On December 10, 1966, the former writes that "in late August and September I was in Lausanne and saw all our chief friends there. I know they too are with you in intention and in prayer."[66] Merton responds in a letter written on Christmas Eve:

> I have not yet written to M. Schuon as I intended. There again, I feel things would be so different if I had only met him personally and spoken to him. As it is, I do not feel it would be anything but artificial for me to write to him about prayer etc. at the moment. Something inside tells one when and when not to move in such instances, and so far I do not have the right impulsion. So it must wait.[67]

There is no reply to this from Pallis in the archived correspondence—only a postcard dated June 21, 1968 (a year and a half later): "Here is the address of my Japanese friend, which was omitted from the air letter posted to you this morning."[68] That letter is missing, as is any note from Merton asking for the addresses (prior to his Asian journey); nor is there any trace of two Pallis letters to Merton mentioned in a letter from Merton to Lord Northbourne in 1967.[69] And, as mentioned earlier, several quotes from "private letters" to Merton from Pallis appear in the notes of Merton's *Asian Journal*, yet none of these letters from Pallis are included in those in the Merton collection at Bellarmine.

Some gaps, some mysteries obviously remain, which is perhaps only appropriate for a correspondence tiptoeing on the edge of secrets.

IV. MERTON CORRESPONDENCE WITH OTHER TRADITIONALISTS

Among Thomas Merton's many other correspondents,[70] there are several others in addition to Marco Pallis with whom he discusses Islam and Sufism: Abdul Aziz from Pakistan; the French Islamic scholar Louis Massignon and his American translator Herbert Mason; the Iranian-born psychiatrist Reza Arasteh; and the Sufi master Sidi Abdeslam, who visits Merton at Gethsemani in 1967.[71] There are also three correspondents with connections to traditionalist ideas: Dona Luisa Coomaraswamy, the widow of Ananda K. Coomaraswamy; and two British associates of Frithjof Schuon, Martin Lings and Lord Northbourne.

Dona Luisa Coomaraswamy writes to Merton in December, 1960, saying she has heard through a mutual friend—Graham Carey, the editor of a journal called *Good Work* to which Merton occasionally contributes—that Merton is interested in her late husband's writings and ideas and might be considering writing an essay about him. She interrupts her own life's work—preparing Coomaraswamy's voluminous writings for publication—to both caution and encourage Merton:

> A. K. Coomaraswamy would object to anything 'personal,' as such, but not if this made possible furthering the understanding of what he wrote, which (was) is not his, but everyman's, yours, and mine. . . . My time is limited, and I must not impose on the work I am responsible to, but I shall be at your disposal in any way I might be able to help, 'for the good of the work to be done.'[72]

Thus begins a fervent dialogue which, for the next nine months, involves not only letters between Merton and Dona Luisa, but also an exchange of books and "offprints" (copies) of articles by Merton and AKC (as Ananda Coomaraswamy is called in the correspondence). Dona Luisa is obviously testing Merton's mettle; she also writes to Graham Carey and another friend and traditionalist scholar, Alvin Moore, to ask their opinions of whether Merton should write about her husband or (as Merton later proposes) publish a limited edition of aphorisms by Coomaraswamy. Both seem to give their blessing, Carey because of his prior knowledge of Merton's own writings and Moore after reading correspondence from Merton forwarded to him by Dona Luisa.[73] When Merton fails to produce the suggested essay or collection of aphorisms, the correspondence trails off politely—sadly so, considering the richness of the existing dialogue.

The letters that the two do exchange reveal Dona Luisa to be, like her exceptionally erudite husband, a scholar and thinker of extraordinary depth. She often challenges Merton to consider questions more thoroughly (very much a traditionalist attitutude) and to reject easy answers and the simplistic reasoning of his contemporaries on spiritual and social issues. Like her late husband, she is also a great lover of language: her letters contain a delightful sense of word-play that stretches conventional meaning and "definition" to insistently explore new territories. Her writing style is full of ellipses and dashes—emblematic perhaps of a mind that doesn't just race, but gallops, from subject to subject, but does so with an ease and a clarity and control that never hint of superficiality.

Perhaps Dona Luisa's allusive letters are too taxing for Merton (or most of us) to follow, like some of the complexities in the writings of Schuon mentioned earlier (and indeed in Ananda Coomarawamy's own demanding works). In her first letter, Dona Luisa, for example, adds somewhat casually:

> Mr. Carey's work on the Four Causes, which Dr. Coomaraswamy thought so very important, was given to an earlier generation—the validity of the subject has not become less, but more important than before . . . what about *you* taking up the issue of understanding Christianity beyond a two-dimensional point of view . . . i.e., the 3rd and 4th (now utterly brushed aside), the allegorical and the Anagogical. Without the 4th cause the 1st is emptied of any meaning! Do let me hear from you.[74]

Merton does indeed respond promptly, but not about allegory, anagogical interpretation, or the Four Causes—allusions which he may or may not have understood. He does mention that among the many offprints he has received from Carey, there was one by AKC "on Kingship, but it was too much for me, I mean there was just too much new material."[75] Instead he expresses, in his own rather down-to-earth style, what his reading of Coomaraswamy has meant to him:

> Ananda Coomaraswamy is in many ways to me a model: the model of one who has thoroughly and completely united in himself the spiritual tradition and attitudes of the Orient and of the Christian West, not excluding also something of Islam I believe. This kind of comprehension is, it seems to me, quite obligatory for the contemplative of our day, at least if he is in any sense also a scholar. I believe that the only really valid thing that can be accomplished in the direction of world peace and unity at the moment is the preparation of the way by the formation of men who, isolated, perhaps not accepted or understood by any "movement," are able to unite in themselves and experience in their own lives all that is best and most true in the various great spiritual traditions. Such men can become as it were "sacraments" or signs of

peace, at least. They can do much to open up the minds of their contemporaries to receive, in the future, new seeds of thought. Our task is one of very remote preparation, a kind of arduous and unthanked pioneering.[76]

Merton hopes to write on Coomaraswamy's ideas as part of such a process and asks Dona Luisa's suggestions about which works, published or unpublished, would be most appropriate:

I will meditate long and happily in silence upon these things, and enrich my life with the symbols, the "mysteries and sacraments" in which he has shown us so many manifestations of God in His world. It is not that I want to write about AKC but rather that I want to enter contemplatively into the world of thought which, as you so rightly say, is for all of us, is not any private property of his, but which nevertheless had to be opened to us by him.[77]

Dona Luisa is a bit cool—or perhaps simply proper and restrained, as befits her aristocratic Argentine Jewish background—to Merton's somewhat effusive enthusiasm: "Forgive me, I do not want to sound authoritative, but I must comment: world peace and unity, *from you*, sounds so Utopian," then adds "'Movements' are usually 'legion,' and you know what that leads to—like good intentions."[78] She admits "the Kingship book is very heavy going"[79] but adds that Merton really should make the effort anyway, no matter how considerable, to understand it: "It is a must for you."

The major portion of her letter, however, evokes a profusion of new (and very old) spiritual ideas, which Merton seems to find fascinating, if a bit daunting (here expressed in Dona Luisa's own very individual "typographic" style):

I have talked with Graham about the need of the equivalent of a sûfî order in Xtianity . . . there comes a time (and this of itSelf) when only the very top-values survive, and these are the same in every tradition, in their diverse dialects; all of them to greater glory of God! There are no exclusions—where man is and God IS—and this applies to the so-called 'barbarians in the remotest parts of the world.' You know this very well, I repeat only as a reminder. There is no monopoly on MONOtheism, never was—can you imagine God objecting, in any way whatever, to what Names He is called! Or what forms one worships Him in! Let us not attribute to HIM our shortcomings.

Levels of reference do exist, and 'bigotry' has its place, and serves a great purpose. Under-the-sun all possiblities have their particular sphere, and these are *what they are*, in order that they may (if they will) work themselves out from one place to another. The *way* is multiple, 'He is multiple, as He is in us, at the same time, He is Unity, as He is in Himself.' Many are called, few are ready, and even of these, fewer are chosen. . . .

Each being must become a "sacrament," in his own tradition. "When God is the teacher all men think alike." What use are other traditions? Great use—when one has bogged down in 'words,' which have lost the reflection of the *Logos* [the Divine Word], as in our present plight, not alone in Xtianity, but in Islam, Hinduism, Jewdaism, etc. etc. . . . *we have to go to that tradition* which has suffered the least 'change.'. . .

To each is given a *sûtra*, a thread, and that is his *tread* (even trade) which is most suit-able to his nature, in his own given life-time.[80]

Two days later, before Merton has time to receive this second letter from her, Dona Luisa sends an addendum, clarifying a description she had sent in the former letter about traditional Jewish prayers and the times of the day in which they are offered (all in response to a somewhat innocent reference by Merton in his first letter about the joys of "saying Mass just at sunrise"). In this P.S., Dona Luisa adds an anecdote that she recalls from memory about her husband and a French correspondent who had written to tell Coomaraswamy, "I have read everything of yours that I could put my hands on, and I am still a Catholic," to which Coomaraswamy replied: "Grateful no end to know this, I should have been embarrassed and deeply disappointed if anything I ever wrote had done otherwise. It is my trust and hope that my writing will make me more what I am, and the reader, what he is, truly."[81]

Merton writes back on February 12, thanking Dona Luisa for her "Two very rich and stimulating letters. So many wonderful openings for new thought, study, and meditation." He is especially intrigued by her reference to Sufism:

> You are right about the Sufis and about the need for Christian equivalents of the Sufis. This kind of need is not something that man thinks up and then takes care of. It is a question of God's honor and glory and of His will. Men do not choose to be Sufis, least of all Christian Sufis so to speak: they are chosen and plunged into the crucible like iron into the fire. I do not know if I have been so chosen but I am familiar enough with the crucible, and I live under the sign of contradiction. Would that I might live so gently, nonviolently, firmly, in all humility and meekness, but not betraying the truth.

> But there is certainly a great need of an interior revival of truth, religious truth. There are everywhere movements which more and more seem to be simply evasions. Collective evasions, with an enormous amount of publicity and false front, with great numbers of speeches and conferences and publications and no one knows what else. And little or no interior fruit, simply a multiplication of addicts and proselytes. Like you, I hate proselytizing. This awful business of making others just like oneself so that one is thereby "justified" and under no obligation to change himself. What a terrible thing this can be. The source of how many sicknesses in the world. [82]

Dona Luisa writes back rather warmly, but zeroes in on one phrase in Merton's response, his reference to living "in all humility and meekness." After stating she finds no such attitude of "humility or meekness" in most standard traditional texts (especially not in the great Hindu heroic epics), she pens in a suggestion (the rest of the letter is typewritten): "Equipoised—not 'umble." Again she simultaneously apologizes for this: "I do not mean to sound off—but this is the only way I know how to speak or write, after 35 years with my nose to this special grind-stone." However, she then goes on to agree wholeheartedly with Merton that there is no difference between art and craft:[83] "Of course there is no distinction between art and craftsmanship . . . but that which the merchants make . . . and this includes the "dealers," in the museums . . . gracious, but they have pulled the wool over our eyes . . ."[84] She then adds another Sufi anecdote:

> One of the old sufis was thought to be stupid by his companions . . . no one would talk to him; but he wanted to share his joy; he had a goat, he tied a cord to its neck and when he was delighted by a word or thought he would pull this cord and the goal would bleat, "bah." In Arabic, "bah" means "yes"!

To this Dona Luisa adds, in reference to Merton's mentioned correspondence with Louis Massingnon, "You should read [Rûmî's] Mathnawi, not Massignon—always the sources, not the sorcerers."

In March, Merton writes again to ask her opinion about his selecting a small collection of her husband's "sayings and aphorisms" to be printed by his friend Victor Hammer (a Swiss-born painter, fine printer, and type designer who is very much an artist and craftsman in the traditionalist vein himself, though not associated with any school). Dona Luisa doesn't immediately respond, but sends Merton a copy of a typescript of an article by her husband entitled "On Being in One's Own Right Mind"—a key traditionalist document—which Merton finds "really fundamental, one of AKC's very best."[85]

Merton writes again in August and September, querying Dona Luisa about the aphorisms project, which he now suggests might be printed by one of his regular publishers, New Directions, instead of by Hammer, if she prefers. In the end, the project never bears fruit, and in December 1963 (some two years later), Merton sends a final letter to Dona Luisa:

> It is a shame that I have not had a chance to do the work on [Coomaraswamy] that I was hoping to do. But one must be realistic and take one thing at a time, and there is always something closer at hand. I do hope, however, that I will always work with something of his spirit. I often think of you and whenever I have a chance to reread something of his it gives me joy, light and peace. I do hope that more of

his great work will be available in print as time goes on. One of his very best things is . . . "On Being in One's Right Mind" and this has always made a deep impression on me, and I am thankful for it.[86]

The correspondence thus terminates. But in the traditional world it is held that, with the right intention, nothing is ever really lost or wasted.

Starting in the spring of 1965, Merton also exchanges several letters with two fellow writers who are close associates of Schuon—Lord Northbourne and Martin Lings. He writes to Lord Northbourne after reading a copy of his *Religion in the Modern World* which had been sent to him by Marco Pallis. Merton thanks Northbourne for having Pallis send the book, which he indicates he has read slowly and carefully and finds "quite salutary and helpful." He goes on to explain:

> It has helped me to organize my ideas at a time when we in the Catholic Church, and in the monastic Orders, are being pulled this way and that. Traditions of great importance and vitality are being questioned along with more trivial customs, and I do not think that those who are doing the questioning are always distinguished for their wisdom or even their information. . . . In particular, I am grateful for your last chapter. For one thing it clears up a doubt that has persisted in my mind, about the thinking of the Schuon-Guénon "school" (if one can use such a term), as well as about the rather slapdash ecumenism that is springing up in some quarters. It is most important first of all to understand deeply and live one's own tradition, not confusing it with what is foreign to it, if one is to seriously appreciate other traditions and distinguish in them what is close to one's own and what is, perhaps, irreconcilable with one's own. The great danger at the moment is a huge muddling and confusing of the spiritual traditions that still survive. As you so well point out, this would be crowning the devil's work.[87]

In regard to his own church, Merton exhibits a definite discomfort with the Vatican II *Gaudium et Spes* "Constitution on the Church in the Modern World" document: "I am disturbed by both those who are termed conservative and some who are called liberal in the Council. . . . I am afraid that on both sides too superficial a view of 'the world' is being taken—whether that view be optimistic or pessimistic. I don't think that the implications of the technological revolution have even begun to be grasped by either side." He goes on:

> Then there is the unfortunate fact that Catholic tradition has become in many ways ambiguous and confused. Not in itself, but in the way in which it is regarded by Catholics. Since people have got into the unfortunate habit of thinking of tradition as a specialized department of theology and since spiritual disciplines have undergone considerable shrinking and drying out by being too legalized, and since the traditional styles of life, worship, and so on have become, for us, merely courtly and baroque to such a great extent, the question of renewal does become urgent.[88]

Merton encloses a copy of his response to the Vatican Council's document, an essay entitled "The Church and the 'Godless' World,"[89] as well as a collection of his poetry, calling Lord Northbourne's attention especially to the prose poem, "Hagia Sophia."

Lord Northbourne answers with a letter and a copy of the journal *Tomorrow*—the same publication Pallis had called Merton's attention to in his first letter to him in the summer of 1963. Merton notes the magazine's "attractive new format"[90] and mentions Lord Northbourne's article on the symbolism and deeper significance of flowers: "The purely utilitarian explanation of the attractiveness of flowers is always annoying, it is so superficial."[91] Merton is no doubt intrigued by the way the article takes a subject distinctly removed from religion or philosophy yet discusses it from a traditional viewpoint. From that article by Lord Northbourne:

> Everyone knows, or thinks he knows, what a flower is: but not until a hundred or so years ago had the modern scientific point of view been applied to flowers, as to everything else. . . . This point of view in fact takes account of nothing but the immediate and tangible advantage, "economic"

in the broad sense of the word, of the individual or the race [of the flower]; it could therefore be described as purely utilitarian. . . . According to this view there exist only blind forces acting upon elementary particles, the resulting associations and dissociations of which constitute the universe and all that it contains. Thus all our experience, all our aspirations, every concepton of beauty or goodness or greatness or any kind of purpose, and of course any kind of theistic conception, while not necessarily neglible to us as human beings, can have no ultimate significance whatever. This is the philosophy of despair.[92]

The real significance of flowers cannot be reduced to such functional or evolutionary expediency, of course:

The attractiveness of flowers to insects bears little relationship to their brilliance or size. . . . In short, the colours and forms of uncultivated flowers cannot be accounted for by any theory that confines the attention to the functional or utilitarian aspect. Let us then assume without more ado that the beauty and fragrance of flowers is not an accident nor yet is it manifested for the exclusive and tangible benefit either of the plants themselves or of man.

In his next letter, Lord Northbourne continues his attack on "humanism" as the same sort of thinking that reduces flowers (and all beauty or truth, which they represent) to the level of materialism:

We live in a "Godless" world . . . [which] substitutes a manmade ideology for revealed religion and its crystallizations, or more simply to the extent that it substitutes humanism for religion. . . . The distinction between the Christian humanism advocated by the Council and the various other brands of humanism is much too subtle to be grasped by a vast majority of those who take interest in the matter at all. . . . I wonder if humanism is not always humanism, whatever its label.[93]

Merton appears to not quite accept Lord Northbourne's distrust of Christian humanism and attempts to clarify his own feelings on the subject in his next letter, referring especially to the Church's work at rectifying the "dreadful destitution" that resulted from the

Western world's displacement of ancient tribal cultures in South
America, Africa, and Asia:

> I see nothing wrong with the Council demanding work for
> a "better world" in this sense. It is not a question of com-
> fort, but of the basic necessities of life and decency. In this
> respect, "humanism" is a matter of simple respect for man
> as man, and Christian humanism is based on the belief in
> the Incarnation and on a relationship to others which
> supposed that "whatsoever you do to the least of my
> brethren you do it to me" (i.e., to Christ). Here I have no
> difficulty. Except of course in the way in which some of
> this might be interpreted or applied. Literacy is not a
> cure-all, and there are plenty of absurd modern social
> myths. Nevertheless, there are realities that must be faced
> in the terms of our actual possibilities, and return to the
> ancient cultures is simply not possible. Though we should
> certainly try to see that their values are preserved insofar
> as they can be.[94]

Earlier in the letter Merton broaches the same dilemma of the corruption of traditional cultures and values by technological "progress":

> Much as we appeciate the great value of ancient and tradi-
> tional cultures, the coming of the industrial and technolog-
> ical revolution has undermined them and in fact doomed
> them. Everywhere in the world these cultures have now
> been more or less affected—corrupted—by modern Western
> man and his rather unfortunate systems. It is simply not pos-
> sible to return to the cultural stability and harmony of these
> ancient structures. But it is hoped that one can maintain
> some sort of continuity and preserve at least some of their
> living reality in a new kind of society. For my part I am
> frankly dubious: I foresee a rather pitiful bastardized culture,
> vulgarized, uniform, and full of elements of parody and car-
> icature, and perhaps frightening new developments of its
> own which may be in a certain way "interesting" and even
> exciting. And terrible. The Council assumes that we just go
> on peacefully progressing and reasonably negotiating obsta-
> cles, making life more and more "human."[95]

The dilemma is one which Merton also has verified personally, in his own day-to-day spiritual struggle between social responsibility and spiritual need:

> Stated in the baldest terms, in my own situation, I meet the problems daily in this form: I can completely turn my back on the whole "world" and simply try to devote myself to meditations and contemplation, silence, withdrawal, renunciation, and so on. I spent at least twelve years of my monastic life with no further object than this. At the end of the time I began to see that this was insufficient and indeed deceptive. It was unreal. . . . I still devote most of my time to meditation, contemplation, reading—in fact I now give more of my time to these things since I am living in solitude: but I also read a great deal more about what is happening and the common problems of the world I live in, not so much on the level of newspapers (I do not get the paper) or of magazines, still less radio or TV (I have barely seen TV once or twice in my life). But I do feel that if I am not in some way able to identify myself with my contemporaries and if I isolate myself so entirely from them that I imagine I am a different kind of being, I am simply perpetrating a kind of religious fraud.

In the last paragraph of the letter, Merton draws the conclusion that his approach and that which Lord Northbourne has been advocating may not be so differerent after all:

> Thus you see that in the end we do meet, though I think there are genuine accidental differences in our viewpoints. I think you are simply more straightforwardly conservative than I am and that for you the conservative position does not present the difficulties that it does for me. You are fortunate, because your position is thus much simpler than mine can be.

Lord Northbourne writes back assuring Merton of a certain sympathy for his dilemma: "You cannot give yourself to man in charity unless you have first given yourself to God. If you try to do so, your gift will be valueless; it will be giving a stone for bread, or worse, giving for a fish a serpent." Merton clearly has understood and lived that lesson, his correspondent acknowledges, though Northbourne still hectors him a bit on the subject of Christian humanism:

> Scientific humanism parodies Christian charity by substituting terrestrial welfare for salvation. Hitherto the Roman Catholic Church has been the arch-opponent of this heresy, she has not only put first things first, but has also appeared to do so. If she ceases to maintain an uncompromising position in this respect, what may not the end be? Quis custodiet ipsos custodes? [Who will watch over the watch-dogs themselves?]

He objects mildly to Merton's reference to the conservative position being a kind of easy way out: "I did not begin to see things as I do now till nearly 50 (I am now 70). . . . I was thoroughly involved in the affairs of a hereditary landowner and farmer, and have been since." To Lord Northbourne the shift in point of view is not to political or social conservatism, but to something deeper and more profound.

On Easter Monday, 1965, another of the British traditionalists, Martin Lings, initiates a brief correspondence with Merton by sending him his new book, *Ancient Beliefs and Modern Superstitions*, along with a short note asking Merton to review it. "This is a very little book," Lings writes, "but I pray it may serve some people as an introduction." Lings then adds, "Marco Pallis, who gave me your address, asked me to ask you if your review of *Comprendre l'Islam* had been published yet?"[96]

Merton responds with some insights into the difficulties he has been having in publishing reviews on books about Sufism in Catholic journals (see section V below for further details):

> Your new book reached me this morning, and I must say it looks extremely interesting. I am not perfectly sure the review of our Order [*Collectanea Cisterciensia*] will want me to review it, this will depend on how germane it is to monasticism. But I think they probably will. On the other hand I have not yet done my review of Schuon's book on Islam. I have a small pile of books on Sufism etc. building up and will probably do them all at once later on.

I must admit that in the review of our Order, still very conservative in a stuffy sense, and slowly evolving to a more open position, it is still quite difficult to know how to handle a review of a book like Schuon's, with which one is in the greatest sympathy. Yet I would still be expected by the censorious to point out small matters that would perhaps call for "criticism" from a strictly Catholic point of view, and to my mind this is not at all worth doing. Quite the contrary. Thus I, who am in any case no professional in dogmatic theology, find myself hesistant. I think that in a little while this will have cleared up sufficiently for me to go ahead without scruple. But not yet.[97]

Merton then moves on to discussing his great appreciation of Lings' earlier book, on the life and teachings of Ahmad al-'Alawî:

On the other hand I was able to give what I felt was a very enthusiastic review to your admirable book on Ahmad al-'Alawî. I am glad of this opportunity to express my thanks. The book was an inspiration to me and I often think of this great man with veneration. He was so perfectly right in his spirituality. Certainly a great saint and a man full of the Holy Spirit. May God be praised for having given us one such, in a time when we need many saints. I hope that in a few days I will have some offprints and will send you a couple.

Meanwhile I am very happy to be in contact with you, as I am with Marco Pallis, whose books have also been a great inspiration to me. I am most indebted to him for sending good books my way, and am in the middle of his translation of Guénon's *Crisis*, which is first-rate. Contact with your "school of thought," shall I say, is of great help to me in rectifying my own perspectives in this time when among Catholics one is faced with a choice between an absurdly rigid and baroque conservativism and a rather irresponsible and fantastic progressivism à la Teilhard. The choice is of course not so restricted, and I am glad of influences that help me to cling, as my heart tells me to, to a sane and living traditionalism in full contact with the living contemplative experience of the past—and with the presence of the Spirit here and now.

When Merton sends the review, Lings responds: "Thank you very much for sending me the review . . . *and also for writing it.* I hope some will take note of the question you put in the last paragraph."[98] He then adds, "I was interested also to see your review of S. Hossein Nasr's book which I also have reviewed. By the way, he is Persian, not Egyptian." Lings also defends the Islamic scholar A. J. Arberry (whom Merton has somewhat dismissed in the review), implying that Arberry may have a more correct attitude toward Sufism than Merton and some others had assumed: "I have always had the impression that he is more and more inclined to look on Sufism as purely Quranic"—i.e., the belief of all Sufis that Sufism, far from being the spin-off or "invented" afterthought that some of its critics maintain, is instead rooted directly in the Divine revelation of the Qur'an, the holy scripture central to all of Islam.

Merton thanks Lings for pointing out his mistake about Nasr: "Do please feel free to advise me and correct errors I may make, and also to send my way anything that will help me get a better understanding of Sufism."[99] Regarding *Ancient Beliefs and Modern Superstitions* (which he is still unsure he will be able to review), he adds:

> Did I give you my final impressions of your own book? I am very much in agreement with you. It is most important to make these points, even though they will not gain a popular hearing. The complacency of modern man makes it impossible for him to conceive that he is in fact dominated by myths as crude and cruder than those which he believes were accepted by primitive man.

Though no review of the new Lings book was forthcoming, Merton lets its author know in that subtle last sentence that he has grasped the scope of the message contained in the book and its title: such confirmation may, indeed, be the best review for which any author can hope.

V. Miscellaneous References in the Merton Collection

The Thomas Merton Center at Bellarmine College in Louisville, Kentucky, houses a true treasure trove of material by and about Merton, revealing the Trappist monk from Gethsemani (some fifty

miles south of Louisville) to have been one of the most prolific writers and thinkers of modern times. Contained there are not only
Merton's many published articles and books (and a multitude of
books and articles about him by others), but also his massive correspondence (he wrote over 3500 letters to some 1000 different
correspondents) and many of the correspondents' responses; his personal journals; his reading notebooks (a kind of multi-volume
commonplace book of quotes and thoughts he jotted down as he
read); and his own library of books, magazines, and offprints
(copies) of the articles and essays of others, some with marginalia,
underlinings, and other notations indicating his responses as he
read the works in question. Exploring these materials, one is struck
most particularly by the scope of Merton's interests: At the same
time that he was reading Reza Arasteh on Rûmî and Sufi psychology, he was also taking notes on Roderick Nash's *Wilderness and the
American Mind*, Ronald Segal's *The Race War*, and I. C. Jarvie's
Revolution in Anthropology, and trying to clarify his thoughts about
the war in Vietnam. At another time, he ricochets back and forth
from notes on Sufism for his series of lectures to the monks at
Gethsemani to readings of theologian Karl Rahner and thoughts
about the character Dilsey in William Faulkner's novel *The Sound
and the Fury*. To say that Merton was, by design, a generalist rather
than a specialist, or that his range of thought has more breadth than
depth, is by no means a derogatory assessment. There is only so
much time in life, as he frequently reminded his correspondents,
and within that time frame, he chose to explore and connect the
many rather than to focus exclusively on the few.

This in no way implies that he was sloppy or casual in his thinking or his writing (though he did occasionally make mistakes both
of fact and interpretation, as he was the first to admit) or that he was
a dilettante pretending to discuss things he did not understand
(whenever the discussion got too deep for him, he usually bowed out
politely, as in his correspondence with Dona Luisa Coomaraswamy).

One can see much about the clear arc of his thinking in Merton's
handwriting, which is controlled, legible, and steady, even in the
presumed rush (or what would be that for many of us) of copying
down favorite quotes in his reading notebooks. In spite of his apol-
ogy to Marco Pallis cited at the beginning of this essay ("I do not

type well, but my writing is worse"), his correspondence, journals, and notebooks all prove, on the contrary, that Merton was a man very much in control of his hands, whether on the keyboard or holding a pen: there are few strikeovers, few cross-outs or omissions, few misspellings or grammatical errors. Here was a man who wrote eloquently, well, and precisely, even when he was writing quickly and for himself alone. At the same time, the handwriting is economical, without flourish or pretense, but avoiding abbreviations and other shorthand shortcuts many writers make when their minds are trying to gallop faster than their pens.

Though he admired scholars such as Massignon, Coomaraswamy, and Schuon, Merton never presumed to be the kind of scholar, thinker, or writer that they were. As he says in his June 20, 1965, letter to Martin Lings: "Actually, I need badly such advice as yours. I am really quite lost in the field of Islamic studies, since obviously I have only the most superficial acquaintance with the field, and it is really rather presumptuous of me to undertake to review books in it for the magazine of the Order. There was another really silly mistake in my review: I confused Ibn Arabî with Ibn Abbad ar Rundi [Ibn 'Abbâd de Ronda]."[100]

Merton did, however, expect his editors to clean up his style before publication. He wrote to Charles Dumont, his editor at *Collectanea Cisterciensia*: "You will have the usual job of correcting my mistakes in French and perhaps typing it up so that it is fit for a printer."[101] Marco Pallis, who once complained to Merton about the misprints in *Seeds of Destruction* "as if the printing had been too much rushed,"[102] would probably have been horrified at what Merton wrote two years later to Father Benjamin Clark, one of the censors of the Cistercian Order who had just read one of Merton's manuscripts: "Yes, you are right that the publisher takes care of style, spelling and all those details."[103]

Here one cannot hope to more than touch on the amount of material about Sufism and traditionalist thought in these miscellaneous writings and readings of Merton. But four areas should be noted as confirmation of Merton's abiding interest in this very fertile field of spiritual understanding: (1) his reviews of Sufi and traditional books for *Collectanea Cisterciensia*; (2) references in his published private journals; (3) selected nuggets of wisdom from the reading notebooks; and (4) marginalia or highlighted passages from books in his personal library.

(1) **The Reviews:** Merton wrote eight short reviews of books about Sufism for the French-language publication *Collectanea Cisterciensia*. These were intended to be grouped together, in two separate issues, under the heading "Moines et Spirituels Non Chrétiens" (Non-Christian Monks and Religous). Only the first four appeared; the second set of four were set in type (there are paged galleys in the Merton Center archives), but were cut from the issue at the last minute, being replaced by other Merton reviews on books about Zen. Appearing in volume 27 (1965) were Merton's reviews of Martin Lings' *A Moslem Saint of the Twentieth Century*, Seyyed Hossein Nasr's *Three Muslim Sages*, Fritz Meier's "The Transformation of Man in Mystical Islam," and Rabindranath Tagore's translation of *One Hundred Poems by Kabir* (the Indian writer who was both a Hindu and a Sufi). Scheduled for volume 29 (1967), but never appearing in print, were reviews of Reza Arasteh's *Final Integration in the Adult Personality* (of which Merton also wrote a long review, in English, for *Monastic Studies*, Volume 6, 1968), Paul Nwyia's *Ibn Abbad de Ronda*, Dom Jean Leclerq's essay "Le Monachism en Islam et Chrétienté," and Cyprian Rice's *The Persian Sufis*.[104]

The history of how Merton came to write the reviews for *Collectanea*—and the difficulties involved—is rather curious, as revealed in the correspondence between Merton and the magazine's editor, Father Charles Dumont. The latter first wrote to Merton, a regular contributor, in April of 1964, suggesting that he might send him something on "'pagan' monasticism—Hindu, Buddhist, Sufi, etc."[105] Merton responded immediately: "I will gladly take responsibility for bulletins in the fields of Hinduism, Buddhism, Sufism, etc."[106] —which unfortunately was not *exactly* what Dumont had requested, i.e., he had not asked him to focus on the religions in general, but on monastic orders within those religions. This misunderstanding leads to much difficulty in the ensuing correspondence.

Merton sends the first review, on Kabir, in June: "You will note . . . that I have been suitably cautious in excising references to 'mysticism' etc. etc."[107] Evidently there were clear ground rules to be observed in this subject area (though the published reviews are full of such references).

Another note of caution comes from Dumont in November: "As regard to Anglican and non-Christian monasticism, either they should have some bearing on monasticism, and then I should think they can easily find a place in the *Bulletin*, under these headings, or they should not be mentioned at all."[108] Merton replies:

> Here is the problem about the non-Christian material I have been doing as "chronique" material. First of all very little of the Islamic or Oriental stuff is really monastic. It is hard to say whether the spiritual movements of Islam are monastic, and the book on Hallâj [by Massignon], or Schuon's book, how shall we regard them? Monastic? I think not.The thing is that such books need a chronique of their own, or else they should be treated as ordinary reviews, but neither of them will qualify for the monastic chronique. I don't know what you will decide to do with the material you now have, but I think we should decide whether in the future this material should have its own chronique, be treated as a "review," or just simply be dropped.[109]

Dumont latches on the final phrase and seems to think the matter is settled: "As regards non-Christian spirituality, I think that the bulletin must keep to monasticism, and for the rest of this field we must leave it to more specialized reviews. Thank you for your clearcut advice."[110] But Merton seems not to have intended Dumont to take him literally about dropping the idea, for he writes in February:

> I have Schuon on Islam and the book on Hallâj, both of which I have been waiting to read, not certain whether you would be expecting a "chronique" on them. Can we decide more or less definitely one way or the other whether I should produce a chronique on non-Christian spiritualities for this year? If so I will gladly go ahead with it, and I have some interesting material which is close to monasticism, even though as the Koran or rather some Hadith asserts, "There is no monasticism in Islam."[111]

After that Merton seems simply to have sent in the reviews, and Dumont printed the first set (though the Lings, Nasr, and Kabir books do not deal specifically with monasticism) but did not, in the end, print the second set. There is no existing correspondence explaining why the four reviews in the second set were not published. Perhaps, indeed, there was simply a lack of space in the issue and Merton himself may have been involved in the decision to run the Zen reviews rather than those dealing with Sufi titles.

There is, however, one curious note in a letter from Merton to Dumont in May, 1966, apparently in response to a query from Dumont about the status of the review of Schuon's *Comprendre d'Islam* (despite the fact that the earlier correpondence implies Dumont was not interested in having it reviewed): "I read F. Schuon's book on Islam but so long ago I have forgotten it and never wrote the review. If you absolutely insist. . . ."[112] Why Merton would say such a thing is puzzling, considering all the history of correspondence on the subject with Lings and Pallis: he is certainly unlikely to "forget" something he invested so much effort in understanding. Only one explanation seems to make a certain amount of sense: This letter to Dumont comes three months after Pallis wrote to Merton giving him new details of Schuon's teaching, and the school or *tarîqah* which he heads. During this period, as his letters indicate, Merton is agonizing over whether he should write to Schuon personally, and he eventually decides against doing so. The prospect of "criticizing" Schuon and his thinking at this juncture is probably not something Merton wants or feels prepared to do: thus, perhaps, a white lie to Dumont is the easiest way out.

(2) **From the Journals:** Merton's journals reveal the private and personal side of his thinking: one of Merton's great gifts, in fact, was his ability to counterbalance the personal and meditative aspect of his life (and writing) with his more theoretical or analytical side (as in his essay "Rain and the Rhinoceros," mentioned above).

One such subjective response to objective thinking comes in his journal entry for May 2, 1961, after he has just read another important traditionalist text, Titus Burckhardt's *An Introduction to Sufi Doctrine*, focusing on the crystalline clarity of Burckhardt's thought:

> Abdul Aziz has sent some books on Islam, including first of all a powerful and concise little volume on Sufism by one Titus Burckhardt, of whom I had not yet heard. Certainly the very finest thing on the subject I have yet touched, marked with a hardness (solidity) and sureness one rarely

finds in western studies of oriental mysticism. . . . This is for me only a first reading of the Burckhardt, which I will go over again more intently. Here's a frankly intellectual mysticism—with real roots. The Truth Itself smashing vanity: and with no separation of knowledge and love.[113]

Two-and-a-half years later, Merton encounters a book by another traditionalist writer (Martin Lings) and another account of Sufi mysticism "with real roots":

Yesterday afternoon I finished a remarkable book—the biography of Shaikh Ahmad al-'Alawî, who died in Algeria in 1934. One of the greatest religious figures of this century, a perfect example of the Sufi tradition in all its fullness and energy. This is one book that I want to read again. The excerpts from his writings are most impressive and I know I have not begun to appreciate their content.[114]

Two days later, the journal contains one of Merton's first reactions (and not a wholly positive one) to the writings of Schuon (one should keep in mind that this is rather early in Merton's reading of Schuon, in 1963):

Two minds more different than those of Karl Barth and Frithjof Schuon would be hard to imagine, yet I am reading them both. Barth with his insistence on "God in the highest" completely unattainable by any human tradition, and Schuon with his *philosophia perennis* (I am reading his excellent book on Islam). True, Barth is a greater mind and there is an austere beauty in his Evangelical absolutism (closer to Islam than one would think!!) but there is another side to him—his love of St. Anselm and of Mozart.

Schuon naturally oversimplifies his "contrast" between Islam and Christianity. One has to know what he's really doing! I wrote this morning to Marco Pallis (who sent the Schuon book) about his *Way and the Mountain* (the other night I dreamed about the way).[115]

That November the journals contain the following reflection:

Technology. No! When it comes to taking sides, I am not with the *beati* [blessed ones] who are open-mouthed in awe at the "new holiness" of a technological cosmos in which man condescends to be God's collaborator, and improve everything for Him. Not that technology is per se impious. It is simply neutral and there is no greater nonsense than taking it for an ultimate value. It is *there*, and our love and compassion for other men is now framed and scaffolded by it. Then what? We gain nothing by surrendering to technolgy as if it were a ritual, a worship, a liturgy (or talking of our liturgy as if it were an expression of the "sacred" supposedly now revealed in techological power). Where impiety is in the hypostatizing of mechanical power as something to do with the Incarnation, as its fulfillment, its epiphany. When it comes to taking sides I am with Ellul [116] and Massignon (not with the Teilhardians).[117]

In June, 1966, Merton's journals recount his having received the "conscience matter" letter from Frithjof Schuon or one of his representatives mentioned earlier. Though Merton does not avail himself of this offer to be in direct touch with Schuon, his contacts with Sufi thought continue until the end of his life, right up to plans for a month-long visit with Seyyed Hossein Nasr in Iran after his journey to Southeast Asia.[118]

Merton's next contact comes in October of 1966, when the Moroccan Sidi Abdeslam, a Sufi teacher from a different branch of the al-'Alawî order, visits Gethsemani.[119] Merton describes the visit in vivid detail in his journal:

> This weekend—momentous visit of Sidi Abdesalam [*sic*],[120] from Algeria. He came with Bernard Phillips from Temple U[niversity] and a disciple (Sidi Hadji) and the latter's wife who translated, as Sidi A. speaks only Arabic.
>
> I can't begin to put down everything, I was so moved by the visit. This is a true man of God, also a man of an ancient and very living (Arabic) culture, and authentic representation of the best in Islam etc. etc. (all that one says sounds stupid—cannot touch the reality). His simplicity, humaneness, directness, friendliness, generosity, warmth etc. . . .
>
> He said I am very close to mystical union and the slightest thing now can so to speak push me over the edge. . . . Sense

of strong bond of friendship between us—I mean him and myself. "Sacramental" quality of simple friendship in our group, 5 of us, sitting in the grass on top of St. Joseph's hill. A real experience of Sufism. I now see exactly what it is all about. Close to monastic spirit. Very close indeed in simplicity, spontaneity, joy, truth. . . . Above all, importance of knowing and following the voice of one's own heart, one's own secret: God in us. Deepening contact with source. Through a friend etc. who understands. Certainly this visit had that effect. A deepening, a clearing of the wells.[121]

The following February, writing about William Faulkner, Merton may be echoing a dilemma he himself is facing at this critical juncture of his life (one that Sufis might describe as the struggle with the *nafs*, or the lower, egotistical self): "The business of taking sides, standing up and being counted, being on the right side—the temptation one has to face above all in his fifties, when he realizes he is on the way out, and tries dishonestly and desperately to *stay*: to leave behind permanent and noble declarations, to prove he was really there."[122] Then, two days later, a reminder, this time clearly of Merton's own *nafs*:

A letter came from Sidi Abdesalam. "Where are you?" Hoping I am not bogged down in words, my own and those of others. What is best is what is not said. True, my meditation is still slack, but I do not want to grip a futility and tighten on something merely imagined, arbitrarily decided. I do still wait, and listen, try for a more total awareness, more simple, and *no phoney absorption*.

The worst thing is, however, this preoccupation with a *persona*, a constructed personal self. This is the danger. Futility of it. Complete waste. The woods save me and the sun and snow. Lovely songs of birds, melting snowfields yesterday afternoon.[123]

Sufism is very much on Merton's mind throughout the last two years of his life, during which he gives a series of lectures on Sufism to the monks at Gethsemani. He also speaks of his deep interest in Sufi thought to a group of Sisters of the Monastery of the Precious

Blood in Eagle River, Alaska, on September 29, 1968;[124] and there are a number of references to Sufism in his Asian journal (October–December 1968).[125] Then, on December 10, 1968, comes the mystical union that Sidi Abdeslam perhaps had foreseen: the moment of departure from the earthy plane that Sufis, of course, do not see as the end of the Path.

(3) **The Reading Notebooks:** From the very personal journals, we move to Merton's reading notebooks, which might be seen as a personal filter of the raw material of the readings he was doing over the years. Since they were his own notations, meant no doubt to jog his memory of the texts he was pursuing—or to hold on to passages he was afraid of losing, for whatever reason—it is sometimes difficult to know where he is quoting verbatim and where the notes are his own comments on the readings. But like the marginalia and underlinings (true raw material, from the books that were in his library), these notebooks show what made an impression on Merton's own mind, and what portions or ideas from the books he took most directly to heart.

For example, Merton might have gone back to notebook 46 (dating from 1961) for advice on the just-mentioned dilemma of the *nafs*. There he quotes a number of early Sufi scholars, including Abu Talib (d. 996): "The carnal self (*nafs*) is by nature prone to action and it has been commanded to be still (that is to be acquiescent to the will of God), so that He afflicts it in order that it might feel the need of its Lord and be cleansed from its own tendencies and desires." Then, a short while later in the same notebook, there is an exceptionally beautiful passage—and an exemplary outpouring of Sufi symbolism—attributed to al-Baydâ bint al-Mufaddal , a woman saint of Damascus (twelfth century or before):

> If you have seen a lover of God you have seen a very wonderful thing—of one in grief not settling in the earth but like a wild bird whose delight in solitude has kept him from rest, while he yearns in remembrance of the Beloved, and his food is love in hunger and his drink is love in thirst and his sleep is the thought of union and his waking hours mean no neglect. . . . At last through love (*shawq*) and long service he attains to the degree of all-absorbing love, then his tranquility returns and his fire dies down and its sparks

are quenched and his grief decreases and he becomes one with the object of his longing.

And on "secrecy," from al-Hujwîrî (d. 1071): "All veils come from ignorance; when ignorance has passed away the veils vanish and this life, by means of gnosis, becomes one with the life to come." This state of knowledge or gnosis, and its connection to what the Sufis call *fanâ*' or extinction fascinated Merton. He quotes al-Junayd (d. 910) "The Lord causes you to die to yourself and live in Him. The *'arif* (gnostic or contemplative) is one from the depths of whose consciousness (*sirr*) God speaks, while he himself is silent." Abu l' Husayn Nuri (d. 907): "The Sufi is one who keeps hold of nothing and is held and bound by nothing."[126]

Merton notes down the seven stages of Sufi development listed by Abu Nasr al-Sarraj (d. 988) in *Kitab al-Luma'* as (1) conversion or repentance (*tawba*), (2) fear of the Lord (*wara'*), (3) renunciation or detachment (*zuhd*), (4) poverty (*faqr*) which implies reliance on God alone, (5) patience or endurance (*sabr*), (6) trust in God (*tawakkul*) or self-surrender, and (7) contentment (*rida*), the state of one who pleases God and is always pleased with Him. Related to the state of *tawakkul* is another note, attributed to al-Ghazâlî (d. 1111) on "*mutawakkil*," as "he who has *tawakkul*," in other words, or "one who has already moved out of the sphere of unaided human striving into that of supernatural prevenience." Unattributed in the notes is the powerful: "On the heart of Poverty three renouncements are inscribed: Quit this world, quit the next world, and quit quitting."

In his extensive notes in notebook 34[127] that Merton made in preparation for the long review he was writing of Iranian psychiatrist Reza Arasteh's *Final Integration*, Merton quotes extensively from Arasteh's thoughts on the poet Rûmî and his mysterious associate, Shams-i Tabrizi:

> [Shams] freed himself from all kinds of authority, internal and external, and frequently criticized traditional scholars and theologians who merely repeated others' opinions. . . . The significance of Rûmî's attachment to Shams, as I see it: it enabled him completely to forget himself; it enabled him to forget about "being anything;" it persuaded him of the supreme reality of *love*.

Shams, for Arasteh, represented "perfect integration . . . beyond the social I (living only by reason) . . . universal man aided by intuition and functioning as a totality with spontaneity and expressiveness." In the next section of the notes, it is difficult to know whether Merton is interpreting, paraphrasing, or quoting Arasteh, but also under "Shams" is the following somewhat unparallel list [taken directly from the notebooks, including the punctuation]:

- to become one with the ocean of kindness from which all love emerges
- to know unity behind plurality and know how unity unfolds in plurality
- one who understands "an ocean of symbols beneath the inward state"
- he had passed from existence to non-existence and beyond it
- he needed no love, no religion, he lacked any sense of guilt and justice: truth and kindness marked his spontaneous acts
- spoke very little, advised Rûmî to "remain deaf externally so that insight might act"

Again Merton notes down the Sufi term *fanâ'*, here with Arasteh's psychological definition, "passing away of the I," and adds Arasteh's interpretation of the related or ensuing state of *baqâ'*, "becoming wholly aware, not I."

Returning to Shams and Rûmî, the notebooks state: "Having been reborn in Shams, Rûmî is now reborn in love. He is beyond Shams and beyond all division. 'I am not Shams of Tabriz, I am pure light. Beware if you see me, don't tell anyone that you have seen me.'"

(4) **Marginalia and Underlinings:** Merton's own Sufi library was largely composed of books sent to him by Marco Pallis and Abdul Aziz. Pallis sent him key books of traditionalist thought (René Guénon's *Crisis in the Modern World*, Frithjof Schuon's *Language of the Self*, Lord Northbourne's *Religion and the Modern World*, Seyyed Hossein Nasr's *Three Muslim Sages*, and his own *The Way and the the Mountain*). Abdul Aziz sent a wide range of material, including traditionalist writings (Nasr's *Ideals and Realities of Islam*, Titus Burckhardt's *An Introduction to Sufi Doctrine*, and Martin Lings' *A Moslem Saint of*

the Twentieth Century), other modern analyses of Sufism (some suspect works, like Idries Shah's *The Sufis*, among them), and key translations of classic Sufi writers such as al-Ghazâlî, al-Junayd, Hujwîrî, Ibn al-Arif, and Ibn 'Abbad de Ronda. Aziz carefully dated each volume he sent to Merton (the first being W. Montgomery Watt's translation of al-Ghazâlî's *Faith and Practice*, sent February 3, 1961, and the last being Nasr's *Ideals and Realities of Islam*, sent March 22, 1968). At times, Aziz apparently gave Merton his own private copies of books, for both the purchase date and the gift date are listed, and there is sometimes a considerable amount of marginalia in Aziz's handwriting, even noting down the dates he read certain chapters or passages. He often objected strongly to certain opinions by translators or commentators, and Merton had the advantage at times of reading not only the books themselves, but a running commentary by a knowledgeable fellow seeker.

Merton's own underlinings and occasional notes are distinguishable from those by Aziz, as the styles of notation (and of course the handwriting) are different. Merton himself used the following marks in his reading (indicating, it seems, increasing levels of relevance—to him, as reader—for the passages thus specified): (1) a single vertical mark in the outside margin of the text, specifying usually a whole sentence or paragraph; (2) underlined text (sometimes just a phrase, but often much more); (3) underlined text within a passage noted by the vertical mark; (4) underlined text within a passage marked by two parallel vertical marks; (5) underlined text within a passage marked by three (or even more) vertical marks; (6) text highlighted by underlining and/or vertical marks as well as an asterisk, check, or question mark next to the vertical marks; and (7) all of the above with a circle around the asterisk. There are occasional, but infrequent, actual marginal comments written next to the text, usually quite brief.

An analysis of Merton's response to these readings would be an exhaustive task, but highlighting a few of them will help indicate the impact some traditionalist and Sufi ideas seem to have had on Merton's thinking in the final seven years of his life.

From the Watt translation of al-Ghazâlî (which is a stunning account of the brilliant philosopher's conversion to Sufism), we see that Merton was especially drawn to the following (underlining is Merton's own):

> It becomes clear to me, however, that what is most distinctive of mysticism is something which cannot be apprehended by study, but <u>only by immediate experience</u> (<u>dhawq</u>—literally 'tasting'), <u>by ecstasy and by a moral change.</u> What a difference there is between *knowing* the definiton of health and satiety, together with their causes and presuppostions, and *being* healthy and satisfied. What a difference between being acquainted with the definition of drunkenness—namely, that it designates a state arising from the domination of the seat of the intellect by vapours arising from the stomach—and being drunk! Indeed, <u>the drunken man while in that condition does not know the defintion of drunkenness nor the scientific account of it; he has not the very least scientific knowledge of it;</u> the sober man, on the other hand, knows the definition of drunkenness and its basis, yet he is not drunk in the very least. . . .
>
> <u>What remained for me was not to be attained by oral instruction and study</u> but only by immediate experience and by walking in the mystic way. Now from the sciences I had laboured at and the paths I had traversed in my investigation of the revelational and rational sciences . . . there had come to me a sure *faith in God most high*, in prophethood (or revelation), and in the last Day.[128]

And a few pages later:

> <u>I learnt with certainty that it is above all the mystics who walk on the road to God;</u> their life is the best life, their method the soundest method, their character the purest character . . . <u>for to the mystics all movement and all rest, whether external or internal, brings illumination from the light of the lamp of prophetic revelation;</u> and behind the light of prophetic revelation there is no other light on the face of the earth from which the revelation may be received. . . . [This is] <u>purification of the heart completely from what is other than</u> God most <u>high;</u> the key to it,

which corresponds to the opening act of adoration in prayer <u>is the sinking of the heart completely in the recollection of God;</u> and the end of it is complete absorption (*fanâ'*) in God.[129]

One of the asterisked sections has a declaration by al-Ghazâlî's that might have been especially meaningful to Merton later as he struggled with his own sexual drives: "I saw that to be ignorant of God is destructive poison, and to destroy him by following desire is the thing which produces the disease, while to know God most high is the life-giving antidote and to obey Him by opposing desire is the healing medicine."[130]

(It is curious to note that during his Asian journey, Merton again encounters the same al-Ghazâlî text—also known as *Deliverance from Error*[131] —in French, apparently not recalling his earlier reading of the Watt translation in early 1961. He writes on August 18, 1968: "Then I went out and read a French translation of Al Ghazâlî's *Error and Deliverance* which is also a magnificent book, one of the greatest" and the next day adds, "The great pages on al-Ghazâlî's conversion to Sufism moved me."[132])

In Hujwîrî's *Kashf al-Mahjub*,[133] which Aziz had sent to him July 31, 1961, along with a number of postcards of mosques and saints' tombs in Morocco (they are still in the book at the Merton Center), Merton takes special note of the clear distinctions the Persian scholar makes between "stages" (or "stations") and "states" in Sufism (a subject which he is again to encounter in simplified form in Cyprian Rice's *The Persian Sufis*, sent to him by Aziz on January 15, 1964; one can't know when Merton made any of his underlinings, of course; though he received the Hujwîrî book in 1961, he might not have read it until he was preparing his lectures for the monks in 1967):

<u>Station (*maqam*) denotes anyone's "standing" in the way of God, and his fulfillment of the obligation appertaining to that "station" and his keeping it until he comprehends its perfections so far as lies in a man's power. It is not permissable that he should quit his "station" without fulfilling the obligation thereof. . . .</u>

<u>State (*hal*), on the other hand, is something that descends from God into a man's heart, without his being able to repel</u>

it when it comes, or to attract it when it goes, by his own effort. Accordingly, while the term "station" denotes the way of the seeker, and his progress in the field of exertion, and his rank before God in proportion to his merit, the term "state" denotes the favour and grace which God bestows upon the heart of His servant, and which are not connected with any mortification on the latter's part. "Station" belongs to the category of acts, "state" to the category of gifts. Hence the man that has "station" stands by his own self-mortification, whereas the man that has a "state" is dead to "self" and stands by a "state" which God creates in him.

In conclusion, you must know that satisfaction is the end of the "stations" and the beginning of the "states": it is a place where one side rests on acquisition and effort, and the other side on love and rapture: at this point mortifications (muahadat) cease. Hence its beginning is in the class of things acquired by effort, its end in the class of things divinely bestowed.[134]

Merton also read and underlined French texts, including Paul Nwyia's study of Ibn 'Abbad de Ronda, which Aziz sent him October 8, 1964 and which includes the following beautiful passage:

The best Invocation is that which bursts forth from the inspiration coming from the Name Invoked—may His memory be glorified!—; such is the secret prayer of the Sufis, an uninterrupted prayer which takes possession of the heart. When one says that this "taking possession" leads the invoker to a state where he loses consciousness of his invocation, this is not a question either of hulûl (incarnation of the Divine in man) nor of ittihâd (union of substance); it is a wisdom and a manifestation of the power of the All-Powerful and the Wise. The meaning of this is that the heart in prayer is emptied of everything; it no longer contains anything but God (bait al-haqq) of which it is full. Thus the invocation bursts forth of itself spontaneously, without premeditation.[135]

Merton also read Schuon's Understanding Islam, a quintessential study of Islam from the traditionalist perspective, in its original

French. His markings in the French text contain a number of question marks, in this case, underscoring his allegation in the journals (October 4, 1963) that he thinks Schuon "oversimplifies the differences between Christianity and Islam." One such objection comes next to Schuon's statement (on page 142 of the equivalent English text) that "the Christian, centered as he is on Christ and on the miracles flowing in essence from that fact, feels an inherent distrust of intelligence—which he is apt to reduce to the 'wisdom after the flesh' in contast to Pauline charity—and in what he believes to be the pretensions of the human mind." But two pages later, Merton marks a passage about active contemplation—a subject which had long interested him—with four vertical lines and a circled asterisk:

> In any case it follows from all traditional definitions of man's supreme function that a man capable of contemplation has no right to neglect it but is on the contrary called to dedicate himself to it; in other words, he sins neither against God nor against his neighbor—to say the least—in following the example of Mary in the Gospels and not that of Martha, for contemplation contains action and not the reverse. If in point of fact action can be opposed to contemplation, it is nevertheless not opposed to it in principle, nor is action called for beyond what is necessary or required by the duties of a man's station in life. In abasing ourselves from humility, we must not also abase things which transcend us, for then our virtue loses all its value and meaning; to reduce spirituality to a "humble" utilitarianism—thus to a disguised materialism—is to give offense to God, on the one hand because it is like saying it is not worthwhile to be overly preoccupied with God and on the other hand because it means relegating the divine gift of intelligence to the rank of the superfluous.[136]

In general, Merton highlights the sections where Schuon is being more straightforward and simple in his reasoning, using poetry and symbolism rather than theological argument or peremptory insistence to state his case. Merton seems to especially like what Schuon says about prayer: "As for the heart, it is the latent remembrance of God, hidden deep down in our 'I'; prayer is as if the heart, risen to the surface, came to take the place of the brain which then sleeps with a holy slumber; this slumber unites and soothes, and its most elementary trace in the soul is peace."[137] Prayer, or invocation of the Holy Name, is both a recollection of what is highest in man and a letting go of what is lowest: "The remembrance of God is at the same time a forgetting of oneself; conversely, the ego is a kind of crystallization of forgetfulness of God."[138] Such remembrance is crystallized in the Divine Name, and particular in the Shahâdah of Islam (lâ ilâha illâ 'Llâh— "There is no god but God"):

> There is necessarily a guarantee of efficacy in the Divine Names themselves. . . . This certitude is derived from the very meaning comprised in the mantram or Divine Name. Thus . . . the Shahâdah comprises the same grace . . . by virtue of its very content: because it is the supreme formulation of Truth and because Truth delivers by its very nature. To identify oneself with Truth, to infuse it into our being and transfer our being into It is to escape from the empire of error and malice.[139]

Schuon's concept of gnosis, of a higher knowledge or wisdom of the heart (the *sophia perennis* of the traditionalists) clearly intrigues Merton, who writes "good" in the middle of a paragraph about the revealed scripture of Islam:

> Pure intellect is the "immanent Quran"; the uncreated Quran—the Logos—is the Divine Intellect, which crystallizes in the form of the earthly Quran and answers objectively to that other immanent and subjective revelation which is the human intellect. In Christian terms it could be said that Christ is like the objectivation of the intellect and the latter is like the subjective and permanent revelation of Christ. Thus there are two poles of the manifestation of Divine Wisdom and they are: firstly, the Revelation "above us" and secondly the intellect "within us;" the Revelation provides the symbols while the intellect deciphers them and "recollects" their content, thereby again becoming conscious of its own substance. Revelation is a deployment and intellect a concentration; the descent is in accord with the ascent.[140]

Finally, let us return to Marco Pallis, and Merton's responses to what is probably his most important text, *The Way and the Mountain*. Three examples will suffice. First on symbolism, the language in which real dialogue, such as that between Merton and the traditionalists, always ultimately takes place:

> It seems hardly necessary to point out that everything enjoying any kind of existence must therefore have its symbolical aspect, which actually constitutes its most profound reality; those who see in symbolism nothing better than an invention of the poets miss the point, unless indeed they are prepared to take the word "invention" in its primitive sense of a "finding" of something that is already and always there to be found—one might also say a "discovery" or even a "revelation."[141]

Also from the title essay, exploring the symbolism of mountains, of climbing, of spiritual aspiration:

> But woe to him who, after having reached the top of one of these secondary eminences, lingers there through letting himself imagine that he has accomplished something final; for then it immediately turns from an aid into a hindrance, from a stage into a barrier, from an open into a closed door, from a symbol into an "idol." This indeed is the essence of "idolatry" against which all the traditions are continually inveighing; nothing can be called an idol itself, but anything, even down to "good works" and "service," can become one if it is for a moment allowed to assert is own independence to the Principle and thus enter into rivalry with it. . . .
>
> So long as there yet exists a step to be taken there are alternatives and hence there are possibillities of comparison, but at the summit all alternative routes become one; every distinction between them, and therefore every opposition, is spontaneously reconciled. The summit itself not only occupies no space, although the whole mountain is virtually contained in it, but it is also outside time and all succession, and only the "eternal" present reigns there. It is

utterly inexpressible in its uniqueness; silent is the Knower of the Summit and the whole Universe strains its ears to catch the accents of his speechless eloquence. . . . [The summit] must be known immediately or not at all; ultimately all roundabout approaches must rejoin the direct route, of which they are but translations in discursive mode, or they will not arrive.[142]

That arrival is at the Summit, the Peak, which is also Center, the Heart: the double metaphor which is the core of Sufism and most traditional teachings. As Merton told the Alaskan Sisters of the Monastery of the Precious Blood at the Day of Recollection September 29 (if the reader will forgive yet one more digression on the way to the peak):

Sufism looks at man as a heart and a spirit and a secret, and the secret is the deepest part. The secret of man is God's secret; therefore, it is in God. My secret is God's innermost knowledge of me, which He alone possesses. It is God's secret knowledge of myself in Him, which is a beautiful concept. The heart is the faculty by which man knows God and there Sufism develops the heart.

This is a very important concept in the contemplative life, both in Sufism and in the Christian tradition: To develop a heart that knows God, not just a heart that loves God, but a heart that knows God. How does one know God in the heart? By praying in the heart. The Sufis have ways of learning to pray so that you are really praying in the heart, from the heart, not just saying words, not just thinking good thoughts or making intentions or acts of the will, but from the heart. This is a very ancient Biblical concept that is carried over from Jewish thought into monasticism. It is the spirit which loves God, in Sufism. The spirit is almost the same word as the Biblical word "spirit"—the breath of life. So man knows God with his heart, but loves God with his life. It is your living self that is an act of constant love for God and this inmost secret of man is that by which he contemplates God, it is the secret of man in God himself.[143]

Like the mountaintop, the secret heart is reachable only through sticking to the path, through whatever difficulties, but its realization of course therefore (and only therefore) transcends the path.

Our third and final quote comes from another essay in *The Way and the Mountain*, where Merton highlights Pallis's summation of all this by discussing, of all things, clothing (that ultimate symbol of the outer to which the inner must respond, of the discipline which precedes any real freedom):

> What individual man is, he owes, positively, to his inherent possibilities and, negatively, to his limitations; the two together, by their mutual interplay, constitute his *svabhava* [mode of existence]. . . . It has been said that there are three degrees of conformity (*islam*) to the truth; firstly, everyone is *muslim* from the very fact of being at all, since, do as he will, he cannot conceivably move one hairsbreadth out of the orbit of the Divine will that laid down for him the pattern of his existence; secondly, he is *muslim* in so far as he recognizes his state of dependence and behaves accordingly—this level is represented by his conscious attachment to a tradition, whereby he is able to be informed of what he is and of the means to realize it; and thirdly, he is *muslim* through having achieved perfect conformity, so that henceforth he is identical to his true Self, beyond all fear of parting.[144]

It is the middle "degree of conformity"—the one where one "recognizes his state of dependence and behaves accordingly . . . represented by his conscious attachment to a tradition"—that Merton marks with three vertical lines. It is the state (or, perhaps more accurately, this "stage" or "station," to use Hujwîrî's terms) in which Merton and most of us find ourselves. But the Summit, the promise of a *state* of mystical union, looms—"State (*hâl*), on the other hand, is something that descends from God into a man's heart, without his being able to repel it when it comes or to attract it when it goes, by his own effort . . . The man that has a 'state' is dead to 'self' and stands by a 'state' which God creates in him."[145] —just over the next ridge.

NOTES

1. Correspondence from Marco Pallis to Thomas Merton, June 25, 1963, Thomas Merton Center, Bellarmine College, Louisville, Kentucky. Hereafter *TMC*.

2. Merton wrote to Dona Luisa Coomaraswamy (the widow of art historian Ananda K. Coomaraswamy) on February 12, 1961: "Yes, I have read Marco Pallis [*Peaks and Lamas*]. We do not have it here, I borrowed it from Victor Hammer's wife (he met AKC once and has some offprints of his). I copied out some of the best bits about Tibetan art and craftsmanship (I make no distinc-tion)." Quoted in Thomas Merton, *The Hidden Ground of Love: Letters on Religious Experience and Social Concerns*, selected and edited by William H. Shannon (New York: Farrar, Straus, & Giroux, 1985; paperback edition: New York: Harcourt Brace Jovanovich, 1993), 128. Hereafter *HGL*.

3. Merton to Pallis, undated letter, *HGL*, 464

4. Brother Patrick Hart, who co-edited *The Asian Journal of Thomas Merton* (New York: New Directions, 1975) with Naomi Stone and Jay Laughlin, thinks these missing letters might possibly be part of the papers left by Laughlin, Merton's longtime editor and publisher at New Direections, to Harvard University on his (Laughlin's) death; these papers are now being catalogued and were unavailable for research when this article was written. Phone con-versation with Brother Patrick Hart, February 22, 1999.

5. Merton to Pallis, March 11, 1966, *HGL*, 475.

6. Merton to Pallis, May 28, 1966, *HGL*, 476.

7. Another possiblility, mentioned above, is that it may be among the James Laughlin papers at Harvard.

8. Personal communication with William H. Shannon, February 4, 1999.

9. See Sidney H. Griffith's study of the Merton–Massignon correspondence in this volume, 51–78.

10. For a full account of Schuon's life and teachings, see the Winter 1998 issue of *Sophia: The Journal of Traditional Studies* (Vol. 4, No. 2), "In Memory of Frithjof Schuon," with articles by a number of today's leading traditionalist thinkers and writers, including Seyyed Hossein Nasr (who edited the issue), Martin Lings, Huston Smith, Whitall Perry, Rama Coomaraswamy, James Cutsinger, and William Stoddart.

11. See Martin Lings, *A Sufi Saint of the Twentieth Century* (Berkeley and Los Angeles: University of California Press, 1961; 3d ed.: Cambridge: Islamic Texts Society, 1993). This book had a powerful influence on Merton and led to his correspondence, discussed later here, with Lings. Merton also reviewed the book in the French publication, *Collectanea Cisterciensia* (27:1), 77; a transla-tion of that review appears in this collection.

12. See Seyyed Hossein Nasr, "In Memoriam: Frithjof Schuon, a Prelude" in the *Sophia* collection cited above, 7–9; and Martin Lings, "Frithjof Schuon: An Autobiographical Approach," 17–19, in the same issue. There was also, as Lings indicates (p. 19), a branch of "African 'Alawis" who carried on the *tarîqah* in Algeria and Morocco. Sidi Abdeslam, who visited Merton at Gethsemani in the fall of 1966, was part of this branch.

13. Nasr, Ibid., 8.

14. In his chapter, "Rediscovery of the Sacred," in the collection *Knowledge and the Sacred* (Albany: State University of New York Press, 1989), Seyyed Hossein Nasr also lists the following thinkers as being strongly influenced by the traditionalism of Guénon, Coomaraswamy, and Schuon: Giulio Evola, Elémire Zolla, Eric Gill, Bernard Kelly, Victor Danner, Mircea Eliade ("at least in his earlier works"), Henry Corbin, Leopold Ziegler, Heinrich Zimmer, Joseph Campbell, Marius Schneider, Gilbert Durand, Kathleen Raine, and E. C. Schumacher (109–10).

15. Re "also": Pallis has just been speaking of Coomaraswamy, with whom he had "corresponded for years, but we never met."

16. Pallis to Merton, June 25, 1973, TMC.

17. Lings in *Sophia*, 16.

18. Shaikh Ahmad al-'Alawî is quoted by Lings as relating the following teaching, learned in turn from his shaikh: "There is only One World, and this is It. What we look on as the sensible world, the finite world of time and space, is nothing but a conglomeration of veils which hide the Real World. These veils are our own senses, our eyes are the veils over True Sight, our ears the veils over True Hearing, and so it is with the other senses. For us to become aware of the existence of the Real World, the veils of the senses must be drawn aside." *Sufi Saint*, 136.

19. Frithjof Schuon, unpublished writings.

20. Lings in *Sophia*, 15.

21. Pallis to Merton, June 25, 1963, TMC.

22. Pallis to Merton, August 8, 1963, TMC.

23. Merton to Pallis, October 4, 1963, TMC; also *HGL*, 466.

24. Pallis to Merton, October 11, 1963, TMC.

25. Merton to Pallis, October 4, 1963. The two sentences in brackets are not included in *HGL* but are in Merton's original carbon letter in the archives at TMC.

26. See Gray Henry's article on Merton and the Lings book in this volume, 163–81.

27. These reviews are translated and included in this volume, 306–18

28. Merton had written Pallis something similar about Schuon and Guénon in his first letter, in the summer of 1963, perhaps with some degree of exaggeration: "I have several works of Schuon in French, also some of René Guénon. I like them both very much, though I have not really got into them thoroughly yet." *HGL*, 464.

29. Merton sent "The Moslems' Angel of Death" to Pallis, who wrote back that it reminded him of some poetry by Martin Lings: "there's a certain kinship of mind there." (Pallis to Merton, October 11, 1963, TMC.)

30. Merton to Pallis, October 4, 1963, TMC. Again the bracketed sentence is not in *HGL*.

31. Pallis to Merton, September 10, 1964, TMC.

32. Pallis to Merton, September 29, 1964, TMC.

33. Pallis to Merton, December 4, 1964, TMC.

34. "The Universality of Monasticism and Its Relevance in the Modern World," which was later published in Schuon's *Light on the Ancient Worlds* (London: Perennial Books, 1965; new ed., Bloomington, Ind.: World Wisdom Books, 1984) and which is reprinted in this volume, 319–34

35. Merton to Pallis, December 10, 1964, *TMC*; also *HGL*, 467–68. Merton may have been being a bit overgenerous (as was sometimes the case in his correspondence) in this assessement of Teilhard de Chardin, whose attempt to conflate Darwinian evolutionism with Catholic theology is so disturbing to traditionalists and Catholic conservatives alike. Merton remained somewhat intrigued by Teilhard de Chardin's ideas about Church and social reform over the next few years (he writes one correspondent in June 1967 that he had recently considered reviewing a book Teilhard but had decided against it), but certainly never became an advocate of his peculiar brand of the scientistic theology. These mixed emotions are reflected in a letter to Rosemary Radford Ruether on September 21, 1966: "I haven't read much Teilhard since an article of mine on *The Divine Milieu* was not allowed to be published by the censors of the Order (Teilhard too wicked). I was not sufficiently concerned to read him when I couldn't do anything with it–and not sold enough on him to read it for pure illumintiation and uplift. So I didn't read him." (*HGL*, 498–99). See also his comment to Lord Northbourne quoted later in this article, where he refers to an "irresponsible and fantastic progressivism à la Teilhard."

36. Merton to Pallis, [undated] 1963, *TMC*; also *HGL*, 464.

37. Pallis to Merton, July 16, 1963, *TMC*.

38. Pallis to Merton, December 17, 1964. Regarding Merton's own correspondence with Lord Northbourne, see Part IV in this article.

39. Merton to Pallis, Easter 1965, *TMC*. Not included in *HGL*.

40. Pallis to Merton, January 23, 1965, *TMC*.

41. In *Seeds of Destruction* (New York: Farrar, Straus & Giroux, 1964), which Merton had sent to him.

42. See Merton's letter to Pallis, June 17, 1965 (*HGL*, 470): "Since you are convinced of the undesirability of that last section on Jihâd . . . I will see that it is eliminated from future editions. I certainly respect your judgment and thank you for it." The section was not eliminated.

43. Merton to Pallis, March 10, 1965, *TMC*; *HGL*, 469.

44. Merton to Pallis, Easter Sunday, 1965, *TMC*; *HGL*, 469.

45. Huston Smith, introduction to revised edition of *The Transcendent Unity of Religions* (Wheaton, Ill.: Quest Books/Theosophical Publishing Co., 1984), x.

46. Merton to Pallis, Easter Sunday, 1965, *TMC*; *HGL*, 469.

47. This section appears to be part of what is missing in the March 10 letter.

48. See section IV below.

49. Pallis to Merton, June 11, 1965, *TMC*.

50. See, for example, the essay, "The Monk in Diaspora," in *Seeds of Destruction* (New York: Farrar, Straus & Giroux, 1964), 199–213.

51. Pallis to Merton, August 13, 1965. *TMC*.

52. Merton to Pallis, June 17, 1965, *TMC*; *HGL*, 470.

53. This sentence is omitted from the published letter.

54. Pallis to Merton, August 13, 1965.

55. Merton's copy of the Nasr book is in the library at the Abbey of Gethsemani. He reviewed it in the same issue of *Collectanea Cisterciensia* (27:1) in which he wrote about Martin Lings' life of Shaikh al-'Alawî. The reviews, originally written in French by Merton, are translated in this volume, 308–10.

56. Pallis to Merton, October 14, 1965. *TMC.*

57. See Lings in *Sophia*, 19.

58. Merton to Pallis, December 5, 1965, *TMC. HGL*, 472–73. Bracketed portion not in *HGL.*

59. Pallis to Merton, February 20, 1966, *TMC.* Since Schuon's death, and the publication of such tributes as the memorial issue of *Sophia*, such basic details are no longer kept strictly private, though at the time of the writing of this letter, that was still very much the case.

60. An apparent reference to Luke 10:42, where Mary has chosen "that good part" ("but one thing needful")—contemplation— while Martha busies herself with being "careful and troubled about many things."

61. *The Journals of Thomas Merton, Vol VI: Learning to Love*, edited by Christine M. Bochen (San Francisco: HarperSanFrancisco, 1997). From the "A Midsummer Diary for M" section of the journals, June 16, 1966. Yet no Pallis correspondence to Merton exists in the files between the February 20 letter and one in December 10, the latter which virtually ignores the question of Merton's contacting Schuon.

62. Pallis had written on February 20 that he had sent Merton's letter about the ikon and the hermitage on to Schuon in Lausanne and "in reply he asked me to give you the message that you have all his good wishes in this new cycle of your spiritual life."

63. Merton to Pallis, March 11, 1966, *TMC; HGL*, 474.

64. Schuon's widow, Catherine, verifies that to the best of her knowledge the two never met or exchanged letters.

65. Merton to Pallis, May 28, 1966, *TMC. HGL*, 476.

66. Pallis to Merton, December 10, 1966, *TMC.*

67. Merton to Pallis, December 24, 1966, *TMC; HGL*, 477.

68. Pallis to Merton, June 21, 1968, *TMC.*

69. Merton to Lord Northbourne, June 4, 1967, *TMC.*

70. There were more than a thousand different correspondents (according to William H. Shannon's introduction to *HGL*, *vi*); most of their letters been preserved, along with carbons or copies of Merton's replies, in the archives of the Thomas Merton Center.

71. See, especially, the essays by Sidney H. Griffith (on Massignon and Abdul Aziz) and Khadidja Benaissa (on Sidi Abdeslam) in this volume, as well as Merton's review of Reza Arasteh's book, *Final Integration.*

72. Dona Luisa Coomaraswamy to Merton, December 22, 1960, TMC.

73. See corresondence between Dona Luisa and Alvin Moore among her letters at the Thomas Merton Center.

74. The ellipses in these letters from Dona Luisa are her own stylistic devices, not editorial omissions.

75. Merton to Luisa Coomaraswamy, January 13, 1961, *TMC*. Unpublished excerpt.

76. Ibid. *HGL*, 126.

77. Ibid., 126–27.

78. An example of Dona Luisa's galloping allusive thought: Christ casting out demons in the New Testament asks the satanic force its name and gets the response: "Our name is legion, for we are many" (just before it invades a herd of swine and runs them over a cliff). The other allusion is to the popular saying, "The road to hell is paved with good intentions." Dona Luisa's attitude toward popular social or political movements is clear.

79. Probably Coomaraswamy's essay on "Spiritual Authority and Temporal Power." The traditionalist idea of "kingship" is a symbolic concept that is especially difficult for Western "democratic" thinkers to understand. See Gai Eaton's *The King of the Castle: Choice and Responsiblity in the Modern World* (Cambridge, England: Islamic Texts Society, 1990; original edition 1977) for a clear exposition of this important cornerstone of traditionalist thought.

80. This last sentence, in particular, with its riff on the words "thread," "tread," and "trade" indicates Dona Luisa's almost Joycean delight in playing around with words of coincidentally similar spellings.

81. Dona Luisa Coomaraswamy to Merton, January 25, 1961, *TMC*.

82. Merton to Luisa Coomaraswamy, February 12, 1961, *TMC*. *HGL*, 128.

83. In his February 12 letter, Merton had mentioned reading Marco Pallis's *Peaks and Lamas*: "I copied out some of the best bits about Tibetan art and craftsmanship (I make no distinction)." *HGL*, 128.

84. Dona Luisa Coomaraswamy to Merton, February 18, 1961, *TMC*.

85. Merton to Luisa Coomaraswamy, September 24, 1961, *TMC*; *HGL*, 130.

86. Merton to Luisa Coomaraswamy, December 18, 1963, *TMC*; *HGL*, 133.

87. Merton to Lord Northbourne, Easter 1965, *TMC*. Included in Thomas Merton: *Witness to Freedom, Letters in Times of Crisis*, selected and edited by William Shannon (New York: Farrar, Straus & Giroux, 1994), 312–13. Hereafter *WTF*.

88. Ibid., 313.

89. It became part of *Redeeming the Time*, a Merton collection published in a British edition by Burns and Oates in 1966; the essay was never published in any of Merton's American collections.

90. Merton to Lord Northbourne, February 23, 1966, *TMC*; *WTF*, 314.

91. Ibid. The copy Lord Northbourne sent (Autumn 1965) is in the Merton Center libary and shows its new design and format, including the Plains Indian "Feathered Sun symbol of the Universe" that is to grace the journal's cover throughout its existence, even after its name is changed to *Studies in Comparative Religion* in 1967.

92. *Tomorrow* (Autumn 1965), 24–25. This issue also contains articles by Schuon ("Some Observations on the Problem of the Afterlife"), Martin Lings

(on the symbolism of Shakespeare), and Whitall N. Perry (on reincarnation), among others.

93. Lord Northbourne to Merton, August 3, 1966, TMC.

94. Merton to Lord Northbourne, August 30, 1966, TMC; WTF, 317.

95. Ibid., 316.

96. Martin Lings to Merton, Easter Monday, 1965, TMC.

97. Merton to Martin Lings, April 24, 1965, TMC; HGL, 453–54.

98. Lings to Merton, April 27, 1965, TMC. The question involves whether or not Christians really admit the "mutual understanding of other religions." (See the translation of Merton's review in this volume.)

99. Merton to Martin Lings, June 20, 1965, TMC. Unpublished portions of letter.

100. Ibid.

101. Merton to Charles Dumont, June 26, 1964, TMC.

102. Pallis to Merton, June 11, 1965, TMC.

103. Merton to Father Benjamin Clark, June 30, 1967. In Thomas Merton, *The School of Charity: Letters on Relgious Renewal and Spiritual Direction*, selected and edited by Brother Patrick Hart (New York: Farrar, Straus & Giroux, 1990), 336.

104. See the English translation of these eight short reviews in this volume. Merton's review of the Arasteh book from *Monastic Studies* is also reprinted here.

105. Father Charles Dumont to Merton, April 2, 1964, TMC.

106. Merton to Dumont, April 8, 1964, TMC.

107. Merton to Dumont, June 26, 1964, TMC.

108. Dumont to Merton, November 27, 1964, TMC.

109. Merton to Dumont, December 4, 1964, TMC.

110. Dumont to Merton, December 19, 1964, TMC.

111. Merton to Dumont, February 14, 1965, TMC.

112. Merton to Dumont, May 27, 1966, TMC.

113. *The Journals of Thomas Merton, Vol IV: Turning toward the World* , ed. Victor A. Kramer (San Francisco: HarperSanFrancisco, 1996), 115 (entry for May 2, 1961).

114. *The Journals of Thomas Merton, Vol. V: Dancing in the Waters of Life*, ed. Robert E. Daggy (San Francisco: HarperSanFrancisco, 1997), 20–21 (entry for October 2, 1963).

115. Ibid., 22 (Entry for October 4, 1963). The editor's rendering "*philosophia humanis* [humanistic philosophy]" is clearly a misreading of Merton's handwriting and has been corrected to the intended "*philosophia perennis.*"

116. Jacques Ellul, author of *The Technological Society*, which Merton once recommended to Pallis (letter of December 10, 1964); HGL, 468.

117. *Dancing in the Waters of Life*, 166.

118. See Nasr's own account of this in the introduction to this volume, 9–10.

119. See the account of the translator, Khadidja Benaissa, elsewhere in the present volume, 182–92.

120. Merton seems to have added an extra "a" to Abdeslam's name, which actually means "slave (abd') of Salem" (Peace, one of the Ninety Nine Names of Allah). Transcriptions of Arabic names into English often undergo odd changes.

121. *Learning to Love*, 152–53 (Entry for October 31, 1966).

122. Ibid., 200 (Entry for February 17, 1967).

123. Ibid.

124. In the lecture to the Sisters, he speaks, for example of early Sufi brotherhoods which were composed of "mystics living in the world in small communities, not formally organized. They did not live in one building, but came together for meetings. This pattern is found in certain parts of Asia today, and I hope I am going to visit some of these people in Indonesia. There is a man there who is known publicly as a very important lawyer in an Indonesian city. But what he really is is the leader of a mystical group that very strongly emphasizes meditation which, they say, is most necessary for their country, because it has a spiritual mission, and if there are not people praying and meditating, the country will not fulfill that mission. It would be wonderful if in this country there were such people—lay people with that sort of outlook, who would like to meditate." Later in the same lecture, Merton speaks of a "very, very deep concept of man" in Sufism about the heart as the path of direct knowledge of God; he adds he hopes "to study these texts further" and to write about them, but adds, "If I don't get around to that writing—the Sufis have this beautiful development of what this secret really is: it is the word 'yes' or the act of 'yes.' It is the secret affirmation which God places in my heart, a 'yes' to Him. And that is God's secret. He knows my 'yes' even when I am not saying it." This lecture, "The Life That Unifies," was transcribed by Naomi Burton and is printed as part of *Thomas Merton in Alaska: The Alaskan Conference, Journals, and Letters*, edited by Robert E. Daggy (New York: New Directions, 1988), 145, 154.

125. Merton met a Muslim professor, Dr. Syed Vahiduddin, in New Delhi, who "told me some good Sufi stories" and "lamented the absence of genuine Sufi masters, though there are some, hidden. And a great number of fakes who are very much in the public eye." [From *The Asian Journal of Thomas Merton*, edited by Naomi Burton, Brother Patrick Hart, and James Laughlin (New York: New Directions, 1973)] This collection also contains Merton's reading notebooks for this period: among the selections he read on his journey were three new articles by Marco Pallis: "Considerations on Tantric Spirituality," from *The Bulletin of Tibetology* (2:2, August, 1965); and "Discovering the Interior Life" and "Is There Room for 'Grace' in Buddhism?" in *Studies in Comparative Religion* (Spring, 1968, and August, 1968); it is not clear whether Merton had the magazines with him or whether Pallis sent him offprints. Also mentioned in the reading notebooks is Titus Burckhardt's "Cosmology in Modern Science," in two parts in the same publication while it was still called *Tomorrow* (Summer/Autumn 1964 and Winter 1965).

126. Both these quotes are from page 33 of Cyrprian Rice's *The Persian Sufis*, as an examination of the copy in Merton's library at Bellarmine reveals. His

listing of the seven states (mentioned in the next paragraph) also appears to have come from Rice.

127. The reading notebooks were not numbered by Merton himself and do not seem to be in chronological order.

128. William Mongomery Watt, *The Faith and Practice of Al-Ghazâlî* (London: Luzac, 1953), 55.

129. Ibid., 60.

130. Ibid, 70.

131. Fons Vitae will reissue a translation of this key al-Ghazâlî text under this title, in a 1980 translation by Richard J. McCarthy, S.J., in the summer of 1999.

132. *The Journals of Thomas Merton, VII: The Other Side of the Mountain*, ed. Brother Patrick Hart (San Francisco: HarperSanFrancisco, 1998), 155–56.

133. Hujwîrî's *Kashf al-Mahjub*, translated by Reynold A. Nicholson (London, Luzak & Co., 1959); its subtitle lists it as "the Oldest Persian Treatise on Sufism."

134. Ibid., 181. Underlinings are by Merton, who also put a circled asterisk by this second paragraph quoted here, and a double vertical line along the third paragraph.

135. Ibn Abbad (1332–90) quoting another Sufi Ibn al-Bannâ' (d. 1320), cited in Paul Nwyia, *Ibn Abbâd de Ronda* (Beruit: Imprimerie Catholique, 1956). Translation: Rob Baker.

136. Frithjof Schuon, *Understanding Islam*, revised and augmented translation (Bloomington, Ind.: World Wisdom Books, 1994), . French edition Paris: Gallimard, 1961; first English translation, London: Allen & Unwin, 1973.

137. Ibid., 149.

138. Ibid., 148.

139. Ibid., 151.

140. Ibid., 57.

141. Marco Pallis, *The Way and the Mountain* (London: Peter Owen, 1960), 15–16. Underlining receives a circled asterisk from Merton.

142. Ibid., 27, 32.

143. "The Life That Unifies," in *Thomas Merton in Alaska*, 153–54.

144. *The Way and the Mountain*, 142–43.

145. As cited previously, from al-Hujwîrî, *Kashf al-Mahjub* Underlinings by Merton.

11

FINAL INTEGRATION
TOWARD A "MONASTIC THERAPY"

Thomas Merton

Aconsiderable amount of uneasiness and ambivalence in the monastic life today is due perhaps to the fact that though we possess clear conceptual formulas to explain what our "contemplative life" is all about, and though those formulas may well accord with what we would like to do, it seems they do not help us much with what we are actually doing. Thus we find ourselves with several different sets of problems which, however, we do not manage to distinguish. We have defined our ends in certain terms (a life of prayer and penance, apart from the world but not alien to it; seeking God alone, but in community and fraternal love; purifying our hearts by renunciation in order to pray more intently and simply, eventually attaining to contemplative experience; thus our community is a living sign of God's presence, etc.). But meanwhile, before we can get around to doing these things, we have to wrestle with a multitude of other problems: how to make our own living efficiently and yet remain "monastic"; how to keep our atmosphere of silence and yet communicate more spontaneously with one another; how to arrange the office, time for work, study, etc.; above all, how to cope with the contradictions in a system which at the same moment—but from different quarters—urges us to go forward and forbids us to move.

Thus, though we may be fairly clear about what we want to do, we are so confused about the way to do it that our ends become almost entirely theoretical, and our energies become involved in a rather different form of life from the one we claim to be living. This naturally causes a lot of anxiety, ambivalence, tension, not to say discouragement and even despair. Then we summon psychiatry to the rescue—and create still further problems: for the kind of adjustment that ordinary psychotherapy calls for is a realistic acceptance of our social situation, an acquiescence in fulfilling a moderately useful role and in being more or less the sort of person our society would like us to be. And yet the monastic role defined by the ideal to which we hold is one thing, and the role as defined by the actual situation of our community and of ourselves in it, quite another. This difficulty becomes all the greater and more confusing when sociology gets into the act, for then we are summoned to live at the same time by an unworldly ideal and by a worldly one: or to be monks according to norms and standards based on statistics which have nothing to do with our kind of life.

To put it quite simply: many people come to the monastery with a strong, if inchoate, sense that they are called to make something out of their lives. But after a few years of struggle they find that this "thing" they are supposed to do is not clarified, and though they may have become acquainted with formulas which explain the monastic life and justify it, they likely still do not feel that they are able to do anything about them. In addition, they begin to question the relevance of such formulas to modern man. The most difficult kind of vocation crisis is that in which a monk with genuine monastic aspirations comes to feel that such aspirations cannot be fulfilled in a monastery. Which means that they probably cannot be fulfilled anywhere.

The idea of "rebirth" and of life as a "new man in Christ, in the Spirit," of "risen life" in the Mystery of Christ or in the Kingdom of God, is fundamental to Christian theology and practice—it is, after all, the whole meaning of baptism. All the more so is this idea central to that peculiar refinement of the theology of baptism which is the monastic *conversatio*—the vocation to a life especially dedicated to self-renewal, liberation from all sin, and the transformation of one's entire mentality "in Christ."

The notion of "rebirth" is not peculiar to Christianity. In Sufism, Zen Buddhism, and in many other religious or spiritual traditions, emphasis is placed on the call to fulfill certain obscure yet urgent potentialities in the ground of one's being, to "become someone" that one already (potentially) is, the person one is truly meant to be. Zen calls this awakening a recognition of "your original face before you were born."

In Asian traditions as well as in Christian monasticism, there has been considerable stress on the need for a guide or spiritual father, an experienced elder who knows how to bring the less experienced to a decisive point of breakthrough where this "new being" is attained. Strictly speaking, Christian monasticism is less dependent on the aid of a guide than some of the other traditions. In Sufism and Zen the spiritual master is as essential as the analyst in psychoanalysis. In Christian monasticism, a fervent community, a living and "spiritual" (*pneumatikos*) celebration of the liturgical mysteries and of the office might compensate, to some extent, for the lack of an experienced and charismatic teacher. But if there is no sense at all of the urgency of inner development, no aspiration to growth and "rebirth," or if it is blandly assumed that all this is automatically taken care of by a correct and communal celebration, something essential is missing.

The monastic life is not justified simply by a sort of contractual fulfillment of a "work" on behalf of the Church—even if it be the spiritual work of the *opus Dei*, the official public celebration of divine praise, or, for that matter, the cultivation of meditative prayer in silence, strict enclosure, in an austere regime. The monastic community does not effectively act as a sign of God's presence and of His Kingdom merely by the fulfillment of certain symbolic functions. For instance, it is not enough to keep the monks strictly enclosed and remote from all external activity—this does not by itself constitute a sign of the eschatological kingdom. On the contrary, very often this limitation constitutes a serious impoverishment of the personalities of the monks and at the same time serves to prevent that impoverishment from becoming public! It is of course perfectly true that solitude and silence are essential to the monastic way of life, and discipline does contribute very much to the ends for which monastic communities exist. But the fact remains that people are called to the monastic life so that they may grow and be transformed, "reborn" to a new and more complete identity, and to a more profoundly fruitful existence in peace, in wisdom, in creativity, in love. When rigidity and limitation become ends in themselves they no longer favor growth, they stifle it.

Sometimes it may be very useful for us to discover new and unfamiliar ways in which the human task of maturation and self-discovery is defined. The book of a Persian psychoanalyst, Dr. Reza

Arasteh, who practices and teaches in America, might prove very valuable in this respect.[1]

Dr. Arasteh has developed and deepened ideas suggested by the humanistic psychoanalysis of Erich Fromm, by existential psychotherapy, and by the logotherapy of Viktor Frankl. But—and this is what is most interesting—he has also incorporated into his theories material from the mystical tradition of Persian Sufism. The *Final Integration* which is the object of his research is not just the "cure" of neurosis by adaptation to society. On the contrary, it presupposes that any psychoanalytic theory that is content merely with this is bound to be inadequate. Dr. Arasteh is interested not only in the partial and limited "health" which results from contented acceptance of a useful role in society, but in the final and complete maturing of the human psyche on a transcultural level. This requires a little clarification.

Contrary to the accepted theory and practice of most psychotherapy derived from Freud and popular in America today, Dr. Arasteh holds that adaptation to society at best helps a man "to live with his illness rather than cure it," particularly if the general atmosphere of the society is unhealthy because of its overemphasis on cerebral, competitive, acquisitive forms of ego-affirmation. Such an atmosphere may favor an apparently very active and productive mode of life but in reality it stifles true growth, leaves people lost, alienated, frustrated and bored without any way of knowing what is wrong with them. In fact, in many cases, psychoanalysis has become a technique for making people conform to a society that prevents them from growing and developing as they should. Quoting E. Knight's book *The Objective Society*, Arasteh says:

> The Western individual, while opposing the integration of the Russian and Chinese models, not only accepts the herd values of his society but he has invented psychoanalysis to prevent him from straying from them. . . . The stresses that modern life often produce in sensitive and intelligent people are no longer considered to call for a change in society; it is the individual who is wrong and he consequently becomes a neurotic, not a revolutionary. No more remarkable device than psychoanalysis has ever been devised by a society for preventing its superior citizens from giving it pain.

This interesting passage, quoted out of context, might give undue comfort to those who assume that, because they enjoy their masochism, they are superior. Nevertheless it does show to what extent psychotherapy and other techniques have been frankly drafted into the service of a massive, affluent organization that is dedicated to "freedom" and yet tolerates less and less dissent, The masochism, the anxiety, the alienation which are almost universal in such a society are forms of organized evasion. The energies that might otherwise go into productive or even revolutionary change are driven into stagnant backwaters of frustration and self-pity. People are not only made ill, but they prefer to be ill rather than face the risk of real dissent. (Note the important distinction between real and pseudo-dissent, the latter being merely a token and a symbol expressing and justifying an underlying neurosis.) We know well enough that this pattern, so familiar in "the world," is even more familiar in "the cloister."

Nevertheless there is an important distinction between mere neurotic anxiety which comes from a commitment to defeat and existential anxiety which is the healthy pain caused by the blocking of vital energies that still remain available for radical change. This is one of the main points made by Dr. Arasteh's book: the importance of existential anxiety seen not as a symptom of something wrong, but as a summons to growth and to painful development.

Carefully distinguishing existential anxiety from the petulant self-defeating sorrows of the neurotic, Dr. Arasteh shows how this anxiety is a sign of health and generates the necessary strength for psychic rebirth into a new transcultural identity. This new being is entirely personal, original, creative, unique, and it transcends the limits imposed by social convention and prejudice. Birth on this higher level is an imperative necessity for man.

The infant who lives immersed in a symbiotic relationship with the rest of nature—immersed, that is, in his own narcissism—must be "born" out of this sensual self-centeredness and acquire an identity as a responsible member of society. Ordinary psychotherapy is fully aware of this. But once one has grown up, acquired an education, and assumed a useful role as a worker and provider, there is still another birth to be undergone. Dr. Arasteh studies this birth to final integration in three exceptional individuals: Rûmî, the Persian mystic and poet; Goethe; and a young modern Turk who was one of Arasteh's patients.

In the past, final integration was generally a matter only for unusually gifted people. We shall return to this point later. Even today, though the need for final integration makes itself more and more widely felt, the majority not only do not try to attain it, but society, as we have seen, provides them with ways to evade the summons. Clearly, in many cases, that summons takes the form of a monastic, religious, or priestly vocation. Clearly, too, there are many who leave the monastery because they feel that the way the monastic life is structured, or the way they themselves are fitted into the structure, makes a genuine response to the summons impossible.

All of us who have had to work through vocation problems with professed monks can, on reflection, easily distinguish obvious neurotics from men whose monastic crisis has taken the form of existential anxiety: this is a crisis of authentic growth which cannot be resolved in the situation in which they find themselves, and the situation cannot be changed. (Very often, in similar situations, it is the mildly neurotic who manage to stay and make some sort of compromise adjustment, nestling fearfully in the protection of the monastery with the obscure sense that further painful growth will not be demanded!)

Since his investigation is purely psychological, not theological, the question of "sanctity" or holiness does not really arise from Dr. Arasteh. But let us make clear that ordinarily a full spiritual development and a supernatural, even charismatic, maturity, evidenced in the "saint," normally includes the idea of complete psychological integration. Doubtless many saints have been neurotics, but they have used their neurosis in the interests of growth instead of capitulating and succumbing to its dubious comforts.

Final integration is a state of transcultural maturity far beyond mere social adjustment, which always implies partiality and compromise. The man who is "fully born" has an entirely "inner experience of life." He apprehends his life fully and wholly from an inner ground that is at once more universal than the empirical ego and yet entirely his own. He is in a certain sense "cosmic" and "universal man." He has attained a deeper, fuller identity than that of his limited ego self which is only a fragment of his being. He is in a certain sense identified with everybody: or in the familiar language of the New Testament (which Arasteh evidently has not studied) he is "all things to all men." He is able to experience their joys and sufferings as his own, without however becoming dominated by them. He has attained to a deep inner freedom—the Freedom of the Spirit we read of in the New Testament. He is guided not just by will and reason, but by "spontaneous behavior subject to dynamic insight." Now, this calls to mind the theology of St. Thomas on the Gifts of the Holy Spirit which move a man to act "in a superhuman mode." Though Dr. Arasteh takes no account of specifically supernatural agencies, it is clear that such considerations might become relevant here. But of course they cannot be investigated by experimental science.

Again, the state of insight which is final integration implies an openness, an "emptiness," a "poverty" similar to those described in such detail not only by the Rhenish mystics, by St. John of the Cross, by the early Franciscans, but also the Sufis, the early Taoist masters and Zen Buddhists. Final integration implies the void, poverty, and nonaction which leave one entirely docile to the "Spirit" and hence a potential instrument for unusual creativity.

The man who has attained final integration is no longer limited by the culture in which he has grown up. "He has embraced *all of life.* . . . He has experienced qualities of every type of life": ordinary human existence, intellectual life, artistic creation, human love, religious life. He passes beyond all these limiting forms, while retaining all that is best and most universal in them, "finally giving birth to a fully comprehensive self." He accepts not only his own community, his own society, his own friends, his own culture, but all mankind. He does not remain bound to one limited set of values in such a way that he opposes them aggressively or defensively to others. He is fully "Catholic" in the best sense of the word. He has a unified vision and experience of the one truth shining out in all its various manifestations, some clearer than others, Some more definite and more certain than others. He does not set these partial views up in opposition to each other, but unifies them in a dialectic or an insight of complementarity. With this view of life he is able to bring perspective, liberty, and spontaneity into the lives of others. The finally integrated man is a peacemaker, and that is why there is such a desperate need for our leaders to become such men of insight.

It will be seen at once that this kind of maturity is exactly what the monastic life should produce. The monastic ideal is precisely this sort of freedom in the spirit, this liberation from the limits of all that is merely partial and fragmentary in a given culture. Monasticism calls for a breadth and universality of vision that sees everything in the light of the One Truth as St. Benedict beheld all creation embraced "in one ray of the sun." This too is suggested at the end of chapter 7 of the Rule where St. Benedict speaks of the new identity, the new mode of being of the monk who no longer practices the various degrees of humility with concentrated and studied effort, but with dynamic spontaneity "in the Spirit." It is suggested also in the "Degrees of Truth" and the "Degrees of Love" in St. Bernard's tracts on humility and on the love of God.

Unfortunately, we can see at once that if too many people developed in this way, if entire communities were all at once to reach final integration, the effect on the community structure itself might be revolutionary. Hence, in fact, our community life is unconsciously organized to make sure that any such development will be subject to human control. We will not let the Holy Spirit get out of hand! And yet with all its shortcomings and deficiencies, the monastic life is charismatic and the Spirit does work in our midst. But in monastic communities as well as in the Church at large we are conscious of the obscure and difficult struggle between charism and institution, in which the overwhelming need to channel and control the energies of the Spirit (and of course to distinguish them clearly from other more destructive energies) has led to a kind of neutralization of Spirit by organization. This institutional straitjacketing does not prevent individuals from breaking through in their own way and achieving an integration that is perhaps warped and singular but nevertheless authentic (sometimes in amusing ways). But the community itself cannot be truly charismatic, except in a very subdued and harmless way. The penalty paid for this is a prevalence of neurosis, of masochism, of obsessions and compulsions, of fanaticism, intolerance, narrow-mindedness, and various petty forms of destructive cruelty which have proved so ruinous in the past. The present changes and relaxations have been first aid measures to relieve these tensions at any price: but merely opening the windows is not enough. We must still be ready to face anxieties, and realize the difference between those that are fruitless and those that offer a promise of fruitful development. Sometimes the latter are even more painful and seemingly more dangerous than the former. After all, the rebirth which precedes final integration involves a crisis which is extremely severe—something like the Dark Night described by St. John of the Cross. And it is evident that anyone who chanced to fall into the Dark Night of the Soul today would (if discovered) soon find himself getting shock treatments, which would effectively take care of any further disturbing developments!

Dr. Arasteh describes the breakthrough into final integration, in the language of Sufism. The consecrated term in Sufism is *fanâ'*, annihilation or disintegration, a loss of self, a real spiritual death. But mere annihilation and death are not enough: they must be followed by reintegration and new life on a totally different level. This reintegration is what the Sufis call *baqâ'*. The process of disintegration and reintegration is one that involves a terrible interior solitude and an "existential moratorium," a crisis and an anguish which cannot be analyzed or intellectualized. It also requires a solitary fortitude far beyond the ordinary, "an act of courage related to the root of all existence." It would be utterly futile to try to "cure" this anguish by bringing the "patient" as quickly and as completely as possible into the warm bosom of togetherness. Jung, with whom Arasteh has much in common, says this:

> [The development of the person to full ripeness] is at once a charisma and a curse because its first fruit is the conscious and unavoidable segregation of the individual from the undifferentiated and unconscious herd. This means isolation, and there is no more comforting word for it. Neither family nor society nor position can save him from the fate, nor yet the most successful adaptation to his environment. . . . [quoted by Arasteh]

Seen from the viewpoint of monastic tradition, the pattern of disintegration, moratorium and reintegration on a higher, universal level, is precisely what the monastic life is meant to provide. In the strictly limited, authoritarian, caste societies of medieval Europe, of India, of China, of Japan, the individual lived within extreme restriction in a framework that denied him social mobility. But the unusual person, from any caste, could become a monk. If he were able to live as an authentic beggar and pilgrim, accept the sacrifices, the insecurities, the risks, the challenges of the solitary adventure, he was freed from social limitations. He was on his own, on the road, in the jungle or in the desert, and he was entitled to develop in his own way, indeed to devote himself with passionate dedication to a freedom even from the limits of his contingency as a creature: he could get lost in the light of eternity, provided he found the way!

In the modern world, things have somehow become reversed. We live in an extremely mobile society in which, though we may not be nearly as free as we think we are, limits are still very flexible and sometimes do not exist at all. To enter into a monastery is to enter into the most restricted form of life there is. This restriction has a purpose: it is imposed in order to liberate us from attachments and from self will. But the big question is: Does it? Yes and no.

The ascesis of communal service and obedience cannot be dismissed as totally irrelevant, antiquated, repressive, and sterile. It is necessary and salutary for people who have had little or no discipline at all. But on the other hand it does definitely operate in such a way that while it initiates a certain growth, it goes only so far. It frustrates and stifles growth beyond a median level. It makes no provision for anything but formal adaptation to a rather narrow and limited communal pattern. Within that pattern it tolerates "safe" moderate growth and blesses lack of growth. In fact, it is in practice more tolerant of those who do not grow.

The crisis, the challenge, and the demands that Arasteh describes in terms of final integration would seldom be really acceptable in a monastery. They would be too disturbing, too exceptional, too "irregular." They would open up possibilities that would be regarded as altogether too hazardous. The result is that for many authentic vocations today the monastery has become merely a way station. To stay in the cloister life would be to renounce their full development. And yet there is no guarantee that by leaving it they will develop any better.

Dr. Arasteh has nothing direct to say about the monastic life, but obviously those who have sufficient background and understanding will be able to apply his principles very fruitfully to our general predicament today. He will help us recover some sense of the real aim of that monastic *conversatio* which we have not only mentally approved but actually vowed. We have dedicated ourselves to rebirth, to growth, to final maturity and integration. Monastic renewal means a reshaping of structures so that they will not only permit such growth but favor and encourage it in everyone.

However, as Christian monks, we cannot properly understand the full meaning of "final integration" if we see it only in the terms of

psychology. For a Christian, a transcultural integration is eschatological. The rebirth of man and of society on a transcultural level is
a rebirth into the transformed and redeemed time, the time of the
Kingdom, the time of the Spirit, the time of "the end." It means a
disintegration of the social and cultural self, the product of merely
human history, and the reintegration of that self in Christ, in salvation history, in the mystery of redemption, in the Pentecostal "new
creation." But this means entering into the full mystery of the
eschatological Church.

Now, as Dr. Arasteh points out, whereas final psychological integration was, in the past, the privilege of a few, it is now becoming a
need and aspiration of mankind as a whole. The whole world is in
an existential crisis to which there are various reactions, some of
them negative, tragic, destructive, demonic, others proffering a
human hope which is yet not fully clear.

The destructive and tragic solutions are not solutions at all: they
simply marshal the immense resources of military, economic, and
political power to block real development and to maintain established patterns—in the interest of those who know best how to profit from them, and at the expense of everybody else.

The humanly optimistic answers foresee radical changes of a
purely secular sort which will initiate a kind of hippie kingdom of
love in a cybernated and peace-loving megacity (presumably with
free LSD for everybody). Many Christians feel that the Spirit is really summoning us to renounce our sense of spiritual privilege and
enter into a fully turned-on solidarity with these secular hopes.
Others, of course, and perhaps the majority, have lined up on the
side of the armies and the "powers" under the mistaken idea that
Christ is fully identified with the capitalist Western establishment
which still refers to itself (when convenient) as "Christian."

At this point, the best one can do is hazard a personal guess that
neither of these solutions is truly Christian, and neither offers a
hope of final, eschatological integration to the individual Christian,
to the Church, or to the monastic community. Both of these are
reducible to identification with one form or other of culture, one
form or other of "given" society. They are historical decisions that
are merely historical and not eschatological. (Though of course they
may contribute in a disastrous way to the ironies of eschatological
judgment upon the organizational Church.)

Where are we to look for the true solutions? Precisely from the Spirit who will speak clearly at the right time through a renewed ecclesiastical and monastic community. The path to final integration for the individual, and for the community lies, in any case, beyond the dictates and programs of any culture ("Christian culture" included).

NOTES

1. Reza Arasteh, *Final Integration in the Adult Personality*, Leiden, E. J. Brill, 1965.

Reza Arasteh also wrote an article on Sufism—viewed from a wholly secular, non-spiritual viewpoint—for a journal that Merton edited at Gethsemani: "The Art of Rebirth," Monks' Pond 2 (Summer 1968); reprinted in Robert E. Daggy, Monks' Pond: Thomas Merton's Little Magazine (Lexington: The University Press of Kentucky, 1989), 89–93. The article reduces Sufi doctrine to a mere psychological theory, with overtones of Teilhard de Chardin's scientific evolutionism, and was not deemed appropriate to include in this volume. —The Editors.

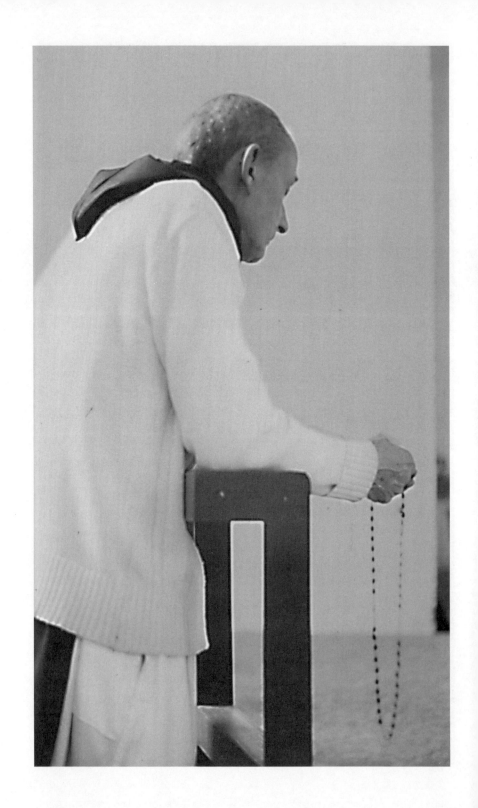

MERTON'S SUFI POEMS

READINGS FROM IBN ABBAD

Note: Ibn Abbad of Ronda was a Moslem, born in the citadel of Ronda, Andalusia, in 1332. In his youth he left Spain to study at Fez in Morocco, a most important religious center for Medieval Islam, and never returned to Spain. He devoted himself to the study of Law and of the Koran,* but finding that Law was "trifling" and looking for the deeper meaning of the Koran he joined a community of Sufis at Sale. Having attained to mystical illumination (at Tangier, 1363?), he returned to Fez to guide and instruct others. About 1380 he was appointed Imam and preacher at the main mosque of the Holy City of Fez and exercised a powerful spiritual influence until his death in 1390 (3 Ragab, 792 A.H.). He is of special interest to students of Western mysticism because some scholars believe that he exercised at least an indirect influence on the Spanish mystic St. John of the Cross. Like St. John of the Cross, Doctor of the "Dark Night of the Soul," Ibn Abbad taught that it is in the night of desolation that the door to mystical union is secretly opened, though it remains tightly closed during the "day" of understanding and light. There is a resemblance between the two teachings, but scholars today do not agree there is clear proof of any influence.

The "readings" which follow are simply meditative and poetic notations made on texts of Ibn Abbad, given in French translation in the recent study by Father Paul Nwyia, S.J., Ibn Abbad de Ronda, Beruit, 1961. The purpose of these notes is to share something of an encounter with a rich and fervent religious personality of Islam, in whom the zeal of the Sufis is revealed, in an interesting way, against the cultural background of Medieval Morocco. There is a mordant, realistic and human quality in the life and doctrine of this contemplative. —*Thomas Merton*

*Editor's Note: Merton's spellings and omission of accents are retained throughout these published poems. This introduction by Merton is not included in *Collected Poems* but exists in a manuscript at the Thomas Merton Center.

1: Ibn Abbad Described by a Friend (Ibn Qunfud)

Among those I met at Fez, let me mention the celebrated
    preacher
The Holy Man Abu Abdallah Mahammad ben Ibrahim ben
    Abbad ar Rundi
Whose father was an eloquent and distinguished preacher.
Abu Abdallah is a sage,
A recollected man in whom renunciation and great kindness are
    one . . .
He speaks admirably of *Tasawwuf*[1]
His writings are worthy to be read to the brothers as they
    practice *Dikr*.[2]
He never returns the visits of the Sultan
But he assists at spiritual concerts (*sama*) on the night of *Mawlid*[3]
I have never found him sitting with anyone in a social gathering.
Whoever would see Abu Abdallah Mahammad must seek him
    out in his own cell.
At times I begged his prayers. This only made him blush with
    confusion.
Of all the pleasures of this world he permits himself none
Save only perfumes and incense
Which he uses lavishly:
Indeed, the Sultan tried to equal him in this
But failed.
And Abu Abdallah Mahammad has taught
That the Holy Prophet himself
Used incense copiously to prepare for his encounters with angels.
He takes care of his own household affairs
And has never taken a wife or a mistress
For above all things he prizes peace
And tranquillity of soul.
At home he wears patched garments
And, when he goes outdoors,
A white or a green mantle.

---

1. *Tasawuuf*—Sufism: the way of poverty and mystic enlightenment.
2. *Dikr*—systematic method of prayer and concentration in which breathing
techniques are united with rhythmic invocation of Allah.
3. Moslem Feast [a celebration of a particular saint or prophet's birthday].

2: The Burial Place of Ibn Abbad

He was buried in a vacant property, for he was a stranger
And had not built himself a tomb in that city, or in any other.
After a few years the wall of the lot fell down
But later, the City Governor
Built the saint a small dome,
Confiding to his secretary the care
To take up the offerings left there
And send them to the saint's family.

Meanwhile the Guild of Shoemakers
Took him as patron. Each year
On the evening of his death in Ragab[4]
They come in procession for a vigil there
With lights, readings and songs,
For in his lifetime
The saint was their friend.
He sat in their shops, conversed with them.
He prayed for the apprentices
To save them from piercing awls
And giant needles.
Often in the Mosque
He led the shoemakers in prayer.
Today, however, he is forgotten.

3: Prayer and Sermon of Ibn Abbad

O Mighty One:
Let me not constrain
Thy servants!

O men:
Your days are not without change and number.
Life passes more quickly than a train of camels.
Old age is the signal
To take the road.
It is death that is truth,

---

4. *Ragab*—June [a month from the Muslim lunar calendar].

Not life, the impossible!
Why then do we turn away from truth?
The way is plain!

O men:
This life
Is only a blinking eye.

O men:
The last end of all our desire:
May He draw close to us
The Living, the Unchanging.
May He move towards us
His huge Majesty
(If it be possible to bear it!)
His Glory!

O men:
Burn away impure desire
In His Glory!

4: Desolation

For the servant of God
Consolation is the place of danger
Where he may be deluded
(Accepting only what he sees,
Experiences, or knows)
But desolation is his home:
For in desolation he is seized by God
And entirely taken over into God,
In darkness, in emptiness,
In loss, in death of self.
Then the self is only ashes. Not even ashes!

5: To Belong to Allah

To belong to Allah
Is to see in your own existence
And in all that pertains to it
Something that is neither yours

Nor from yourself,
Something you have on loan;
To see your being in His Being,
Your subsistence in His Subsistence,
Your strength in His Strength:
Thus you will recognize in yourself
His title to possession of you
As Lord,
And your own title as servant:
Which is Nothingness.

6: *Letter to a Sufi Who Has Abandoned Sufism to Study Law*

Well, my friend, you prefer jurisprudence to contemplation!
If you intend to spend your time collecting authorities and
    precedents
What advice do you want from me?
I can tell you this: each man, today,
Gets what he wants,
Except that no one has discovered a really perfect
Way to kill time.
Those who do not have to work for a living
Are engrossed in every kind of nonsense,
And those who must gain their livelihood
Are so absorbed in this that they
Have time for nothing else.
As to finding someone capable of spiritual life
Ready to do work that is clean of passion
And inordinate desire
Done only for love of Allah—
This is a way of life in which no one is interested
Except a few who have received the special
Mercy of Allah.
Are you aware of this? Are you sure of your condition?
Well then, go ahead with your books of Law,
It will make little difference whether you do this
Or something else equally trivial.
You will gain nothing by it, and perhaps lose nothing:
You will have found a way to kill time.

As you say: you prefer to spend your time doing things you are
 used to.
Drunkards and lechers would agree:
They follow the same principle.

7: To a Novice

Avoid three kinds of Master:
Those who esteem only themselves,
For their self-esteem is blindness;
Those who esteem only innovations
For their opinions are aimless,
Without meaning;
Those who esteem only what is established,
Their minds
Are little cells of ice.

All these three
Darken your inner light
With complicated arguments
And hatred of Sufism.

He who finds Allah
Can lack nothing.
He who loses Allah
Can possess nothing.

He who seeks Allah will be made clean in tribulation,
His heart will be more pure,
His conscience more sensitive in tribulation
Than in prayer and fasting.
Prayer and fasting may perhaps
Be nothing but self-love, self-gratification,
The expression of hidden sin
Ruining the value of these works.
But tribulation
Strikes at the root!

8: *To a Novice*

Be a son of this instant:
It is a messenger of Allah
And the best of messengers
Is one who announces your indigence,
Your nothingness.
Be a son of this instant
Thanking Allah
For a mouthful of ashes.

9: *To a Novice*

The fool is one
Who strives to procure at each instant
Some result
That Allah has not willed.

10: *Letter to One Who Has Abandoned The Way*

Our friend X brought me your letter—*one* letter—informing me of your present state. One letter, not two or three as you contend. And thank God for it, since if there had been two or three I would have had to answer them all and I have no taste for that.

Since you have left me, your conduct is an uninterrupted betrayal of Allah, the Prophet, the Law and the Way of Sufism. And yet Allah had ennobled you in the state of poverty, and had bound you more tightly than others to religion and *Tasawwuf,* so that your admiration of the friends of God had become your life's breath. Thus you were obligated to remain faithful and preserve this vocation from all that might corrupt it!

Yet you did nothing of the kind. You have taken the exact opposite path. You have made all reconciliation impossible. And worse: you have cast off religion entirely to run after trifles that even fools would despise, let alone men of reason.

And on top of all that you have betrayed me for an onion, for a turd, rather, since an onion can have some use!

Yet in spite of all this, there is the will of Allah which I do not measure; there is the power of Allah to which no limit can be imposed; and if Allah wishes to give the lie to my doubts of your possible conversion, that is not hard for Him to do.

As for me, I can help only by prayer.

But what help is that, if you do not help me by a sincere return?

EAST WITH IBN BATTUTA

1. Cairo 1326

Cloisters (khanqahs) of Darvishes
Built by aristocrats
Have silver rings on their doors
The mystics sit down to eat
Each from his private bowl
Each drinks
From his own cup
They are given
Changes of clothing
And a monthly allowance
On Thursday nights
They are given sugar
Soap and oil
For their lamps
And the price of a bath.

In the great cemetery
They build chambers
Pavilions
Hire singers
To chant the *Koran*
Day and night among the tombs
With pleasant voices.

Convent at Dayr at-Tin:
A piece of the Prophet's
Wooden basin with the pencil
With which he applied kohl
The awl

With which he sewed his sandals
Bought by the founder
For a hundred thousand dirhams.

2. Syria

Ma'arra and Sarmín: towns
Of abominable Shi'ites
Who hate the Ten Companions
And every person called Omar

In Sarmín (where scented soap
Is made and exported
To Damascus and Cairo)
These heretics so hate the Ten
They will not even say "Ten"
Their brokers at auctions
When they come to "ten"
Say "Nine-plus-one"

One day a faithful Turk
At one of their markets
Heard the broker call "Nine-plus-one"
He went for him with a club, shouting
"You bastard, say TEN!"

"Ten with a club"
Wept the broker.

3. The Nusayris

These heretics hate all true believers and when ordered by
     the Sultan
To build mosques build them far from their homes
Keep asses and cattle in them let them fall into disrepair.
If a true believer coming from another country
Stops in a ruined mosque and sings the call to prayer
The infidels say: "Stop braying,
We will bring you a little hay."

Once a stranger came to the Nusayris and told them he was
     the Mahdi

He promised to divide Syria among them
Giving each one a city or a town.
He gave them olive leaves and said:
"These will bring you success. These leaves
Are warrants of your appointment."

They went forth into city and town
And when arrested, each said to the Governor:
"The Imám al-Mahdi has come. He has given me this town!"

The Governor would then reply: "Show me your warrant."

Each one then produced his olive leaves
And was flogged.

So the stranger told the heretics to fight:
"Go with myrtle rods," he said
"Instead of swords. The rods
Will turn to swords at the moment of battle."

They entered a town on Friday when the men were at
        the mosque.
They raped the women and the Muslims
Came running out with swords
And cut them to pieces.

News was sent to the capital by carrier pigeon.
    The Governor
Moved out with an army. Twenty thousand heretics
Were slaughtered. The rest hid in the mountains.
They offered one dinar per head if they were spared.
This news went by pigeon to the Sultan
Who said: "Kill them."

But the General
Said these people would be useful
Working on the land
And their lives were spared.

4. Mecca

"The Meccans are very elegant and clean in their dress, and
most of them wear white garments, which you always see

fresh and snowy. They use a great deal of perfume and
kohl and make free use of toothpicks of green arák-wood.

"The Meccan women are extraordinarily beautiful and very
pious and modest. They too make great use of perfumes to
such a degree that they will spend the night hungry in order
to buy perfumes with the price of their food.

"They visit the mosque every Thursday night, wearing their
finest apparel; and the whole sanctuary is saturated with the
smell of their perfume. When one of these women goes
away the odour of the perfume clings to the place after she
has gone."

5. Isfahan

In Isfahan the fair
Surrounded by orchards
(Apricots and quinces
Pears and melons)
The people out-do one another
In banquets
"In the preparation for which
They display all their resources"
One corporation entertained another with viands
Cooked over candles
"The guests returned the invitation
And cooked their viands with silk."

6. Delhi

In the Sultan's apartments
I saw a *Júgi*
Sitting in midair
I fell in a faint
They had to give me a drink
To revive me

And there he was
Still sitting in midair
His companion

Took a sandal from a bag
Beat it on the ground
Til it rose in the air
All by itself and poised
Over the floating one
And it began hitting him
On the back of the neck
Until he floated down
And landed.

"I would tell them to do something else,"
Said the Sultan, "If I did not fear
For your reason."

7. Calicut

Chinese vessels at anchor in the harbor
One of the largest in the world. Malabar
Coast of ginger pepper spice
Four decks with cabins saloons
Merchants of Canton Sumatra
Ceylon stay locked in cabins
With wives and slave girls
Sailors bring their boys to sea
Cultivate salads and ginger
In wooden vats

In Calicut I missed my boat
To China and my slave
Girls were all stolen by the King
Of Sumatra and my companions
Were scattered over China
Sumatra and Bengal

When I saw what had happened
I sailed for the Maldives
Where all the inhabitants
Are Muslims

Live on red fish lightly cooked
Or smoked in palmleaf baskets
It tastes like mutton

These natives wear no pants
Only aprons
Bathe twice a day
Use sandalwood and do not fight
Their armor is prayer.

LUBNAN

Idris—Ilyas: two names
One star, one prophet
Throned in the sun (Idris)
And coming down
The ladder of alchemy and metals
To Baalbeck
Red hot earth
Whose temples are furnaces
He did not stop half way
To rutting Bedlam
Tried out all the dreams
Wasted his demon machine
In a university of lepers
And lost the faculty of speech.

One day the stonewall mountain
Cracked its blue dome
Let out a horse harnessed in flame
A car of fire
Which Ilyas happened to notice

Green green are the waters
Gone the rider in the green night
And Bedlam bells
Quiet

Far away the red saint rides the shouting fire of that horse
Idris—Ilyas one interpreter
May be back tomorrow morning
When the vision
Will be total.

TOMB COVER OF IMAM RIZA

At Meshed, Iran

Here is the threshold of holiness in the dust of the road
    where mighty kings have laid their heads and crowns
Men and spirits, birds and beasts, fairies and demons
    all have laid their heads down in the court of His presence.
No wonder that they lay the head of service and obedience
    on the threshold of Him descended from the Prophet
For having laid the hand of seeking on the skirt of Haidar
    their desire is fulfilled
Seeking for grace the holy cherubim have spread
    their pinions under the footsteps of His visitors.

For the being of Abbas the nine round canopies of heaven
    were raised
    for the life of Abbas and the enduring of his line.

In the hand of heaven the radiant sun was fixed
    to light the steps of those who came before His court
The dust of their passing is a lure baited with mush
    and the earth of their footsteps a snare with ambergris
They are drunk as with wine in union with the Friend's
    beauty
    or even as if they had set foot in paradise

Without weariness of the road they reach the fountain of life
    and leave to Alexander for his portion the realms of
    darkness.
Greater joy than the water of life is their pleasure
    who give their hearts to the winebearer of Kanthar [Kauthar].

SONG FOR THE DEATH OF AVERROËS
(from Ibn Al Arabi, after the Spanish version of Asin Palacios)

i

My father sent me on an errand to the house of his friend Averroës,
    one of the cadis of the city, the great one, the wise Averroës, son
    of Aristotle

Averroës had manifested a desire to see me and to learn if it were
    true that God had spoken to me in solitude.

So I came to the house of Averroës, in Cordova. I was still at that season so young that my beard had not grown, but God had spoken to me.

And when I entered the house of Averroës and reached the apartment in which he was engaged in thought,

He rose from the place where he was sitting and came towards me with affection and respect.

He took me in his arms and said in a questioning tone: "Yes?"

I said: "Yes."

My answer increased his joy.
For he saw that I had understood him right away.

But I realized the source of his satisfaction, and I said immediately: "No."

For though I have understood him, he had not understood me.

Then Averroës was overcome with distress. He turned pale.
He began at that moment to doubt.
The whole truth of his own teaching was now in question.

He asked me, then: "So, you have learned the answer: but how?
By the Spirit? By His Light? What answer?
Is it perhaps the same answer that we have learned from reason?"

I answered: "Yes and No.
Between the 'yes' and the 'no' spirits fly forth from matter,
Between 'yes' and 'no'
The living neck bone is set apart from flesh!"

Then Averroës grew very pale, and sat down in the grip of fear.
He seemed to be overcome by stupor
As though he had by chance
Caught the gist of my allusions.

ii

Averroës, an eminent philosopher, dedicated entirely to a life of thought, study, and rational investigation, could not but give thanks to God for having been permitted to live in a time when he might see with his own eyes a human being who had entered, ignorant, into the spiritual sanctuary and who had emerged as Averroës himself,

Without the help of any education, without study, without books, without teacher.

For this reason he exclaimed: "Here now is that spiritual state the existence of which we have long defended with rational proofs, without ever encountering anyone who had experience of it.

"Praise be to God who had made us live in this time when there exists one of those endowed with mystical gifts, one able to unlock His door, and praised be He for granting me, in addiition, the favor of seeing one such person with my own eyes."

I desired to meet Averroës again, and by the mercy of God he was shown to me at a time when I was in ecstacy. But I saw him under such a form that there appeared to be between his person and myself a very thin curtain, through which I could observe him without his being able to see me, or to become aware of the place which I occupied.

There he was, in abstraction, thinking deeply within himself.

And I said: "It is true, then. There is no way that he can be brought into the place where we others are."

iii

I never saw Averroës again until he died.

His death was in the year 595,* in a city of Morocco, and he was translated most solemnly to Cordova, the place of his sepulchre, where he lies today.

* of the Hegira

When the body of Averroës was brought once more to Spain, and when the people of Cordova were gathered to watch its return to the city of burial,

The coffin containing his remains was mounted on one side of a beast of burden. And on the other side, for counterweight, what did they hang but all the books Averroës had written!

I too was watching, in the company of the scholar Benchobair, and of my disciple, Benazzarach, the copyist.

Turning to us, the young one said: "Do you not observe what it is that hangs as counterweight to the Master Averroës as he rides by? On one side goes the Master, and on the other side his works, that is to say the books which he composed!"

Then Benchobair explained: "No need to point it out, my son, for it is clearly evident! Blessed be thy tongue that has spoken it!"

I took careful note of this word of my disciple, and I set it apart for future meditation, as a reminder of this event.

For this was the word that held the secret of the occasion, the seed of truth, shown to the disciple, at the burial of Averroës:

I planted the seed within myself thus, in two verses:

> "On one side the Master rides: on the other side, his books.
> Tell me: his desires, were they at last fulfilled?"

Three of us friends together stood by and saw, when Averroës was brought to Cordova for burial.

Of these three, two are now gone. May God have pardoned them.

THE NIGHT OF DESTINY*

In my ending is my meaning
Says the season.

---

* "The Night of Destiny" celebrates the end of the Moslem fast, Ramadan, and commemorates the giving of the Koran to Mohammed. Hence it has something of the Spirit of Christmas, a feast when the heavens open and the "Word" is heard on earth.

No clock:
Only the heart's blood
Only the word.

O lamp
Weak friend
In the knowing night!

O tongue of flame
Under the heart
Speak softly:
For love is black
Says the season.

The red and sable letters
On the solemn page
Fill the small circle of seeing.

Long dark—
And the weak life
Of oil.

Who holds the homeless light secure
In the deep heart's room?

Midnight!
Kissed with flame!

See! See!
My love is darkness!

Only in the Void
Are all ways one:

Only in the night
Are all the lost
Found.

In my ending is my meaning.

THE MOSLEMS' ANGEL OF DEATH
(Algeria 1961)

Like a jeweled peacock he stirs all over
With fireflies. He takes his pleasure in
Lights.

He is a great honeycomb of shining bees
Knowing every dust with sugar in it.
He has a million fueled eyes.

With all his eyes he explores life.

The firefly city stirs all over with knowledge.
His high buildings see too many
Persons: he has found out
Their times and when their windows
Will go out.

He turns the city lights in his fingers like money.

No other angel knows this one's place,
No other sees his phoenix wings, or understands
That he is lord of Death.

(Death was once allowed
To yell at the sky:
"I am death!
I take friend from friend!
I am death!
I leave your room empty!")

O night, O High Towers! No man can ever
Escape you, O night!

He is a miser. His fingers find the money.
He puts the golden lights in his pocket.

There is one red coal left burning
Beneath the ashes of the great vision.
There is one blood-red eye left open
When the city is burnt out.

Azrael! Azrael!
See the end of trouble!

MERTON'S BOOK REVIEWS FROM COLLECTANEA CISTERCIENSIA

(The following short book reviews were written by Father Louis [Thomas Merton] for the publication Collectanea Cisterciensia, *published in French by the Cistercian order. They were planned as constituents of a two-part series entitled "Moines et Spirituels Non-Chrétiens" [Non-Christian Monks and Spirituals], which also included some more reviews by Merton and others of books about Zen and Hindu monasticism as well. The first four appeared in issue # 27 in 1965; the last four were intended for issue # 29 in 1967. Though page proofs were sent to Merton and are now in the archives at the Thomas Merton Center, the second quartet of reviews never appeared in the journal itself but were replaced by other reviews by Merton on books about Zen Buddhism.)*

One Hundred Poems of Kabir, translated by Rabindranath Tagore, assisted by Evelyn Underhill (London: Macmillan & Co., 1962)

L et us welcome this new edition of an extraordinary book, a selection of 100 poems by Kabir, translated by the great Tagore, and introduced by Evelyn Underhill. A weaver in Benares in the fifteenth century, Kabir, the son of poor Muslim parents, was accepted by a Hindu master and, though remaining a Muslim and a layman, had a hand in the renewal of Indian spirituality, inspired by his master Ramananda. The spirituality of Kabir, without being overly concerned about orthodoxy, reconciled Sufism and Brahmanism in divine love poems which are among the most beautiful in the world. We find in them not only the accents of the great Persian spiritual poets—'Attâr, Rûmî and Hâfiz—and those of the Hindu *Bhakti,* but echoes of Christian mysticism as well, for Kabir is always careful to respect the distinction between God and man. In the hymns of joy and ecstatic love, Kabir sings of the "cosmic game" and the "invisible dance" between the eternal Lover and His creation: This is the very ancient theme of the "dance of Shiva" celebrated as the expansion of all the "spiritual senses" of the ascetic, who recognizes himself as the mysterious and eternal chosen one of the divine Lover:

> Gorakhnath asks Kabir: "Tell me, O Kabir, when did your
>   vocation begin? Where did your love have its rise?"
> Kabir answers:
> "When He whose forms are manifold had not begun His play;
>   when there was no Guru, and no disciple: when the world
>   was not spread out: when the Supreme One was alone—
> Then I became an ascetic; then, O Gorakh, my love was drawn
>   to Brahma.[1]

Indeed, in this beautiful small book we find echoes of the *Canticum Sponsi et sponsae*, which were heard in Cistercian monasteries in the seventeenth century, and even more of the poetry which makes us think of the Rhenish and Flemish mystics (Hadewijch for example). Listen to this:

> The shadows of evening fall thick and deep, and the darkness of
>   love envelops the body and the mind.
> Open the window to the west, and be lost in the sky of love;
> Drink the sweet honey that steeps the petals of the lotus of the
>   heart.
> Receive the waves in your body: what splendour is in the region
>   of the sea!
> Hark! the sounds of conches and bells are rising.
> Kabir says: "O brother, behold! the Lord is in this vessel of my
>   body."

Here again, recalling the traditional theme of monastic vigilance:

> O my heart! the Supreme Spirit, the great Master, is near you:
>   wake, oh wake!
> Run to the feet of your Beloved: for your Lord stands near to
>   your head.
> You have slept for unnumbered ages: this morning will you not
>   wake?

This is obviously not a completely Christian mysticism, and though we can always debate the exact scope of this experience of

God, we cannot deny its profundity, its sincerity, or the splendor of its poetic expression.

*

* *

Martin Lings, *A Moslem Saint of the Twentieth Century, Shaikh Ahmad al 'Alawî* (London: George Allen & Unwin, 1961).

"North African Europeans live as a rule in such ignorance of the inner workings of Islam, that for them a Shaikh or a Marabout is a kind of wizard, without any importance except for what political influence he may have." These are the words of a French doctor, who in 1920 for the first time encountered the grand spiritual master of North African Islam, Shaikh Ahmad al-'Alawî (who died in 1934). But this most important Sufi master of our century, who was conscious of being an instrument of spiritual renewal in Islam, remained unknown even to scholars and Islamicists, even though he published a dozen important books. Louis Massignon mentions him only in passing. Martin Lings, of the Library [2] of the British Museum, has just published a remarkable study of the spiritual teaching of the Shaikh, with translations of some of his poems.

To the same skeptical doctor who had in a way discovered him, Ahmad al-'Alawî said: "Do you know what is lacking in you? . . . To be one of us and to see the Truth; you lack the desire to raise your Spirit above yourself. And that is irremediable." The essence of Sufism is the elevation of the spirit to God through the *dhikr*, an uninterrupted "remembering"—a rhythmic invocation, synchronized with breathing, movement, and repose—which puts the Name (of Allah) inside the heart, between the microcosm and the macrocosm, and ultimately between time and eternity. By the dance and the *dhikr*, by purification in the silence and solitude of the *khalwah* (a retreat of up to forty days, more or less), by fasting, and by meditation on the Qur'an, the Sufi seeks the interior and spiritual concentration which elevates him to gnosis, the knowledge of the heart which pierces the exterior of things in order to be able "read" these things or to decipher them as symbols. But, indeed more than that, the heart of the Sufi loses itself in the mystery of God to such a point that God becomes, through his love, "the ear with which he hears, the eye with which he sees, the hand with which he touches, and the foot with which he walks."

This contemplation is not, in al-'Alawî's teaching, the affair of the majority. A few may reach it. All can aspire to it, and those who do not achieve it will at least have a certain interior peace proportional to their efforts and their fidelity. But, he says, "beneath the religion there is the teaching"—the exterior practice of religion must be completed by a contemplative deepening. There are two sorts of knowledge: that of the tongue, and that of the heart. That which is [only] of the tongue bears witness against the disciple who does not possess the knowledge of the heart. "Let him examine his conscience: if what his heart possesses is more precious than what his tongues pronounces, then he is one of those whom his Lord has made certain."

This grand Shaikh had even a certain universalist and ecumenical spirit. He knew the Gospel of St. John, the Letters of St. Paul, and unlike most Muslims, he at least understood what the Christian belief in the Holy Trinity means to say. According to the author, the Shaikh would have liked to find some Christian of his own spiritual level, but "Christianity seldom admits mutual understanding on the part of other religions." These words are not those of the Shaikh, but of his English disciple. Are they just? In practice, the majority of Christians have been allowed to believe that this is so. But the times are changing. Let us remember what the Qur'an says on the subject of Christians, especially monks: "And when they listen to the revelation received by the Messenger, thou wilt see their eyes overflowing with tears, for they recognize the truth." (Sûrah V, 82–83). It is thus our part, in the face of Islam, to be ready to understand everything which is authentic in the aspirations of Sufism.

*

* *

Seyyed Hossein Nasr, *Three Muslim Sages* (Adapted from The Harvard Lectures on World Religion; Cambridge, Mass.: Harvard University Press, 1964).

The most important of the grand masters of Sufism, Ibn 'Arabi, was born in Spain in 1165. It is he who, according to the opinion expressed long ago by Asin Palacios, perhaps left his traces in the mystical teaching of St. John of the Cross.[3] An outline of this teaching of Ibn 'Arabî has just been given in these lectures at Harvard by a scholarly Egyptian,[4] Seyyed Hossein Nasr, who considers Ibn 'Arabî to be the person who systemized Sufism in order to integrate it definitively into the the common tradition of Islam. "His aim was not to give an explanation [of the belief of Islam] that would satisfy the intelligence and be be acceptable to reason, but *a true theory or vision of its reality*, which was not attained without the practice of various methods." The author studies this gnostic as a spiritual textual-interpreter of the world of the Qur'an, the transition-ground between exterior reality (*zahir*) and interior reality (*batin*) through the mediation of symbol, produced by the creative spiritual and mystical imagination. It is thus a very interesting teaching to compare with the *théoria physikè* of the Alexandrine and Cappadocian Fathers. Sufism looks at the world with a frankly mystical eye, for to the Sufi the Creation is epiphany, which can be seen even as theophany. Is Sufism thus a teaching foreign to the Qur'an? Not at all. The author ranges those who accept Sufism as fully Quranic (such as Massingon, Corbin, and others) against those who maintain the outdated position which seeks to attach Sufism chiefly to Hinduism, Christianity, or Mazdaism (like Zaehner, Arberry,[5] Nicholson, and Asin Palacios.)

*

* *

Fritz Meier, "The Transformation of Man in Mystical Islam," *in Man and Transformation*, Papers from the Eranos Yearsbooks, vol. 5, Bollingen Series 30 (New York: Pantheon, 1964), 37–68.

The mystical aspirations of Sufism collided early on with the dogmatic intransigence of Islam regarding the unity and transcendance of God. How does one arrive at union with the Unique, the Only, who does not allow any other being even to come close to Him? If Abû Yazîd al-Bistâmî (ninth century of the Christian era) could say "I am God" without being punished, it is because Allah alone spoke through him. Al-Hallâj had less luck. For having proclaimed his union with the Truth, this "mystical martyr of Islam" was crucified.

Fritz Meier, a professor at the Universtiy of Basle, studies the degrees of mystical transformation in Sufism in a fashion that is so simplified that it leaves aside numerous formal stages and reduces them more or less to three. The aspiration to union is justified among Sufis by *tawhîd* (profession of the Unity of God, then negation of the duality of God/man through mystical love). Al-Balki (tenth century) defines the mystical life in a way quite acceptable to Islamic orhtodoxy: "the life of the heart with God"—total submission to the will of God by enduring all the transformations required by him (which links this reading by Meier to another in the same volume, by Father [Jean] Daniélou on a similar subject[6] in St. Gregory of Nyssa.)

Conversion (*tawba*) is the work of God, not of the faithful. The novice places himself immediately under a master (*shaikh*) whom he obeys in all things as if he were the Angel Gabriel who spoke to the prophets. The novice should reveal to the master not only all his thoughts and spiritual experiences, but also all his dreams, which the shaikh will interpret. "Whoever has no shaikh, has Satan for his guide," says a Sufi maxim. Under the direction of the shaikh, the novice practices a severe ascesis. According to Meier, the word Sufi itself refers to the hair shirt which these ascetics wear, in imitation of Christian monks. (Not all are in agreement on this last point.) When he has made notable progress, the novice may enter into a period of absolute seclusion (*khalwah*) in a cell with no light in order to remain in silence, solitude, and strict fasting with no occupation other than the *dhikr Allah* (constant remembrance of God by repeating either His Name, or the the consecrated formula, "There is no god but God," etc.). This practice is called "thinking of God inside the heart" and it should lead to mystic or gnostic knowledge (*ma'rifah*) in which the heart enters within the luminous shadow (*shekinah*) of God. One sees that Sufism reproduces many of the traits of mystic monastic Christianity, especially Eastern Christianity. One finds there especially a mystical exegesis of the Qur'an, of Biblical history, and of the Islamic traditions [or hadiths] which approximate the spiritual interpetations by the Church Fathers of The Song of Songs and the Old Testament. One notes also that for the Sufi, as for St. John of the Cross, visions are rather symbolic obstacles to be discarded. They are, says Kubra, like the walls of a prison which keep you from entering freely into contact with God inside the luminous cloud. The true objective of the Sufi is the dissolution of the "I" contingent in God.

Was Meier always right in his choice of terms? Is the experiencing of "the light of a contranatural reality" really "against nature"? Is it true to say that the introversion of Sufis was their "weak point," since they thus remained "in contact with the real world" and with their brothers? And especially, is it just to blame Sufi introversion for the "cultural decadence of Islam"? The author himself points out the abundance of good works, brotherly love, and social conscience among the Sufis. One must in the same manner admit the possibility of a more profound conception of "reality," which without impugning the value of everyday reality, refuses to admit that it is the only true one.

Let us remember that beautiful story of Rûmî (thirteenth century) who, when he heard that there was a Turk in the street calling out that he had a fox (*dilkü*) for sale, believed that he heard instead the Persian phrase *dil-kû* ("Where is your heart?") and fainted for love.

*

*   *

A. Reza Arasteh, "Final Integration in the Adult Personality," *American Journal of Psychoanalysis* 25:1 (1965).[7]

To describe the full integration of the person and his maturity, psychologists and psychoanalysts generally take as their point of departure infancy or mental illness. It is less current to encounter one who, to describe this final integration in an adult, takes his givens from the life and writings of the mystics. In this perspective, a Persian psychoanalyst, who is a professor in the United States, has written a very suggestive article, in which he is above all interested in the tradition of Persian Sufism, and especially in Rûmî. We find here as well some references to other Eastern mystical traditions, particularly Zen, which has attracted the attention of some Western analysts. Dr. Reza Arasteh comes to the conclusion that the way of the mystics is that of full integration. It opens the person to the "void" of Self through the dissolution of the empirical "I," the "I" constituted by its ties to social realities. The dissolution of this "social and cultural I" does not come without a feeling of great agony; it is in fact a sort of death. Few men are capable of it; few are capable of passing beyond what Arasteh calls an "existential moratorium" in order to reach a reintegration in a consciousness that is higher and more universal, in which is found a true creativity and the "perception of multiple realities" unified in the One. It is a question of a "transcultural state" in which (the experience of)[8] the distinction between subject and object disappears. The "fully integrated" man is the one who has thus become "perfectly one" in a "state of ultimate rebirth." Careful to remain within the framework of modern science, the author treats his subject phenomenologically rather than theologically, and he does not refer to the mystic state as such, that is to say, as union with God. He makes no allusion to the Christian mystic. We can see ourselves in this excellent and very suggestive study, which establishes that full integration of the human personality is not acquired merely by "sublimation" and adjustment to society, but that it is found at the end of the long hard road of spiritual search, which demands sacrifice. The monastic ideal has always been centered on this aspect of a pilgrimage of discovery of the inner and outer light in the ordinary frame of social and cultural forms.

*

*   *

Paul Nwyia, *Ibn 'Abbâd de Ronda* (Beruit: Institute of Oriental Studies, 1961)

In Islam, spiritual direction is not regarded as necessary, and when it occurs, it is rather exceptional. However, the Sufis hold it as absolutely essential to the higher degrees of spiritual life, and as very useful for a life of average piety. Discussing the intense spiritual fervor of the Sufi centers of Morocco in the fourteenth century, Paul Nwyia illustrates this subject abundantly through his account of the writings and the teaching of Ibn 'Abbâd de Ronda and his entourage. In choosing a guide, novices were given counsel to avoid three types of men: the prideful and the vain, who are blind to their own conceit; the innovator who has lost his way and strayed into error; and the narrow-minded conformist who cannot free himself from the servitude to stereotypical rules and practices, who interprets them literally in a spirit of servile fear. The guide whom the disciple needs to pick is one who is "a friend for whom the way to follow is not a secret," and quite particularly, one who knows thoroughly the end and the means, who would know not only how to formulate the general principles, but how to impose himself as a guide in concrete circumstances. A director of this quality is a gift from God to the sincere man who truly challenges his own "I." No one else deserves such a gift. The best directors, according to Ibn 'Abbâd, inculcate the "way of gratitude," akin to the grace that the "son of the present moment" holds. This gratitude attests that nothing which comes from God is not good. And the "filial" attitude inside the present moment lets us discover in it a gift of love that God brings us. The guide should not "make life painful" for us. On the other hand, the advantageous way of helping the disciple proceed with "ease" is meant not to steer the disciple toward self-indulgence, but toward faith, leading him to see God in everything, relying on Him for everything, and not on the feeble means at his own disposal. Thus the disciple will eventually be led to *fanâ'* which is the elimination of self by totally surrendering it to God, which is the summit of Sufism. But never, so the Sufis believe, will one arrive at this without a spiritual guide. "He who has no shaikh (master), has Satan for a shaikh." Whoever finds a master in any of the spiritual ways, should never cease to thank God.

(*Note*: It was maintained wrongly—in our review of Seyyed Hossein Nasr's *Three Muslim Sages* in #27 of *Collectanea*—that Asin Palacios suspected an influence by Ibn 'Arabî on St. John of the Cross. Actually it was Ibn 'Abbâd whom Asin Palacios took as a possible Islamic influence on the mystic of Carmel. We take this opportunity to correct that mistake.)

*

* *

Dom Jean Leclercq, O.S.B., "Le Monachisme en Islam et Chrétienté." *in Images de Toumliline* (Morocco: 1963), 1–5.

Recent studies have demonstrated the inexactitude of the cliché which has, for a long time, held that there is "no monasticism in Islam." The Qur'an shows that the Prophet [Muhammad] not only did not blame (Christian) monks, but even came to regard them with a certain respect, finding the humble among them "the closest, in love, of believers" (Sûrah V). History also holds some proofs of a certain monasticism in Islam itself. The Benedictine Dom Jean Leclercq, in a compilation of studies concerning this subject, attests that each of the "four species of monk" described by St. Benedict in the first chapter of his Rule, are found in Islam and comprised, until the eighteenth century, undercurrents of a character like that of a St. Benedict Labre.[9] Some rather close comparisons have been made, in the past, between Christian monks and Sufis or holy men in Islam. St. John of Damascus considered Islam rather indulgently, and, in the ninth century, in the East, a cordial understanding reigned between Muslims and Christian monks who consulted each other mutually. In the West, Monte Cassino[10] was a place of encounter, at least on the cultural and scientific planes, between Christianity and Islam. Moreover there is the question of contacts in Spain. Cistericians and Muslims met during the Crusades in less friendly connections. Dom Leclercq concludes; "If Islam has inherited certain Christian influences, emanating from those of Christian monasticism, which are destined to make their imprint on (Muslim) monaticism, these influences or examples have not always been the best ones." But, he adds, "the hour is coming for a better understanding, and, on both sides, one admits the need for a very big initiative, for a study without prejudice, for a frankness of dialogue." One awaits a better conclusion, following the monastic conference in Morocco with the monks of Toumliline,[11] none of whom is ignorant of the ecumical dimension.

*

* *

Cyprien Rice, *The Persian Sufis* (London: George Allen and Unwin Ltd., 1964).

Father Cyprien Rice, who was trained at Cambridge in the Consular Services of the Levant[12] prior to World War I and learned Arabic, Persian, and Turkish there, became a Dominican in 1919. It was as a Dominican that, during the 1920s, he was sent to Persia on the invitation of the Apostolic Delegate and there encountered a number of

Persian intellectuals, poets, and dervishes. His study of Persian Sufism can thus be called a firsthand documentation, one made from personal contacts as well as direct recourse to sources. We have now a clear account, one both interesting and favorable, of the Muslim mysticism one encounters in Persia. We discover in Sufism, if not a monastic institution, at least an incontestably monastic spirit of spiritual poverty, surrender, and interior renunciation, coupled with submission to the guidance of a spiritual father and the search for the union with God, all of this often in complete solitude, at least part of the time. Father Rice is in agreement with many other scholars in maintaining that Sufism, certainly that founded strictly on the Muslim faith in the One God, is a tributary, in its development, of the Christian monasticism of Syria, which he described as "capital and the most dynamic." The Sufi literature abundantly deals with the ascetic "degrees" [or stages] and the mystic "states," which the author descibes for us succinctly. The Sufi manner of prayer is centered on the *dhikr* or "remembrance," that is, the rhythmic and recollected repetition of the name of Allah, for the purpose of eliminating all other thought and to introduce the Name into the sanctuary of the heart. This invocation goes hand in hand with a controlled breathing, sometimes with movements of the body, and even with dance. Given the fact that Sufism has known, since its origins, a certain openness toward Christian mysticism, and that the mystic devotion of the great Sufi poets of Persia, awakens, for the most part, familiar resonances in the Catholic reader, one understands why Father Rice sees in Sufism one of the great ecumenical bridges between Catholicism and Islam. It is necessary however to take account of the fact that Sufism has not always had the unreserved approval of [that part of] Islam that is strictly and rigidly orthodox.

—Translated by Rob Baker

NOTES
1. All quotes from the Underhill and Tagore translation of *One Hundred Poems of Kabir*, originally entitled *Songs of Kabir* (New York: Macmillan Co., 1915/1961).

2. Martin Lings's actual title was Curator of the Department of Oriental Printed Books and Manuscripts for the British Museum at this time.

3. See Merton's correction of this error in his Nwyia review below. It was Ibn 'Abbâd de Ronda who Asin Palacios thought might have influenced St. John of the Cross, not Ibn 'Arabî.

4. Nasr is actually Persian (Iranian).

5. After reading this review, Martin Lings wrote to Merton (on June 15, 1965) that he thought Merton had been unfair to lump the Islamicist A. J. Arberry in with those who found Sufism derivative: ". . . at the end, I think you do Arberry an injustice. He recently wrote an article in the Bulletin of the School of Oriental and African Studies entitled *Bistamiana*, in which he ridicules Zaehner's theories about the origins of Sufism. Incidentally, it was only through Arberry's strong recommendation that my book was published; and he has invited me to write the chapter on Sufism in a forthcoming Cambridge University Press book on 'Religion in the Middle East.' I always have the impression that he is more and more inclined to look on Sufism as purely Quranic." (Letter in the Thomas Merton Center, Bellarmine College, Lousiville, Kentucky.)

6. In the French, "epectase," for which no translation could be found.

7. Arasteh later expanded this magazine piece into a book, which Merton also reviewed in the essay "Final Integration," which is included in this collectiion.

8. Parentheses are in Merton's original French.

9. For a clarification of Merton's reference here, the translator is indebted to Brother Patrick Hart of Gethsemani, who immediately recognized the comparison to the little known St. Benedict Joseph Labre (1748–83), a wandering homeless solitary who as a young man was refused admission by both the Trappists (twice) and the Carthusians. He decided instead to spend four years wandering on foot to the holy pilgrimage places of Europe, then settled in Rome where he visited churches by day and slept in the Colisseum at night. As Merton seems to be implying, he was a bit of a Sufi in spirit. Butler's *Lives of the Saints* indicates that even as a child, "the boy, however, had already begun to realize a call to serve God in complete abandonment of the world." From a very young age, "His one ambition was now to retire into the most austere religious order he counld find." Failing at that, he took to the road, sleeping in barns and fields and eating only what others gave to him in charity, and thus found his true vocation: "Not by shutting himself up in any cloister was he to abandon the world, but by obeying the counsel of perfection without turning his back on the world." Small wonder some religious historians dismissed him as "a social misfit" (John Coulson, *The Saints*) or "a representative example of those who, at all times in Christian history, have refused to be 'respectable.'" (Donald Attwater, *A Dictionary of Saints*) and many reference sources, including *The Catholic Encyclopedia*, do not list him at all. His death, after collapsing on the steps of a church during Holy Week in 1783, was greeted by crowds of children running through the streets of Rome proclaiming, "The saint is dead!" One hundred years later the Church agreed and canonized him. His day is April 16.

10. The mother house of the Benedictine Order, located between Naples and Rome.

11. Monastery of the Benedictine Order in North Africa. Merton had suggested to Leclercq that he visit there on a planned trip to Africa in 1963. In a letter published in *The School of Charity: Letters on Religious Renewal and Spiritual*

Direciton, ed. Brother Patrick Hart (New York: Farrar, Straus & Giroux, 1990), Merton writes: "I envy you going to Africa. I think it is a very important place now. Toumliline is a place I admire greatly. Dom Denis Martin met and spoke to me briefly here. Naturally I did not have permission to visit with him; he is one of those 'dangerous' Benedictines who are experimenting with a new kind of monastic life." (letter of July 23, 1963, *School of Charity*, 179).

12. The countries of the eastern Mediterranean, from Turkey to Egypt.

THE UNIVERSALITY OF MONASTICISM

AND ITS RELEVANCE IN THE MODERN WORD

Frithjof Schuon

(Of this piece Merton wrote [1964], "Schuon's really remarkable essay on monasticism . . . I like it very much, and like the whole tone of it from beginning to end. It is a much saner and more realistic approach to the question of 'the monk and the world' that is being taken at times by some of the monks." Marco Pallis sent a copy of this article by Frithjof Schuon to Merton in the fall of 1963. It was later published as part of Light on the Ancient Worlds, *[London: Perrenial Books, 1965; new ed., Bloomington, Ind.: World Wisdom Books, 1984]. Merton held Schuon's writings in high regard, especially* Understanding Islam, *and particularly his explication there of the Basmalah, the phrase meaning "In the Name of God.")*

The finding of a common denominator for phenomena as varied as the different monasticisms of the West and of the East does not appear at first sight to be an easy task, for in order to be able to define, one must have found a point of view that makes definition possible. There is however a point of view that seems to arise without difficulty out of the nature of things, granted that it is impossible to give an account of human nature otherwise than by way of its attachment, either positively or negatively, to God, for without God there is no such thing as man. From that point of view it can be said that the effort to reduce the complexity of life to a simple formula, and to a formula that is essential and liberating, arises out of whatever is most whole and most profound in the human condition, and that this same effort has led, in the most diverse spiritual climates, to the sort of institutional sanctity that constitutes monasticism.

Man was created alone and he dies alone; monasticism aspires to preserve this solitude in its metaphysically irreplaceable aspects: it aims to restore to man his primordial solitude before God, or again, it wants to bring man back to his spiritual integrity and to his totality. A perfect society would be a society of hermits, if so paradoxical a statement be admissible; nevertheless, that is exactly what the monastic community seeks to realize, for monasticism is in a certain sense an organised eremitism.

The reflections contained in the next few paragraphs may perhaps seem to some people to be truisms, but they are concerned with mental habits so ineradicable that it is difficult to underestimate their importance if one looks at the matter in the light of fundamentals. The point at issue is this: according to current opinion, monasticism is a matter of "vocation," but not in the proper sense of the word; for when a man is simple enough to take religion literally, and when he commits the indiscretion of allowing rather too spiritual opinions or attitudes to appear, people do not scruple to tell him that his place is "in a monastery," as if he were a foreign body with no right to existence outside the walls of the appropriate institution. The idea of "vocation," in itself positive, then becomes negative: the man who "receives a call" is not one who lives in the truth and is "called" because he lives in it, but one who disturbs society by causing it to become involuntarily aware of what it is. According to this more or less well-established way of looking at things, an absence of vocation or, to put it plainly, worldliness exists *de jure* and not merely *de facto*, and this implies that perfection exists as an optional speciality, and thus as a luxury; it is reserved for monks, and nobody thinks of wondering why it is not for everybody.

A monk will certainly never blame any man simply for living in his own age; this is self-evident, having regard to the secular clergy and lay saints; what is blameworthy is not living "in the world," but living in it badly, and thus in a certain sense creating it. When anyone reproaches a hermit or a monk for "running away from" the world, he commits a double error: firstly, he loses sight of the fact that contemplative isolation has an intrinsic value that is independent of the existence of a surrounding "world"; secondly, he pretends to forget that there are escapes that are perfectly honorable and that, if it is neither absurd nor shameful to do one's best to run away from an avalanche, it is no more so to run away from the temptations or even simply from the distractions of the world, or from our own *ego* insofar as it is rooted in this vicious circle; and let us not forget that in disencumbering ourselves of the world we disencumber the world of our own sufferings. In our days people are very ready to say that to escape from the world is to shirk "responsibilities," a completely hypocritical euphemism that dissimulates behind "altruistic" or "social" notions a spiritual laziness and a hatred of the absolute; people are happy to ignore the fact that the gift of oneself for God is always the gift of oneself for all. It is metaphysically impossible to give oneself to God in such a way that good does not ensue to the environment: to give oneself to God, though it were hidden from all men, is to give oneself to man, for this gift of self has a sacrificial value of an incalculable radiance.

From another point of view, to work for one's own salvation is like breathing, eating, or sleeping; one cannot do these things for anyone else, nor yet help anyone else by abstaining from them. Egoism is taking away from others what they have need of; it is not taking for oneself something of which they know nothing or for which they have no desire.

It is not monasticism that is situated outside the world, it is the world that is situated outside monasticism. If every man lived in the love of God, the monastery would be everywhere, and it is in this sense that one can say that every saint is implicitly a monk or a hermit. Or again: just as it is possible to introduce the "world" into the framework of monasticism, since not every monk is a saint, so also it is possible to transfer monasticism, or the attitude it represents, into the world, for there can be contemplatives in any place.

*

* *

If monasticism is defined as a "withdrawal for God," and if its universal and inter-religious character is recognized on the grounds that the thirst for the supernatural is in the nature of normal man, how can this definition be applied in the case of spiritual men who are Moslems and do not withdraw from society, or who are Buddhists and do cut themselves off but do not seem to have the idea of God? In other words, as far as Islam is concerned, how can there be a spirituality in a religion that rejects monasticism, or again, why is monasticism excluded from a religion which never-theless possesses a mysticism, ascetic discipline, and a cult of saints? To that the answer must be that one of the *raisons d'être* of Islam is precisely the possibility of a "monastery-society," if the expression be allowable: that is to say that Islam aims to carry the con-templative life into the very framework of society as a whole; it suc-ceeds in realizing within that framework conditions of structure and of behavior that permit of contemplative isolation in the very midst of the activities of the world. It must be added that what corre-sponds to the monastery for the Moslem is above all an initiatic attachment to a brotherhood and his submission—*perinde ac cadav-er*—to a spiritual master, as well as the practice of supererogatory orisons, together with vigils and fasts; the isolating element with respect to the worldly is strictness in the observation of the *sunna*; the surrounding society would not think of opposing this strictness in a Moslem country, thus it takes the place in practice of the walls of a monastery. It is true that the dervishes assemble in their *zawiyas* for their communal practices and make retreats in them lasting sometimes for several months; a few live there and consecrate their whole lives to prayer and the service of the *Shaikh*; but the result is not monasticism in a strict sense, comparable to that of Christians or Buddhists. However that may be, the famous "no monasticism in Islam" (*lâ rahbâniyah fî'l-islâm*) really means, not that contempla-tives must not withdraw from the world, but on the contrary that the world must not be withdrawn from contemplatives; the intrin-sic ideal of monasticism or of eremitism, namely asceticism and the mystical life, is in no way affected. And let us not forget that the "holy war" is accompanied in Islam by the same mystical justifica-tion as in Christian chivalry, notably that of the Templars; it offers a way of sacrifice and of martyrdom which united Christians and Moslems at the time of the crusades in one and the same sacrificial love of God.

In the case of Buddhism the difficulty lies in the fact that this religion, while it is essentially monastic, and is so to a degree that cannot be surpassed, seems to ignore the idea of God. Now it goes without saying that an "atheistic spirituality" is a contradiction in terms, and in fact Buddhism possesses completely the idea of a tran-scendent Absolute, and it possesses likewise the idea of a contact between this Absolute and man. Although Buddhism has not got the idea of a "God" in the Semitic or Aryan sense of the word, nonetheless it is in its own way just as conscious of the divine Reality, for it is far from neglecting the crucial ideas of absoluteness, of transcendence, of perfection, and, on the human side, of sacrifice and of sanctity; though doubtless "non-theist," it is quite certainly not "atheist." The aspect of a "personal God" appears notably in the *mahâyânic* cult of the Buddha Amitabha—the Japanese Amidism— wherein it is combined with a perspective of redemptive Mercy. Christian influences have been suggested; this is not only false, but even improbable from more than one point of view; it is forgotten that it is in accordance with the fundamental nature of things that phenomena analogous at least in their forms should occur wherev- er the circumstances are favorable. This prejudice concerning "influences" or "borrowings" brings to mind the ethnographer who found among the Red Indians the myth of the deluge, and ingenu- ously concluded that missionaries had been in touch with them; whereas this myth — or rather this recollection — is found among almost all the peoples on earth.

These last remarks afford an opportunity for a few words on the current confusion between syncretism and eclecticism, although this may perhaps carry us a little away from our subject. Syncretism is never an affair of substance: it is an assembling of heterogeneous elements into a false unity, that is to say, into a unity without real synthesis; eclecticism on the other hand is natural wherever differ- ent doctrines exist side by side, as is proved by the integration of Platonism or Aristotelianism with Christianity. The important thing in any case of the kind is that the original perspective should remain faithful to itself and should accept alien concepts only inso- far as they corroborate its faithfulness by helping to illuminate the fundamental intentions of its own perspective. The Christians had no reason at all for refusing to be inspired by Greek wisdom since it was at hand, and in the same way the Moslems could not help mak- ing use to a certain extent in their mystical doctrine of Neoplatonic concepts as soon as they became aware of them; but it would be a serious mistake to speak of syncretism in these cases, on the false assumption of an analogy between them and artificial doctrines such as those of the modern Theosophical Society. There have never been borrowings between two living religions of essential elements affecting their fundamental structures, as is imagined when Amidism is attributed to the Nestorians.

As examples of Asiatic monasticisms, that of the Hindus and that of the Taoists may be mentioned, but they can scarcely be said to present difficulties comparable to those already spoken of in connection with Islam and Buddhism. Difficulties connected with religious differences are of course of very general occurrence, but that is a complex problem which the present somewhat synthetic view of monasticism as a phenomenon of humanity need not take into account.

*

* *

A world is absurd exactly to the extent that the contemplative, the hermit, the monk appear in it as a paradox or as an "anachronism." The monk however is in the present precisely because he is timeless: we live in an epoch of idolatry of the "age"; the monk incarnates all that is changeless, not through sclerosis or through inertia, but through transcendence.

This leads to certain considerations that may seem to diverge from our subject, but they bring negatively into relief the burning actuality of the monastic ideal, or simply of the religious ideal, which in the last analysis amounts to the same thing. In this world of absurd relativism in which we live, anyone who says "our times" thinks he has said all that is necessary; to identify phenomena of any kind with "other times," or still more with "times gone by," is to liquidate them; consider the hypocritical sadism concealed by words like "gone by," "outdated" or "irreversible," which replace thought by a sort of imaginative suggestion, a "music of prejudice" one might say. If it is found, for example, that some liturgical or ceremonial procedure offends the scientific or demagogic tastes of our age, people are relieved when they recall that the usage in question dates from the Middle Ages, or perhaps that it is "Byzantine," because they can then conclude without further ado that it has no longer any right to existence; they forget completely that there is only one question that must always be asked, namely, *why* the Byzantines did such a thing; more often than not one finds that the answer to this *why* is situated outside time, and that the reason for the existence of such a usage arises out of timeless factors. The identification of oneself with this "age," thereby removing from things all, or nearly all, intrinsic worth, is quite a new attitude, and it is arbitrarily projected into what we call retrospectively "the past." In reality our ancestors did not live in a "time," speaking subjectively and intellectually, but in a "space," that is to say, in a world of stable values wherein the flux of duration was only so to speak accidental; they had a marvelous sense of the absolute in things, and of the rooting of things in the Absolute.

Our age tends more and more to cut man off from his roots; but in seeking to "start again from scratch" and to reduce man to the purely human it succeeds only in dehumanizing him, which proves that the "purely human" is but a fiction; man is fully man only in rising above himself, and he can only do so through religion. Monasticism is there to remind us that man exists only by virtue of his permanent consciousness of the Absolute and of absolute values, and that the works of man are nothing in themselves. The desert Fathers, or Cassian, or St. Benedict, or their like, have shown that before acting one must be, and that actions are precious to the extent that the love of God animates them or is reflected in them, and tolerable to the extent that they are not opposed to that love. The fullness of being, which depends on the spirit, can in principle dispense with action; action does not carry its end in itself; Martha is certainly not superior to Mary. Man is distinguished from the animals in two essential respects, firstly by his intelligence that can reach the absolute and is consequently capable of objectivity and of a sense of the relative, and secondly by his free will, capable of choosing God and attaching itself to him; the rest is but contingency, and this is notably true of that profane and quantitative "culture" totally unknown to the primitive Church and now made into a pillar of human value, in defiance of current experience and of the evidence.

In our age man is defined, not by reference to his specific nature—which cannot be defined otherwise than in a divine context—but by reference to the inextricable consequences of a Prometheanism that has become secular: it is the works of man, or even the remote consequences of these works, which in the minds of our contemporaries determine and define man. We live in a scene-shifter's world wherein it has become almost impossible to get into touch with the primordial realities of things; at every step the prejudices and reflexes inseparable from an irreversible glissade intervene; it is as if before the Renaissance, or before the Encyclopaedists, man had not been wholly man, or as if, in order to be man, it were necessary to have passed by way of Descartes, Voltaire, Rousseau, Kant, Marx, Darwin, and Freud, not forgetting—most recent of all—the inevitable Teilhard de Chardin. It is sad to see how religious convictions are all too often enveloped in an irreligious sensibility, or how such convictions are accompanied by reflexes directly opposed to them. Religious apologetics tend more and more to take their stand on the wrong ground, on which their victory is anyhow impossible, and to adopt a language that rings falsely and can convince nobody, discounting an occasional propagandist success which in no way serves religion as such; when apologetics rub shoulders with demagogy they enter upon the road to suicide. Instead of keeping to the pure and simple truth—a truth that quite obviously cannot please everyone—apologists allow themselves to be fascinated by the postulates of the adversary, as well as by his self-assurance, his dynamism, his easy success and his effective vulgarity. On the pretext of not wanting to "keep the religious message to oneself" it is extrinsically and imperceptibly "falsified," but belief in the existence of such a danger and the mention of such a word are carefully avoided; the very most that is admitted is a danger of "attenuating the message," a euphemism of which the bias is evident.

"Have dominion over the earth" says the Bible, and the partisans of progress do not miss the chance of exploiting that command to justify the ever more totalitarian industrialism of our age and to extol a "spirituality" that conforms to it. In reality it is a very long time since man has obeyed that injunction of the Creator; in order to grasp its true intention and its limits one must remember the divine command to "take no thought for the morrow" and other similar junctions.[1] It is pure hypocrisy to make much of the Biblical sentence first quoted without situating it in its full context, for according to that style of logic it would be right to attribute an equal and absolute force to the words "be fruitful and multiply"[2] and to abolish all chastity in Christianity, and even to return to the polygamy of the Hebrews. This strange eagerness to follow the "commandments of God" might well lead, or so it seems, to many scriptural discoveries besides that of the passage that concerns agriculture, fishing, hunting and stock-rearing, and to many spiritual concerns other than the industrialization of religion.[3]

*

* *

Inferiority complexes and mimetic reflexes are bad counsellors: how often does one meet with absurd reproaches leveled not only at the religion of the Middle Ages but also at that of the nineteenth century which at least was still not "atomic," as if all men who lived before ourselves had been struck with an inexplicable blindness, and as if it had been necessary to await the advent of such and such an atheistic philosopher to discover the light of a new knowledge both decisive and mysteriously unknown to all the saints. It is too readily forgotten that, if human nature has a right to its weaknesses today, which nobody disputes, it had the same right to them in the past; "progress" is most often but a transference, the exchange of one evil for another, otherwise our age would be perfect and sanctified. In the world of man, as it is in itself, it is scarcely possible to choose a good; one is always reduced to the choice of a lesser evil, and in order to determine which evil is the less, there is no alternative but to relate the question to a hierarchy of values derived from eternal realities, and that is exactly what "our age" never does.

In the Middle Ages one started from the idea that man is bad because he is a sinner, whereas in our century man is good because sin does not exist, so much so that evil is first and foremost whatever makes us believe in sin; modern humanitarianism, convinced that man is good, purports to protect man: but from whom? From man evidently, but from what man? And if evil does not come from man, from whom does it come, given the conviction that nothing intelligent exists outside the human being nor more particularly above him?

There is the prejudice of science and the prejudice of society; monasticism insists on the "one thing needful" and practices a collective pauperism free from all envy and perfectly concrete as far as individuals are concerned though the monastery itself be rich; it thus offers in its own way the answer to these two stumbling blocks. What is a science that takes account neither of the transcendent and conscious Infinite, nor of the hereafter, nor of basic phenomena such as Revelation, miracle, pure intellection, contemplation, sanctity; and what is a social equilibrium that abolishes all real superiority and takes no account of the intrinsic nature of man nor of his ultimate destiny? The Biblical account of the creation raises a smile, but nobody understands the Semitic symbolism, which furnishes the key to things apparently naive; it is claimed that the

Church has always been "on the side of the rich," and it is forgotten that from the point of view of religion there is only man, be he rich or poor, man made up of flesh and of spirit, always exposed to suffering and dedicated to death; and if the Church as a terrestrial institution has been forced to lean on the powerful who protected her—or were supposed to protect her—she has never refused herself to the poor, and she compensates to a great extent her accidental and human imperfections by her spiritual gifts and her numberless saints, not forgetting the permanent spiritual presence which is precisely what monasticism actualizes. The Catholic Church has been reproached for its "self-sufficiency": now the Church has a thousand reasons for being "self-sufficient," since she is what she is, and offers what she offers; it is not for her to be uneasy, nor to produce her own "self-criticism," nor to "go off on a new tack," as she is expected to do by those who have no sense of her dignity. The Church has the right to repose in herself; her frontline troops are the saints; she has no need of busy demagogues who make play with "drama" and "death throes." The saints suffice her, and she has always had them.

The success of atheistic materialism can be explained in part by the fact that it represents an extreme position; that kind of extremism fits easily into the framework of a tottering world, and is well adapted to the psychological elements to which it appeals. Christianity also represents an extreme position, but, instead of the fact being given its full value, it is dissembled—this at least is the tendency that seems to prevail—and the Christian position is adapted to that of the adversary, whereas it is precisely the extremism of the Christian message, if it is affirmed without disguise, but also without any forced "dynamism," that has the gift of fascinating and convincing. A conscious or unconscious capitulation before the arguments of the adversary evidently originates in a desire to give him the impression that the Christian absolute realizes the same kind of perfection as the progressive and socialist absolute, and any of the aspects, however essential, of the Christian absolute are disowned if they cut across the adverse tendencies, in such a way that nothing is left wherewith to oppose those tendencies except a half-absolute devoid of all originality; for there are two false attitudes: to say that one has never had anything in view but social progress, which is a ridiculous falsehood wholly unrelated to the Christian perspective, or to accuse oneself

—promising the whole to do better in future—of having neglected social progress, and that is purely and simply a betrayal. What ought to be done is to put each thing in its place and to insist at every turn on what, from the religious point of view, man, life, the world, and society are. Christianity is an eschatological perspective, it envisages things in relation to the hereafter or it does not envisage them at all; to pretend to adopt some other way of looking at things, or to adopt it in fact, while remaining within religion is an incomprehensible and disastrous inconsistency.

The relevance of monasticism is that it incarnates, whether one likes it or not, precisely that very thing in religion that is extreme and absolute and is of a spiritual and contemplative essence; terrestrial charity has no meaning save in connection with celestial charity. "Seek ye first the kingdom of God, and His righteousness. . ."

It is evident and inevitable that religion can and sometimes must adapt itself to changed circumstances; but care must be taken not to decide *a priori* in favor of circumstances, and not to look on them as norms just because they exist and because they please a majority. In proceeding to an adaptation it is important to adhere strictly to the religious perspective and to the hierarchy of values it implies; the inspiration must come from a metaphysical and spiritual body of criteria, and one must not give way to pressures nor especially allow any contamination by a false evaluation of things. Do we not hear of a "religion orientated towards social needs," which is either a pleonasm or else an absurdity, and even of a "spirituality of economic development" which, apart from its monstrosity, is a contradiction in terms? According to that way of thinking, error or sin need no longer be subordinated to the imperatives of truth and of spirituality, but on the contrary it is truth and spirituality that must be adapted to error and to sin; it is the opinion of the adversary that is the criterion of truth and falsehood, of good and evil.

*

* *

But let us return for a moment to the modern scientific outlook, since it plays so decisive a part in the modern mentality. There seems to be absolutely no reason for going into raptures about spaceflights; the saints in their ecstasies climb infinitely higher, and these words are used in no allegorical sense, but in a perfectly concrete sense that could be called "scientific" or "exact." In vain does modern science explore the infinitely distant and the infinitely small; it can reach in its own way the world of galaxies and that of molecules, but it is unaware—since it believes neither in Revelation nor in pure intellection—of all the immaterial and supra-sensorial worlds that as it were envelop our sensorial dimensions, and in relation to which these dimensions are no more than a sort of fragile coagulation, destined to disappear when its time comes before the blinding power of the Divine Reality. To postulate a science without metaphysic is a flagrant contradiction, for without metaphysic there can be no standards and no criteria, no intelligence able to penetrate, contemplate and coordinate. Both a relativistic psychologism which ignores the absolute, and also evolutionism which is absurd because contradictory (since the greater cannot come from the less) can be explained only by this exclusion of what is essential and total in intelligence.

In former days it was the object that was sometimes questioned, including the object that can be found within ourselves—an "object" being anything of which the subject can be distinctively and separatively conscious, even if it be a moral defect in the subject—but in our days there is no fear of the contradiction inherent in questioning the subject, the knower, in its intrinsic and irreplaceable aspect; intelligence as such is called in question, it is even "examined," without wondering "who" examines it—is there not talk about producing a more perfect man—and without seeing that philosophic doubt is itself included in that same devaluation, that it falls if intelligence falls, and that at the same stroke all science and all philosophy collapse. For if our intelligence is by definition ineffectual, if we are irresponsible beings or lumps of earth, there is no sense in philosophizing.

What we are being pressed to admit is that our spirit is relative in its very essence, that this essence comprises no stable standards of measurement—as if the sufficient reason of the human intellect were not precisely that it should comprise some such standards!—and that consequently the ideas of truth and falsehood are intrinsically relative, and so always floating; and because certain consequences of accumulated errors fall foul of our innate standards and are unmasked and stigmatized by them, we are told that it is a question of habit and that we must change our nature, that is to say, that we must create a new intelligence that finds beautiful what is ugly and accepts as true what is false. The devil is essentially incapable of recognizing that he is wrong, unless an admission to that effect is in his interest; so it is error become habitual that must be right at all costs, even at the cost of our intelligence and, in the last analysis, of our existence; as for the nature of things and our faculty of equating ourselves thereto, ideas of that sort are all "prejudice."

It has been said and said again that monasticism in all its forms, whether Christian or Buddhist, is a manifestation of "pessimism;" in this way the intellectual and realistic aspect of the question is evaded either through opportunism or through stupidity, and objective authentications, metaphysical ideas and logical conclusions are reduced to purely sentimental attitudes. A man who knows that an avalanche is an avalanche is accused of "pessimism"; an "optimist" is one who prefers to think that it is a patch of mist; to think serenely of death while despising distractions is to see the world painted in dark colors, but to think of death with repugnance, or to avoid thinking of it at all, while finding all the happiness of which one is capable in transitory things, that, it seems, is "courage," and shows a "sense of responsibility." It has never been easy to understand why those who put their hope in God, while possessing enough discernment to be able to read the "signs of the times," are accused of bitterness, whereas others are credited with strong and happy natures because they mistake mirages for realities. It is almost incredible that this false optimism, which is totally opposed to the Scriptures on the one hand and to the most tangible of criteria on the other, should win over men who profess to believe in God and in the future life.

*

* *

An attempt must now be made to describe in a certain way—though there would be a thousand other ways of doing so—how the man who has attached himself to God is spiritually situated in existence, or how he takes his stand in face of the dizzy abyss that the world is. The condition of the monk—for it is he in whom interest is centred here, though the same considerations could be applied to contemplatives in general—the condition of the monk constitutes a victory over space and time, or over the world and life, in the sense that the monk situates himself by his attitude at the center and in the present: at the center in relation to a life full of phenomena, and in the present in relation to a life full of events. Concentration of prayer and rhythm of prayer: these are in a certain sense the two dimensions of spiritual existence in general and of monastic existence in particular. The monk withdraws from the world, he fixes himself in a definite place, and the place is central because it is consecrated to God, morally he shuts his eyes and remains where he is awaiting death, like a statue stood in a niche, as St. Francis de Sales says; by this "concentration" the monk places himself under the divine axis, he already partakes of Heaven by attaching himself concretely to God. In so doing the contemplative also withdraws from duration, for through prayer—that permanent actualization of a consciousness of the Absolute—he situates himself in a timeless instant: prayer, or the remembrance of God, is now and always, it is "always now" and already belongs to Eternity. The life of the monk, by the elimination of disordered movements, is a rhythm; now rhythm is the fixation of an instant—or of the present—in duration, in the same way as immobility is the fixation of a point—or of the center—in space; this symbolism, founded as it is on the law of analogy, becomes concrete by virtue of a consecration to God. Thus it is that the monk holds the world in his hands and that he dominates life as well: for there is nothing precious in the world which we do not possess in this very place, if this point where we are belongs to God and if, being here for God, we belong to him; and in the same way, all our life is in that instant in which we choose God and not vanities.

In the temporal dimension that stretches ahead of us there are only three certitudes: that of death, that of Judgment, and that of the Eternal Life. We have no power over the past and we do not know the future. As far as the future is concerned we have but these three certitudes, but we possess a fourth in this very moment, and that fourth is all: it is that of our actuality, of our present liberty to choose God and thus to choose our whole destiny. In this instant, this present, we hold our whole life, our whole existence: all is good if this instant is good, and if we know how to fix our life in this hallowed instant; all the secret of spiritual faithfulness lies in dwelling in this instant, in renewing it and perpetuating it by prayer, in holding on to it by means of the spiritual rhythm, in enclosing wholly within it the time that floods over us and threatens to drag us far away from this "divine moment." The vocation of the monk is perpetual prayer, not because life is long, but because it is only a moment; the perpetuity—or the rhythm—of the orison demonstrates that life is but an ever-present instant, just as the spatial fixation in a consecrated place demonstrates that the world is but a point, a point however which belongs to God, and is therefore everywhere and excludes no bliss.

This condensation of the existential dimensions—insofar as they are indefinite and arbitrary—into a hallowed unity is at the same time the very thing that constitutes the essence of man; the rest is contingency and accident. This is a truth that concerns every human being; the monk too is not a being apart, but simply a prototype or a model, or a spiritual specification, a landmark: every man, because he is a man, should realize in one way or another this victory over a world that disperses and over a life that enslaves. Too many people think that they have not time to pray, but this is an illusion due to that indifference which is, according to Fénélon, the worst sickness of the soul; for the many moments we fill with our habitual dreams, including our all too often useless reflections, we take away from God and from ourselves.

The great mission of monasticism is to show to the world that happiness does not lie somewhere far away, or in something situated outside ourselves, in a treasure to be sought or in a world to be built, but here where we belong to God. The monk represents, in face of a dehumanized world, what our true standards are; his mission is to remind men what man is.

NOTES
1. "For what is a man profited, if he shall gain the whole world, and lose his own soul?" (Matt. 1: 26).
2. "Be fruitful, and multiply, and replenish the earth, and subdue it; and have dominion over the fish of the sea, and over the fowl of the air, and over every living thing that moveth upon the earth" (Genesis 1:28).
3. The partisans of this "forcing into step" must be answered by the Scriptures; "Whoso therefore will be a friend of the world is the enemy of God" (James 4:4). "And be not conformed to this world: but be ye transformed by the

renewing of your mind, that ye may prove what is that good, and acceptable, and perfect, will of God" (Rom. 12:2). In our days it is the other way round: it is atheistic scientism, it is demagogy, it is the machine that decides what is good, what should be pleasing to God, what is perfect. "Woe unto you, when all men shall speak well of you! for so did their fathers to the false prophets" (Luke 6:26). "Love not the world, neither the things that are in the world. If any man love the world, the love of the Father is not in him" (I John 2:16). And St. Francis of Sales addresses the human soul in these words: "God did not put you into this world because of any need that he had of you, who are quite useless to him, but only that he might exercise in you his goodness, giving you his grace and his glory. To this end he has given you understanding wherewith to know him, memory wherewith to remember him, will wherewith to love him, imagination that you might picture his benefits, eyes that you might see the marvels of his works, a tongue wherewith to praise him, and likewise with the other faculties. Being created and put into this world with that intention, all intentions contrary thereto must be rejected and avoided, and those that in no way serve this end must be despised as being vain and superfluous. Consider the misfortune of the world which thinks not at all of this, but lives as if thinking that it had been created only to build houses, plant trees, amass riches and disport itself" (*Introduction to the Devout Life*, chapter 10).

CONTRIBUTORS

NICOLE ABADIE (KHADIDJA BENAISSA) was born in Oran, Algeria, the daughter of a prominent French surgeon. She completed her graduate and postgraduate studies at the Sorbonne in Paris. She became a Muslim in 1953 and married a disciple of Shaikh Sidi Hadj Adda who succeeded the Shaikh al-'Alawi. Mrs. Benaissa has worked as a translator and interpreter throughout her life, most recently for the United Nations.

ROB BAKER, editorial director of Fons Vitae, is former co-editor of *Parabola: The Magazine of Myth and Tradition* (1987–1992) and has worked as a critic (music, theater, dance, and film), writer, and editor for a number of publications, including *Dance Magazine*, *The Chicago Tribune*, *The (New York) Daily News*, and *The Soho Weekly News*. He is the author of *Planning Memorial Celebrations: A Sourcebook* (Bell Tower Books, forthcoming) and is currently working on a comparative study of sacred musics of the world for the same publisher. His translation of René Guénon's short work, *Saint Bernard*, appeared in a recent issue of *Sophia: The Journal of Traditional Studies* and his translation of Titus Burckhardt's *A Spiritual Key to Muslim Astrology in the Writings of Ibn 'Arabî* will be published by Fons Vitae.

WILLIAM C. CHITTICK is Professor of Comparative Religious Studies at State University of New York, Stony Brook. He has published numerous books, among them *Imaginal Worlds: Ibn al-'Arabî and the Problem of Religious Diversity; Faith and Practice of Islam; Three Thirteenth-Century Sufi Texts; The Sufi Path of Knowledge: Ibn al-'Arabî's Metaphysics of Imagination; The Sufi Path of Love: The Spiritual Teachings of Rûmî; A Shi'ite Anthology; and The Self-Disclosure of God: Principles of Ibn al-'Arabî's Cosmology*, all published by SUNY Press.

BERNADETTE DIEKER graduated summa cum laude with a B.A. in English from Bellarmine College. Her senior thesis is entitled

Chicana Sexuality, Spirituality, and La Virgen de Guadalupe: An Exploration through Ana Castillo and Sandra Cisneros. Other publications include an essay, "Responsibility in Detail," in an upcoming work on the New England poet Jane Kenyon (Spring 2000). She is currently Assistant Director of Fons Vitae Publishing.

SIDNEY H. GRIFFITH, S.T., is a professor in the Department of Semitic and Egyptian Languages and Literatures at the Catholic University of America in Washington, D.C., and secretary general of the department's Institute of Christian Oriental Research. Since 1984 he has been director of the graduate program in Early Christian Studies. His specialty is Syriac and Arab Christian literature, especially from the early Islamic period, with a particular interest in the history of Muslim/Christian relations. Publications include numerous articles on topics in these areas of study, as well as the following recent publications: *Arabic Christianity in the Monasteries of Ninth-century Palestine* (1992); *Faith Adoring the Mystery; Reading the Bible with St.Ephraem the Syrian* (1997); *Theodore Abu Qurrah; A Treatise on the Veneration of the Holy Icons.*

NICHOLAS HEER retired in 1990 as chairman of the Near Eastern Languages and Civilization department at the University of Washington in Seattle. He had been associated with the university there since 1965, first as associate professor of Arabic then as full professor. He previously taught in the Arabic departments at Stanford University and Harvard University and was a visiting lecturer at Yale, from which he received his B.A. in 1949, taking his Ph.D. at Princeton in 1955. From 1955–57 he worked as translation analyst for the Arabian American Oil Company in Saudi Arabia; between that and his teaching career, he served one year as curator of the Middle Eastern collections of the Hoover Insititution at Stanford University. His publications include an Arabic edition of 'Abd al-Rahman al-Jami's *al -Durrah al-Fakhirah* (Wisdom of Persia Series 19, Tehran, 1980) and an English translation of the same work under the title *The Precious Pearl* (Albany: SUNY Press, 1979).

GRAY HENRY took her B.A. from Sarah Lawrence College in Comparative Religion and Art History and later completed her M.A. in Education and Curriculum Development. Presently she is in the process of completing a doctoral dissertation in Divinity at Canterbury. She also studied from 1969–78 at Al Azhar University in Cairo. She is a co-founder and trustee of the Islamic Texts Society and Quinta-Essentia in Cambridge, England, and at present directs Fons Vitae Publishing in Louisville, Kentucky. She is also a contributing editor at *Parabola: The Magazine of Myth and Tradition*. She serves on the Board and Programs Committee of the Thomas Merton Center Foundation.

SEYYED HOSSEIN NASR, an Iranian by birth, is a graduate of MIT and Harvard University; former professor of history of science and philosophy, dean of the Faculty of Letters, and vice chancellor at Tehran University; and former president at Aryamehr University. Nasr served as a visiting professor at Harvard in 1962 and 1965. In 1964–65, he was the first Aga Khan professor of Islamic Studies at the American University of Beirut. He is the founder and first president of the Iranian Academy of Philosophy. Dr. Nasr was the first distinguished professor of Islamic studies at the University of Utah and was professor of Islamic studies at Temple University from 1979 to 1984. He is currently University Professor of Islamic Studies at George Washington University. The author of over twenty books and over two hundred articles, on aspects of Islamic studies and Sufism, comparative philosophy and religion, philosophy of art, and the philosophical and religious dimensions of the environmental crisis, Dr. Nasr has lectured widely throughout the United States, Western Europe, most of the Islamic world, India, Australia, and Japan. Nasr's publications include *Three Muslim Sages, Introduction to Islamic Cosmological Doctrines, Science and Civilization in Islam, Man and Nature, Knowledge and the Sacred, Ideals and Realities of Islam, Sufi Essays*, and *Religion and the Order of Nature*.

ERLINDA G. PAGUIO was born in Manila, Philippines. She began her graduate studies in the history of religions and obtained her M.A. in African History and Modern European History from the University of Illinois, Chicago. She attended courses on the history of Islam at the Ateneo de Manila University and Indiana University in Bloomington, Indiana. She has been Treasurer of the International Thomas Merton Society since 1991. She also was Secretary of the Thomas Merton Center Foundation. She has given several talks on "Merton and Meister Eckhart," "Merton and Ananda Coomaraswamy," "Merton and Sufism," "Merton and the Carmelite Saints,"and "Merton, D. T. Suzuki, and John Wu." She is currently Research Coordinator at the University of Louisville's Development Office.

FRITHJOF SCHUON (1907–1998) was born in Basle, Switzerland, of German parents. As a youth he went to Paris where he studied for a few years before undertaking a number of trips to North Africa, the Near East, and India in order to contact spiritual authorities and gather material for his writings. After World War II, he traveled to the American West, in view of studying the religion of the Plains Indians. Schuon's writings on comparative religion made him a world-renowned authority on *sophia perennis*. His writings include *The Transcendent Unity of Religions*, *Understanding Islam*, *Esoterism as Principle and as Way*, *Logic and Transcendence*, *Spiritual Perspectives and Human Facts*, *To Have a Center*, *The Eye of the Heart*, *Stations of Wisdom*, and *Sufism, Veil and Quintessence*.

BONNIE THURSTON, an ordained minister and professor of New Testament at the Pittsburgh Theological Seminary in Pittsburgh, Pennsylvania, is a founding member of the International Thomas Merton Society, wrote her doctoral dissertation on Thomas Merton at the University of Virginia, and has published eighteen articles on various aspects of Merton's work, as well as a number of books on the New Testament and the Early Church. She has previously served ITMS as secretary, vice-president, and president.

BURTON B. THURSTON earned the Th.D. from Harvard Divinity School and was for many years professor at the American University of Beirut, Beirut, Lebanon. An ordained pastor in the Christian Church, Dr. Thurston retired from Bethany College, Bethany, West Virginia, as Professor of Middle Eastern Studies. He was especially interested in Muslim/Christian dialogue. He died in 1990.

ACKNOWLEDGMENTS

Unpublished material from the collection in the Thomas Merton Center at Bellarmine College in Louisville, Kentucky, is included here with the permission of the Trustees of the Merton Legacy Trust. This includes the Merton correspondence with Louis Massingnon and Abdul Aziz (in the two chapters by Sidney H. Griffith) and with Marco Pallis, Dona Luisa Coomaraswamy, Lord Northbourne, Martin Lings, and Charles Dumont (in Rob Baker's chapter), as well as quotes from Merton's reading notebooks and the transcriptions of his lectures to the novices on Sufism.

Books and articles quoted or cited in the text under the usual fair use allowances are acknowledged with full publication credits in the endnotes to each chapter.

Longer excerpts from previously published Merton books are reprinted by permission of the following institutions:

Farrar, Straus, & Giroux Inc.: *The Hidden Ground of Love: Letters on Religious Experience and Social Concerns*. Copyright © 1985 by the Trustees of the Merton Legacy Trust. © 1985 by Farrar, Straus & Giroux, Inc. *Witness to Freedom: Letters in Times of Crisis*. © 1994 by the Trustees of the Merton Legacy Trust. © 1994 by Farrar, Straus & Giroux Inc.

HarperSanFrancisco: *The Journals of Thomas Merton, vol. IV: Turning Toward the World*. © 1996 by the Trustees of the Merton Legacy Trust. © 1996 HarperSanFrancisco. *The Journals of Thomas Merton, vol. V: Dancing in the Waters of Life*. © 1997 by the Trustees of the Merton Legacy Trust. © 1997 HarperSanFrancisco. *The Journals of Thomas Merton, vol. VI: Learning to Love*. © 1997 HarperSanFrancisco.

"Readings From Ibn Abbad" by Thomas Merton, from RAIDS ON THE UNSPEAKABLE. Copyright ©1966 by The Abbey of Gethsemani, Inc. Reprinted by permission of New Directions Publishing Corp. "The Moslems' Angel of Death," "Song for the Death of Averroes," "East with Ibn Battuta," "The Night of Destiny" by Thomas Merton, from THE COLLECTED POEMS OF THOMAS MERTON. Copyright ©1948 by New Directions Publishing Corporation. Reprinted by permission of New Directions Publishing Corp.

In addition, the following chapters originally appeared in some other form:

William C. Chittick's "Sufism: Name and Reality" was delivered as a lecture to the Merton Society at Bellarmine College on June 28, 1998. Printed here by permission of the author.

Burton B. Thurston's "Thomas Merton's Reflections on Sufism" first appeared in *The Merton Seasonal* 15:3 (Summer 1990). It is reprinted by permission of the Thomas Merton Center, publishers of the *Seasonal*, and Bonnie Thurston.

Bonnie Thurston's "Thomas Merton's Interest in Islam: The Example of Dhikr," first appeared in *The American Benedictine Review* 45:2 (June 1994). Permission granted by Father Terrance G. Kardong, O.S.B., Editor, and by the author.

Sidney H. Griffith's "Merton, Massingnon, and the Challenge of Islam" first appeared in *The Merton Annual* 3 (New York: AMS Press, 1990): 151–72, in a slightly earlier form. Reprinted by permission of the Thomas Merton Center and the author.

Nicholas Heer's translation of al-Tirmidhî's *Bayân al-Farq bayn al-Sadr wa al-Qalb as al-Fu'ad wa al-Lubb (The Elucidation of the Difference between the Breast, the Heart, the Inner Heart, and the Intellect)* originally appeared in *Muslim World* 51:1 (1981), 25–36. It is reprinted by permission of the Hartford (Connecticut) Seminary Foundation, the publisher of *Muslim World* and the author. A new edition of the complete version forthcoming from Fons Vitae Press.

Frithjof Schuon's "The Universality of Monasticism and Its Relevance in the Modern World" is reprinted from *Light on the Ancient Worlds* (new edition, World Wisdom Books, 1984), 119–35. Reprinted by permission of the Estate of Frithjof Schuon.

On the heart of Poverty three renouncements are inscribed: Quit this world, quit the next world, and quit quitting.

—UNATTRIBUTED QUOTE FROM
MERTON'S READING NOTEBOOKS

Each thing hath two faces, a face of its own, and a face of its Lord; in respect of its own face it is nothingness, and in respect of the Face of God it is Being. Thus there is nothing in existence save only God and His face, for everything perisheth but His Face, always and forever.

—AL-GHAZALI (D. 1111)
PASSAGE UNDERLINED BY THOMAS MERTON

If you have seen a lover of God you have seen a very wonderful thing—of one in grief not settling in the earth but like a wild bird whose delight in solitude has kept him from rest, while he yearns in remembrance of the Beloved, and his food is love in hunger and his drink is love in thirst and his sleep is the thought of union and his waking hours mean no neglect. . . . At last through love (shawq) *and long service he attains to the degree of all-absorbing love, then his tranquility returns and his fire dies down and its sparks are quenched and his grief decreases and he becomes one with the object of his longing.*

—BAYDÂ BINT AL-MUFADDAL
A WOMAN SAINT OF DAMASCUS (C. TWELFTH CENTURY)
FROM MERTON'S READING NOTEBOOKS

Set in Goudy Type
on a Macintosh Computer
by Watersign Resources
Lexington, Kentucky

Printed by
V. G. Reed & Sons
Louisville, Kentucky